Developing Advanced Literacy in First and Second Languages

Meaning With Power

Developing Advanced Literacy in First and Second Languages

Meaning With Power

Edited by

Mary J. Schleppegrell
M. Cecilia Colombi
University of California, Davis

2002

LAWRENCE ERLBAUM ASSOCIATES, PUBLISHERS
Mahwah, New Jersey   London

Lawrence Erlbaum Associates, Inc., Publishers
10 Industrial Avenue
Mahwah, NJ 07430

Cover design by Kathryn Houghtaling Lacey

Library of Congress Cataloging-in-Publication Data

Developing advanced literacy in first and second languages: mean-
ing with power / edited by Mary J. Schleppegrell, Cecilia Colombi.
     p.   cm.
Includes papers presented at a conference held Feb. 2000, University
of California, Davis.
   Includes bibliographical references and index.
   ISBN 0-8058-3982-8 (cloth : alk. paper)
   ISBN 0-8058-3983-6 (pbk. : alk. paper)
1. Literacy—Study and Teaching—Congresses. 2. Language and
languages—Study and teaching—Congresses. I. Schleppegrell,
Mary. II. Colombi, Cecilia.
P53.475 .D48 2002
302.2'244—dc21
                                                    2001040700
                                                    CIP

Books published by Lawrence Erlbaum Associates are printed on acid-
free paper, and their bindings are chosen for strength and durability.

Printed in the United States of America
10 9 8 7 6 5 4 3 2 1

Contents

Preface

This book addresses the challenges that advanced literacy presents for students from all backgrounds in our ever-changing society. As directors of university programs in which students from diverse linguistic and social backgrounds are learning to write in Spanish and English at advanced levels, we recognize the need for more research that explores the issues involved in the development of advanced literacy. Our book brings together work that addresses a range of student populations and disciplinary contexts.

In February 2000, we invited many of the contributors to this book to a conference on advanced literacy at the University of California, Davis, sponsored by a grant from the Humanities Research Institute of the University of California at Irvine. This book includes some of the findings presented there together with work from other scholars. It offers insights into the social and linguistic challenges that face students as they engage in academic tasks that require advanced levels of reading and writing. It is intended to serve researchers, teachers, and students, presenting both theory and practice related to the literacy contexts and genres that engage students from the late elementary grades through secondary and tertiary education. Disciplinary areas that are addressed include science, history, language arts, and teacher education.

This book illustrates approaches to research and pedagogy appropriate for first-language development across languages as well as second-language development. It brings together research on students' development of advanced literacy skills in English and Spanish, with a focus both on bilingual contexts and English as a second language (ESL) contexts. It also addresses the challenges of advanced literacy for native speakers of English, including students for whom standard English is a second dialect.

This research spans a range of theoretical orientations and analytic approaches, drawing especially on work in functional linguistics and sociocultural theory. Students in an academic environment have to use language to negotiate different social identities as they interact with new textual genres. This book emphasizes the linguistic perspective on these challenges, while still highlighting the more widely studied social perspective.

Research on register and genre has shown that there are clear grammatical and discourse-organizational differences between ordinary conversational language and the language expected of students at school. These differences become most apparent as students move from early literacy into the contexts of advanced literacy, where the demands of schooling increase and students are asked to participate in new social contexts with their associated genres. Learning to use language in ways that meet the school's expectations for advanced literacy tasks is a challenge for all students who have little opportunity for exposure to and use of such language outside of school.

One approach that informs several of the chapters in this volume is systemic-functional linguistics (SFL). SFL is currently not well known in the United States, although it is a major influence on work in other parts of the world. Because of its focus on the interrelationship between meaning and form, we believe that SFL can play an important role in increasing our understanding of the linguistic challenges that first- and second-language readers and writers face in participating in advanced literacy texts and contexts. Other approaches to research in language development are also represented, including sociocultural approaches that highlight the challenges students face in participating in unfamiliar discourse communities.

OVERVIEW

What unites all of these authors is an interest in providing a clear picture of the challenges of literacy beyond the early years of schooling. Although much is known about early literacy, much less has been written about the development of literacy as students move into secondary education and beyond. This is the fundamental contribution of this book. The authors are all committed to a view of literacy that emphasizes both the social contexts and the linguistic challenges. Our hope is that this book will make a substantive contribution to those interested in research and pedagogy for the multilingual and multicultural students in today's classrooms, including first- and second-language learners of English and students who wish to develop advanced literacy in languages other than English in a bilingual context.

The chapters need not be read in sequence, but they have been ordered to highlight the particular emphases of the volume. Our introductory chapter frames the theoretical issues that underlie the research presented here and raises the practical pedagogical issues that the authors address throughout the book. In chapter 2, Lemke then raises many of the themes that the volume addresses, as he defines advanced literacy in the context of both academic and popular science, showing how all literacy is embedded in social contexts that reflect a community's values and beliefs.

The next two chapters describe some grammatical features of the registers and genres that are featured in advanced literacy tasks and provide some analytic tools for charting the development of students' proficiency with these registers and genres. In chapter 3, Christie does this in the context of adolescents' writing development in English as a subject area, providing an overview of the grammatical challenges that the complex genres of secondary schooling pose for all students. This focus on issues of advanced literacy development is then also taken up by Colombi in chapter 4, in regard to Spanish, as she explores the development of academic writing of bilingual university students who are writing in academic Spanish for the first time.

Chapters 5 and 6 address genre-related issues, focusing on the challenges for students in history and science. In chapter 5, Martin describes the key genres students read in secondary level history classes, explicating their grammatical and discourse challenges, especially for developing students' critical literacy skills. He demonstrates that students need to draw on grammatical options that enable the "expanded meaning potential" required for critical literacy. Schleppegrell's focus in chapter 6 is the ESL student at the postsecondary level and how discourse and grammatical challenges can prevent them from realizing the interpersonal and textual meanings that make their presentation of ideas most effective. She provides examples from laboratory reports to demonstrate the strategies that students use when their grammatical resources are inadequate for construing the meanings they intend.

This linguistic focus on the challenges of advanced literacy development for students who have learned English as a second language is then taken up in chapter 7 by Celce-Murcia, who describes some grammatical features of the registers of advanced literacy and points out how these grammatical features need to be taught in appropriate discourse contexts. She argues that even advanced ESL students need continued support in postsecondary contexts for development of discourse-level competence with grammatical features that are seldom addressed in standard pedagogical approaches to ESL.

Moving from a more linguistic to a more social perspective on these issues, Gee focuses in chapter 8 on the discourse communities we are preparing students to participate in and the way language positions students. He points out that students need to be made aware of how identities are mediated through the social practices for which advanced literacy skills are functional, arguing that literacy is more than textual practice and that achieving effective participation in a discourse community means accepting the ways of using language that are taken for granted in that community. In chapter 9, Baugh addresses these issues in the context of African-American communities, reviewing social, educational, and linguistic factors that have affected students' development of advanced literacy, and providing suggestions for how we might more effectively work with students who speak nonstandard dialects.

The community that Ramanathan then addresses in chapter 10 is that of teachers in training, suggesting that we raise their meta-awareness about the communities that they are being initiated into as a means of helping them become more aware of the social and institutional constraints and expectations of the discourses into which they will initiate their students, so that they in turn can raise their students' consciousness about social identity and social practice.

The next set of chapters returns to second-language issues from a pedagogical perspective. In chapter 11, Scarcella identifies a number of factors that have not been given enough emphasis in research on ESL, arguing especially for the need for more "excellent instruction" if we are to move students beyond basic knowledge of English into advanced literacy skills. Merino and Hammond show in chapter 12, the need for focus on genres other than the narrative in the context of late primary school science instruction. Finally, in chapter 13, Garcia brings several of the book's themes together as she talks about the development of advanced biliteracy in Spanish native speakers who are preparing to be bilingual teachers.

We thank the University of California, Davis, Second Language Acquisition Institute and the University of California Humanities Research Institute for their support for the Conference on Advanced Literacy at UC Davis in February, 2000. The conference was also supported in part by a grant from the Spencer Foundation. The views expressed are, of course, solely the responsibility of the authors. We also thank the editors and reviewers at Lawrence Erlbaum Associates, especially Naomi Silverman, senior editor. Finally, we thank the students who were the inspiration for this book.

—*Mary J. Schleppegrell*
M. Cecilia Colombi

1

Theory and Practice in the Development of Advanced Literacy

M. Cecilia Colombi
Mary J. Schleppegrell
University of California, Davis

"Advanced literacy," as we present it in this volume, refers to the kind of meaning-making that is typical of secondary and postsecondary schooling, and that is also required for participation in many of the professional, technical, bureaucratic, and social institutions of our world. We focus particularly on educational contexts, where students need to work in content areas that have particular ways of making meaning. Students' learning of disciplinary knowledge requires participation in social contexts where texts are actively constructed. Students need to be able to participate in literacy in ways that enable them to contribute to the evolution of knowledge by shaping what is learned and shared, or by challenging current practices and developing new ways of using language in advanced literacy contexts. With full participation by all students, from all backgrounds and experiences, the disciplines and institutions of our society can evolve in new ways that take account of the diversity of experiences and needs that these students represent. Without full participation by all, the inequities that characterize our society will continue to be reproduced.

Literacy is often talked about as if it were an attribute of a person (she is literate); or, on the other hand, as something that someone *has* or doesn't have (he has functional literacy). But in today's complex world, literacy means far more than learning to read and write in order to accomplish particular discrete tasks. Continual changes in technology and society mean that literacy tasks are themselves always changing, calling for skills in handling technical, bureaucratic, and abstract language; often simultaneously requiring that people get meaning from print, visual, electronic, and other kinds of media. In this context of change, literacy cannot be thought of as something that is *achieved* once and for all. We need to understand literacy as a process of meaning-making that continuously evolves both in society and in the individual. This book contributes to such an understanding by focusing on advanced literacy contexts where meaning-making depends on control of a range of semiotic resources as well as on an understanding of social and linguistic expectations for participation in those contexts.

Literacy is a social semiotic (Halliday, 1978; Lemke, 1989); a form of social action where language and context coparticipate in the meaning-making enterprise. Meaning is not inherent in texts; it comes from "how they are used and interpreted in communities" (Lemke, chap. 2, this volume). Lemke stresses the connection between the local context and the larger society, saying that "the meanings we make on any occasion are both uniquely emergent and culturally typical; they depend both on local contexts and on other meanings made in other times and places." The kinds of meanings that are made in the institutions of learning and working and living today are complex meanings that call for complex uses of language and other semiotic resources. The development of advanced literacy is also a social process of enculturation into the values and practices of specialist communities. Lemke emphasizes how language is integrated with other semiotic resources in advanced literacy tasks, describing, as an example of this, the "multiple semiotic modalities" employed in "doing science" in school, in professional contexts, and in scientists' communication with the public.

At the level of society, new kinds of literacy are constantly evolving. We have seen in recent history the development of new material means of making meanings (electronic, video, and others) along with new contexts of meaning-making in all domains of inquiry. Every discipline is continually evolving new ways of seeing, investigating, discussing, and evaluating knowledge, creating new contexts and new ways of *doing* literacy. These new ways of doing literacy that evolve at the level of society also continually put new demands on individuals. An individual's growth and development and ability to participate in the powerful institutions of our society require ever expanding knowledge and control over meaning-making in new contexts and through new semiotic resources. This means that control over the basic resources of print (learning to read and write) is only the first step in developing the complex set of understandings, skills, and social forms that enable participation in the many institutions of our world that are partially constructed and maintained through the process of literacy.

This has major implications for our schools. Students need move beyond the basics to *do* science, history, and other subjects; to construct arguments and critique theories; and to integrate print, visual, interactional, and electronic means of developing and sharing knowledge—in other words, to develop advanced literacy skills. The challenge to educators is to make advanced literacy possible for all students.

The wide range of backgrounds and experiences that students bring to our classrooms makes the pedagogy of advanced literacy a complex endeavor. Our schools serve students who speak different languages and dialects, who have been socialized in different ways, and who face vastly different challenges in their daily lives. We can not rely on methods of literacy development that assume a homogeneous group of students who share similar cultural backgrounds and language experiences. In order to enable all students to participate in the institutions in our society, we need a new understanding of the literacy demands of those institutions and approaches that provide students with the experiences they need to enter into dialogue with others.

Multicultural classrooms are the norm in our schools today. The 2000 U.S. Census reported a population of over 280 million people in the United States, and of those more than 30% consider themselves ethnic minority. Together with these demographic changes come new educational challenges. Although much research has described the diversity of student populations and different ways of interacting in their communities, the focus in literacy research has concentrated primarily on the early stages of literacy development. But students need to move beyond initial literacy if they are to become full participants in the dialogue and texts that provide access, power, and opportunity in today's world. Learning to use language in ways that meet the school's expectations for advanced literacy tasks is a challenge for all students, but it is especially difficult for those who have little opportunity for exposure to and use of such language outside of school. Students have different experiences of language use in their homes and communities, and teachers are often not prepared to recognize and build on the experiences of students whose backgrounds are different from their own. Students whose cultural practices are similar to those of the school are able to transfer those practices to the school setting, but students from other backgrounds need to engage in meaningful experiences of authentic social practices involving speech, writing, tools, and technologies, and to focus on the ways that different semiotic systems, especially language, contribute to meaning making in those social contexts, in order to develop advanced literacy.

A great part of the diversity in our school-age populations is linguistic, and this linguistic diversity is clearly related to the challenges and problems of developing advanced literacy skills. Linguistic diversity manifests itself in different ways. Some students are bilingual, some are learning English, and some speak varieties or dialects of English that are not recognized and valued in school. This book brings together research on advanced literacy from a variety of contexts, including Spanish in a bilingual context, English as a second language (ESL), and standard English as a second dialect.

Latinos are the fastest growing population in the United States, with a total of 35.3 million, roughly equal to that of African Americans. Latinos are people of any race who (themselves or their ancestors) come from Spanish-speaking countries; in the United States, about two thirds of them are of Mexican descent with the largest concentration in the Southwest (California, Colorado, New Mexico, Arizona, Texas, and Nevada). The Latino population of the east coast presents a different profile. New York City, for example (García, chap. 13, this volume) has a Latino population of 30%, and of those, 40% were born in the United States. New York Latinos born in Spanish-speaking countries come mostly from Puerto Rico, the Dominican Republic, Colombia, Ecuador, and México. This makes Spanish the most frequently spoken language in the United States, after English. In some parts of the country, such as California, Spanish speakers make up more than one third of the total population. Spanish language students are more than 70% of all English learners in our schools, but many other languages are also spoken at home by our students, as one in seven school-aged children is not from an English speaking background (McKay & Wong, 2000).

In our current educational system, many students fail to continue development of their first languages as they become proficient in English. Even when students are provided with instruction in their mother tongues, such as in bilingual programs, the focus has typically been on developing their English skills so that they can make a transition into English-only classrooms. This means that bilingual students rarely develop advanced biliteracy. When literacy skills are taught in a language other than English, development frequently ends with initial literacy. This is a loss for the individual students and for society, as we know that bilingualism and biliteracy provide cognitive and social advantages to students (Bialystock & Hakuta, 1994; Cummins, 1983; 1989; Hakuta 1986), and that L1 academic language skills can serve as a basis for development of L2 literacy skills (Cummins & Danesi, 1990; Verhoeven 1991; see also chapters in Faltis & Wolfe, 1999, and Pérez, 1998). Maintaining and developing the first language facilitates the development of the second language, particularly at the levels of advanced literacy, and promotes bilingualism, a benefit for us as a society.

The chapters by Colombi and García (chaps. 4 and 13 respectively, this volume) discuss issues of advanced literacy development in Spanish-speaking students, focusing on helping these students develop full biliteracy. García, for example, shows how bilingual student-teachers working toward certification face major roadblocks in developing advanced literacy in Spanish (their first language) and English. She attributes their difficulties to the lack of venues in which the rich cultural and rhetorical traditions of Spanish advanced literacy can be meaningfully experienced in the U.S. context, where monolingualism is valued over bilingualism; and to the simplified version of the English rhetorical tradition that these students have been taught in school. Colombi offers a more positive outlook on this issue by showing how university students who have never had the opportunity to develop advanced literacy skills in Spanish, their first language, can develop their writing from more oral styles toward more written styles as they learn to make grammatical choices that structure their texts in more academic ways.

Another population addressed by this volume is second language learners of English. Students whose first language is not English are themselves diverse. They may be bilingual students who are developing linguistic skills in more than one language, or they may be losing their first languages as they move toward monolingualism in English. They may have been educated to levels of advanced literacy in their first languages, or they may have no first language literacy skills. Almost 3.4 million students in the United States are in programs for students who are limited in their English proficiency (Macías, 2000). Students who are learning English as a second language are at great risk for school failure, as research suggests that with current practice it takes students many years to develop the advanced literacy skills that enable them to do grade-level work in English (Collier, 1987). Many ESL students spend years in classrooms where they are expected to *pick up* English through immersion; losing valuable time in which they could be developing language skills through structured opportunities to learn the genres and registers that are important for school success.

Scarcella (chap. 11, this volume) identifies a series of factors that affect the development of advanced literacy in ESL students, including first language literacy skills, good oral English skills on entry to school, and opportunities to interact with speakers of standard English. She suggests that the most important factor in ensuring success for all language learners is the opportunity to engage in instructional activities that help students learn how to do advanced literacy tasks.

Many of the contributors to this volume consider the explicit teaching of language an important aspect of effective instruction in advanced literacy. It is important to understand the demands of language learning beyond basic conversational competence to enable second language learners of English to participate in ever more abstract and demanding contexts of learning. Celce-Murcia (chap. 7, this volume) provides examples of three grammatical structures that are typically taught only at the sentence level and shows how we need to help learners understand how such structures function in extended discourse. Schleppegrell (chap. 6, this volume) shows how university ESL students in chemical engineering courses are unable to draw on the linguistic strategies that their native-speaker peers use to structure lab reports and discuss experimental results. She shows how a sentence-level focus on correcting their grammatical errors does not address the deeper challenges these students face in constructing authoritative and well-organized texts. Merino and Hammond (chap. 12, this volume) provide suggestions for how skills in this lab report genre might begin to be developed by bilingual students or second-language learners even in the upper-elementary grades. They argue that the development of advanced literacy must be scaffolded from the early years by engaging students in academic language tasks, and not just the personal and narrative tasks that are typically assigned to students in the early grades.

The third population that this book addresses are native speakers of English who speak nonstandard dialects, or whose socialization has prepared them to use language in ways that are not valued at school. These students also face great challenges; similar to the challenges faced by bilingual students and second language learners. African American students are the largest population of nonstandard dialect speakers, but students from many backgrounds speak varieties of English that are not recognized and supported through school literacy tasks. As Baugh (chap. 9, this volume) reports, sociolinguistic studies have demonstrated that a nonstandard dialect such as African American English (AAE) is a fully formed linguistic system that has emerged under particular historical and social circumstances. Baugh provides background on the situation of African American students and outlines the challenges that African American speakers of nonstandard English face in developing advanced literacy in mainstream schools. Sociolinguists have shown the variability and richness of linguistic resources and purposes for literacy that characterize populations of nonstandard dialect speakers, and have urged that other dialects also be maintained and developed (e.g., Wolfram, Adger, & Christian, 1999).

Although these studies have made major contributions to the ways we see and understand other varieties of English, the work that has followed from the sociolinguistic studies has not focused on how students who speak nonstandard dialects might be guided in the development of advanced literacy skills. In addition, the challenges faced by students who speak nonstandard dialects can also face students whose dialects are close to standard English but whose life experiences have not prepared them for the kinds of literacy tasks they are expected to participate in at school. As with the other populations we have discussed, research with speakers of nonstandard dialects has typically focused primarily on the context of initial literacy; on the early stages of reading and writing and on remedial programs for older students. For advanced literacy, accepting that students come to school speaking different dialects that need to be respected is not enough. As Delpit (1995, 1998) has pointed out, in addition to recognizing and valuing what students bring to the classroom from their ways of using language in their home communities, we also need to help students develop new ways of meaning that enable them to participate successfully in advanced literacy contexts. Students also have to gain access to ways of making meaning that are currently socially distributed in ways that leave out many segments of society.

This book addresses issues of advanced literacy development common to all of the student populations we have described. What all of these students share is a need for experience in the sociocultural contexts of advanced literacy and knowledge about how linguistic choices enable participation in new ways of making meaning in society.

LITERACY AS SOCIAL ACTIVITY

There are two major theoretical orientations toward literacy that inform the authors of this volume; a focus on literacy as social activity and a focus on literacy as linguistic activity, as literacy researchers often have a primary focus either on the social contexts in which literacy is *done* and developed, or on the linguistic challenges that these literacy contexts present. Approaches that focus on literacy as a social activity highlight the socialization of the individual into various discourse communities as their basic point of departure, examining the social contexts of literacy and the variability of meaning in texts according to context. Approaches that focus primarily on literacy as a linguistic activity, on the other hand, highlight the role of language in construing social contexts, examining the features of texts that instantiate various contexts. Both perspectives are represented here, but the analytical distinction and the emphasis on one or the other should not obscure the fundamental inseparability of social context and linguistic realization that must be recognized in any approach to literacy research and pedagogy.

A focus on literacy as social activity highlights the interactional construction of meaning in particular social and cultural contexts. One of the major figures contributing to a theoretical perspective that sees literacy as social activity is Vygotsky (1896–1934; e.g., Vygotsky, 1986). Vygotsky was most interested in how people construct meaning through joint activity, using the tools of their culture. He demonstrated how social interaction is crucial to the development of language and thinking, showing that new skills develop in collaboration with a more proficient interlocutor who scaffolds tasks for the novice so that the learner can do more than he or she would be able to do alone. Different sociocultural expectations that are part of the particular social context in which the individual develops mean that children develop different ways of using language. How people learn and learn through language depends on the kinds of tools that their cultures use and the ways of interacting that are particular to their situations. Vygotsky also makes a distinction between "everyday" concepts and "scientific" concepts, where everyday concepts are those that we are socialized to understand unconsciously, and scientific concepts are those that are consciously learned, typically through language. This distinction is important for understanding the contribution of schooling to the development of language and thought.

The Vygotskian perspective has influenced many scholars working with first-language development in schools as well as some scholars working with ethnic minority students and second-language learners (e.g, Lantolf & Appel, 1994; Lee & Smagorinsky, 2000; Pérez, 1998). The primary emphasis of this social activity view of literacy has been on the importance of collaborative inquiry in the construction of meaning, suggesting teaching practices that view the learner and learning process as situated in social contexts where learning (and literacy development) emerge within specific cultural practices.

This perspective is also relevant to the development of advanced literacy. The same kind of scaffolding with a knowledgeable mentor is required for the development of advanced literacy as is needed for initial development of mother tongue and basic reading and writing skills. The tools that are part of today's cultures include material, social, and semiotic resources that together enable the making of a vast assortment of ordinary, technical, and abstract meanings. Advanced literacy makes it possible for students to work with concepts that are not part of the everyday world.

The social activity view of literacy puts language itself in the background as it focuses on the social contexts in which literacy tasks occur. Gee (1990, p. 137) argues that "the focus of literacy studies cannot be, and ought not to be, on language, or even literacy itself as traditionally construed. Rather the focus must be on the social practices." In this volume (chap. 8), Gee points out how achieving effective participation in a discourse community means being fully aware of the ways of using language that are taken for granted in that community. He provides an overview of his theory of "Discourses" and points out that schooling is a process through which students add secondary discourses to the primary discourse they have been socialized into in their families and home communities. He shows how cultural practices that are appropriate for certain communities of practice may confer the wrong message when used in a different community, and demonstrates how form and function work together in specific ways within specific discourses. For him, understanding grammar and meanings requires knowing how to situate the meanings "within specific Discourse models connected to the values and interests of specific Discourses." He argues that understanding the values and interests of various discourses is necessary for participation in them, and suggests that raising learners' meta-awareness of these values and interests, as well as providing them with experience within contexts where these discourses are valued, is crucial for providing access to all students.

Discourses are embedded in "communities of practice" (Lave & Wenger, 1991), including the subject-matter and disciplinary communities into which students begin to be socialized at the secondary and postsecondary levels. Becoming a member of a community of practice means adopting the discourse that is recognized and used by the established members of the community. Students gain "insidership" by engaging in the mutual construction of the discourse that community members recognize and use to discuss and critique their knowledge system. Ramanathan (chap. 10, this volume) adopts a related notion, that of the "thought collective," and argues for raising prospective teachers' meta-awareness about the disciplinary communities (thought collectives) that they are being initiated into. She lays out an agenda for developing such consciousness that includes heightening teachers' awareness of how their thought collectives function as activity systems, having them recognize how the activities they are engaged in lead them to new ways of thinking and understanding, and having them recognize the roles they themselves play in the stability and growth of the elements that make up the thought collective that is their discipline. She suggests that doing this will help prospective teachers become more aware of the social and institutional constraints and expectations of the discourses into which they will in turn initiate their students.

This social activity view of literacy also informs much recent research in composition, where writing in higher education is viewed as socially situated and constructed (e.g., Harklau, Losey, & Siegal, 1999), and as "a dynamic process of negotiation, involving both adaptation and resistance, and involving both teachers and students" (Zamel & Spack, 1998, p. xii). García (chap. 13, this volume) takes up this point, demonstrating how bilingual teachers in New York have no contexts in which to develop advanced literacy skills in Spanish, so their Spanish-speaking *voices* are stifled without interlocutors for meaningful dialogue. In addition, their advanced literacy skills in English have been limited by a pedagogy that reflects an impoverished view of meaning-making by imposing rhetorical forms that do not construe meaningful and empowering genres. She explains how the difficulty achieving advanced biliteracy in New York is directly related to the sociolinguistic and historical conditions of the United States as "a society that doesn't value bilingualism and whose schools do not develop biliteracy," and suggests that "advanced biliteracy can only be developed if there are meaningful purposes and authentic audiences for which the two languages are read and written." She points out, however, that in the United States, there are few reasons why advanced literacy in Spanish (or in any other minority language) is needed.

Thus, the social activity view of literacy focuses on how social contexts, discourse communities, and the cultural expectations of those communities interact with individuals' specific situations, facilitating or impeding their development of advanced literacy. Researchers who take a social activity approach to literacy stress the importance of creating contexts in the schools that will enable students from diverse ethnic and class backgrounds to develop advanced literacy and consequently to be able to participate actively and fully in today's world.

LITERACY AS LINGUISTIC ACTIVITY

A focus on literacy as linguistic activity highlights the way that language as a semiotic tool interacts with social contexts in making meaning. Language is the primary resource for meaning-making both in emergent and in advanced literacy contexts, so a theory of language is also needed for full understanding of the demands and challenges of advanced literacy. The theory of language that is currently informing much of the work on literacy as linguistic activity is M. A. K. Halliday's systemic functional linguistic (SFL) theory (Halliday, 1994; Martin, 1992; Matthiessen, 1995). Halliday suggests that language is a "theory of human experience" that children learn as they enact their culture, and that understanding language better can help us understand how this learning happens (Halliday, 1993c). From the linguistic activity perspective, then, literacy is both product and process.

SFL is not a linguistic theory that considers language outside of social contexts; to the contrary, it highlights the ways that language actively *construes* contexts. Language and context are mutually constitutive. A functional grammar connects the linguistic and the social by offering descriptions of language form in relation to semantics, and descriptions of semantic categories in relation to the contexts of social living. It offers, therefore, a theoretically coherent means of describing how and why language varies in relation both to groups of users and uses in social context (Halliday & Hasan, 1989).

The social theory that informs many SFL researchers is that of Basil Bernstein (Bernstein, 1990; 1996; Hasan, 1999). Bernstein suggests that people have different ways of using language, or "coding orientations," which are manifested in the ways they participate in interaction. People are positioned differently, with different senses of what is significant and relevant, based on the social relations that are characteristic of their experiences in a particular social class and culture, which in turn are affected by the amount of power and control that people in that social group are able to exercise in their material lives, among other things. These different coding orientations mean that even when participating in the same contexts, such as schooling, students from different backgrounds will use language in different ways.

Hasan (1999) shows how Bernstein's social theory can fruitfully engage in dialogue with Vygotsky's theory, as both are concerned with finding systematic relationships between context and use of language. Hasan's research focuses on explaining in functional terms the relationship of linguistic choices to the situational contexts in which language is used in order to demonstrate how people from different social groups exploit the meaning potential that grammar provides in different ways, and what the results of that are for the kinds of contexts that are construed. (See also Wells [1994] for another view on the complementarity of Vygotsky's and Halliday's approaches.)

SFL uses the notion of linguistic "register" to illuminate the relationship between language and context. Halliday proposes that a register is the constellation of lexical and grammatical features that realizes a particular situational context (Halliday & Hasan, 1989). Registers vary because what we do with language varies from context to context. Texts produced for different purposes in different contexts have different features, because different lexical and grammatical options are related to the functional purposes that are foregrounded by speakers/writers in responding to the demands of various tasks. A register reflects the social context of a text's production and at the same time realizes that social context through the text. The social context includes what is talked about (field), the relationship between speaker/hearer or writer/reader (tenor), and expectations for how particular texts should be organized (mode; Halliday, 1994). Speakers and writers simultaneously present content, negotiate role relationships, and structure texts through particular grammatical choices that make a text the kind of text it is.

Along with this theory of the construal of social context through linguistic register, SFL theorists also interpret the context of culture through a focus on "genre." Genres are staged, goal-directed activities that are functional for achieving cultural purposes (Christie, 1985). Every culture has genres that are realized through various configurations of register variables and that are recognized as meaningful and appropriate for achieving social purposes.

This linguistic activity perspective focuses on the active role that grammatical and lexical choices play in realizing advanced literacy contexts. For example, Halliday (1993b) has shown how written language has co-evolved historically with new social processes such as scientific experimentation. From this perspective, writing is not only a different medium of expression than oral language but also a means of constructing a semiotic system that adds to the everyday language that we already have. People use the writing system to construct new forms of social action, new contexts that are different from those of daily spoken interaction. These contexts then bring about new grammatical patterns, which in turn enable other new registers to evolve.

This way of thinking about literacy helps us understand how developing new ways of using language also leads to new ways of thinking and new forms of consciousness in students. Constructing new contexts through advanced literacy tasks, using language in new ways, means seeing the world in new ways. Halliday suggests, for example, that it is not possible to "do science" using ordinary language; that the language of science has evolved in the way it has because the kinds of meanings that are made in scientific discourse call for new ways of using the resources of the grammar. From this perspective, learning new ways of using language is learning new ways of thinking, and developing new cognitive skills. To believe this does not mean devaluing the ordinary language that students bring to school from their homes and communities, but suggests that learning new registers will increase students' repertoires in ways that enable them to participate in new contexts.

Halliday's theory explicitly addresses the linguistic challenges of advanced literacy through his construct of "grammatical metaphor," a process whereby some semantic component is construed in the grammar in a form other than that which is prototypical (see Christie & Martin, chaps. 3 and 5 respectively, this volume, for more on grammatical metaphor). Through grammatical metaphor, *everyday* meanings are construed in new ways by the grammar; ways that enable the abstraction, technicality, and development of arguments that characterize advanced literacy tasks. Halliday suggests that "as grammatical generalization is the key for entering into language, and to systematic common-sense knowledge, and grammatical abstractness is the key for entering into literacy, and to primary educational knowledge, so grammatical metaphor is the key for entering into the next level, that of secondary education, and of knowledge that is discipline-based and technical" (Halliday, 1993c, p. 111).

Halliday has characterized the major differences in the continuum between oral and written language (1987, 1994), describing written English as having a denser pattern of lexicalized content than spoken English. A high lexical density (the number of lexicalized elements in the clause) as well as grammatical meta-phor are characteristic of the kinds of written texts that are relevant to advanced literacy tasks. Halliday suggests that being literate means being able to effectively use the lexicogrammatical patterns that are associated with particular kinds of written texts.

Every language and culture has an array of advanced literacy tasks and ways of using language to accomplish those tasks that require conscious study and focus, but the main features of advanced literacy can be described in general terms that are relevant to all students' language development. Halliday (1993a) has shown the similarities between English and Chinese in the ways they construct scientific meanings, and Colombi (chap. 4, this volume) demonstrates how grammatical constructs that describe advanced literacy in English can also illuminate the devel-opment of advanced literacy skills in Spanish.

SFL theory provides a means of identifying the grammatical features that make a particular genre the kind of text it is, so that the relationship of linguistic choices to the situational contexts in which the language is used can be explained in func-tional terms. Because the meaning-making systems of language vary according to social contexts, and not everyone in the community has access to all the possible contexts, one of the major goals of SFL researchers has been to describe academi-cally valued contexts of use, elucidating the features of the genres of schooling and showing the challenges that those features present to students who are developing advanced literacy skills (see, for example, Christie, 1999b; Christie & Martin, 1997; Christie & Misson, 1998; Halliday & Martin, 1993; Hasan & Williams, 1996; Lemke, 1990; Martin & Veel, 1998; Unsworth, 2000).

Christie's and Martin's chapters in this volume make similar contributions. Christie demonstrates the grammatical features that students need to draw on in order to write the genres that are typically expected in secondary-school language arts classes. Illustrating her points through student texts that are examples of com-mon genres of secondary school English, including narratives, book reviews and "opinionated pieces", she describes the grammatical systems that are important for writing texts of these types. Martin focuses on the discourse of history, presenting and describing the variety of texts that constitute a pathway into the kinds of read-ing and writing tasks that advanced literacy in history requires. He analyzes the grammatical and discourse-organizational features of recount, account, explana-tion, exposition, and discussion genres, arguing that control of these genres is nec-essary if students are to be able to engage in the critical analysis that we expect in advanced literacy tasks.

Thus, this view of literacy as linguistic activity emphasizes how language means in a social context and how the social context is construed through language. SFL, as a theory of grammar, provides a tool for investigating the ways that language construes social context and culture by demonstrating how a text means what it does through the grammatical and lexical choices that realize it.

Both social activity and linguistic activity theories of literacy are concerned with scaffolding advanced literacy development for the diverse students and con-texts in which advanced literacy is taught in our schools today. Both perspectives recognize that what we ask students to do in schooling cannot depend on knowl-edge of social contexts and socialization practices outside of school because children's out of school experiences vary widely and prepare them to quite varying extents for the kinds of tasks that schooling requires. So for investigating the development of advanced literacy, both perspectives point us toward a focus on interaction and the scaffolding of tasks in ways that make the demands of the tasks explicit, and both focus us on the literacy demands of different disciplines and discourse communities. Advanced literacy skills enable participation, and it is only through the participation of all that we can truly ensure that all voices are heard. Helping students develop advanced literacy, then, can strengthen democracy and enable society to achieve greater equity.

IMPLICATIONS FOR PEDAGOGICAL PRACTICE

All texts function socially and politically within communities, and it is important that we understand what the demands of advanced literacy are and the consequences of teaching or not teaching students to engage with certain kinds of texts and contexts and not others. Lemke (chap. 2, this volume) points out that a social semiotic perspective on literacy is explicitly political. "We encounter in texts all the values and beliefs of [a] community, all its attitudes and orientations, alliances and conflicts, categories and classifications." This means that we need to ask some key questions about the texts we ask students to read and write at school: "which activities, which settings, which persons and artifacts are connected by these texts? How are they used similarly and differently by those who typically handle them? And how is immediate behavior, and larger-scale social order, different because these texts with these beliefs and values circulated where they did rather than other texts with different beliefs and values?" (Lemke, chap. 2, this volume). By asking such questions about the texts, we can be more deliberate in our choice of the texts and tasks in which we engage students, and understand their implications more clearly.

Different uses of literacy are not neutral; they inevitably contribute to maintaining or challenging the way things are. Engaging in critical dialogue with institutions and social forms requires understanding how the ideas, beliefs and attitudes that make up a world view or a political position are embedded in texts and literacy practices (Hasan, 1996). This is not possible without access to those institutions and forms, and access requires tools for engagement. Advanced literacy is such a tool; with control of advanced literacy, students can engage in the areas of their interest and choice; they can support or resist the current social order. Without control of advanced literacy, students remain marginalized. Enabling students to develop the ability to participate in advanced literacy texts and contexts gives them opportunities and the choice to challenge or support current institutions and social forms, as advanced literacy involves the capacity to understand how language functions to establish and maintain social practices and to articulate different ideological positions (Fairclough, 1992; Gee, 1990; Lemke, 1995).

Some ideological positions achieve positions of power and are taken for granted as the natural and obvious order of things. Both Martin and Gee (chaps. 5 and 8 respectively, this volume) provide examples of this, describing how history is written and historical positions are construed through particular linguistic choices that naturalize certain ideological positions. A critical approach to literacy pedagogy can prepare students to question such ideological positions and provide the tools to make them explicit. Gee points out, for example, that by juxtaposing different models of discourse and different ways of situating meanings we can "get people to reflect overtly on meaning making and the sociopolitical functioning of Discourses in society." But developing such abilities in students is not a task to be taken lightly. Following his detailed description of the genres of the secondary school history curriculum, Martin points out that "this is a lot to learn, especially in education sectors where teachers and students do not share a meta-language for talking about discourse, and where pedagogic principles are influenced by the 'progressive' ideology that direct teaching is an impediment to learning."

A critical approach to literacy "recognizes how traditional forms of instruction can work to maintain literacy deficits and support the differential positioning of students within the social structure" (Walsh, 1991, p. v). Making the expectations of advanced literacy explicit is a way for educators to examine the expectations of schooling. Forms of instruction that rely on an implicit pedagogy put students at risk. Bernstein (1996, p. 112) characterizes pedagogic practice as "visible" or "invisible." In visible pedagogical practice the "hierarchical relations between teacher and pupils, the rules of organization (sequence pace) and the criteria [are] explicit and so known to the pupils. In the case of *invisible* pedagogic practice the hierarchical rules, the rules of organization and criteria [are] implicit and so not known to the pupils." Invisible pedagogy is prevalent in U.S. schools; as, for example, in writing classrooms, where process-oriented pedagogies that do not incorporate explicit instruction and oppose explicit grammar teaching are so dominant that alternatives are rarely considered (Cazden in Cope & Kalantzis, 1993b).

In second-language teaching, too, an invisible pedagogy is the norm. Influenced by Krashen's theory of comprehensible input as the primary motivator of language development, pedagogical approaches to second-language teaching have tended to focus only on immersing students in meaningful input, de-emphasizing or even advising against focus on form in language teaching. Scarcella (1996 and chap. 11, this volume) criticizes the pedagogy that has followed from such research and points to the inadequacy of immersion in comprehensible input as an approach for many of the second-language learner populations in our schools. She, along with others, has suggested that explicit teaching and focus on form is needed for the development of advanced levels of language ability (see, e.g., the chapters in Doughty & Williams, 1998). Celce-Murcia (chap. 7, this volume) argues for the explicit teaching of academic language structures that are not regularly taught, helping students learn when and for what purpose particular structures are used, as this is important knowledge for students who want to develop advanced literacy skills.

The theoretical orientations that inform this volume focus us on the need for a pedagogical approach that is explicit about what is to be taught and learned. If learning happens through scaffolding by more expert others, the expert others have to be aware of what it is they are scaffolding and what they are aiming to achieve. From the linguistic perspective, if we recognize that particular texts are valued in particular social contexts, such as schools, we need to provide opportunities for students to develop an understanding of how those valued texts make the meanings they make through grammatical and lexical choices.

Especially in a diverse, multi cultural environment, it is important to be clear about what it is we want to teach. Because not all students come with similar backgrounds, we need to develop ways of teaching that provide the scaffolding and explicit knowledge that enable all students to develop advanced literacy skills. Research that focuses on differences between children's home cultures and school expectations has made contributions to our understanding of the literacy demands of school, but as Bartolomé (1998) has pointed out, the notion of cultural incongruence or mismatch as an explanation for students' failure at school perpetuates the notion that the practices of school are appropriate as they are. She argues for a re-evaluation of teachers' practices in terms of how such practices consistently and automatically undervalue and disrespect different communication skills, as well as for a more explicit teaching of the academic practices that are valued in schools in the context of culturally appropriate student–teacher interaction.

Researchers working from an SFL perspective have been major proponents of teaching functional grammar as a way of helping students to analyze the literacy tasks that they are expected to engage in. Their goal is to develop a literacy pedagogy that can help learners gain access to educational discourses of the kind that they might otherwise not become familiar with in their daily life. Just giving students opportunities to read and write about what they already know from their personal experience is not enough for the development of advanced levels of literacy. Christie (1999a, p. 157) suggests that the teaching of a functional grammar "develops a critical capacity to interpret and challenge the ways language makes meanings." She gives an example of a language arts curriculum that expects students to read literature and adopt a position that is their *own*, without any explicit analysis of the texts they are reading that would reveal the many and varied embedded cultural meanings. Such an implicit pedagogy puts at risk all those students whose socialization has not prepared them to relate to the embedded meanings, those students who have not had opportunities outside of school to engage in the kind of discussion and critique that prepares them for such tasks in school.

Teaching a metalanguage for talking about texts is also one of the goals of Christie, (chap. 3, this volume), who suggests that the features she describes as characteristic of advanced literacy can and should be explicitly taught, to avoid a "hidden curriculum" that disadvantages those students who do not otherwise have access to such knowledge. This is especially important for the diverse populations in our schools today. As Christie argues, we must identify the texts that are valued in schools and provide access to knowledge about such texts to all students so that none are disadvantaged.

In Australia, the genre-based writing movement has provided descriptions of the main stages of educationally valued genres, with a focus on the register features that make those genres the kinds of texts they are (Christie, 1986; Martin, 1989). Genre-based pedagogy (Christie, 1997; Martin, 1993; Rothery, 1996) takes an explicit approach to literacy instruction with a goal of providing equal opportunities for all students to read and write the genres that will allow them to participate successfully in school, in science and technology, and in other institutions of our society. The genre approach means "being explicit about the way language works to make meaning ... engaging students in the role of apprentice with the teacher in the role of expert on language system and function ... [with] emphasis on content, on structure and on sequence in the steps that a learner goes through to become literate in a formal educational setting" (Cope & Kalantzis, 1993a, p. 1). Many children have been barred from access to "text, knowledges and 'genres' that enable access to social and material resources" because of invisible pedagogies that do not push students to move beyond what they already know (Cope & Kalantzis, 1993b, p. vii). Overt instruction foregrounds the patterns and relationships in the language and practices being taught and helps students gain an understanding of their position in the systems of knowledge and social relations. Learning the standard genres of school-based language and social practices gives students tools for using such genres in their own social, cultural, and political interests.

Christie and Martin (1997, p. 2) present some critical theoretical perspectives that have shaped the discussion of genre based pedagogy, examining genres of the workplace and community such as science, technology, administration, or schooling as well as oral and written texts. They focus on the role of genre in the social construction of experience, suggesting that educational processes are crucial for the building of various social positionings of relevance in the wider world beyond school, the world of work and community. Explicit teaching of the features of the genres of schooling can give students control of the discourses that are powerful in building technology and affecting policy (Martin, chap. 5, this volume).

Second-language researchers are also increasingly arguing for more explicit instruction as a way of increasing students' capacities to be critical. Belcher and Braine (1995, p. xv) suggest, for example, that the current interest in cognitive and social aspects of writing is "informed by the belief in the power of explicit cognitive awareness of the text, subtexts, and contexts of academic discourse to enable individuals to join the collectivist endeavors that academic communities are without loss of the 'home perspectives' that students bring to this endeavor." They favor "explicit presentation and explication of the rules of the academic culture of power" (1995, p. xvi) as a way of helping students learn how to negotiate in the rhetorical communities of academia, as explicit teaching of academic discourse can promote critical participation. "If academic discourse is presented in a framework that highlights its variability, which is both cause and effect of its epistemic nature (how it helps us see our world) and its transformative capabilities (how it helps us shape our world), then the very real privileges that students can enjoy as consciously purposeful users of this privileged discourse should become much more apparent to them" (1995, p. xvi).

Being explicit about what is to be learned does not mean forcing every student to conform to some kind of predetermined format or style. In fact, an explicit approach to pedagogy that makes clear the expectations of the school for particular genres can also recognize the unique perspectives that second-language students and other marginalized students bring to the literacy classroom (Cope & Kalantzis, 1993b). As Cope and Kalantzis suggest,

> an explicit pedagogy for inclusion and access is not the same as an enforced cultural assimilation which teaches the use of alien social tongues for social purposes.... [F]ar from being disadvantaged, students whose first languages are not derived from socially dominant discourses are in a uniquely advantageous position to deconstruct the grammar of dominant discourses simply because they are less influenced by the cultural as-

sumptions of literate culture and the secondary orality that comes with it....
Difference ... does not have to be erased in an explicit curriculum that is aimed at in-
clusion and access. It can be reaffirmed by using it as a resource. (1993a, pp. 85–86)

Students can accept or reject dominant ways of communication by the ways
they use language. They can develop strategies to analyze the ways language is used
in school to serve dominant interests and silence particular groups (Walsh, 1991),
and to examine how institutions and social organizations are maintained and reproduced through the use of language. Martin (chap. 5, this volume) points out
that the texts of advanced literacy "give controllers the meaning potential to intervene across a range of sites, as they so choose, which would otherwise be closed—
to enact bureaucracy for example, or build technology." He suggests that controlling advanced literacy is not just a question of "sounding literate or learned," but
rather it is a question of having power through those texts to effect change. Having
a critical orientation depends on control of "both the discourse under critique and
the discourses used to critique" (Martin, 1999, p. 130). Students cannot contribute to or criticize what they are unable to participate in. Literacy education is about
equity, and giving access to students who would not otherwise be able to engage in
advanced literacy is a way of enabling them to participate in and, if they choose, to
challenge the structures of society that maintain inequality.

The values and hierarchies related to academic genres are not obvious or evident without explicit instruction. Approaches to teaching literacy that draw on
linguistic analysis, particularly register analysis, to understand the discipline-specific nature of writing tasks can be combined with approaches that emphasize the social and discursive practices through which a discipline constitutes
itself, recognizing the complexity and specificity of these contexts (see, for example, Baynham, 1995).

The contributors to this volume present a variety of perspectives and approaches that provide an agenda for the teaching of advanced literacy skills to all
students. By seeing the challenges and benefits of achieving advanced literacy, and
implementing an active pedagogy that teaches about text in social contexts, we
can overcome the labels that separate students into different categories and social
groups, and focus on the common agenda of enabling them gain control over the
texts that have the power to shape the future that they share.

REFERENCES

Baynham, M. (1995). Literacy practices: Investigating literacy in social contexts. London:
    Longman.
Bartolomé, L. (1998). The misteaching of academic discourses: The politics of language in the
    classroom. Boulder, CO: Westview Press.
Belcher, D., & Braine, G. (Ed.). (1995). Academic writing in a second language: Essays on re-
    search and pedagogy. Norwood, NJ: Ablex.
Bernstein, B. (1990). Class, codes and control, Vol. 4: The structuring of pedagogic discourse.
    London: Routledge.
Bernstein, B. (1996). Pedagogy, symbolic control and identity: Theory, research, critique. Lon-
    don: Routledge & Kegan Paul.

Bialystok, E., & Hakuta, K. (1994). In other words: The science and psychology of second-language acquisition. New York: Basic Books.

Christie, F. (1985). Language and schooling. In S. Tchudi (Ed.), Language, schooling and society (pp. 21–40). Upper Montclair, NJ: Boynton/Cook.

Christie, F. (1986). Writing in schools: Generic structures as ways of meaning. In B. Couture (Ed.), Functional approaches to writing: Research perspectives (pp. 221–239). London: Frances Pinter.

Christie, F. (1997). Curriculum macrogenres as forms of initiation into a culture. In F. Christie & J. R. Martin (Eds.), Genre and institutions: Social processes in the workplace and school (pp. 134–160). London: Cassell.

Christie, F. (1999a). The pedagogic device and the teaching of English. In F. Christie (Ed.), Pedagogy and the shaping of consciousness: Linguistic and social processes (pp. 156–184). London: Continuum.

Christie, F. (Ed.). (1999b). Pedagogy and the shaping of consciousness: Linguistic and social processes. London: Continuum.

Christie, F., & Martin, J. R. (Ed.). (1997). Genre and institutions: Social processes in the workplace and school. London: Cassell.

Christie, F., & Misson, R. (Ed.). (1998). Literacy and schooling. London: Routledge.

Collier, V. P. (1987). How long: A synthesis of research on academic achievement in a second language. TESOL Quarterly, 23, 509–531.

Cope, B., & Kalantzis, M. (1993a). The power of literacy and the literacy of power. In B. Cope & M. Kalantzis (Eds.), The powers of literacy: A genre approach to teaching writing (pp. 63–89). London: The Falmer Press.

Cope, B., & Kalantzis, M. (Ed.). (1993b). The powers of literacy: A genre approach to teaching writing. London: The Falmer Press.

Cummins, J. (1983). Language proficiency, biliteracy and French immersion. Canadian Journal of Education, 8(2), 117–138.

Cummins, J. (1989). Language and literacy acquisition. Journal of Multilingual and Multicultural Development, 10(1), 17–31.

Cummins, J., & Danesi, M. (1990). Heritage languages. The development and denial of Canada's linguistic resources. Toronto, CA: Garamond Press.

Delpit, L. (1995). Other people's children: Cultural conflict in the classroom. New York: The New Press.

Delpit, L. (1998). The politics of teaching literate discourse. In V. Zamel & R. Spack (Eds.), Negotiating academic literacies: Teaching and learning across languages and cultures (pp. 207–218). Mahwah, NJ: Lawrence Erlbaum Associates.

Doughty, C., & Williams, J. (Eds.). (1998). Focus on form in classroom second language acquisition. Cambridge, UK: Cambridge University Press.

Fairclough, N. (Ed.). (1992). Critical language awareness. London: Longman.

Faltis, C., & Wolfe, P. (Eds.). (1999). So much to say: Adolescents, bilingualism and ESL in the secondary school. New York: Teachers College.

Gee, J. P. (1990). Sociolinguistics and literacies: Ideology in discourses. London: Falmer Press.

Hakuta, K. (1986). Mirror of language: The debate on bilingualism. New York: Basic Books.

Halliday, M. A. K. (1978). Language as social semiotic. London: Edward Arnold.

Halliday, M. A. K. (1987). Spoken and written modes of meaning. In R. Horowitz & J. Samuels (Eds.), Comprehending oral and written language (pp. 55–82). San Diego, CA: Academic Press.

Halliday, M. A. K. (1993a). The analysis of scientific texts in English and Chinese. In M. A. K. Halliday & J. R. Martin (Eds.), Writing science: Literacy and discursive power (pp. 124–132). Pittsburgh, PA: University of Pittsburgh Press.

Halliday, M. A. K. (1993b). The construction of knowledge and value in the grammar of scientific discourse: Charles Darwin's *The Origin of the Species*. In M. A. K. Halliday & J. R. Martin (Eds.), *Writing science: Literacy and discursive power* (pp. 86–105). Pittsburgh, PA: University of Pittsburgh Press.

Halliday, M. A. K. (1993c). Towards a language-based theory of learning. *Linguistics and Education, 5*(2), 93–116.

Halliday, M. A. K. (1994). *An Introduction to Functional Grammar* (2nd ed.). London: Edward Arnold.

Halliday, M. A. K., & Hasan, R. (1989). *Language, context, and text: Aspects of language in a social-semiotic perspective* (2nd ed.). Oxford, UK: Oxford University Press.

Halliday, M. A. K., & Martin, J. R. (Eds.). (1993). *Writing science: Literacy and discursive power.* Pittsburgh, PA: University of Pittsburgh Press.

Harklau, L., Losey, K., & Siegal, M. (Eds.). (1999). *Generation 1.5 meets college composition: Issues in the teaching of writing to U.S.-educated learners of ESL.* Mahwah, NJ: Lawrence Erlbaum Associates.

Hasan, R. (1996). Literacy, everyday talk and society. In R. Hasan & G. Williams (Eds.), *Literacy in society* (pp. 377–424). Harlow, Essex, UK: Addison Wesley Longman.

Hasan, R. (1999). Society, language and the mind: The meta-dialogism of Basil Bernstein's theory. In F. Christie (Ed.), *Pedagogy and the shaping of consciousness: Linguistic and social processes* (pp. 10–30). London: Continuum.

Hasan, R., & Williams, G. (Ed.). (1996). *Literacy in society.* Harlow, Essex, UK: Addison Wesley Longman.

Krashen, S. (1982). *Principles and practice in second language acquisition.* Oxford, UK: Pergamon Press.

Lantolf, J. P., & Appel, G. (Eds.). (1994). *Vygotskian approaches to second language research.* Norwood, NJ: Ablex.

Lave, J., & Wenger, E. (1991). *Situated learning: Legitimate peripheral participation.* Cambridge, UK: Cambridge University Press.

Lee, C. D., & Smagorinsky, P. (Eds.). (2000). *Vygotskian perspectives on literacy research: Constructing meaning through collaborative inquiry.* Cambridge, UK: Cambridge University Press.

Lemke, J. (1989). Social semiotics: A new model for literacy education. In D. Bloome (Ed.), *Classrooms and literacy* (pp. 289–309). Norwood, NJ: Ablex.

Lemke, J. (1990). *Talking science: Language, learning, and values.* Norwood, NJ: Ablex.

Lemke, J. L. (1995). *Textual politics: Discourse and social dynamics.* London: Taylor & Francis.

Macías, R. F. (2000). The flowering of America: Linguistic diversity in the United States. In S. L. McKay & S.-L. C. Wong (Eds.), *New immigrants in the United States* (pp. 11–57). Cambridge, UK: Cambridge University Press.

McKay, S. L., & Wong, S.-L. C. (Eds.). (2000). *New immigrants in the United States.* Cambridge, UK: Cambridge University Press.

Martin, J. R. (1989). *Factual writing.* Oxford: Oxford University Press.

Martin, J. R. (1992). *English text: System and structure.* Philadelphia: Benjamins.

Martin, J. R. (1993). Genre and literacy—Modeling context in educational linguistics. *Annual Review of Applied Linguistics, 13,* 141–172.

Martin, J. R. (1999). Mentoring semogenesis: 'Genre-based' Literacy Pedagogy. In F. Christie (Ed.), *Pedagogy and the shaping of consciousness: Linguistic and social processes* (pp. 123–155). London: Continuum.

Martin, J. R., & Veel, R. (Eds.). (1998). *Reading science: Critical and functional perspectives on discourses of science.* London: Routledge.

Matthiessen, C. (1995). *Lexicogrammatical cartography: English systems.* Tokyo: International Language Sciences Publishers.

Pérez, B. (Ed.). (1998). *Sociocultural contexts of language and literacy.* Mahwah, NJ: Lawrence Erlbaum Associates.

Rothery, J. (1996). Making changes: Developing an educational linguistics. In R. Hasan & G. Williams (Eds.), *Literacy in society* (pp. 86–123). Harlow, Essex, UK: Addison Wesley Longman.

Scarcella, R. (1996). Secondary education in California and second language research: Instructing ESL students in the 1990s. *CATESOL Journal, 9*(1), 129–152.

Unsworth, L. (Ed.). (2000). *Researching language in schools and communities: Functional linguistic perspectives.* London: (Continuum) Cassell.

Verhoeven, L. (1991) Acquisition of biliteracy. In J. H. Hulstijn & J. F. Matter (Eds.), *Reading in two languages* (pp. 61–74). Amsterdam: *Association Internationale de Linguistique Appliquée (AILA) Review, 8.*

Vygotsky, L. (1986). *Thought and language.* Cambridge, MA: MIT Press.

Walsh, C. (Ed.). (1991). *Literacy as praxis: Culture, language, and pedagogy.* Norwood, NJ: Ablex.

Wells, G. (1994). The complementary contributions of Halliday and Vygotsky to a "Language-based theory of learning." *Linguistics and Education, 6*(1), 41–90.

Wolfram, W., Adger, C. T., & Christian, D. (1999). *Dialects in schools and communities.* Mahwah, NJ: Lawrence Erlbaum Associates.

Zamel, V., & Spack, R. (Eds.). (1998). *Negotiating academic literacies: Teaching and learning across languages and cultures.* Mahwah, NJ: Lawrence Erlbaum Associates.

2

Multimedia Semiotics: Genres for Science Education and Scientific Literacy

---

Jay L. Lemke
CUNY Graduate Center

WHY SCIENTIFIC MULTIMEDIA?

The acquisition of advanced literacy is a social process of enculturation into the values and practices of some specialist community. In the case of scientific literacy this is the community of professional scientists, and their literate practices are normally conducted in multimedia genres where meanings are made by integrating the semiotic resources of language, mathematics, and a variety of visual-graphical presentations. I consider here the nature and extent of the multimedia literacy demands of (1) the advanced secondary-school curriculum in science, (2) the multimedia genres of traditional scientific print publication, and (3) the internet-based multimedia genres that professional scientists are developing to communicate with one another and to the public. A survey of these three domains of scientific literacy can provide a useful foundation for defining both the goals of advanced literacy in science and measures of proficiency in this globally significant literacy.

As writers and scholars we know that no discussion of such important and complex topics can be complete in itself. I focus here on more recent explorations of internet-based multimedia science genres and only briefly summarize work reported elsewhere on science classrooms (Lemke, 1990a; 2000a) and scientific print publications (Lemke, 1998a). I also cite other discussions of basic theoretical and conceptual issues in the analysis of literacies and semiotic practices that I have published over nearly 20 years. In those can be found extensive reference to the large literatures on these subjects, which can hardly be summarized here. Indeed, as bodies of scholarship grow in extent to unprecedented new scales, I believe we must abandon all pretense in individual works to exhaustive citation of the relevant literature. What I write here can only make full sense to those who read not only my cited references, but a substantial portion of the larger web of relevant literature, which is in turn cited in those references. These vast webs of intertextuality are both powerful resources for meaning-making in general and specifically relevant to the nature of scientific literacies (Lemke, 1985, 1990a, 1990b, in press a).

Before looking in detail at specific examples of the multimedia literacy demands of scientific genres, I want to sketch in some general conceptual background that will inform what I say about the examples.

LITERACY AND SOCIAL SEMIOTICS

For some time now I have been trying to develop a discourse about literate social practices that is informed by a theoretical perspective often referred to as social semiotics (e.g., Halliday, 1978; Hodge & Kress, 1988; Lemke, 1989, 1995). The basic principle of social semiotic analysis is that meanings are made by selective contextualization: Each entity that we take to be a sign we make meaningful by considering its syntagmatic, paradigmatic, situational, and intertextual contexts, both actual and potential (Lemke, 1985). We do this in relatively automated ways that represent the typical and repeated meaning-making practices of the communities to which we belong, and in ways that are specific to cultures and subcultures, topics, participants, and settings. Making meaning is a process that takes place in material systems that include but extend beyond ourselves as biological organisms; these systems include the material texts, tools, and artifacts of a community, as well as other persons and nonhuman participants, and extend over multiple spatial and temporal scales from the local setting and immediate moment to the whole history of a widespread community. The meanings we make on any occasion are both uniquely emergent and culturally typical; they depend both on local contexts and on other meanings made in other times and places.

In this view the broadest sense of "literacy" is identical to meaning-making or semiosis in general. A narrower definition of literacy may be constructed by focusing on meaning-making in which complex configurations of artifacts or natural structures play a critical role, as "text," in the meanings we make on some occasion. In this sense a geologist may "read" the Grand Canyon as a text, just as she or he may "read" a photo-montage of the canyon, a geological map of its strata and topography, or a verbal account of its stratigraphy. In fact the meanings made by such a geologist, and the typical genres of diagrammatic and verbal texts in geology, presume that verbal accounts are typically made sense of in relation to relevant maps, diagrams, photographic records, and personal field experience. Each of these is in turn to be interpreted in relation to all the others, including a large intertextual web of verbal and multimedia texts. Actual scientific texts are almost never in fact purely verbal (Lemke, 1998a; Roth, Bowen, & McGinn, 1999).

The narrowest definition of literacy would focus solely on verbal literacy with written media, but this definition is intellectually untenable today. Efforts to say what distinguishes "writing" (e.g., Harris, 1995; Lemke, 1997), unless they arbitrarily restrict themselves to signs interpreted only in terms of the semantics of the linguistic system, find that the boundaries between written text and mathematical or chemical symbolism are hard to declare or justify; indeed, both of these latter instances arguably descend from language historically and remain partially interpreted linguistically. From text to table, table to chart, chart to graph, graph to diagram, diagram to picture there are historical continuities and contemporary unities in practice (Lemke, 1998a). Developmentally, speech and gesture derive from common motor routines, pictures descend from the lasting traces of gestures, and writing is a differentiated form of expressive speech-accompanying gesture, not initially separated from depiction. Semiotically, we never in fact make meaning with only the resources of one semiotic system: words conjure images, images are verbally mediated, writing is a visual form, algebra shares much of the syntax and semantics of natural language, geometric diagrams are interpreted verbally and pictorially, even radio voices speak to us of individuality, accent, emotional state, and physical health through vocal signs not organized by the linguistic code. All semiotics is multimedia semiotics; all meaning is made in the integration of resources from only analytically separable semiotic resource systems.

In the perspective of social semiotics, meaning making is social, and material, and semiotic, and so therefore is literacy. Because it is material, no actual phenomenon of literate practice can ever be exhaustively analyzed by specifying the formal relations by which it instances one semiotic, or even all known semiotics (the consequence here has long been recognized by phenomenology, the cause is a bit more mysterious; Lemke, 2000b). Because it is semiotic, our accounts of what and how it means must consider the state of affairs it presents, how it orients itself in the system of intertextual alternatives, and what unifies it as a "text" (Halliday's 1978, 1994 "ideational, interpersonal, and textual" linguistic meta-functions, and see generalizations in Kress & van Leeuwen, 1996; Lemke, 1998a; O'Toole, 1990, 1994). Because it is social, we must explicate its social functions, both local and immediate and larger-scale and longer-term, to understand its meanings in the widest sense.

CRITICAL LITERACY

Every literacy has evolved historically to fulfill some social function. Literacies in general assist cooperative activity in communities, and in particular they help us integrate short-term activities across longer time scales (Lemke, 2000c). A "text" in the sense of some material artifact that survives on a timescale that is long compared to that of its production, and that circulates in a community over this longer timescale, comes to play a role in many specific short-term activities in which it is semiotically interpreted, and thereby functions most basically to tie together longer-term, larger-scale social processes and networks.

We can see, therefore, in texts the semiotic lifeblood of a community circulating through the body politic. We encounter in texts all the values and beliefs of that community, all its attitudes and orientations, alliances and conflicts, categories and classifications. We learn what it regards as normal and surprising, assured and doubtful, desirable and undesirable, necessary, permitted, forbidden, and optional. But to understand the wider functions of the beliefs and values embodied in texts we must also study how they circulate: which activities, which settings, which persons and artifacts are connected by these texts? How are they used similarly and differently by those who typically handle them? And how is immediate behavior and larger-scale social order different because these texts with these beliefs and values circulated where they did rather than other texts with different beliefs and values?

A social semiotic perspective on literacy is explicitly political. Because it does not see meaning as inherent in texts, but rather in how they are used and interpreted in communities, it points outward to the social functions of texts and not just inward to their formal patterns. Because it sees meaning-making not as an interior mental process but as an ecological, material process in an emergent self-organizing system larger than the isolated organism, it poses questions about the social and material effects of texts and not just about the organismic physiology of their production or interpretation. Because it seeks to understand both the semiotic and material bases of social organization, it regards every text as having a political function on some social scale.

I believe the goal of education, all education, is to nurture the development of critical intellectual capabilities. The responsible exercise of the power that knowledge gives us requires that we assess the implications, consequences, and alternatives of our actions as best we can. Every text we make, every text in whose circulation we participate, every discourse formation or multimedia genre we adopt and use has larger political and social functions. Ethically and morally we must know what we do. Politically and personally we must learn enough to help our communities do better.

Advanced multimedia literacy in the genres of science and scientific education confers great power in our society. To empower a wider range of people, we need to understand the specific semiotic and social demands of this literacy. To empower them responsibly, we need to understand equally well its social and political consequences.

THE MULTIMEDIA LITERACY DEMANDS
OF SCIENTIFIC EDUCATION

For most of us our first encounters with the multimedia literacies of science come in school. School science and its texts are not examples of the genres of professional science, not even in the advanced secondary school curriculum or in most of tertiary education (Lemke, 1994; Roth et al., 1999). They do however initiate students into its multimedia literacy demands (Lemke, 2000a). Science textbooks contain not just words in sentences and paragraphs, but tables, charts, diagrams, graphs, maps, drawings, photographs, and a host of specialized visual representations from acoustical sonograms to chromatography strips and gene maps. In many cases they also contain mathematical formulas and algebraic derivations.

But it is not just the print materials that make these demands. In a recent analysis of videotape data following one student through a day of advanced chemistry and physics classes (Lemke, 2000a; see also Cumming & Wyatt-Smith, 1997), I observed that in his chemistry lesson this student had to interpret a stream of rapid verbal English from his teacher; the writing and layout information on an overhead transparency; writing, layout, diagrams, chemical symbols, and mathematical formulas in the open textbook in front of him; the display on his handheld calculator; more writing, layout, diagrams, symbolic notations, and mathematics in his personal notebook; observations of gestures and blackboard diagrams and writing by the teacher; observations of the actions and speech of other students, including their manipulation of demonstration apparatus, and the running by-play commentary of his next-seat neighbor. In fact he quite often had to integrate and coordinate most of these either simultaneously or within a span of a few minutes. There is no way he could have kept up with the content development and conceptual flow of these lessons without integrating at least a few of these different literacy modes almost constantly.

In one episode in the physics lesson, there is no role for the notebook, and not even a diagram, but a pure interaction of language and gestural pantomime, including whole-body motion. The teacher, Mr. Phillips, is standing just in front of the first (empty) row of student desktables, at the opposite end of the room from where the student, John, is sitting. John sees his teacher's hands cupped together to form a sphere, then the hands move a foot to the left and cup together to make another sphere. Then back to the first, and one hand and Mr. Phillips' gaze make a sweeping gesture from one to the other; then Mr. Phillips begins to walk to the left, repeating these gestures and walking down toward John's end of the room. Fortunately, Mr. Phillips is also talking and John is listening; by integrating the teacher's precise and conventionalized mime with his accompanying technical speech, John can interpret that the cupped hands are atoms, the sweeping hand a photon, emitted by the first, traveling to the second, absorbed there, re-emitted after a while, passing on down through a ruby crystal, producing a snowball effect of more and more photons of exactly the same energy. In other words, the crystal is a laser.

Mr. Phillips says he's going to add more complexity to the picture now. An atom might shoot out a photon in this direction—gesture away from the axis of the room-sized imaginary ruby crystal toward the students—or in this one—gesture back toward the blackboard—or … —oblique gesture. How do we get a laser beam then? He walks back and forth between the ends of his now lasing, imaginary ruby crystal, describing the mirrors he gestures into being at each end, but saying they differ in reflectivity and transmissivity, to build up and maintain the avalanche of photons, while letting some out in the form of the laser beam. John has seen mimes like this before; he has seen diagrams of atoms and crystals, of photons being absorbed and emitted by atoms. Intertextually, he can use the visual literacy of these past diagrams, together with his literacy in pantomime, and his verbal discourse literacy in atomic physics to synthesize a model of how a laser works.

John is lucky. He does appear to have the required literacies, and to be able to combine and synthesize them across media, events, and semiotic modalities. There is a great deal that John must already know in order to make sense of what he is learning in these lessons minute to minute. Not just language and verbally expressed discourse formations (such as the intertextual thematic formations I have described in Lemke, 1983, 1995, and elsewhere), but conventional diagrams of atomic arrangements in a crystal, standard graphs of energy levels of atoms, typical ways of gesturing directionality in space, and common notations for the algebraic and symbolic representation of chemical reactions and stoichiometric calculations of concentrations and the pH of solutions. His literacy extends to motor routines in operating a calculator, social discourse routines of question and answer in a classroom, and technical practices in manipulating a spectroscope and diluting a solution. He must constantly translate information from one modality to another: numerical to algebraic, algebraic to graphical, graphical to verbal, verbal to motor, pantomime to diagrammatic, diagrammatic to discursive. But simple translation is not enough; he must be able to integrate multiple media simultaneously to re-interpret and recontextualize information in one channel in relation to that in the other channels, all in order to infer the correct or canonical meaning on which he will be tested. In most cases, the complete meaning is not expressed in any one channel, but only in two or more, or even only in all of them taken together (see detailed examples in Lemke, 2000a; Roth & Bowen, 2000; Wells, 2000).

Even if we restrict our attention to the interpretation of printed text, scientific genres remain highly multimodal.

MULTIMEDIA GENRES OF SCIENTIFIC PRINT PUBLICATIONS

In another recent study (Lemke, 1998a), I examined the semiotic forms found in the standard genres of research articles and advanced treatises of professional scientific publication. In a diverse corpus, across disciplines and publication venues, the clear finding was that there is typically at least one and often more than one graphical display *and* one mathematical expression per page of running text in typical scientific print genres. There can easily be three to four each of graphics displays and mathematical expressions separate from verbal text *per page.*

In one prestigious journal of the physical sciences, each typical three-page article integrated *four* graphical displays and *eight* set-off mathematical expressions. Some had as many as three graphical displays per page of double-column text, or as many as seven equations per page. In another journal, in the biological sciences, each typical page had two nontabular visual-graphical representations integrated with the verbal text, and each short (average length 2.4 pages) article typically had six graphics, including at least one table and one quantitative graph.

To appreciate the absolutely central role of these nonverbal textual elements in the genres being characterized, it may help to ponder a few extreme (but hardly unique) cases:

- In one advanced textbook chapter, a diagram was included in a *footnote* printed at the bottom of the page.
- In one seven-page research report, 90% of a page (all but five lines of main text at the top) was taken up by a complex diagram and its extensive figure caption.
- The main experimental results of a two and one half-page report were presented in a set of graphs occupying one-half page and a table occu-

pying three fourths of another. The main verbal text did not repeat this information but only referred to it and commented on it.

- In most of the theoretical physics articles, the running verbal text would make no sense without the integrated mathematical equations, which could not in most cases be effectively paraphrased in natural language, although they can be, and are normally meant to be read out as if part of the verbal text (in terms of semantics, cohesion, and frequently grammar).

A more detailed analysis in this study showed how absolutely normal and necessary it is to interpret the verbal text in relation to these other semiotic formations, and vice versa. It is not the case that they are redundant, each presenting the complete relevant information in a different medium; rather the nature of the genre presupposes close and constant integration and cross-contextualization among semiotic modalities.

Why? Why is science not content with verbal linguistic expression? Why have the forms of verbal expression it does use co-evolved so as to mainly make sense only when interpreted in close association with mathematics, diagrams, graphs, tables, maps, and so on? One reasonable hypothesis (for more discussion see Lemke, 1998a, in press b) is that in attempting to describe the quantitative covariation of continuously variable phenomena (shape, temperature, velocity, angle, color, voltage, concentration, mass, and so on) scientific discourse came up against the limitations of language as a semiotic resource. The semantics of natural language specializes in categorization—in discretely nameable things and processes and in classifying their relationships. Language is not very good at describing complex shapes, shades of color, or degrees of temperature. For these purposes visual and spatial-motor representations are much better suited. To achieve precision however in relating one representation to another, the semantics of natural language also had to be extended historically to describe quantitative variation and relationships. Language remained the main tool of conceptualization and classification, but it was of use only when integrated with mathematical and visual representation. All these representations were and are themselves useful primarily as adjuncts to practical, technical, and experimental activity (see for example Lynch & Woolgar, 1990). The operational conventions of scientific procedures themselves constitute yet another semiotic modality to be integrated with the others.

SCIENTIFIC LITERACIES AND NEW MULTIMEDIA GENRES

When we seek to educate students to use advanced scientific literacies, we are participating in their socialization into global communities. Scientific discourse formations and multimedia genres, at least in their print forms, are today international in their scope and global in their reach. In order to be perceived in the scientific and technical community as deploying them appropriately, students need to learn and adopt, even with reservations, certain values and identities. To *think like a physicist* (or biochemist, or chemical engineer), to write like one, to make sense of technical genres as do those who create them authoritatively, students need to understand the larger value assumptions and subcultural conventions of the scientific community. They need to know what is regarded as of greater relative importance and how to signal such importance. They need to know how conflict and adversarial relationships are managed in this community. They need to understand how the texts of technoscience not only serve internal functions within the community, but how they link the community to its larger social, economic, and political functions in the wider society.

It is part of internal ethos or ideology of science about itself that it is an activity of pure human good, and that any discernable link to matters economic or political distances science from its ideal and is to that extent not truly science. Historically this isolationism arose from the conflicts between the grounds of scientific authority and those of religious and political authority (e.g., Shapin & Schaffer, 1985) in times of great social unrest and violence. We see its effects today in the restricted semantic register of scientific language, where evaluations of warrantability are manifold and explicit, but other dimensions of evaluative and expressive meaning (Lemke, 1998b) must be inferred on the basis of often distant or unwritten intertexts. Scientific texts are written as if they were only about matters of fact and explanation, when of course every text makes meaning about desirability, importance, permissibility, expectedness, and all the other value dimensions.

From the viewpoint of social semiotics, scientific multimedia genres are as they are not just because they are fit to the internal functional needs of the scientific community, but also because they play a role in linking that community within the wider social, economic, and political institutions that make their continued existence possible.

It is more or less the case today that all professional science is *big science* (i.e., it is funded and supported by large-scale social institutions, whether universities, foundations, or increasingly, and always so historically, governmental and military agencies). One such agency, responsible for the support of a great deal of scientific research in the United States, is NASA, the National Aeronautics and Space Administration. It was created to separate secret and restricted military research from research that would potentially have wider economic impact and political support. In fact there is relatively little difference between a missile and a "launch vehicle" so far as technology is concerned, and even less between a military spy satellite and a civilian "earth observing platform." NASA is increasingly driven by its potential economic impact and its need for the political support that derives from economic benefits to turn its technologies toward the earth rather than the stars.

NASA also maintains one of the largest systems of scientific and technical communication and publicly available information databases in the world. Scientific teams and high technology companies look to NASA, as to its sister institutions (such as NOAA and the U.S. National Laboratories) to maintain the complex networks of nonprint communication on which they depend, and to supply them with the results of taxpayer-supported scientific research. Indeed the global technoscience community, and not just the United States, depends on NASA's networks of information.

The global communications and information technology infrastructure known as the internet was initially created to permit continuous military communications under conditions of nuclear warfare. It was then parasitized by the communication needs of scientists doing contract research for the U.S. military, and later by the wider scientific community whose research was funded by the U.S. government and seen to be in the national interest. For much longer than the commercial internet has been in the public eye, the scientific internet existed to permit rapid transmission of technical information among distant research centers doing related projects. The model of information on which it is based was designed to allow all forms of meaning: verbal, graphical, numerical, to be exchanged with equal ease. Very powerful computing facilities were, and largely still are, needed to convert these information streams into forms of which humans can make sense (text, images, numbers), but in the last few years, as we all know, smaller computers have acquired the power to participate in this communications network and to transform at least small data streams into the beautiful text, images, animations, audio, and video of the World Wide Web.

NASA maintains a very large website as the primary interface to its enormous databases of satellite-derived information and many other technical resources. Because it is a governmental agency, and so a political as well as a scientific institution, NASA also uses its website to build popular and business support for its agendas. Conveniently for researchers interested in the multimedia literacy demands of scientific information on the internet, its webpages are also in the public domain.

In a study I am currently engaged in, I am looking at the presentation of scientific information of essentially the same kind and from the same source in two different parts of the NASA website (actually it is a meta-site, a large number of interlinked websites spread across the component institutions in the nasa.gov domain). In one of these sites, the NASA Earth Observatory (http://earthobservatory.nasa.gov), data on conditions of the atmosphere, oceans, land, and biosphere of the earth as observed from space are presented for science teachers, students, and interested members of the educated public. In the other, the Goddard Space Flight Center's Earth Sciences (GES) Distributed Active Archive Center (DAAC, http:// daac.gsfc.nasa.gov/DAAC_DOCS/gdaac_home.html) this same information is made available to professional scientists, in strikingly parallel fashion. (In fact I suspect the Earth Observatory site may have been modeled after Goddard's. For all web figures below, the original screen shots are archived in color at http://academic.brooklyn.cuny.edu/education/jlemke/webs/nasa/Davis-NASA.htm.)

The level of multimedia literacy demands at the Earth Observatory (EO) site is hardly minimal. Users of these webpages confront the complexities of not just simplified scientific text, but an interactive glossary function, links to background information in documents accessed from a Library page, links to closely related websites documenting research projects on related scientific topics (the Study), and most notably the option of linking to an interactive system for scientific visualization of relevant satellite data (the Observation Deck, Fig. 2.1a). It is the main Observation Deck page that is organized along strikingly parallel lines with the Goddard GES DAAC main page. By selecting a "parameter" (i.e., type of data derived from satellite sensors, e.g., Vegetation) and a time range (see Fig. 2.1b), users can display, in the form of color-coded maps (Fig. 2.1c), an animated display that shows changes in the values of this parameter worldwide over the chosen time range, and even display side by side for comparison maps coded for

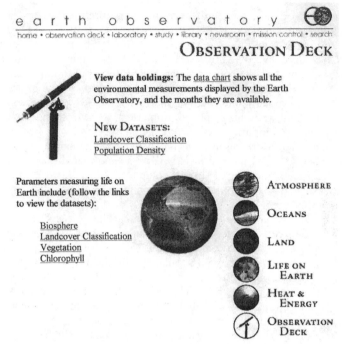

two different parameters. Users have the choice of three display modes:
mercator-like projection maps in an animated strip (Fig. 2.1c, rather like cartoon
frames that can be flashed by quickly to show a single dynamically changing image), a grid or matrix table of maps each for a different fixed time within the
range, and a globe that shows only a single time frame, but can be rotated to show
the color-coded values of the parameter(s) at all points on the earth, or as seen
from any direction in space above the earth.

Moreover, the color-coding is quantitatively based, and a key is provided that
shows a continuously variable color-spectrum and the corresponding numerical
values (Figs. 2.1b, 2.1c). Along with this is an explanatory paragraph discussing
what the color-coded image maps show that is of scientific importance, and in
some cases what the technical nature of the parameter is and from what satellite instrument it is derived (e.g., Fig. 2.1b, truncated at bottom). These latter facts are
not usually fully explained, even if they are mentioned.

The Earth Observatory site in fact also includes a "Style Sheet" for potential
contributors, and this makes it clear that its genre conventions, at least verbally,
are journalistic. It aspires to something like the level of sophistication and public
accessibility of a print publication such as *Scientific American*. There is almost no
mathematics in the EO site, but regular use of both numerical values and visual

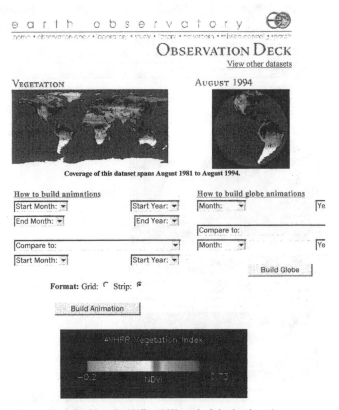

FIG. 2.1b   NASA Earth Observatory: Life on Earth, Vegetation Dataset Webpage (January 2000, http://earthobservatory.nasa.gov/Observatory/Datasets/ndvi.avhrr.html).

representation of quantitative information and relationships. In making use of the Observation Deck's scientific visualization facility, visitors must integrate scientific language, specialized visual display genres, quantitative values, and time-dependent animation. The latter is also interactive; the user employs a motor routine to control the animations by dragging the mouse over the images while a counter changes to show the month and year of each frame.

The demands of the EO site represent the minimal goals of scientific multimedia literacy in the current school curriculum, according to generally agreed on national standards (American Association for the Advancement of Science, 1996;

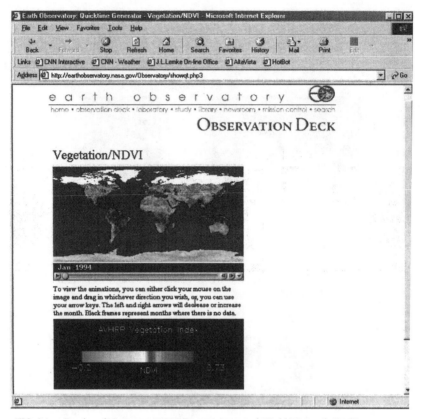

FIG. 2.1c   Display of Vegetation NDVI Data in Animated World Map with Key (January 2000, http://earthobservatory.nasa.gov/Observatory/showqt.php3).

National Research Council, 1996). They would not be sufficient for tertiary study of a scientific or technical field, or even for the work that John was doing in his advanced science classroom in a secondary school. They do show us, however, how print genres of sophisticated popularized science are evolving to take advantage of the new computational possibilities of internet-based multimedia.

To gain a better sense of the dimensions of increasing semiotic sophistication that are needed beyond the EO site's level, we can turn to its sister site for professional scientists. It is not in fact easy for the casual visitor to the NASA website to find the GES DAAC. Most of the pages that are readily accessed from the NASA homepage (www.nasa.gov) are oriented to informing the general public and have the production values of a news magazine or advertising poster. You can get to the EO site by looking through the prominently displayed "Cool NASA Sites" on the homepage. EO can be reached by just two hypertext jumps from the NASA homepage. GES DAAC on the other hand took quite a lot of hunting to find in the absence of knowledge of the correct specialized search terms. A relatively direct path, seeking information on earth sciences data, takes six such jumps, most of them far from obvious choices in menus with several other plausible options. A slightly shorter path leads to a search engine, which, if one knows the correct technical terms, would bypass the GES DAAC and lead directly to the possibility of downloading the raw data that the GES DAAC pages describe. There is also information available on how to turn this raw data into useful visualizations, but only for those using high-end scientific workstation computers.

At the Goddard Earth Sciences DAAC homepage, we find a marvelous analogue of the EO Observation Deck page. Both contain menus of links to information on topics such as the earth's atmosphere, oceans, biosphere, and so on. The respective menus are:

Earth Observatory Observation Deck:

Atmosphere—rainfall, ozone, cloud fraction

Oceans—chlorophyll, sea temperature

Land—vegetation, fires, surface temperature

Life on Earth—biosphere, vegetation, chlorophyll

Heat and Energy—surface temperature, outgoing radiation

GSFC Earth Science DAAC:

Atmospheric Chemistry

Atmospheric Dynamics

Field Experiments (meteorological variables)

Hydrology (global precipitation)

Interdisciplinary (global land, ocean, and atmospheric parameters)

Land Biosphere (vegetation and infrared brightness)

Ocean Color

On the EO page, passing the cursor over each menu item heading (at right) leads to the appearance of a colored (2-D) globe of the earth showing a typical pattern for one of the parameters under that heading and beneath it a list of links to the visualization engine for various specifically related data parameters. (See Fig. 2.1a.)

On the DAAC page, passing the cursor over each menu item (at left) leads to the appearance in a frame on the right of a colored graphic image and paragraph long caption. The images are in two cases color-coded earth globes (Figs. 2.2a and 2.2b), exactly as on the EO page, but other images include a complex data graph showing atmospheric carbon dioxide and global temperatures as a function of time

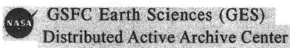

Atmospheric Chemistry Ozone and other trace gas compositions, dynamics and energy interactions of the upper atmosphere.

Atmospheric Dynamics 3-dimensional dynamic and thermodynamic state of the earth-atmosphere system, from satellite measurements and assimilation systems.

Field Experiments Aircraft and ground based measurements of meteorological variables designed to improve science algorithms and validate satellite-derived data products.

Hydrology Global precipitation, its variability, and associated latent heating, important for studying the global hydrological cycle, climate modeling and applications.

Interdisciplinary Global land, ocean and atmospheric parameters mapped to uniform spatial and temporal scales for basic research and applications studies.

Land Biosphere Long time-series vegetation and thermal infrared brightness temperature data sets for global change research.

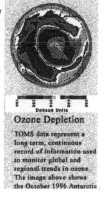

Ozone Depletion

TOMS data represent a long term, continuous record of information used to monitor global and regional trends in ozone. The image above shows the October 1996 Antarctic.

FIG. 2.2a   NASA Goddard Space Flight Center Earth Sciences Distributed Active Archive Homepage, Cursor over Atmospheric Chemistry link, Displaying Ozone Depletion (January 2000, http://daac.gsfc.nasa.gov/DAAC_DOCS/gdaac_home.html).

(years and decades, Fig. 2.2c) and a topographic visualization of the vector flow of air and ocean currents in a monsoon (Fig. 2.2d). Beneath one of the globe images is a color-spectrum quantitative key for ozone concentrations (Fig. 2.2a). The captions tend to give more technical descriptions of the nature of the data as well as of its scientific importance. On this one DAAC page the multimedia literacy demands are already in excess of those for the entire sequence on the EO site leading to interpretation of the visualized coded data maps. These users begin already past the point where the EO users end.

If we try to locate comparable information to that in the EO site (e.g., its Life on Earth: Vegetation data, which shows the greening of the earth with the seasons and the extent of polar snowfields in the north and south year by year) we select Land Biosphere from the DAAC menu and are taken first to the option to browse and select the data we want by means of a search page that has drop-down boxes like those on the EO visualization page (Fig. 2.3a, compare Fig. 2.1b) listing the various parameters available (in DAAC these are datasets, but classified by their typical scientific uses) and similarly, again like EO, for the time ranges. In the DAAC site, time can be specified to the day, not just the month as in EO, and geographical regions can also be isolated. But once a data set is selected, our

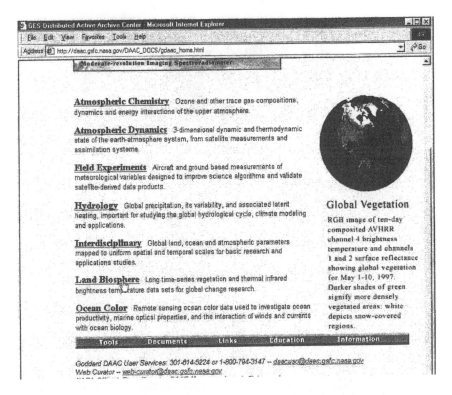

FIG. 2.2b   NASA GSFC DAAC Homepage, Cursor over Land Biosphere link, Displaying Global Vegetation (same URL as for Fig. 2.2a, different cursor position).

choice is either to download it by FTP (the faster forerunner of HTTP on the web), typically 35 megabytes, or to browse it … but this is only possible if we have a unix-based workstation computer, not an ordinary PC. True scientific users would then have a comparable experience to the EO visitor. Further technical literacy is required to make use of the instructions given on how to set up the browser function on the workstation.

Unlike at the EO site, browsable images here do not include brief color-key codes and an explanatory paragraph. Rather, there is an entire menu of resources and documentation to assist the technical user in interpreting the data displays. In some cases this includes links to the researchers who have created the datasets; and in all cases links to the published scientific literature describing all aspects of the production of the data. If we in fact look at some of this documentation (there is a 96-page printable manual you can download for the data we are interested in here on vegetation cover), we find after three more jumps a sample of the displays of our data, in low resolution, as a grid of maps, very similar to what

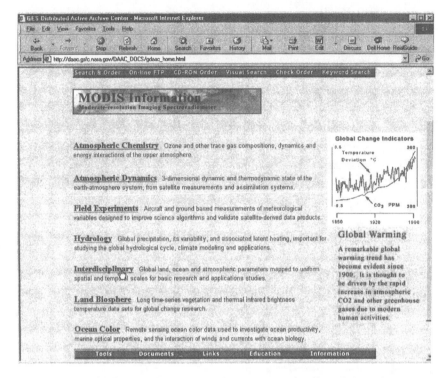

FIG. 2.2c   NASA GSFC DAAC Homepage, Cursor over Interdisciplinary link, Displaying
Global Warming (same URL as for Fig. 2.2a, different cursor position).

we can get in the EO visualization (see Fig. 2.3b). It is accompanied by a reference
to the published literature, and the key explanation:

The Climate Data Set is a 1 degree by 1 degree product for use in global, coarse resolution modeling studies. The Climate data set is a global, 1-degree × = 1-degree, NDVI
field. This is derived from the Composite Data Set by calculating a mean Channel 1
reflectance and a mean Channel 2 reflectance for each 1-degree area in which 50% or
more of the 8 km pixels are identified as land pixels.

There is no automatic glossary function here as there is in the EO site, but we
can use the online documentation to unpack the meaning of much of the technical
language. In doing so, we get some sense of the multimedia literacy demands of professional scientific genres. For example, "composite data set" leads back to "daily
data set" and its description is primarily in the form of a table:

Daily Data Set Layers

Layer	Units	Range
NDVI	-	−1 to +1
CLAVR flag	-	0 to 31
QC flag	-	0 to 31
Scan Angle	radians	−1.047 to +1.047
Solar Zenith Angle	radians	0–1.396
Relative Azimuth Angle	radians	0–6.283
Ch1 Reflectance	%	0–100
Ch2 Reflectance	%	0–100
Ch3 Brightness Temps	Kelvin	160–340
Ch4 Brightness Temps	Kelvin	160–340
Ch5 Brightness Temps	Kelvin	160–340
Date and Hour of Obs	DDD.HH	1–366.23

[http://daac.gsfc.nasa.gov/CAMPAIGN_DOCS/LAND_BIO/Daily_ds.html]

The actual parameter in the data set that underlies the images of interest to us, and that is in fact identified, but not explained, even in EO is 'NDVI'. Following on to the basic documentation for this we find:

> The Normalized Difference Vegetation Index (NDVI), which is related to the proportion of photo synthetically absorbed radiation, is calculated from atmospherically corrected reflectances from the visible and near infrared AVHRR channels as:

> (CH2 − CH1) / (CH2 + CH1)

> Where CH1 is the reflectance in the visible wavelengths (0.58–0.68 um) and CH2 is the reflectance in the reflective infrared wavelengths (0.725–1.1 um). The principle behind this is that Channel 1 is in a part of the spectrum where chlorophyll causes considerable absorption of incoming radiation, and Channel 2 is in a spectral region where spongy mesophyll leaf structure leads to considerable reflectance (Tucker 1979, Jackson et al., 1983, Tucker et al., 1991).

[http://daac.gsfc.nasa.gov/CAMPAIGN_DOCS/LAND_BIO/ndvi.html]

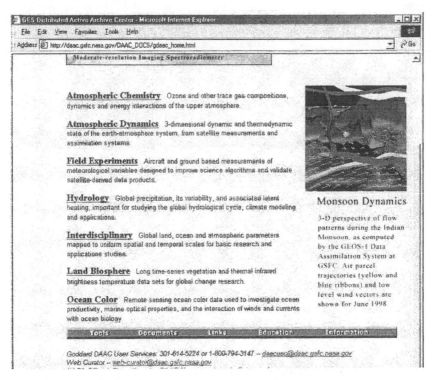

FIG. 2.2d   NASA GSFC DAAC Homepage, Cursor over Atmospheric Dynamics link,
Displaying Monsoon Dynamics (same URL as for Fig. 2.1a, different cursor position).

This paragraph is perfectly typical of mathematical-scientific register: the set-off
algebraic formula expression, followed by the "Where …" definitions, the citations
to the literature, as well as the use of technical terms, and embedded numerical expressions with units of measure. Note the hypertext link on "reflectances" that is a
new feature of this medium. It leads in fact not to a simple text definition, but to a
complex page dominated by black-and-white images showing the differences between the channel 1 and channel 2 data used in NDVI calculations; this
reflectances page also contains embedded quantitative data with measure units
and a link to the published literature.

The literacy demands here are quite comparable to those of scientific print publications (Lemke, 1998a), but go beyond them in the specific matter of hypertext
(or hypermedia) literacy. In print genres, the scientific citation is a standard
intertextual referring device; to make use of it requires not just language literacy
skills to interpret the citation, but also the activity skills needed to physically locate
the printed text referred to. That latter demand is being simplified by the hypertext
links of web-based genres (although it is still present here; the links to the citations
lead not to the original papers but only to the detailed citation information in an

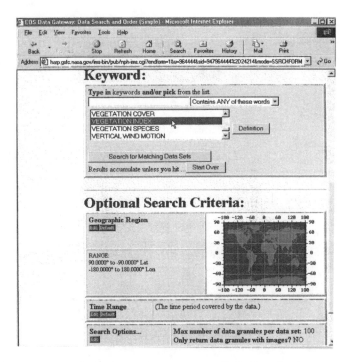

FIG. 2.3a   NASA EOS Data Gateway: Data Search and Order Form Page (Access via link: Enter as Guest from http://harp.gsfc.nasa.gov/~imswww/pub/imswelcome/plain.html).

online bibliography). At the same time, it becomes easier in the new medium to increase the density of links, and so the complexity of the intertextual web that users must integrate in order to make full sense of any part of it.

Hypertext literacy is a large subject in itself (e.g., Reinking, Labbo, McKenna, & Kiefer, 1998; Rouet & Levonen, 1996), raising basic questions of how people navigate through large hypertextual webs, and how we make meaning across both short-term, small-scale trajectories of sequentially linked webpages and also longer-term, larger-scale trajectories that may eventually include a large fraction of all the locally linked pages at a site (or within a meta-site). Hypertext literacy is feature of the emerging extended literacy of computer-based multimedia (Lemke, 1998c), which happens to have its leading developmental edge in the domain of scientific communication.

CONCLUSIONS AND INITIATIVES

It is too early in my ongoing studies of web-based multimedia genres to draw firm conclusions about the dimensions and directions of advanced literacy beyond

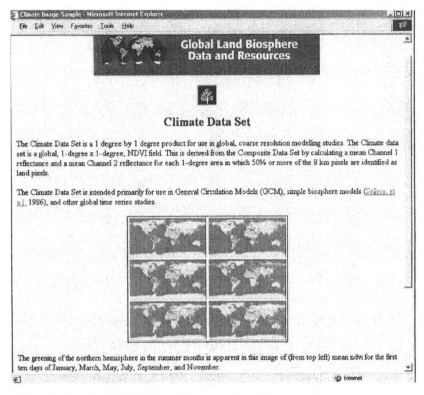

FIG. 2.3b   NASA GSFC Global Land Biosphere Data and Resources, Climate Data Set
Webpage (January 2000, http://daac.gsfc.nasa.gov/CAMPAIGN_DOCS/LAND_BIO/
Climate_ds.html).

what carries over, transformed, from print literacies. It will be important to compare not just public-interest versus professionally oriented websites, but also scientific websites (which are somewhat conservative in conserving the substantial
cultural capital already invested in scientific print literacies) versus more *avant
garde* experiments with the semiotic affordances of web-based media. It is typical in
the evolution of any medium that it first seeks to replicate familiar genres (e.g.,
early live television and theatre, photography and painting, email and office
memos, web chat and conversation), but then creates new genres of its own (music
videos, strobe photographs, list groups, the emerging distinctive CHAT register).
The webpage itself is a new proto-genre, evolving away from its antecedents in
printed-page composition, and it will likely diverge into many new genres fitting
specialized functional niches.

Meanwhile, analysis of web-based scientific genres continues to show us the institutional connections of scientific texts in ways that may be more obvious on the
web than in print. The NASA homepage shows ample evidence of political inten-

tions (e.g., its anti-drug message), and elsewhere in the site it is easy to trace the new emphasis on *doing business* that has been added to the original mission of *doing science*. It would be interesting to know how many links there are from webpages in the .mil (military) domain to those in nasa.gov. The site also shows the many means by which different kinds of users are differentiated, from "kids" to "educators" to "business" and "commercial technology," from the general public to professional scientists. Institutionally, and ecologically, all these different actors and activities form a single system. We have already seen briefly here how similar presentations can be for technical and nontechnical audiences; it is obvious that one is in some sense derived from the other, and it is likely that in a larger view intertextual influences circulate full-circle and the forms of technical genres take into account— even in their reactions to or efforts at distinguishing themselves from—less technical genres. Although the differences between pages for "kids" and those for professional scientists may be striking, contrasts with pages for businesses are likely to be less so, and it may be quite difficult to distinguish messages for the general public, messages for scientists as citizens, and messages for political sponsors of the NASA budget. Accordingly it becomes more and more likely that genre and register conventions, or rhetorical means, will tend to diffuse between sets of pages designed for these different user groups.

Studying a complex web domain such as *nasa.gov* also provides the opportunity to follow the connections, and disconnections, among materials created for the entire gamut of users from children to professional scientists, all within a single institutional framework. This is not possible, for example, with the print publishing industry; there are probably not very many institutions that span this range. Government science agencies in the United States may be unique in addressing such a broad spectrum of reader-users. Social semiotics emphasizes the institutional contexts of literate practices, and if we wish to understand how our society constructs degrees of literacy, from elementary to advanced, within a single domain such as science, it may be more useful to examine various examples all within a single discernable institutional framework, rather than institutionally unconnected instances.

Finally, any enumeration of the contexts of use of these multimedia texts must include not just those of production and circulation, but also those of the local end-users. A complete social semiotic analysis would therefore add, as additional and for some purposes privileged intertexts, interview reports and on-site field notes and recordings of how people actually make use of and interpret NASA webpages. In what institutional contexts (school, business, military R&D, scientific research) do people with various science literacy backgrounds make use of these pages, and for what purposes? Whom do these pages' designs and contents serve well, and for whom are they difficult or intractable?

Many users of NASA webpages are located outside the United States (for the Earth Web Server, mainly nontechnical, but with links to technical data: about 15% of all accesses were from Europe, 4% from Asia, 2% from Latin America; for comparison 8% were from U.S. university domains, 16% from U.S. commercial domains that include most private individuals connecting to the internet; comparable data for a more exclusively technical website at GSFC was not recently available). Technical users presumably have no difficulty accessing the pages in English, which is the dominant language of international science and technology, but those less proficient in either or both the English language and the thematic formations of relevant scientific subfields in any language will have particular difficulty. There are webpage translation engines, but they are general purpose and do not do well with technical registers, although for a specialized translation engine these predictable and routinized registers are rather easily translated. I suspect that familiarity with the conceptual semantics of the relevant scientific field in any language is more relevant to successful understanding of a scientific text in English than is general English proficiency, at least beyond a very rudimentary skill in the language. If this is true, then teachers of science may be better prepared to teach scientific English than are teachers of the English language, at least in the sense that they could acquire the necessary language concepts in far less time than language teachers would require to master the necessary scientific ones. In fact, New York State now requires six credits of study in language acquisition and literacy development for all teachers, including all secondary school teachers of science (New York State Education Department, 1999).

It is commonly believed that the presence of mathematical and visual-graphical elements also aids scientific comprehension in a second language. Whether this is so may depend not so much on the debatable *universality* of the nonlinguistic semiotics (they are in any case internationally standardized in science across languages) as on whether students have learned their conventional forms and meanings by having previously integrated them with verbal text in any language.

It is presumably easier, especially at later ages, to teach students the necessary multimedia forms and conventions in a language in which they are proficient and otherwise experienced in dealing with scientific topics, and then assist them to make similar connections of mathematical formulas, diagrams, graphs, and so on, to English text, once the combined meanings of text and image have initially been grasped. In a social semiotic perspective there is far less difference between *learning science* and *learning scientific English* (Lemke, 1990a) than in theories that describe language entirely as a matter of forms, separable from semantic content and function, or that regard "science" or "scientific knowledge" as objective or mental realities separable from using language and other semiotic resources in social practices. There is no science without language, and no mastery of scientific English separate from the comprehension of some set of scientific concepts.

If we extend this view to the integrated deployment of multiple semiotic modalities, then scientific "concepts" are themselves multimedia entities (Lemke, 1998a). What it means to understand a scientific concept is to be able to mean with it, and we normally make scientific meaning only in some combination of words, images, and mathematical and graphical signs. Advanced scientific literacy means both using advanced literacy skills specific to scientific activity and making specialized scientific meanings that cannot be made without using some language, in conjunction with other semiotic resources. It is particularly clear in the domain of scientific activity that language skills as such are not separable in practice from the particular kinds of meanings to be made, nor from the other semiotic resources needed to do so.

REFERENCES

American Association for the Advancement of Science. (1996). *Benchmarks for science literacy.* Washington, DC: AAAS Press.

Cumming, J., & Wyatt-Smith, C. (Eds.). (1997). *Examining the literacy-curriculum relationship in post-compulsory schooling.* Brisbane, Qld: Griffith University.

Halliday, M. A. K. (1978). *Language as social semiotic.* London: Edward Arnold.

Halliday, M. A. K. (1994). *An introduction to functional grammar* (2nd ed.). London: Edward Arnold.

Harris, R. (1995). *Signs of writing.* London: Routledge.

Hodge, R., & Kress, G. (1988). *Social semiotics.* Ithaca, NY: Cornell University Press.

Kress, G., & van Leeuwen, T. (1996). *Reading images.* London: Routledge.

Lemke, J. L. (1983). Thematic analysis: Systems, structures, and strategies. *Semiotic Inquiry, 3*(2), 159–187.

Lemke, J. L. (1985). Ideology, intertextuality, and the notion of register In J. D. Benson & W. S. Greaves, (Eds.), *Systemic perspectives on discourse,* (pp. 275–294). Norwood, NJ: Ablex.

Lemke, J. L. (1989). Social semiotics: A new model for literacy education. In D. Bloome, (Ed.), *Classrooms and literacy* (pp. 289–309). Norwood, NJ: Ablex Publishing.

Lemke, J. L. (1990a). *Talking science: Language, learning, and values.* Norwood, NJ: Ablex.

Lemke, J. L. (1990b). Technical discourse and technocratic ideology. In M. A. K. Halliday, John Gibbons, & Howard Nicholas, (Eds.), *Learning, keeping, and using language: Selected papers from the 8th AILA world congress of applied linguistics, Sydney (1987, Vol. II,* pp. 435–460). Amsterdam: John Benjamins.

Lemke, J. L. (1994, April). *The Missing Context in Science Education: Science.* Paper presented at American Educational Research Association annual meeting, Atlanta, GA. Arlington VA: ERIC Documents Service (ED 363 511).

Lemke, J. L. (1995). *Textual politics: Discourse and social dynamics.* London: Taylor & Francis.

Lemke, J. L. (1997). Review of: Roy Harris, *Signs of writing. Functions of Language 4*(1): 125–129.

Lemke, J. L. (1998a). Multiplying meaning: Visual and verbal semiotics in scientific text. In James R. Martin & Robert Veel (Eds.), *Reading Science,* (pp. 87–113). London: Routledge.

Lemke, J. L. (1998b). Resources for attitudinal meaning: Evaluative orientations in text semantics. *Functions of Language 5*(1), 33–56.

Lemke, J. L. (1998c). Metamedia literacy: Transforming meanings and media. In D. Reinking, L. Labbo, M. McKenna, & R. Kiefer (Eds.), *Handbook of literacy and technology,* (pp. 283–301). Hillsdale, NJ: Lawrence Erlbaum Associates.

Lemke, J. L. (2000a). Multimedia demands of the scientific curriculum. *Linguistics and Education., 10*(3), 1–25.

Lemke, J. L. (2000b). Material sign processes and ecosocial organization. In P. B. Andersen, C. Emmeche, & N. O. Finnemann-Nielsen, (Eds.), *Downward causation: Self-organization in biology, psychology, and society,* (pp. 181–213). Denmark: Aarhus University Press.

Lemke, J. L. (2000c). Across the scales of time: Artifacts, activities, and meanings in ecosocial systems. *Mind, Culture, and Activity 7*(4), 273–290.

Lemke, J. L. (in press a). Ideology, intertextuality, and the communication of science. In P. Fries, M. Cummings, D. Lockwood, & W. Spruiell (Eds.), *Relations and functions in language and discourse.* London: Cassell.

Lemke, J. L. (in press b). Mathematics in the middle: Measure, picture, gesture, sign, and word. In M. Anderson, V. Cifarelli, A. Saenz-Ludlow, & A. Vile (Eds.), *Semiotic perspectives on mathematics education.*

Lynch, M., & Woolgar, S. (Eds.). (1990). *Representation in scientific practice*. Cambridge, MA: MIT Press.

National Research Council. (1996). National science education standards. Washington, DC: National Academy Press.

New York State Education Department. (1999). Registration of curricula in teacher education. [http://www.highered.nysed.gov:9220/teach/app5221.htm]

O'Toole, L. M. (1990). A systemic-functional semiotics of art. *Semiotica*, 82, 185–209.

O'Toole, L. M. (1994). *The language of displayed art*. London: Leicester University Press.

Reinking, D., Labbo, L., McKenna, M., & Kiefer, R. (Eds.). (1998). *Handbook of literacy and technology*. Hillsdale, NJ: Lawrence Erlbaum Associates.

Roth, W.-M., Bowen, G. M., & McGinn, M. K. (1999). Differences in graph-related practices between high school biology textbooks and scientific ecology journals. *Journal of Research in Science Teaching, 36,* 977–1019.

Roth, W.-M., & Bowen, G. M. (2000). Decalages in talk and gesture. *Linguistics and Education 10*(3), 335–358.

Rouet, J. F., & Levonen, J. (1996). Studying and learning with hypertext: Empirical studies and their implications. In J. F. Rouet, J. J. Levonen, A. Dillon, & R. J. Spiro (Eds.), *Hypertext and cognition*. Mahwah, NJ: Lawrence Erlbaum Associates.

Shapin, S., & Schaffer, S. (1985). *Leviathan and the air-pump*. Princeton, NJ: Princeton University Press.

Wells, G. (2000). Modes of meaning in a science activity. *Linguistics and Education, 10*(3), 307–334.

3

The Development of Abstraction in Adolescence in Subject English

Frances Christie
University of Melbourne

When I was invited to contribute to a volume devoted to "advanced literacy," I did wonder a little at the theme: In what sense was the word "advanced" intended? Did it mean advanced in the sense that it concerned older students at advanced (i.e., tertiary) levels? Or did it mean advanced in the sense that it involved thinking about literacy at some level *beyond the basics*, however we conceived those? Or did it, perhaps relatedly, mean advanced in the sense that it suggested developing students who could take up challenging (i.e., advanced) positions in their writing, in which case it might suggest some interest in critical literacy, and all that that implies? It might in fact mean all these, although it will be as well if I begin by setting some constraints on what I intend in responding to the notion of the acquisition of advanced literacy.

The thesis I shall propose here is that:

- advanced literacy is developed in the secondary years;
- the movement to the secondary experience is as much a rite of passage as is the entry to the kindergarten and lower primary school;
- it is with the transition to the secondary school that students must learn to handle the grammar of written English differently from the ways they handled it for primary schooling, and that it is these changes that constitute the "advanced literacy" that is needed for future participation in further study and many areas of adult life;

- the changes in the grammar, which I want to talk about with respect to subject English, are various, although collectively they create the capacity in the successful writer, to handle the building of generalization, abstraction, argument, and reflection on experience that advanced literacy seems to require.

I might of course choose to look at development of literacy across different subjects. A great deal of relevant work has been done by Martin, Rothery and their colleagues in the so-called "Write it Right Project" of a few years ago (see several papers in Christie & Martin, 1997, for a discussion of some of the work that emerged from that project). However, I have chosen to look at English for several reasons:

- It happens to be the school subject whose teaching I have been researching most closely for the last 2 years;
- English interests me anyway, because it is the one compulsory subject in all states in Australia for all the years of secondary school, so it is clearly perceived as important in the culture;
- While the teaching of literacy is an important issue in all other subjects, it is subject English that, ostensibly at least, is committed to the teaching of language itself as an overt object of study;
- Finally, although there are features of literacy performance that are common across the secondary subjects, there are also features peculiar to each subject and its discourse. In the interests of economy, I am thus going to look at only English.

I should note as I proceed that the focus of my discussion will be on students' writing, although I would argue that what I shall say has consequences for reading and its teaching as well.

ESTABLISHING SOME TERMINOLOGY

It will perhaps be useful briefly to establish several of the terms I shall use, most of them drawn from systemic functional (SF) linguistic theory, and all of them generally relevant to building my arguments concerning development of capacities for abstraction, generalization, and argument, as features of advanced literacy. The first of the terms I shall refer to is that of "abstractness," a term to be used here in a reasonably orthodox sense, in that it involves uses of abstract nouns, such as "quality," in an expression such as "she has good qualities." Abstractness is not a feature of early writing, and we may reasonably assume that a degree of life experience is required before children give expression to it, especially in their writing. Another term is that of "technicality," used here to refer to those linguistic items that are used in establishing the technical language of some discourse. The following is an example of a sentence taken from a 9-year-old child's writing, demonstrating both that she understands the meaning of the technical item "erosion" and that she is able to deploy it in a piece of writing:

"Erosion is the gradual wearing away of the soil by wind, running water, waves and temperature."

Emergent control of technicality in language is a necessary feature of the development of advanced literacy.

Another, often related term to be used here is that of "grammatical metaphor" (Halliday, 1994, pp. 342–367), an expression that has come into use to refer to the ways in which the "congruent expressions" of the grammar of speech are turned into the "noncongruent," or metaphorical, expressions of the written mode. The congruent way to represent experience in the English clause is in a process (expressed in a verbal group), associated participants (expressed in nominal groups), and where needed, associated circumstance(s), expressed either in a prepositional phrase or an adverbial group:

1. *The soldiers* (Participant; nominal group) *attacked* (Process; verbal group) *the town* (Participant; nominal group) *with guns* (Circumstance; prepositional phrase).

The congruent way to link the experiential information of this clause to another is by means of a conjunctive relationship, thus:

The soldiers attacked the town with guns <u>*and then*</u> *removed the treasures.*

If we were to represent these two clauses in a noncongruent or metaphorical manner, we would write:

2. *The soldiers' attack on the town with guns* (Participant; nominal group containing two prepositional phrases in Postmodifier position to the noun *attack*); *led to/was followed by* (Process; verbal group) *the removal of the treasures* (Participant; nominal group containing one prepositional phase).

Why term this metaphorical? The answer to that rests on acceptance of the notion that the congruent is the unmarked way we represent experience, and that the alternative or marked realization, in that it plays with and changes the grammar, is a form of metaphor. Thus, in our metaphorical example in (2), the two independent clauses in (1), expressed as we typically might say it in speech, have been turned into the one clause of writing, by a process that (i) turns the action of a clause (*the soldiers attacked the town*) into the nominal group of writing (*the soldiers' attack on the town*), and (ii) buries the conjunctive relationship between the original two clauses (*and then*) in the new verbal group (either *led to*, or *was followed by*). Emergent control of noncongruent expression, or grammatical metaphor, so Halliday (1994) has written, is a phenomenon of late childhood at the earliest, although my own observation is that for many students it emerges in adolescence, and even then very unevenly.

Apart from instances of grammatical metaphor that are experiential in character, like those I have just discussed, where it is the elements that construct experiences that are made noncongruent, there are other examples of grammatical metaphor that are interpersonal, where it is the perspective or stance of the writer toward those elements of experience that is expressed metaphorically. Interpersonal meaning is expressed in the resources of mood and modality. A congruent expression might read: *Certainly he told the truth*, where *certainly* carries modal significance, expressing the writer's judgement. A noncongruent way to express this might be: *I'm sure he told the truth*, or perhaps *It is obvious he told the truth*. We can demonstrate that *I'm sure* is metaphorical, by using Halliday's test of a tag question to establish the subject of the clause: *I'm sure he told the truth, didn't he?*, not *I'm sure he told the truth, aren't I?* The expression functions as an alternative to *certainly*. As for *it is obvious*, this is simply one of the many expressions available in English for asserting opinions, all of them carrying modal significance, and constituting substitutes for modal adverbs such as *probably* or *certainly*. The development toward control of generalizations and abstractions that characterize advanced literacy includes developing control of interpersonal metaphor, for this is involved in the related development of capacity for judgment and expression of opinion. As I shall suggest later, emergent capacity for judgment expresses itself in more than one way, for adverbs other than those having a direct modal significance seem to be involved.

These matters having been established, we can now move to consideration of a range of written texts by Australian school students, selected because they represent examples of texts produced in subject English classrooms across several years of schooling. Subject English—at least in Australia—seems to value and reward a particular range of text types: narratives, especially in the primary and junior secondary years; a number of text types I would loosely group as "literary critical," including book (or film) reviews and character studies, especially in the junior secondary years, and, by the mid secondary years, literary critical pieces, involving expository texts discussing major themes in literary works; and finally, what I shall term "opinionated pieces," generally about social issues, such as drug abuse, and selected because they are current, and because they are intended to allow students opportunity for expression of personal opinion. The latter texts seem to emerge by the mid secondary years, although the pattern is variable.

For the purpose of developing this discussion, I shall examine three instances of narratives, then I shall go on to examine two literary critical pieces, and finally I shall discuss two opinionated pieces about social issues. The seven texts have been selected both because they offer a range of text types or genres found in subject English, and because they are drawn from across the primary and secondary years. All but one of the texts were collected in Australian schools, and I know something of the contexts for writing in which they were produced. They were written by both L1 and L2 students, and were not drawn from privileged schools. In fact, with the exception of the last text I shall use, taken from the pages of a Melbourne newspaper, the texts were drawn from students in schools in some reasonably under privileged areas. I should note in addition, that although I would suggest the texts are representative of Australian experience across the years of schooling, all the texts used (with the exception of the one printed in the newspaper, where a teacher's opinion was not sought) were judged by their teachers to be good.

NARRATIVE TEXTS

The first narrative to be displayed here was written by a bilingual speaker of English and Russian, when she was 6 years old. It is a reasonably complete, if rudimentary, instance of a narrative genre, although my interest is less in establishing its generic structure, and rather more in establishing those features of the child's uses of language that mark this as a young text, written by a child who does not control grammatical metaphor. For convenience, I shall set the text out showing the elements of structure. I shall also mark in italics those aspects of the story which reveal aspects of the characters, either what they are like, or how they respond to events. Capacity to *intrude* observations about responses into the unfolding of those events is an important aspect of narrative writing.

Text 1

Orientation

Once upon a time there was a Fairy who was pretty. She had one child. *She was good to people and animals.* She went to the fairy shop and got a toy bear for her girl. She washed the bear when she came home. *Her child was happy.*

Complication/Resolution

When the bear tore Mum mended it. Mum loved the child.

Closure

We say goodbye.

As noted, Text 1 is rudimentary, and it has an extremely simple Complication, yet for a child of her years it is a successful piece. It makes fairly successful use of reference, the naming and linking through anaphora of the participants in the narrative, and this is unusual in my experience in such a young child. My overwhelming observation is that young children in the first years of schooling take some time in sorting out the nature of the referential items to be used in writing, and that is because they understand reference much more fully as a feature of the language of speech, where a great deal of reference is exophoric, referring to elements in the shared context of speaking. Learning to handle the endophoric references needed to create a successfully coherent written text takes some time. The endophoric reference here works to assist in holding all elements of the story together in a reasonably coherent way. However, having said that, we should also note that the young writer is confused, in that she begins her tale by writing of *a Fairy*, although toward the end of the story she has become *Mum*. The text is set out as Fig. 3.1.

The nominal group structures in which participant roles are realized are extremely simple: *she, her child, the bear*. The process choices, realized in the verbal groups, sometimes express action as in *she washed the bear*, or sometimes they build attributes as in *her child was happy*, and once Anna uses a mental process of affect, *Mum loved the child.* Two prepositional phrases build Circumstances: *to the fairy*

Once upon a time there was a Fairy

who was pretty.

She had one child.

She was good to people and animals.

She went to the fairy shop

and got a toy bear for her girl.

She washed the bear

when she came home.

Her child was happy.

When the bear tore

Mum mended it.

Mum loved the child.

We say goodbye.

FIG. 3.1.   Reference in Text 1.

shop and *for her girl*. Most of the topical Theme choices are unmarked, apart from the opening Theme *Once upon a time*—in itself a very common feature of young children's stories.[1] In fact, for the most part topical Themes conflate with the Subjects of the verbs, so that the commonest Theme choice is *she*. Overall, then, this is a simple instance of a narrative, using a series of clauses that construct information in congruent ways, and showing a commendable grasp of the needs both to create a

---

[1]The term "Theme" is used in systemic functional theory to refer to what is thematic in the clause (Halliday, 1994). Theme is defined as "the point of departure for the message of the clause." In English, but not in many other languages, Theme comes in first position in the clause. Theme itself has three potential elements, which correspond to the major metafunctions recognized. Topical (or experiential) Theme refers to what is the experiential focus of the clause. Interpersonal Theme builds some aspect of relationship in that some interpersonally relevant information is made the focus, as in the use of the finite: *Would you like this?* Or in the use of a vocative: *Mary, did you see that?*, or in the use of an adverb that builds judgment: *Certainly you can come to our house.* Textual Theme corresponds to the textual metafunction, and is to do with the role of "tying clauses together." Textual Theme is typically realized in a conjunction. Where the three types of metafunctions occur, they do so in the order: textual, interpersonal, topical. Topical theme is of course the commonest Theme choice, and it may be either marked or unmarked. The usual or unmarked topical Theme conflates with the Subject of the clause. However, English speakers and writers often employ marked topical Themes, sometimes expressed in a prepositional phrase, sometimes in an adverb, sometimes in a dependent clause. Thematic progression in texts is very important, for it is a major resource for carrying the text forward. Achieving control of Theme is an important developmental task for children.

FIG. 3.2   Timmy the clock was published by Deakin University Press in the Deakin University Bachelor of Education Children Writing Study Guide, published in 1989. Efforts to trace the writer have proved unsuccessful.

FIG. 3.2 continued.

sense of internal coherence in the text, and to order it in such a way that it builds a sense of generic completeness.

Text 2 is an instance of a narrative written by a boy in the last year of primary school, about 11 or 12 years old.

My discussion of Text 2 will be in some ways incomplete. It was originally written as a little book, so that each double page involved an illustration on one page and an accompanying page of text on the other. The story is told through a great deal of the information in the accompanying pictures, and because I do not intend to consider these, I fail to do the writer full justice. The story of "Timmy the Clock" was written as part of a class activity devoted to researching and then writing stories for young readers. My object in looking at the text is to offer some commentary on the linguistic changes in such a text by a writer some years older than Anna, who wrote Text 1. For convenience, I have set out the text here, commenting on some linguistic features down the side.

The text is identifiably by an older writer, although its clause structures are still entirely congruent. Like the earlier example of a narrative, this one interweaves Process types, some to do with actions (*he would set off his alarm*), and a number to do with establishing attributes of the main character (*he was shy*), whereas two are mental processes of affect (e.g., *he had liked the girl*). The nominal group structures realizing the Participant roles are again simple, although a little more varied than was the case in Text 1: *Timmy the Clock, a little girl*. There are two principal differences compared with the first text. One difference is the more varied range of conjunctive relations between clauses, involving some to do with cause (*because he was shy*), others to do with additive and time relations (*and he didn't put his alarm on; un-*

Orientation One day Timmy the Clock was in the store window. **Complication** No one would buy him because he was so shy. *Every time people looked him, he would set off his alarm clock, until he bounced around to face the other way.* *He always did this, because he didn't like the looks of the people.* One day a little girl came past, and he didn't put his alarm on. He liked her very much, but then she went away. *Timmy was sad because he had liked the girl.* **Resolution** The next day the girl came back again. *He was so happy that he put on his alarm, and started shouting for joy.* The little girl bought him *and he was so happy.* *But he was still shy. Every time some one looked at him, he would put on his alarm and turn around.* *Except when the girl looked at him.*	Text has a series of clauses which build information in a congruent way. Marked topical Themes signal the passage of time. Protagonist's feelings & responses to events in italics. Few Circumstances (realised in prepositional phrases) e.g. *in the store window*

FIG. 3.3   Schematic structure and some salient linguistic features in Text 2.

til be bounced around), and others of a contrastive nature (*but he was still shy*). The other difference is that Text 2 has a much more varied range of topical Themes, including several marked ones that serve to signal the passage of time: *one day, the next day,* and so on. In the case of Text 1, as we saw, the topical Themes were not varied, and for the most part, they identified the mother in the story: *she.* Development of control of Theme in writing would seem to be a feature of the primary years. Like the development of control of reference, to which I alluded in the case of Text 1, achieving control of thematic progression in writing is a developmental task of some significance, principally because the thematic organization of written language is very different from that of spoken language. However, one qualification needs to be noted: It is that thematic progression in writing varies considerably, depending on the target genre and its goals.

In summary then, Text 2 succeeds on a number of grounds. It has a reasonably successful sense of the target generic structure—a characteristic in which it does better than Text 1, in fact; it makes successful use of thematic progression to unfold the events of the story; it interplays some clauses that build events and others that construct responses to events; and it builds a range of conjunctive relationships between its clauses, all of them helping to advance the overall organization of the story and its meanings. Like Text 1, its clause structures are congruent, while its nominal groups are still reasonably simple, and it uses few prepositional phrases to build circumstantial information.

The third narrative I shall consider was written by a student of non-English-speaking background, though he was by no means a recent arrival in Australia, and he was in year 8, about 14 years old. His narrative is far too long to reproduce, and with some regret therefore, I must simply cite extracts from it. I shall select the opening phase of the narrative, and the closing phase. The story concerns a group of people who plot to steal a fabulous diamond brooch from a museum, an activity in which they almost succeed, but they are finally stopped and their leader is shot. The opening is set out first, and as above, I shall offer some running commentary on the linguistic features, before discussing it below. I should note that in this text, unlike the earlier ones, there are several instances of embedded clauses (Halliday, 1994, pp. 242–248), so-called because they are said to be embedded within other linguistic entities that have rank. For example, in the following there is said to be one clause, which contains an embedded clause within in, shown with the notations [[ ]]: *The man [[who spoke to me]] was a visitor to this country.* Here *The man [[who spoke to me]]* is the nominal group that expresses the Subject of the clause, and the embedded clause has no status as an independent clause. Interestingly the 14-year-old writer of Text 3 uses embedded clauses as a useful resource in expanding his nominal groups and sometimes also within his prepositional phrases. The emergence of such features in his writing has developmental significance.

Several linguistic measures mark this narrative as written by an older writer than Texts 1 and 2. The opening sentence *sets the scene,* using, among other things, an identifying process realized in the verb "to be," and employing a cluster of embedded clauses, which are made most apparent if we set them out thus:

tonight was the night [[when one of the greatest burglary plans [[ever known to man's history was being put together]]]].

<u>Orientation</u> It was one cold, stormy winter night, not your usual winter night because tonight was <u>the night [[when one of the greatest burglary plans [[ever known to man's history was being put together]]]]</u> <u>Down in a small village just outside a small town two men [[called Jack and Small]]</u> and a lady were sitting near an old fireplace in a small broken down house waiting for their boss. <u>As they sat there</u> the door swung right open and in that moment lightning struck. The shadow of a tall big man appeared in the doorway. All three of them felt their hearts jump up into their throats and then back down due to the fright they got. A deep voice but in a soft town (tone) asked, "Do you know why I called you here?" "Yes, so we could reunite our old gang", the small fat dark-haired fellow answered. "That's correct, Small, but that isn't just the reason" the shadow replied. He continued to walk towards them out from the dark corner of the room to the brighter area of the fire. The shadow slowly disappeared and <u>a clear image of a tall, huge looking man [[dressed in a black coat]]</u> appeared in the chair beside them. He looked at each person waiting for an answer but they just sat there blankly staring at him.	Identifying process to set the scene. Clause embeddings expanding the nominal group (double underlines). Marked topical Theme choices underlined (single underlines). Several expanded nominal group structures (e.g., *the shadow of a tall big man*). Circumstances realised in prepositional phrases: *down in a small village outside a small town; in that moment; near an old fireplace in a small broken down house; out from the dark corner of the room to the brighter area of the fire.* Two adverbs realize different circumstantial information: *slowly; blankly.* Clause embedding expanding nominal group structure.

FIG. 3.4   Some salient linguistic features in the opening of Text 3.

The effect of the clause embeddings here is to *pack in* information in the nominal group structure, in a manner particularly characteristic of written language. The capacity to exploit the resources of the nominal group structure here and elsewhere in Text 3 is in considerable contrast to the extreme simplicity of the nominal group structures in the earlier two narratives. Other instances, not always employing embedded clauses, include: *one cold, stormy winter night; the shadow of a tall big man; a clear image of a tall, huge looking man [[dressed in a black coat]].* Clearly, the nominal groups in which participant roles are realized suggest considerable confidence in manipulating the grammar of writing, especially for the construction of experiential information. Another resource used successfully is that of the prepositional phrase, creating important circumstantial information: *down in a small village outside a small town; near an old fireplace in a small broken down house; out from the dark corner of the room to the brighter area of the fire.* Interestingly, two adverbs realiz-

With the awakening of the sun's rays thousands of curious people were on their way to see the spectacular display of jewellery in the enormous newly-opened museum. Outside a line had developed all awaiting for the moment [[the doors opened]]. The pushing and shoving of the crowd was getting bigger until finally the doors burst open and the crowd rushed in, all with mouths open, astonished with their first glimpse of the wonderful Museum.	Grammatical metaphors involved in building expanded nominal groups: *the awakening of the sun's rays; the enormous newly opened museum; the pushing and shoving of the crowd.*
.... Text omitted	Marked Topical Themes (single underlines)
The boss at that time was still holding the brooch in his hand as if nothing would make him let go. Then he jumped up, aimed with his gun at the security guard and... BANG! a shot from behind him.	
.........................Text omitted The boss just fell flat on top of the table for he had been shot in the head. Blood was slowly dripping down the side of his face and dripping off the edge of his cheek. He was positioned like a drowning man [[reaching for a life guard]] and there in the palm of his huge hand <<still dazzling with shininess>> lay the Golden Brooch.	Adverb to build more circumstantial information

Prepositional phrase with embedding to create Circumstance: *like a drowning man [[reaching for a life guard]]*

Enclosed clause (<< >>) strategically placed to enhance Circumstance: in the palm of his huge hand <<still dazzling with shininess>> |

FIG. 3.5   Some salient linguistic features in the closing stage of Text 3.

ing circumstantial information appear in this text: *the shadow slowly disappeared,* and *they just sat there blankly staring at him.*

Students in the primary years typically make little use of such adverbs. Some adverbs of intensity may appear, such as "so" in the story of "Timmy the Clock," just as we can also find evidence of modal adverbs, like the one used by the writer of Text 3 in *they just sat there.* However, more often than not, circumstantial information is not considerable in the writing of primary aged children, and, so I have also found, it does not necessarily develop for some time into the secondary years. The commonest circumstantial information, where it appears, is realized in prepositional phrases, as was the case in Texts 1 and 2. We have also noticed the appearance of such information in Text 3, where indeed it is more abundant. What significance, then, might be attached to the appearance of the adverbs in Text 3, written by a boy in adolescence? Circumstantial information expressed in prepositional phrases, of the kind found in Texts 1, 2, and 3 is all to do with time (*once upon a time*) or place (*out from the dark corner of the room to the brighter area of the fire*). As resources for building circumstantial information, what adverbs seem to offer is capacity to introduce information about manner: This is certainly true of the two I have identified in Text 3. It would seem that this kind of facility for constructing information to do with manner is essentially a characteristic of the relatively greater maturity of adolescence, and of the developing capacity to use language for the expression of judgments about behavior.

I shall now turn to the last phase of the story of the Diamond Brooch. I should note that the story unfolds with an account of the crowds forming outside the museum to see the diamond brooch, and the coming of the burglars, who succeed in gaining entry to the museum and in getting the diamond brooch, although they are nonetheless foiled in their attempt to escape with it.

Several instances of grammatical metaphor are noticeable here, the first of them in the marked topical Theme in the first clause: *with the awakening of the sun's rays*. This is in fact an example where the metaphor is both grammatical and lexical. Expressed congruently, this would read: *When the sun rose*. Other instances of grammatical metaphor may be found in: *the enormous newly opened museum*, and *the pushing and shoving of the crowd*. The effect, in both the latter two cases, is to create nominal groups, whose function in the story is to help build the experiential information on which the tale depends. The embedded clauses, as I noted previously, are interesting, not least because there are several of these, helping to expand the experiential information in both Participant roles and Circumstances. One enclosed clause falls towards the end of the text: *and there in the palm of his huge hand <<still dazzling with shininess>> lay the Golden Brooch*. The latter type of clause, unlike the embedded clause, is not down ranked within another entity: Instead, it is a dependent clause that is redeployed from its usual or unmarked position, to achieve some particular linguistic effect.

The text overall reveals considerable differences compared with the earlier narratives. First, it makes extensive use of quite elaborate nominal group structures to build both its Participant roles and the prepositional phrases that build Circumstances. Second, in creating several of these it employs grammatical metaphor, demonstrating that the writer has begun to understand how to exploit such a resource to good effect, and to write what are instances of noncongruent realizations. Third, as noted earlier, it makes effective use of several adverbs, all of them to do with the manner by which someone or something behaves. Adverbs create different circumstantial information from prepositional phrases, as I have noted, and it is significant that they appear in this narrative, although not in those by the younger writers.

LITERARY CRITICAL PIECES

I examine here two texts, the first by a student in year 8, and about 14 years old, the other by a student in year 10, and about 16 years old. As I indicated earlier in this discussion, literary critical texts appear to be required in the English program of the junior secondary school, although they are not extensively found in the primary years as far as I can tell. Text 4, written by a boy of second language background (although not recently arrived) is a character description of the central character in the Australian novel, *Thunderwith*, written by Libby Hathorn. It will be apparent immediately that because the genre is different from the narrative, it makes somewhat different demands on the language used. For convenience I have again set the text out with some commentary down the side.

Character discussion is very heavily involved with the building of abstractions, and one measure of this and of how different are the grammatical realizations involved, compared with those of narratives, is the fact that in this text there are very few processes of action. On the contrary, the majority, realized in the verb "to be," build attributes of Lara, such as *Lara is a young, reliable, teenage girl*. Occasionally, the writer uses an identifying process to build a strong statement of opinion about the character as in: *other qualities of Lara are her determination and her reliability*. Lexical metaphor (Lara uses *her "reservoir" of emotional strength* or *I would describe her as an army tank in emotional traumas*) help develop the character description. These seem rather forced to me, by the way, although my observation during the years I taught in high schools myself was that sometimes adolescents did strain to achieve successful effects when using metaphorical language, and I believe this is itself a developmental matter. Topical Theme choices are varied, many of them unmarked, although the marked Themes have a major function in constructing the development and progress of the text: *after the recent death of her beloved mother; throughout the book; despite her extraordinary resistance to emotion*. At times too, this student uses an interpersonal Theme choice, as in: *In my eyes, Lara is an exceptionally determined person*. In the last concluding paragraph, he uses textual Theme to signal closure: *To sum it all up*. Later in the last paragraph, he uses a dependent clause in Theme position, whose effect is to foreground the fact that he is stating his opinion of the character: *If I were to change one part of Lara, I would change her ability to fight back*. One further matter to do with expression of judgment needs to be mentioned: It is the cluster of uses of modal verbs in the last paragraph, where, as is the convention for such a genre, several observations construct statements of opinion: *without one of these elements, Lara would not be herself; without Thunderwith, Lara would not have able to pull through the period of sadness; if I were to change one part of Lara, I would change her ability to fight back; with a little bit more aggression, Lara would be a much better person*. Finally, and bearing in mind my earlier observations about the emergence of uses of adverbs in adolescence, it will be noticeable that the young writer here makes use of several adverbs all having significance for their roles in building judgment about the character: *unbelievably, surprisingly*, and *exceptionally*.

No easy comparison with the narrative texts is possible or even sensible because the genres differ and their social purposes are very different. However, we can make some observations about the developmental changes apparent in a student who writes as in Text 4, some of which at least accord with the observations made about Text 3, which as we saw was written by a student of a similar age to the writer of Text 4. The most notable of the changes are apparent in the writer's capacity to employ abstractions, constructed either in the uses of abstract nouns such as *qualities, determination*, or *reliability*, or through the use of grammatical metaphor, creating nominal groups such as *her extraordinary resistance to emotion*. Many of the nominal

Character Introduction Lara is <u>a young, reliable teenage girl in the book</u> <u>'Thunderwith'</u>. <u>After the recent death of her</u> <u>beloved Mother Cheryl</u>, Lara needs to come to terms with <u>the fact [[that she has to move in with</u> <u>her step family]]</u>. **Description** Lara has many distinctive qualities. The most distinct of these qualities, is her emotional strength. <u>Throughout the book</u>, Lara needs to use her 'reservoir' of emotional strength against her step mother Gladwyn <u>and the bullying of Gowd</u> <u>Gradley.</u> *Lara is an unbelievably strong person. I* *would describe her as an army tank in emotional* *traumas.* However, <u>despite her extraordinary resistance to</u> <u>emotion,</u> Lara does not stand up to the bullies. She takes life as it comes and does not make any attempt to change it. *This is one of the weaknesses of* *Lara. I think that if Lara was a little bit aggressive, her* *life at Wallingat would have been surprisingly different.* Other qualities of Lara are her determination and her reliability. *In my eyes, Lara is an exceptionally* *determined person.* She has set out to do something and there is no turning back. Lara's canine companion, Thunderwith is an addition to her positive attitude. Lara thinks of Thunderwith as a reincarnation of her Mother. Thunderwith gives Lara the strength when she needs it. It is only at the end that the horrible truth faces Lara. The loss of Thunderwith. **Evaluation** To sum it all up, Lara has a very interesting character and personality. Her determination, emotional strength and reliability make Lara what she is. <u>Without one of these elements, Lara would</u> not be herself. Thunderwith <u>is a major part of</u> Lara as well. *Without Thunderwith, Lara would not* *have been able to pull through the period of sadness that* *she experienced.* <u>If I were to change one part of Lara,</u> *I* *would change her ability to fight back. With a little bit* *more aggression, Lara would be a much better person.*	Expanded nominal group structures (double underlines) Marked topical Theme (single underlines) Abstractness: *distinctive* *qualities; emotional strength.* Lexical metaphor: *reservoir* *of emotional strength* Expanded nominal group using grammatical metaphor. Many processes build attributes of Lara (e.g., *she is* *an unbelievably strong person*). Marked topical Theme. Italics to indicate judgments re the character Abstractness: *one of the* *weaknesses of Lara; her* *determination & her* *reliability.* An identifying process builds strong statement about character. Several modal adverbs help build judgments re the character: *unbelievably,* *surprisingly, exceptionally.* Textual Theme: *to sum it all* *up.* Marked topical Theme Building of judgment through abstraction: *her* *determination, emotional* *strength & reliability make* *Lara what she is.* Marked topical Theme.

FIG. 3.6   Schematic structure and some salient features in Text 4.

groups in which Participant roles are constructed are quite elaborate, making effective use of this resource for constructing experiential information. Theme
choices, some marked and others unmarked, show a good sense of ordering of the
overall text. Other Themes, chosen for their interpersonal significance, show
emergent control of capacity to express judgment and opinion, although it needs to
be acknowledged that such expressions were not required in the narrative texts.

I shall now turn to the second of the literary critical pieces I have chosen. This
one is far too long to reproduce, so regretfully I shall reproduce only two small sections of the essay. It is an essay written by an L1 student, about 15 years old, and she
had been asked to discuss the major themes in the novel *To Kill a Mockingbird*. In
Fig. 3.7 I reproduce only the opening paragraph in which she sets out what her thesis is to be, and then her concluding paragraph.

The writer of Text 5 understood that in this kind of literary critical piece, the
skill was in doing more than simply retelling the story of the novel. On the contrary,
the object in such a piece is to abstract away from the events (although the writer
must demonstrate a familiarity with them) and to generalize about life and experience from the events. Hence she positioned herself very cleverly with the opening
generalization about life in the first clause (*Life is about growing up, learning new
things, meeting different people*), followed by the second clause that establishes a link
between that generalization and the novel (*and the book To Kill a Mockingbird is
about all of these*). As was the case in Text 4, many of the processes here are realized
in the verb "to be," for their role is in building generalizations about the book and
its themes, or statements about the characters. I should note that many of the para-

Life is about growing up, lea~~rning new things,~~ meeting different people, and the book *To Kill a Mockingbird* is about all of these. Many situations throughout the book show the children's reactions and emotions. Jem and Scout are the main characters in the story and being children, they view everything with a fresh and unprejudiced outlook. They are guided by the steady hand of their father - Atticus Finch, the local lawyer and distinguished member of the town's society. He helps them deal with life's blows, the good times and the bad.	Opening generalization about "Life". Abstract notion: *life.* Instances of grammatical metaphor: *they view everything with a fresh & unprejudiced outlook; they are guided by the steady hand of their father; he helps them deal with life's blows.*
Text is omitted	
Yet, it is agreeable that the novel *To Kill a Mockingbird* is all about children growing up as that is what children do best. They try new things, figure stuff out, cope with their own struggles and the rest of the world's, while at the same time just try to have some adventure and little fun.	Closing generalization: (growing up) is [[what children do best]].

FIG. 3.7   Some salient linguistic features in Text 5.

graphs within the body of the essay did employ other process types, as details of the novel's events were told. Participant roles are often here expressed as abstractions: *life; children's reactions and emotions*. Instances of grammatical metaphor build propositions about the novel and its themes, as for example, in the expression *they view everything with a fresh and unprejudiced outlook*, where the Circumstance *with a fresh and unprejudiced outlook* is offering essentially an abstract idea, based on observation of the children's behavior in several situations in the novel. The closing generalization has two parts, built in the two clauses in the sentence, *It is agreeable that the novel To Kill a Mockingbird is all about children growing up, as that is [[what children do best]]*. It is of course, something of a cliché to say that growing up is what children do best. This too, it seems to me, is an instance of a student striving to establish what is expected of her for this kind of genre.

Overall, the student in this text has demonstrated capacity to abstract away from the events of the novel, and to build observations about life and its themes. Subject English appears to value the writing of such literary critical genres, and it rewards them in young writers.

OPINIONATED TEXTS

The last two texts I shall examine typify those texts that English requires for the expression of opinion. The first is by a student in Year 8, whose class had been discussing the values of using animals for entertainment, as in circuses. She wrote a discussion genre, in which she set out to indicate the issue, provide arguments both for and against the use of animals in such a manner, and then provide her own point of view. The realizations here are largely congruent, although the young writer demonstrates that she is in control of a number of aspects of the grammar of written language. The text is set out in Fig. 3.8.

The target genre in Text 6 is rather different from that in either Text 4 or Text 5. This one sets out to review arguments for and against, and then to offer an opinion. The opening paragraph states the issue briefly, using an identifying process, where one Participant has an embedded clause in it: *the name of the topic [[we're talking about in this essay]]*. Several Processes are realized in verbs of behaving (*in the report [[we read]]*) and of saying (*it said*), revealing that the writer is aware she is reporting on matters read about and researched. Generic references (*to people* and *most people*) indicate the writer is aware that she is offering general statements about the attitudes of certain groups, rather than dealing with individuals, where specific references would be more appropriate. Topical Theme choices are both unmarked and marked, and they serve to structure the overall text in an orderly way (*in the report [[we read]]*), whereas some textual Themes also have an important role in structuring the text (*but then on the other hand*). The adverbs used are significant for their modal roles: *they're nearly always in confined spaces; the animals are not usually kept … ; they can't exactly force people to join*.

I now turn to Text 7, the only text used here that did not come from an Australian classroom. It was written by a school girl, called Lauren Kiratzis, who was, at the time, 16 years of age, and in Year 11 of her schooling. The letter appeared in the major Melbourne newspaper *The Age*. I have selected the text, although it is not from any of the classrooms I have researched, because it represents a type of opin-

Statement of issue	Opening statement of the
"Should we use animals for entertainment" is the name of the topic [[we're talking about in this essay]]. Below, I have stated the positive and negative points for this issue.	issue. Expanded nominal group with embedded clause
	Verbal process (said) &
Arguments for	behavioural processes
In the report [[we read]], it said that <<in order to let a particular species survive >> we need to at least capture a few to show to the public, to let them learn about the animals and then maybe the public would do something to help the endangered animals. It said the animals are never hurt or tortured during training or the performances and they are kept in very clean, natural yards while not performing. At one stage it said that animals are the core element of circuses and the statistics proved that people like the animals best at the circus, therefore, human circuses would not meet the public demand. Most people judge circuses on their old ways, not on the current, improved ways.	(read) Enclosed clause to foreground an important point. Marked topical Themes Lexical metaphor: *animals are the core element of circuses.* Varied range of conjunctive relationships: *in order to; and then; therefore; so; and; which.*
Arguments against	
But then on the other hand, animals like the elephants and bears are very prone to stress so they make a habit of standing in one place and rocking or swaying, which is bad for their joints and feet. Things like constant travelling and performing in front of very large audiences nearly every day affect this. They're nearly always in confined spaces and the biggest places [[they are ever in]] are the circus arena or tent, which is also really small. The animals are not usually kept in their natural habitat, which stops their basic instincts like fighting for mates, building nests, hunting, etc, from being used to such a large extent like they do in the wild. An alternative is to use humans in circuses because they can't exactly force people to join, they have to be voluntary.	Textual Theme signals shift in the construction of the text's arguments. Large nominal group in topical Theme position Abstract nominal group: *their basic instincts* Some modal adverbs: *nearly; usually; exactly.*
Recommendation	
After looking at all these facts, I believe that it's wrong for us to keep animals in circuses for our entertainment. We should be able to entertain our selves, not rely on animals. For this reason, and the ones [[I have mentioned before]], I believe it is wrong for us to train and force animals to perform in circuses.	Strong assertion of opinion, using marked topical Theme & modal adjunct *I believe*; also use of modal verbs: *we should be able to entertain ourselves.*

FIG. 3.8   Schematic structure and some salient features in Text 6.

ionated text that is regularly encouraged in the upper secondary English class-rooms. The text was inspired by the advertising campaigns run on television by a weight loss organization called Gloria Marshall. The advertisements were designed to persuade even teenage girls of the need to diet and change their shapes if they were to be considered feminine. Such aggressive advertisements have been criti-cized more than once in Australia, as providing poor information to many adoles-cents. Text 7 is set out in Fig. 3.9.

Abstract As an average-sized, year 11 student, *I feel compelled to express my concern at the current Gloria Marshall Weight Loss Program advertisement on television.*	Marked topical Theme. Strong interpersonal statement: *I feel compelled to express*
Statement of Issue The advertisement portrays a girl of average weight and her mother shopping without success for a formal dress, thus prompting the girl to suggest that they should both join the Gloria Marshall program. The advertisement continues by showing the girl as slim and glamorous in an evening gown, as she greets her formal partner. Having recently experienced my year 11 formal I can relate to the dilemma of[[being unable to find a dress [[that looks and fits perfectly]]]]. However, *I am greatly angered by the fact[[that Gloria Marshall is using an average-sized teenager as the basis of her advertisement]].*	Varied range of dependent clauses: *thus prompting the girl to suggest...;* *having recently experienced my year 11 formal* Marked topical Theme Embedded clauses in nominal groups
Argument 1 Although the average Australian woman is size 12 to 14, we are constantly bombarded with the exaggerated and incorrect notion [[that teenagers should all aspire to be size 8 or 10 like the models [[filling the pages of fashion magazines]]]]. Therefore, although the girl in the Gloria Marshall advertisement is not overweight, the pressure [[placed on teenagers [[to attain the "perfect body"]].]] makes her desire [[to lose weight]] understandable.	Marked topical Theme Clause embeddings to build complex nominal groups Textual Theme to shift argument forward More embeddings in nominal group structures.
Argument 2 The pressure on many Australian teenagers, especially girls, due to this type of advertising is disturbing. *It is of great concern that a reputable company such as Gloria Marshall is encouraging young women to conform to society's unreasonable and blatantly incorrect expectations.* With anorexia nervosa and bulimia so prevalent in our society how is this latest campaign, helping the self-esteem of the average sized (12 to 14) teenage schoolgirl?	Interpersonal metaphor: *it is of great concern..* Forceful adverb Marked topical Theme Rhetorical question
Recommendation Teenagers should not be trying to lose weight while their bodies are still growing. It is obvious that this advertisement is sending the wrong message to teenagers.	Modal verb: *should* Interpersonal metaphor: *It is obvious*

FIG. 3.9 Schematic structure and some salient linguistic features in Text 7. Text from *The Age*, October 7, 1998. Text reprinted with permission of the author, Lauren Kiratzis.

This text shows considerable skill in deploying the resources of written language. It uses several key marked Themes, signaling steps in progress of the argument: *as an average-sized year 11 student; although the average Australian woman is size 12 to 14; with anorexia and bulimia so prevalent in our society.* It makes very successful use of interpersonal Themes: *it is of great concern that a reputable company....; it is obvious that this advertisement....* The text makes considerable use of modal adverbs: *I am greatly angered; we are constantly bombarded; the pressure placed on many Australian teenagers, especially girls.* The text creates a number of participant roles using expanded nominal groups, at least several of which involve clause embeddings. Some at least of the nominal groups involved build abstractions: *the* dilemma of [[being unable to find a dress [[that looks and fits perfectly]]; the exaggerated and incorrect notion [[that students should all aspire to size 8 or 10 like the models [[filling the pages of fashion magazines]]]]. It is around the creation of such abstractions that much of the argument of the text depends. Unlike the earlier texts by much younger writers, such as Texts 1 and 2, this one shows greater facility in the uses of various dependent clauses, some of them nonfinite, such as: by showing the girl as slim and glamorous in an evening gown; thus prompting the girl to suggest that they should both join the Gloria Marshall program; having recently experienced my year 11 formal. The writer of Text 3, the narrative by a 14-year-old student, did have some similar expressions: he looked at each person waiting for an answer but they just sat there blankly staring at him. A greater facility in uses of various clause dependencies would appear to be one of the measures of growing maturity in writing.

CONCLUSION

In this discussion, I have sought to review the common range of text types taught in subject English in Australian schools, and to develop some measures by which the nature of students' control of written language must change if they are to achieve the kinds of advanced literacy that participation in a complex early 21st century will require. I have suggested that although the particular configurations of linguistic features required for different text types will always differ, there are nonetheless certain linguistic features that the evidence suggests must change if students are to attain adequate advanced literacy. As I noted much earlier, all the texts (with the exception of Text 7) were regarded as good by the teachers concerned. The texts did not for the most part come from privileged schools, although having said that, I should also observe that the fact that some students produced the texts I have discussed does not mean that all the students in the various classes were able to do as well. Learning to write is actually quite hard, and one of my principal reasons for undertaking the analyses here is to arrive at some explanation of the features of developing maturity in literacy, so that we can use that knowledge to devise better teaching programs. Hence in the following discussion, I attempt to summarize what appear to be measures of developing success in writing.

First, control of reference, especially those properties that build endophoric reference to make a coherent written text, is very important in the developmental processes of learning to handle written language. The writer of Text 1, it will be recalled, was reasonably successful in this regard, although she did manage to confuse the manner of referring to one of the protagonists in her story. Most primary school students learn to handle reference in writing. However, it is my observation that some of the weakest students in the secondary school still have trouble controlling reference in written language, tending instead to rely on the features of reference in speech, with confusion often resulting.

Second, control of Theme would seem to be a very important aspect of learning to handle written language. As I hope my discussion has revealed, Theme choices are very important in ordering and progressing a text forward. Theme is different in writing from speech, and one of the earliest developmental tasks involves a recognition of this. With growing maturity, writers learn to deploy a range of Theme choices, and although their configurations differ say, in a narrative, compared with an opinionated text, in both cases, much depends on facility in use of Themes, both for linking to what has gone before in the text, and for pushing the discourse forward. By the end of the primary school, many students have developed considerable facility with Theme, and I believe that control of this must be one of the early measures of success in control of writing.

Another observation I would make about writing development is that although primary-age writers produce clauses that offer congruent realizations, it will be into the secondary years that noncongruent realizations appear. The writers of Text 3, Text 4, Text 5, and Text 7 all showed some facility with grammatical metaphor, causing them to create at least some noncongruent realizations in their texts. A third, sometimes related, feature of developing writers is a growing facility with handling of abstractions. Creating an abstraction does not always depend on grammatical metaphor, for, as we have seen, it can be constructed by the use of various abstract nouns as in Text 6. But the effect of developing control of writing is that capacity to handle abstraction becomes more marked.

A related, but perhaps less well-noted observation about the grammatical features of maturing writing lies in the proportionally greater uses of processes of being of various kinds, realized in the verb "to be," or one of its equivalents. Once a writer moves into construction of abstractions and generalizations of various kinds, the tendency is to build either identifying statements (e.g., [growing up] is what children do best), or statements that build attributes (e.g., Lara is a young, reliable teenage girl in the book Thunderwith.) It does not follow that processes of action, of mental activity or of behavior necessarily disappear (in fact the types of processes used are a condition of the type of genre). However, it does follow that the more texts become discussions that involve abstractions, arguments, and generalizations, the more the tendency will be there to build "being" statements around these things.

A fifth and again related feature of developing control of writing lies in development of considerable facility in creating elaborate nominal groups, sometimes including clause embeddings, although they are not a necessary feature. It is these that are heavily involved in the building of abstractions and generalizations just alluded to. The general effect of uses of complex nominal group structures is that the writer is able to pack in a great deal of information, and it is this feature, as much as anything, that accounts for the greater density of writing over a great deal of speech. Mature writers can say a lot more things than can young writers, such as the writer of Text 1.

Another resource that writers learn to exploit in order to provide a great deal of information is that of the Circumstance. The first sources of circumstantial information in young writers are prepositional phrases, and they create either Circumstances of place (in the store window) or of time (once upon a time). But these are reasonably sparse in young writers, emerging in greater quantity in older writers. As for the other principal means by which circumstantial information is created—adverbs—these would seem to be not a frequent feature in the writing of primary-age students. They appear more commonly in the secondary years, and on the evidence I have provided, they may be loosely grouped into two categories: those of manner (slowly; blankly), and modal adverbs (nearly; constantly). Both types of adverbs are actually involved in expression of opinions and/or judgments, and it seems that it is only with developing maturity that these begin to feature in students' writing.

Finally, what can we conclude from all this of what it is that subject English values and rewards? It seems that subject English—at least as it is taught in Australia—values and rewards capacity to write narratives, various literary critical pieces, and certain opinionated pieces. Narratives are valued because they offer opportunity to express truths about human experience and opportunity for self expression. The literary texts and the opinionated texts, both of which belong to the secondary years, are valued because they promote capacity to express personal opinion. In my observation, subject English attaches great significance to personal opinion and self expression, although it needs to be noted that the English teaching profession is sometimes rather naive about its claims in these areas. The narratives that are sought and rewarded in schools are essentially orthodox in terms of structure and ideology, and the other texts devoted to literary works or to critical social issues are also essentially of an orthodox kind. Furthermore—a worrying aspect of the naivete I have referred to—many English teachers subscribe to the view that in the interests of promoting self expression and personal opinion, teachers should leave a great deal of the decisions about *what* to write about, and *how* to write about it, to their students. Among the many problems this creates is the lack of a technical language in subject English that can be used, among other matters, to refer to grammar in writing instruction. That is because many English teachers do not believe it is their role to teach a knowledge about language so they employ no metalanguage either for discussing the types of texts to be written, or the linguistic features of these. Much of the significant knowledge of English, then, remains tacitly part of the curriculum, available to those students who, by life circumstance and opportunity, are enabled to develop the necessary facility with language for success in the subject. But for many other students, what represents success in English remains elusive, part of the "hidden curriculum" of schooling. When one considers, as I noted in my opening remarks, that subject English is the one subject that remains compulsory for all the years of secondary schooling, we perpetuate significant social injustice when we leave access to useful knowledge about language as a matter of chance.

Whatever the particular text type sought in the English program, what is overwhelmingly valued in the texts of developing maturity—and hence of advanced literacy—is the capacity to deploy language in ways that abstract away from immediate, lived experience, to build instead truths, abstractions, generalizations, and arguments about areas of life of various kinds. Capacity to handle these things can be taught. Let's teach!

REFERENCES

Christie, F., & Martin, J. R. (Eds.). (1997). Genre and social institutions: Social processes in the workplace and school. London: Cassell Academic.
Halliday, M. A. K. (1994). An introduction to functional grammar (2nd ed.). London: Edward Arnold.

4

Academic Language Development in Latino Students' Writing in Spanish

M. Cecilia Colombi
University of California, Davis

This chapter analyzes the development of academic writing in Spanish as a native minority language in a bilingual context from the perspective of systemic functional linguistics (SFL). This project is part of a longitudinal study that examines written texts of Latino college students in opinion essays (expository texts) during 1 academic year (three quarters) in a program of Spanish for Native Speakers. The students in this program are second-generation immigrants who are the first in their families to access higher education. The Spanish for Native Speakers program aims to develop academic proficiency in oral and written modes using a Freirian and process-writing oriented methodology (multiple version assignments, peer editing, tutors). The longitudinal study attempts to discover the extent to which Latino college students develop full control of literate language.

Halliday (1996, pp. 339–343) characterizes the concept of literacy from a linguistic point of view (i.e., "[1] treating literacy as something that has to do with language; and [2] using the conceptual framework of functional linguistics as a way of understanding it.… Literacy can be conceived as activity rather than as knowledge … being literate means engaging with language and its written form: distinguishing what is writing from what is not writing." For Halliday (1996, p. 368) it is through the written language that the writer can engage with the material environment to produce abstract symbolic objects (i.e., through writing, the world can be "objectified as the basis for systematic knowledge"). He points to lexical density, nominalization, and grammatical metaphor as the main lexicogrammatical characteristics of written language.

This linguistic framework sees language as a strategic, meaning making resource, allowing us to relate lexicogrammatical forms to specific functions in certain contexts that achieve particular purposes. For example, we can see in these essays how, as students become more aware of the academic register, they make different lexical and grammatical choices as they provide information, present a point of view, and structure their texts. From the SFL perspective, registers are a combination of lexicogrammatical features that characterize different genres, reflecting the social context in the ideas, role relationships, and text organizational patterns that they realize. Thus, the study of lexical and grammatical features can demonstrate the extent to which students make the choices that approximate the grammatical conventions of different text types. Christie (1986), for example, demonstrates how different grammatical choices make a text a narrative, a report, or a literary study.

Many studies have described the resources language has to condense and compact information in the sciences, such as by use of grammatical metaphor. Grammatical metaphor is a resource language uses to condense information by expressing concepts in an incongruent form. The use of grammatical metaphor is considered an essential characteristic of scientific and academic language (Halliday, 1993a, 1993b, 1998; Veel, 1998). Some studies have looked at differences in the use of grammatical metaphor in science and in the humanities (Martin, 1991; Unsworth, 1999). Eggins, Wignell, and Martin (1993), for example, discuss the lexicogrammatical characteristics of the discourse of history and of different history text types. Other studies have used this approach to identify genre and register characteristics that can help second language learners understand English in the professional and academic environment (Drury, 1991; Jones, Gollin, Drury, & Economou, 1989; Martin, 1993, 1996; Ventola & Mauranen, 1991). Taking a functional perspective, these studies show how different choices make a text the type of text it is.

Few researchers have applied SFL to the analysis of registers in Spanish (see Burdach, Millan, & Tonselli, 1994; Whittaker & Rojo, 1999). One study particularly relevant to this chapter is Gibbons (1999), which explores the differences between English and Spanish, applying Halliday's concepts of Mode, Field, and Tenor to characterize the academic register. Gibbons uses four measurements: lexical density, phrasal intricacy, syntactic intricacy, and grammatical metaphor, to describe two pairs of texts from natural science and one pair from history, in elementary and secondary school contexts. He points out that English and Spanish use some similar devices to realize academic language, but that there are also differences. In Spanish, for example, the most typical complex noun group is formed with the "*of* construction," as opposed to English, which modifies one noun with another. For example, *language loss* is expressed in Spanish as *the loss of language* (*la pérdida del lenguaje*). Gibbons concludes that the mastery of grammatically metaphorical forms is a very valuable indicator of textual competency in Spanish as well as in English.

A functional approach to language helps us understand how students' writing develops along a continuum of language competence, recognizing students' strengths, even when their writing still shows many weaknesses. Especially with Spanish as a minority language in a bilingual context, identifying how students improve over time is often difficult. As some studies have demonstrated, improvement in students' writing cannot be assessed only by counting the number of errors or the growth in vocabulary (Casanave, 1994). A functional approach goes beyond analysis of students' errors to look at the lexicogrammatical choices that students make and how they change over time, moving or not moving in the direction of academic language.

In this chapter I focus on nominalization and clause combining choices students make as a means of demonstrating their writing development. Studies of English as a first language have shown that as students develop, their writing moves from more coordination (oral-like structure) to more written styles, achieved primarily through a reduction in clausal structures (Crowhurst, 1990; Menyuk, 1988). Researchers in second-language writing have also noted this developmental tendency from oral/conversational uses to more literate ones characterized by the use of subordination and higher lexical density (Bialystok, 1991; Connor, 1990).

Within SFL, strategies of clause-linking are central to register differences. At the clausal level, language users make choices that constitute their writing as more or less appropriate for the genres they are attempting. These choices reveal them as more or less successful in adopting the appropriate register. Halliday (1994, p. 350) points out that "typically, written language becomes more complex by being *lexically dense*: it packs a large number of lexical items into each clause; whereas spoken language becomes complex by being *grammatically intricate*: it builds up elaborate clause complexes out of parataxis and hypotaxis." In spoken language we tend to chain clauses together one after another, often resulting in very long sentences, whereas in written language we tend to use relatively few clauses per sentence, packing more information into each clause through nominalization and grammatical metaphor (Eggins, 1994).

Although the written dimension does not correlate precisely with an academic register, as texts can be written without being academic, and spoken language can also adopt an academic register, for purposes of this study, it is helpful to consider the extent to which features of more formal written registers are found in students' texts. Academic language is different from interactional registers in its grammar and discourse structure (Valdés & Geoffrion-Vinci, 1998; Ventola & Mauranen, 1996), and my previous research (Colombi, 1997) has demonstrated that native speakers learning to write in academic Spanish often draw on informal, oral-like registers, frequently giving the appearance of immature writing (see also Schleppegrell, 1996, for similar conclusions about English and second language students).

The goal of this study is to demonstrate that students' development of academic registers in Spanish as a minority language can be measured through analysis of their use of nominalization in combination with clause-combining strategies, and that those strategies interact with the discourse organizational demands of writing assignments (i.e., the way they use lexicogrammatical devices to achieve different functions). In an earlier study (Schleppegrell & Colombi, 1997) we showed that writers' organizational structure is reflected in the types of clause combinations they choose. We characterized students' writing as highly planned, condensed and tightly constructed on the one hand, or as emergent, elaborated, and loosely connected on the other hand. The writer who uses a strategy of simple sentences or clause embedding, with a high level of nominalization, typically realizes a more academic register, whereas the writer who uses a strategy of clause-chaining, linking multiple clauses in longer sentences, realizes a more oral register, with greater grammatical intricacy. This study shows how writers begin to move from the oral style that characterizes their immature academic writing toward the clause condensation and nominalization that makes their writing more like what is typically expected in academic contexts.

THE LEXICOGRAMMATICAL FEATURES
OF EXPOSITORY WRITING

This study analyzes the writing of native speakers of Spanish enrolled in university courses in Spanish composition. These bilingual students' future careers will require that they function in both English and Spanish in formal environments using academic registers, but this population of students is much more familiar with informal conversational registers. They use Spanish at home with their families and friends, but have not used it in many formal contexts. They are now focusing on improving their academic writing skills.

For this chapter, I illustrate the developmental trends in these students' writing by focusing on two students' expository essays that demonstrate the direction of academic writing development of a larger group (30 students under study). I analyze two essays by each student; one written at the beginning of their academic writing courses and another written at the end of the 9 months of instruction. All are first drafts of expository essays. The composition courses they took are typical of university writing courses, where students read essays or other texts and respond with essays that recapitulate the author's points and then go on to present a thesis with supporting arguments. The courses do not focus on grammatical structure in the functional ways proposed here; in other words, these students did not receive explicit instruction about register development or academic strategies for clause combining. However, a functional linguistic look at the different ways these two students move along the continuum of academic language development can give us a description of the relevant lexicogrammatical features of academic genres (expository essays, in this case) that can inform instruction in these courses in a more explicit way.

I analyzed the clause-combining strategies used by the student writers, characterizing each clause as main, hypotactic, paratactic, or embedded. Then I calculated the grammatical intricacy of each essay, comparing the earlier essays with the later essays to see the developmental trends. Finally, I looked at what students achieved from a discourse organizational perspective by making these clause-combining choices.

These definitions draw on Halliday (1994):

- Main clause: The main clause is the only clause in a simple sentence, the initiating clause in a paratactic sequence, or the dominant clause in a hypotactic clause complex.

- Hypotactic clause: Hypotactic clauses are dependent on but not con-stituents of another clause. Examples of hypotaxis are nonrestrictive relative clauses, adverbial clauses, and clauses projected through verbs of saying or thinking (Halliday, 1994, p. 220).
- Paratactic clause: Paratactic clauses are linked to the main clause with a coordinating conjunction or merely juxtaposed. This category in-cludes both clauses traditionally analyzed as coordinated clauses as well as direct quotations.
- Embedded clause: Embedded clauses are distinguished from hypotactic clauses (both of which are part of the traditional category, "subordinate clause") because embedding is not a relationship between clauses. An embedded clause is a part of the clause in which it is embedded; for exam-ple, as a postmodifier. A hypotactic clause is dependent on another clause, but is not a part of that clause. Embedded clauses include restric-tive relative clauses, comparative clauses, and nominalized clauses that function as subject or complement. It is precisely in this point that the Hallidayan functional perspective departs from traditional notions of subordination. A distinction between embedded and hypotactic clauses can yield more precise characterizations of students' writing develop-ment than studies that do not distinguish between these clause types.[1]

For this analysis, "clauses" are defined as structures with finite verbs. I analyze only finite clauses, because it is the presence of hypotactic and paratactic finite clauses that contributes to the spoken-like register. Every orthographic sentence that contains a subject and finite verb is analyzed as either a simple sentence (main clause only) or a complex sentence (main clause plus associated clauses). Each clause is then coded as main, paratactic, hypotactic, or embedded. My interest is in demonstrating how the clause combining choices contribute to the organization of the essay. For this reason, I identify only the clauses in the essay at the level of the major constituents that make up each sentence. (1) is an example of this analysis:

(1) Rosa's[2] first essay

La ciudad de Los Angeles, por ejemplo, es una de las cuantas ciudades [(en) que uno puede observar la cantidad de razas [[que viven ahí]].

The city of Los Angeles, for example, is one of the many cities in which one can observe the quantity of races that live there.

This sentence has one main clause with an embedded relative clause as a modi-fier. I do not further analyze the embedded clause (which also has an embedded rela-tive clause) because the second embedded clause does not contribute directly to the structure of the discourse. This analysis, then, gives us results that show the propor-

---

[1]See Schleppegrell and Colombi (1997) for further discussion of these constructs.
[2]Not their real names.

tion of hypotactic, paratactic, and embedded clauses to main clauses, allowing us to see the degree to which students rely on oral strategies in their written texts. The lexical density of these texts is another measure that can help us see how students move in the continuum toward more academic language. The lexical density has been calculated here by expressing the number of content carrying words in the texts as a proportion of all the words in the texts (Eggins, 1994). Content-carrying words are lexical items that include nouns, adjectives, verbs, and some adverbs. Grammatical items, on the other hand, are those that function in closed systems in the language: determiners, pronouns, conjunctions, prepositions, some adverbs, and some verbs (traditionally called "auxiliaries"). Another aspect to consider when we discuss academic language is frequency of occurrence (i.e., with the lexis of any language there are a number of highly frequent words; gente, cosa, hace, tiene, muchos, bien, bueno/ *people, thing, do, have, many, well, good,* etc.) on the borderline of grammar that contribute very little to the lexical density (Halliday, 1985/89).

Table 4.1 presents a quantitative analysis of Rosa's essays, giving us a picture of the student's grammatical choices in clause-combining, illustrating the direction in which her writing develops over the time of the study.

Table 4.1 presents the clause combining strategies Rosa uses in her first and final essays. It shows her development from a higher use of paratactic and hypotactic clauses (32.81%) in the first essay to a higher use of main and embedded clauses (46.57% and 28.76%, respectively), in the final essay. These figures exemplify Rosa's movement from a more oral register to a more written one. Looking at the period of time and the rate of movement from more paratactic and hypotactic clauses to the use of more condensed language, realized in a higher number of main clauses, we can say that the movement has been very slow (these essays were written 9 months apart). This shows that students will move in the direction of academic language with practice in writing and reading, but raises a question about how much faster these students could develop academic genres and registers if they had an explicit pedagogy that made them aware of the lexicogrammatical features that characterize those genres and registers.

This movement toward academic language is also reflected in the results of the grammatical intricacy and lexical density analysis presented in Table 4.2.

Grammatical intricacy is defined as the number of main, paratactic and hypotactic clauses divided by the number of orthographic sentences that appear in the text. Embedding is not subsumed under grammatical intricacy because it represents intricacy at the level of the nominal group. As we can see, Rosa moves from a grammatical intricacy of 1.75 in her early essay to a less intricate 1.52 in her later one. She moves from a lexical density of 43.1% to 50.5% in her last essay. The complexity of written language is lexical, whereas that of spoken language is grammatical. In Rosa's case, her grammatical intricacy decreases as her lexical density increases.

These quantitative conclusions can be illustrated with examples from Rosa's essays that demonstrate how she moves from grammatical choices that reflect oral registers toward more written-like grammatical options. In her first essay Rosa begins by introducing the issue she will discuss: the racial conflicts that the United States is facing. She starts by saying that many years ago the United States had con-

TABLE 4.1

Rosa's Grammatical Development

Essays (Rosa)	#1 1st Quarter (688 words)		#3 3rd Quarter (762 words)	
Clause type	Number of Clauses	Percent of Clauses	Number of Clauses	Percent of Clauses
Main clauses				
In simple sentences	14		6	
In complex sentences	14		28	
Total main clauses	**28**	**43.75%**	**34**	**46.57%**
Hypotactic clauses	12		12	
Paratactic clauses	9		6	
Total paratactic plus hypotactic clauses	**21**	**32.81%**	**18**	**24.65%**
Embedded clauses	**15**	**23.4%**	**21**	**28.76%**
Total Clauses	**64**	**100%**	**73**	**100%**

TABLE 4.2

Rosa's Grammatical Development

Rosa's Essays	Lexical Density	Grammatical Intricacy
#1	(297/688) 43.1 %	(49/28) 1.75
#3	(387/762) 50.5 %	(52/34) 1.52

Oral	⟶	Written
Grammatically Intricate	⟵⟶	Lexically Dense

flicts with races that did not belong to the Anglo-Saxon culture and explains that that created divisions among the races. She then emphasizes that nowadays that problem still exists and presents some examples. She continues by asking why. Her oral register in the first essay evidences itself most clearly in the way she combines clauses with hypotactic and paratactic links. (2) is an example of her clause combination in this first essay of the academic year, analyzed in Table 4.3. We see that Rosa responds to her own question by chaining her arguments one after another.

(2) Rosa's first essay

¿Por qué?

Simplemente porque no conviven con diferentes razas y no quieren ver la realidad que ocupan y necesitan de las demás identidades, como los hispanos

As example (2) and Table 4.3 show, to answer the question *¿Por qué?*, Rosa chains one idea after the other with the connector *y* (*and*), using hypotactic and paratactic clauses without any main clause. This is typical of oral language, where we tend to add one thought after the other as they come to our mind while we are speaking. This clause complex represents a good example of the grammatical intricacy that spoken language has. The ideational content is strung out in clausal patterns. It is more "choreographic" (Halliday, 1994). On the other hand, in written language, the clausal patterns are typically more simple; but the ideational content is densely packed in nominal constructions; more "crystalline," in Halliday's terms. Let's compare this clause complex with another from her last essay to see how her writing is developing toward a more written academic style.

TABLE 4.3

Clause Analysis of (2)

Clause	Type
¿Por qué? Why?	(Minor sentence)
Simplemente porque no conviven con diferentes razas Simple because they do not live with different races	Hypotactic
y no quieren ver la realidad and do not want to see reality	Paratactic
que ocupan they occupy	Embedded
y necesitan de las demás identidades, como los hispanos. and need of the different identities, like the Hispanics.	Paratactic

[Lexical density $(10/24) = 41\%$]

In her final essay, Rosa compares the situation in a play the students have read in class to the political situation in Mexico. Here, in (3), analyzed in Table 4.4, she uses just one sentence (made up of a main clause modified by an embedded clause) to express her main point:

(3) Rosa's last essay

El Gesticulador de Rodolfo Usigli indudablemente representa la decepción y el engaño que frecuentemente ocurre en el sistema político de México.

TABLE 4.4

Clause Analysis of (3)

Clause	Type
El Gesticulador de Rodolfo Usigli indudablemente representa la decepción y el engaño The Gesticulator by Rodolfo Usigli undoubtedly represents the deception and fraud	Main
que frecuentemente ocurre en el sistema político de México. that frequently occurs in the political system of Mexico.	Embedded

[Lexical density (12/21) = 57%]

We see that Rosa's language has now become more lexically dense: There are 12 lexical items in a total of 21, giving a lexical density of 57%, as opposed to the example from her first essay where she uses 10 lexical items out of 24 words, a ratio of 41%. In (3) the ideational meaning is lexically condensed, whereas in (2) it is strung out over many clauses. (2) is grammatically intricate, whereas (3) is lexically complex, as Rosa condenses information in prepositional phrases (which are also embedded and downranked constituents) such as *el Gesticulador de Rodolfo Usigli* and *sistema político de México*.

A closer look at how she expresses her thesis in these essays also shows us her development toward a more academic register over the course of a year. From the point of view of the discourse organization in the essay, the thesis functions as the idea put forward by the writer in the introduction that will be supported with premises and warrants. In other words, the writer tells us in the thesis what she or he will write about in the essay. The following is a comparison of Rosa's introductory paragraphs for her first and final essays.

(4) Rosa's first essay

California y "el otro"

Hace muchos años atras, los Estados Unidos tuvo conflictos con razas que no eran o pertenecían a la cultura anglosajon. Nomas porque no querían aceptar la diversidad entre culturas. Lo cual pudo haber causado las barreras y divisiones entre muchas razas. Actualmente, todavia existe este problema. Simplemente en los estados al este de los Estados Unidos, (como Virginia, Carolina de Sur), se niegan aceptar que el mundo se esta haciendo diverso cada vez más. ¿Por qué? Simplemente porque no conviven con diferentes razas y no quieren ver la realidad que ocupan y necesitan de las demás identidades, como los hispanos. En cambio, el estado de California, tiene tanta diversidad multicultural que, se puede decir que, California está preparado para enfrentarse con "el otro" atravéz de diversos lenguajes, contribuciones y la diversidad racial.

California and "the other"

Many years ago, the United States had conflicts with races that were not or did not belong to the Anglo-Saxon culture. Mainly because they did not want to accept the diversity among cultures. Which could have caused barriers and divisions among races. Nowadays, this problem still exists. Simply in the states in the east of the United States, (like Virginia, South Carolina), they refuse to accept that the world is becoming more diverse every time. Why? Simply because they do not live with different races and they do not want to see the reality they occupy and they need of the different identities, like the Hispanics. On the other hand, the state of California, has so much multicultural diversity that, we can say that, California is ready to face the "other" through different languages, contributions and racial diversity.

(5) Rosa's last essay

La verdad nos grita

El Gesticulador de Rodolfo Usigli es una novela dramática que trata el tema de la mentira entre una familia. Antes de publicarse en 1963, esta novela fue llevada al teatro en numerosas ocasiones. Inclusivemente, ha sido traducida en varios idiomas como el inglés, alemán y el francés. Tal y como lo indica su título, esta novela oculta los secretos de sus personajes. El Gesticulador refleja el engaño y la decepción que ocurre entre el sistema político de México representado a través de la familia Rubio.

The truth shouts at us

The Gesticulator by Rodolfo Usigli is a dramatic novel that develops the theme of deceit in a family. Before its publication in 1963, this novel was staged in theaters on many occasions. Inclusively, it has been translated into several languages, such as English, German and French. As the title indicates, this novel hides the secrets of its characters. "The Gesticulator" shows the fraud and deception that occurs in the political system of Mexico represented through the Rubio family.

In her first essay, (4), Rosa presents her thesis in stages; there is not one statement that summarizes it. She first introduces the topic of racial conflicts. Then she states that the problem still exists and at the end of her introduction she presents California as an example of a state that is dealing with the problem and is prepared to face the "other" (see the highlighting in the text). This strategy of information presentation draws on the sequential structure of oral exposition; the pseudodialogic use of rhetorical questions and answers is reminiscent of oral argumentation and lecturing. This oral style is also reflected in the "fragmentation" of some of her sentences and the repetitions in the language she uses (e.g, *diverso, diversidad*). She has used four main clauses and five hypotactic and paratactic clauses, an intricate and dynamic grammatical style typical of oral registers.

On the other hand, Rosa's thesis in the introductory paragraph of her last essay, (5), is more focused and clear. She presents it in the last sentence of the paragraph: *El Gesticulador refleja el engaño y la decepción que ocurre entre el sistema político de México representado a través de la familia Rubio.* She uses five main clauses with two embedded ones, a less grammatically intricate and more lexically condensed style. She condenses information by using nominalizations such as *antes de publicarse en 1963, representado a través ...* and embedded clauses such as *que trata el tema de la mentira entre una familia, que ocurre entre el sistema político de México.* These features together with others like the use of passive structures (*fue llevada al teatro, ha sido traducida*) give the text a more academic register. She does not use a dialogic style with rhetorical questions, but presents information in a more impersonal, detached and condensed way.

This analysis shows what I mean by movement from a more oral style, characterized by the use of hypotactic and paratactic clause combination, to a more academic register characterized by a greater use of main clauses with embedding and nominalization.

In the analysis of the students' texts, nominalization emerged as the most significant feature of their development from more oral language to a more academic register. "The nominal group is the primary resource used by the grammar for packing in lexical items at high density," according to Halliday (1994, p. 351). This makes nominalizing the single most powerful resource for creating grammatical metaphor. By this device, processes (congruently worded as verbs) and properties (congruently worded as adjectives) are reworded metaphorically as nouns. Instead of functioning in the clause as Process or Attribute, they function as Thing in the nominal group (Halliday 1994, p. 352).[3] The recursive principle of language makes it possible for such nominal groups to function inside prepositional phrases and for prepositional phrases to function inside nominal groups; these elements are then said to be "down-ranked" or "embedded." This structure can accommodate a great deal of lexical material, enabling the more dense presentation of information that characterizes the academic register.

The analysis of the different linguistic resources that Roberto uses to support his ideas in the first and last essays he wrote shows his language growth through the use of nominalization and grammatical metaphor.[4] In his first essay there are only two instances in which he expresses causation, whereas in his last essay he expresses causal relationships to support his ideas six times. Analysis of his expressions of causation shows how his grammatical choices change over time.

(6) Roberto's first essay

Esta variedad cultural en los Estados Unidos se debe a una fluición de inmigrantes quienes llegan de México y el resto de Latinoamérica.

---

[3]SFL uses the functional labels Process (verb), Thing (noun), and Attribute (adjective).
[4]The tables of the clause combining analysis together with the lexical density and grammatical intricacy of Roberto's essays are presented in Table 4.5.

TABLE 4.5

Roberto's Grammatical Development

Essays (Roberto)	#1 1st Quarter (494 Words)		#3 3rd Quarter (762 Words)	
Clause type	Number of Clauses	Percent of Clauses	Number of Clauses	Percent of Clauses
Main clauses				
In simple sentences	6		8	
In complex sentences	14		25	
Total main clauses	**20**	42%	**33**	**39%**
Hypotactic clauses	10		15	
Paratactic clauses	12		12	
Total paratactic plus hypotactic clauses	**22**	47%	**27**	**32%**
Embedded clauses	**5**	11%	**25**	**29%**
Total Clauses	**47**	100%	**85**	**100%**

Essays	Lexical Density	Grammatical Intricacy
#1	(222/494) = 44.9%	(42/20) 2.10
#3	(350/762) = 45.9%	(60/33) 1.81

In (6) Roberto uses the relational Process *deberse/ to be due* to support his idea. This is one of the few cases where he presents his own point of view in this first essay. In the main, he supports his ideas by referring to other sources. In (6), he is using a Process (*deberse*) in a incongruent way (i.e., integrated into the grammar to make the causal connection between the two ideas). It represents a clear attempt toward a more written style. In (7), on the other hand, analyzed in Table 4.7, he uses a prepositional phrase as a conjunction of cause, more typical of an oral style.

TABLE 4.6

Clause Analysis of (6)

Clause	Type
Esta variedad cultural en los Estados Unidos se debe a una fluición de inmigrantes. This cultural variety in the U.S.A. is due to the flow of immigrants	Main
quienes llegan de México y el resto de Latinoamérica. who come from Mexico and the rest of Latin America.	Embedded

[Lexical density 11/23) =47.82%]

TABLE 4.7

Clause Analysis of (7)

Clause	Type
Leyes como la de proposición 187 crean una actitud contra la inmigración. Laws like Prop.187 create an attitude against immigration	Main
y la hace parecer como un problema, and make it look like a problem,	Paratactic
a pesar de que el gobierno sabe despite of that the government knows	Hypotactic
que necesita la inmigración de trabajadores; that it needs the immigration of workers;	Hypotactic
por esta razón, estas leyes for this reason, these laws	Paratactic
que tienen que "arreglar el problema de la inmigración" that have to "resolve the immigration problem"	Embedded
terminan siendo inefectivas. end up being ineffective.	

[Lexical density 19/49) =38%, grammatical intricacy 5]

(7) Roberto's first essay

Leyes como la de proposición 187 crean una actitud contra la inmigración y la hace parecer como un problema, a pesar de que el gobierno sabe que necesita la inmigración de trabajadores; por esta razón, estas leyes que tienen que "arreglar el problema de la inmigración" terminan siendo inefectivas.

(7) represents a good example of the oral register that most of these students exhibit at the very beginning of the year; they link one idea after the other through hypotactic and paratactic clauses.

In his final essay, on the other hand, Roberto is able to use of a variety of resources to convey reason or causal links. He uses the conjunction *porque* (*because*) twice, *causar* (*cause*) as a Process twice, and *causar* once each as a noun (*la causa*), and as part of a prepositional phrase (*a causa*), as we see further on.

Conjunction porque (because)

(8) Roberto's last essay

Yo pienso que toda la pelea fue inútil porque nada se mejoró con la guerra sino que con la comunicación que solo empezó mucho después que haya terminado la violencia.

(9) Roberto's last essay

Pero la realidad se hizo evidente muy pronto porque ellos seguían con hambre y seguían trabajando para los hacendados.

TABLE 4.8

Clause Analysis of (8)

Clause	Type
Yo pienso que I think that	Main
toda pelea fue inútil all the fight was useless	Hypotactic
porque nada se mejoró con la guerra because nothing improved with the war	Hypotactic
sino que con la comunicación but with the communication	
que solo empezó mucho después that started only much after	Embedded
que haya terminado la violencia the violence had finished.	Embedded

[Lexical density (10/29) = 34.48%; grammatical intricacy 3]

TABLE 4.9

Clause Analysis of (9)

Clause	Type
Pero la realidad se hizo evidente muy pronto But the reality became evident soon	Main
porque ellos seguían con hambre because they continued to be hungry	Hypotactic
y seguían trabajando para los hacendados. And continued to work for the landowners.	Paratactic

[Lexical density (7/19) = 36.8%; grammatical intricacy 3]

Examples (8) and (9), analyzed in Tables 4.8 and 4.9, continue to present an oral style with many hypotactic and paratactic clauses. Here we can see that as Roberto's language is developing he still makes use of clause combinations that are characteristic of oral language. When we look further at other examples, however, we see how he is moving toward the written language.

Process causar (to cause)

It is through the use of different grammatical resources than the causative conjunction *porque* that nominalizations began to appear in the text. Still in the process of development and not always with a felicitous realization, Roberto's use of *causar* as a Process points in the direction of more written language with a higher use of nominalization and consequently a higher lexical density, as we see in (10), analyzed in Table 4.10.

(10) Roberto's last essay

La infelicidad con el gobierno corrupto __causó__ un levantamiento armado y el derrocamiento de la dictadura de Porfirio Díaz y poner un fin de una vez al porfirismo.

Two long nominalizations are joined by the material Process *causar*. *La infelicidad con el gobierno corrupto*, with a grammatical metaphor, *infelicidad*, congruently a Quality, is here incongruently presented as a Thing that can be modified by *con el gobierno corrupto*. The second nominalization is made up of two nominal groups joined by the conjunction *y*: *levantamiento armado y el derrocamiento de la dictadura de Porfirio Díaz*. Both nominalizations present a grammatical metaphor with a Process (*levantar, derrocar*) functioning as a Thing.

TABLE 4.10

Clause Analysis of (10)

Clause	Type
La infelicidad con el gobierno corrupto **causó** The unhappiness with the corrupt government caused	Main
un levantamiento armado y el derrocamiento de la dictadura de Porfirio Diaz an armed insurrection and the overthrow of the dictatorship of Porfirio Diaz	
y poner un fin de una vez al porfirismo. and (to) put an end for ever to the 'porfirismo'.	{Paratactic}

[Lexical density (14/28) = 50%]

Prepositional phrase *a causa (due to)*

(11) Roberto's last essay

Es obvio ahora que nada fue resuelto <u>a causa</u> de la guerra civil.

In (11), analyzed in Table 4.11, *causa* is nominalized as a Thing and functions as head of the prepositional phrase with another prepositional phrase functioning as a postnominal modifier.

TABLE 4.11

Clause Analysis of (11)

Clause	Type
Es obvio ahora It is obvious now	Main
que nada fue resuelto **a causa** *de la guerra civil.* that nothing was resolved due to the civil war.	Embedded

[Lexical density (6/13) = 46.1%]

Thing *causa (cause)*

(12) Roberto's last essay

La dominación del hacendado sobre poblaciones pequeñas de peones era <u>la causa</u> de tensión a través del país que se hacía peor cada año hacia el final del siglo XIX.

TABLE 4.12

Clause Analysis of (12)

Clause	Type
La dominación del hacendado sobre poblaciones pequeñas de peones era The landowners' domination over small populations of peasants was	Main
la causa de tensión a través del país the cause of tension through the country *que se hacía peor cada año hacia el final del siglo XIX.* that was getting worse every year towards the end of the XIX Century.	Embedded

[Lexical density (12/29) = 41.3%]

In (12), analyzed in Table 4.12, we can see how Roberto uses nominalizations to compact information and present his ideas. This sentence is constructed of two clauses; the main clause uses a relational Process (*era/ was*) to link two nominal groups. *La causa* is an incongruent realization of the Process *causar*. By nominalizing it and using it as a Thing, Roberto is able to qualify and determine it, packing more information into the nominal group. There are other grammatical metaphors in this example: *dominación*, an incongruent realization of the Process *dominar* (*to dominate*) and *tensión*, an incongruent realization of the Quality *tenso* (*tense*). (12) clearly demonstrates how Roberto's writing development is incorporating the resources of nominalization and grammatical metaphor.

We can use another indicator of lexical growth in the nominal group by looking at the nominal structure (or phrasal intricacy; Gibbons, 1999) of the essays to measure the extent that they use more complex noun groups and consequently more nominalizations. The nominal structure in this study has been determined by dividing the number of complex noun groups by the number of clauses. A complex noun group is defined as one that contains more elements than one determiner (and/or adjective) plus one noun. Table 4.13 presents the nominal structure of these students' essays.

TABLE 4.13

Nominal Structure

Students	First Essay	Last Essay
Rosa	(31/64) 48 %	(58/73) 79 %
Roberto	(26/47) 55 %	(50/85) 58 %

As we can see, although there are differences between Rosa and Roberto, both students move in the direction of higher nominal structure at the end of the academic year. Rosa's difference between the two essays is larger than Roberto's and this difference may be due to various and individual factors. However these results indicate that as these students' writing progresses toward a more academic register, their lexical density as well as their nominal structure increases.

CONCLUSIONS

This study has presented how two bilingual students move in the direction of developing academic registers in their essay writing in Spanish at the university level. Two essays by each student were analyzed, the first from the very beginning of the year and the second written at the end of the academic year (about 9 months difference). Their clause-combining strategies together with measurements of lexical density, grammatical intricacy, and nominal structure were used to determine their growth. The results show that although there are differences, both students move in the direction of a more literate or "written" language. At the clause combining level, they move from more informal registers that draw on paratactic and hypotactic clauses to more formal registers that use main clauses with embedded clauses. Although this is a very slow process, the direction of this progress can be seen by analyzing their clause combining strategies and understanding the functions that different clause combinations help them accomplish.

These findings suggest that analysis of nominalization together with clause-combining strategies can provide a means of charting the development of academic writing skills. It shows that as their writing develops toward more academic registers their lexical density and nominal structure will grow while the grammatical intricacy will decrease. It also demonstrates that the use of nominalization and grammatical metaphor play an important role in the understanding of academic writing development.

An understanding of the functional meanings that are conveyed by different clause-combining choices can provide teachers with a useful framework for effectively incorporating grammar into writing instruction, making explicit how different grammatical choices help students produce the types of texts that are expected in academic contexts. Rather than relying on paratactic and hypotactic clause combinations, familiar to them from spoken discourse, students at this level need to adopt strategies of clause condensation and nominalization in order to achieve an academic register. Bilingual writers, in particular, who have acquired their native language in informal situations, may benefit from explicit linguistic focus on the ways of condensing information that are typical of many academic tasks.

It is important to emphasize that the students in this study were not shown explicitly the difference in clause combination that oral and written styles reflect. Guided instruction about the grammatical choices that realize academic registers could help students increase the rate at which they progress in the development of their academic writing. The development of academic Spanish in the United States is a long endeavor, but guided focus on grammar at the level of the text can facilitate and accelerate this process. A functional approach that helps students recognize how the elements of linguistic structure contribute to the presentation of ideas, the interpersonal stance, and the organization of their texts can inform instruction in Spanish academic registers at all levels.

REFERENCES

Bialystok, E. (1991). *Language processing in bilingual children*. New York: University of Cambridge.
Burdach, A. M., Millan, A. M., & Tonselli, M. (1994). Aplicación del modelo de conjunción como recurso de cohesión de Halliday y Hasan a una muestra del español [Application of the Halliday and Hasan conjunction model as a resource of cohesion to a Spanish sample]. *Revista del Instituto de Letras de la Pontificia Universidad Católica de Chile, 19,* 167–180
Casanave, C. P. (1994). Language development in students' journals. *Journal of Second Language Writing, 3*(3), 179–201.
Christie, F. (1986). Writing in schools: Generic structures as ways of meaning. In B. Couture (Ed.), *Functional approaches to writing: Research perspectives* (pp. 221–239). London: Frances Pinter.
Colombi, C. (1997). Perfil del discurso escrito en textos de hispanohablantes: Teoría y práctica [Profile of the written discourse in Spanish-speakers texts: Theory and practice]. In M. C. Colombi & F. X. Alarcón (Eds.), *La enseñanza del español a hispanohablantes* Teaching Spanish to Spanish-speakers (pp. 175–189). Boston: Houghton Mifflin.
Connor, U. (1990). Linguistic/rhetorical measures for international student persuasive writing. *Research in the Teaching of English 24,* 67–87.
Crowhurst, M. (1990). The development of persuasive/argumentative writing. In R. Beach & S. Hynds (Eds.), *Developing discourse practices in adolescence and adulthood* (pp. 200–223). Norwood, NJ: Ablex.
Drury, H. (1991). The use of systemic linguistics to describe student summaries at university level. In E. Ventola (Ed.), *Functional and systemic linguistics: Approaches and uses: Trends in linguistic studies and monographs.* (pp. 431–456). Berlin, Germany: Mouton de Gruyter.
Eggins, S. (1994). *An introduction to systemic functional linguistics.* London: Pinter Publishers.
Eggins, S., Wignell, P., & Martin, J. R. (1993). The discourse of history: Distancing the recoverable past. In M. Ghadessy (Ed.), *Register analysis: Theory and practice* (pp. 75–109). London: Pinter Publishers.
Gibbons, J. (1999). Register aspects of literacy in Spanish. *Written Language and Literacy, 2*(1), 63–88.
Halliday, M. A. K. (1985) *Spoken and written language.* Geelong, Vic.: Deakin University Press.
Halliday, M. A. K. (1993a). On the language of physical science. In M. A. K. Halliday & J. R. Martin (Eds.), *Writing science: Literacy and discursive power,* (pp. 54–68) Pittsburgh: University of Pittsburgh Press.
Halliday, M. A. K. (1993b). Some grammatical problems in scientific English. In M. A. K. Halliday & J. R. Martin (Eds.), *Writing science: Literacy and discursive power,* (pp. 69–85). Pittsburgh: University of Pittsburgh Press.
Halliday, M. A. K. (1994). *An introduction to functional grammar.* London: Edward Arnold.
Halliday, M. A. K. (1996). Literacy and linguistics: A functional perspective. In R. Hasan & G. Williams (Eds.), *Literacy in society,* (pp. 339–376). Harlow, Essex, UK: Addison Wesley Longman.

Halliday, M. A. K. (1998). Things and relations. In J. R. Martin & R. Veel (Eds.), *Reading science: Critical and functional perspectives on discourse of science*, (pp. 185–235). London: Routledge.

Jones, J., Gollin, S., Drury, H., & Economou, D. (1989). Systemic-functional linguistics and its application to the TESOL Curriculum. In R. Hasan & J. R. Martin (Eds.), *Language development: Learning language, learning culture*, (pp. 257–328). Norwood, NJ: Ablex.

Martin, J. R. (1991). Nominalization in science and humanities: Distilling knowledge and scaffolding text. In E. Ventola (Ed.), *Functional and systemic linguistics: Approaches and uses* (pp. 307–337). Trends in Linguistic Studies and Monographs. Berlin, Germany: Mouton de Gruyter.

Martin, J. R. (1993). Genre and literacy-modeling context in educational linguistics. *Annual Review of Applied Linguistics, 13*, 141–172.

Martin, J. R. (1996). Waves of abstraction: Organizing exposition. *The Journal of TESOL-France, 3*(1), 87–105.

Menyuk, P. (1988). *Language development: Knowledge and use*. Glenview, IL: Scott, Foresman and Company.

Schleppegrell, M. (1996). Conjunction in spoken English and ESL writing. *Applied Linguistics, 17*(3), 271–285.

Schleppegrell, M., & Colombi, C. (1997). Text organization by bilingual writers. *Written Communication, 14*, 481–503.

Unsworth, L. (1999). Developing critical understanding of the specialised language of school of science and history texts: A functional grammatical perspective. *Journal of Adolescent and Adult Literacy, 42*(7), 508–521.

Valdés, G., & Geoffrion-Vinci, M. (1998). Chicano Spanish: The problem of the "underdeveloped" code in bilingual repertoires. *The Modern Language Journal, 82*(4), 473–501.

Veel, R. (1998). The greening of school science. In J. R. Martin & R. Veel (Eds.), *Reading science: Critical and functional perspectives on discourse of science* (pp. 114–151). London: Routledge.

Ventola, E., & Mauranen, A. (1991). Non-native writing and native revising of scientific articles. In E. Ventola (Ed.), *Functional and systemic linguistics: Approaches and uses: Trends in linguistic studies and monographs.* (pp. 457–492). Berlin, Germany: Mouton de Gruyter.

Ventola, E., & Mauranen, A. (Eds.). (1996). *Academic writing: Intercultural and textual issues*. Amsterdam: Benjamins.

Whittaker, R., & Rojo, L. M. (1999). A dialogue with bureaucracy: Register, genre and information management as constraints on interchangeability. *Journal of Pragmatics, 31*, 149–189.

5

Writing History: Construing Time and Value in Discourses of the Past

James R. Martin
University of Sydney

WHAT HISTORY?

In a postcolonial world, our history comes back to haunt us and it becomes difficult to move forward without dealing with the past. In Australia, the issues of land rights and stolen generations dominate the politics of reconciliation, with diverse voices contesting both the history and what to do about it. Debates are highly charged, and for many commentators John Howard's conservative government has not dealt productively with the situation:

> On taking office the Howard government mounted a cynical and sustained campaign to discredit the institutions of Aboriginal welfare and the processes of self-determination and reconciliation, culminating in Howard's shameful refusal to apologise on behalf of the nation for the policies of forced removal of Aboriginal children from their parents. The prime minister invited the outpouring of racial hatred through the calculated persecution of the "Aboriginal industry" and his attacks on the "black arm-band view" of Australian history. (Hamilton, *Guardian Weekly* June 21, 1998, p. 12)

From a social semiotic perspective, a concern with reconciliation makes the discourses of history every bit as important to salvaging humanity as discourses of science are to salvaging the environment. But research funding, and thus scholarly enterprise, do not reflect a balance of this kind. For science we have *Talking Science* (Lemke, 1990), *Writing Science* (Halliday & Martin, 1993), *Reading Science* (Martin & Veel, 1998), *Explaining Science in the Classroom*, (Ogborn, Kress, Martins, & McGillicuddy,

1996), *Genre Analysis* (Swales, 1990), *Writing Biology* (Myers, 1990), *Shaping Written Knowledge* (Bazerman, 1988), *Scientific Discourse in Sociocultural Context* (Atkinson, 1999, Wallace & Louden, 2002) … the list goes on. Quite a canon! But for history … just what springs to mind? Beyond this, in Australia's public education sector, history is rapidly declining as a subject choice in secondary school. What effect, one wonders, will this have on our readings of the past—on just who will make them and who will read them, and on how critically any of this will be done?

In this chapter I'd like to redress this balance a little, drawing on literacy research undertaken by colleagues from the so-called "Sydney School" (Martin, 2000a). I'm interested in the kind of discourse that makes and remakes history, and in the implications of this for teaching literacies of history in university and school.

WHOSE HISTORY?

Let's begin by setting some parameters, drawing on the highly charged reconciliation theme introduced earlier. First, some oral history, from Archie Roach, a well-known Aboriginal singer and songwriter. The song in question has become one of the anthems of the stolen generations movement; in the verses reproduced here, Roach recounts his own experience of having been stolen from his family by white Australia.

[1] One dark day on Framingham

Came and didn't give a damn

My mother cried go get their dad

He came running fighting mad

Mother's tears were falling down

Dad shaped up he stood his ground

He said you touch my kids and you fight me

And they took us from our family

Took us away

They took us away

Snatched from our mother's breast

Said this was for the best

Took us away … (Roach, 1990)[1]

Roach is in the fortunate position of being able to sing his history to an appreciative audience in the field of popular culture. Most personal history on the other hand is never recorded, let alone heard. The oral history movement represents an attempt by historians to give a voice to nonliterate histories, and it has had some impact on Australian schools—with, for example, students interviewing relatives about mi-

---

[1] Lyrics are from "Took the Children Away" written by Archie Roach (Mushroom Music Publishing). Reprinted with permission.

gration or Aboriginal elders visiting schools on "Sorry Day"[2] to talk about their experiences as stolen children. Hardy (1968, a popular writer) and Rose (1991, an academic) are two influential Australians who have given voice to Aboriginal history along these lines. Recently, the federal government report on the stolen generations, *Bringing Them Home*, included an unparalleled amount of testimony from stolen Aboriginal Australians in textually prominent positions throughout the document.

Next, some written history, from Vicente Rafael (1988), a postcolonial scholar dealing with the colonization of the Philippines by the Catholic church. In chapter 3 of his treatise, Rafael turns to the logic of confession:

[2] ... This internalisation of an exterior hierarchy consists of two interrelated procedures: the accounting of past events and the reproduction of the discourse of interrogation contained in the confession manuals.

First, the process of accounting. All confession manuals contain the unconditional demand that all sins be revealed ...

The Spanish demand is that nothing be held back in confession. One is to expend all that memory can hold in a discourse that will bring together both the self that recalls and that which is recalled. The present self that confronts the priest in confession is thus expected to have managed to control his or her past—to reduce it, as it were, to discursive submission. Whereas the examination of conscience requires the division of the self into one that knows the Law and seeks out the other self that deviates from it, a "good confession" insists on the presentation of a self in total control of its past. It is in this sense that confessional discourse imposes on the individual penitent what Roland Barthes called a "totalitarian economy" involving the complete recuperation and submission of the past to the present, and by extension of the penitent to the priest (Barthes, 1976: 39–75).

Unlike Roach's song, this text is not written for a mass audience, but for a community of academic peers who can handle discourse at this level of abstraction. As we might expect from his poststructuralist stance, Rafael treats colonization as a discourse interpellating subjects as the church's emerging hegemony prescribes. This reading of the past is a long way from common sense discourse; it deconstructs the naturalizing story of civilization and salvation we might uncritically expect. Discourse of this order has also had some impact on Australian schools, as part of the critical literacy movement—with prominent educators promoting deconstructive readings from the beginning of every lesson from the beginning of school (cf. Morgan, 1997; Muspratt, Luke, & Freebody, 1997; Walton, 1996). In order to understand how to manage this for history, we need to look closely at texts like Rafael's and the discourses they build on to see what kind of discourse postcolonial critique involves—so that we don't fall into the trap of writing as if critical literacy is a stance outside of discourse that students can be directed to assume.

---

[2]The anniversary of the release of the government's *Bringing Them Home* report; now referred to by some organizers as "Journey of Healing." Around Australia grass-roots commemorative meetings are held in recognition of the stolen generations.

MARKING TIME

What I want to do now is proceed by factoring out some distinctive features of history discourse, across a range of genres—taking texts like Roach's as point of departure and eventually ending up with texts like Rafael's. In each phase of this procedure, I'll use contrasting texts to highlight the variables in question; and I'll provide a functional linguistic reading of relevant factors based on Halliday (1994) and Martin (1992). The tradition of reading history I'm following here is based on Coffin (1997); Eggins, Wignell, and Martin (1993); Martin (1993a, 1993b, 1996, 1999a, 1999b, 2000b); Martin and Plum (1997); and Veel and Coffin (1996).

To begin, consider Text 3, a personal recount written after a class trip to the zoo. This genre is deployed to recount personal experiences that unfold over a relatively short time frame, with an ongoing prosody of evaluation giving meaning to events for family and peers (Martin, 1985/1989; Martin & Plum, 1997). It features actions sequenced in time by both implicit and explicit temporal connections (explicit links are underlined in Text 3 below).

[3] Taronga Park Zoo

Last Wednesday all Year 1 went to Taronga Zoo.

First we went to have a lesson. We all saw a ringtail possum and the teacher showed us a koala's hand. We saw a great white shark's mouth and I saw a lion.

We saw a peacock while we were having lunch and my Dad came to the Zoo with me and monkeys and a big gorilla and we saw zebra and a giraffe and I had a good time at the Zoo. I went back to school. I felt good.

I liked the lion and the elephant and giraffe but the best thing was going on the train and the ferry and the bus and I felt good going back home and when I got back home I felt exhausted and we had a snack.

From these links we can reconstruct the sequence of events through which the text unfolds, as we might have done for Roach's personal recount above (implicit links in parentheses below).

First   We went to have a lesson.

(then)   We all saw a ringtail possum

And (then)   The teacher showed us a koala's hand.

(then)   We saw a great white shark's mouth

And (then)   I saw a lion.

This kind of personal recount can be usefully contrasted with Text 4, an historical recount, whose function is to manage generalized events involving whole classes of participants that typically unfold over a relatively longer time frame. Text 4 covers

1000 years of whaling, as related by a retired marine biologist to the Canadian Wildlife Federation in 1989. It features activities positioned in the past by circumstances of location in time that appear initially in the clause as Theme (as underlined below).

[4] <u>For one thousand years</u>, whales have been of commercial interest for meat, oil, meal and whalebone. <u>About 1000 A.D.</u>, whaling started with the Basques using sailing vessels and row boats. They concentrated on the slow-moving Right whales. <u>As whaling spread to other countries</u>, whaling shifted to Humpbacks, Grays, Sperms and Bowheads. <u>By 1500</u>, they were whaling off Greenland; <u>by the 1700s</u>, off Atlantic America; and <u>by the 1800s</u>, in the south Pacific, Antarctic and Bering Sea. <u>Early in this century</u>, the Norwegians introduced explosive harpoons, fired from guns on catcher boats, and whaling shifted to the larger and faster baleen whales. The introduction of factory ships by Japan and the USSR intensified whaling still further.

The global picture, then, was a mining operation moving progressively with increasing efficiency to new species and new areas. Whaling reached a peak during the present century.

<u>While this high-seas drama was unfolding</u>, coastal, shore-based whaling developed around the world. In Canada, for example, it was native whaling for Belugas and Narwhal in the Arctic, and commercial whaling from northern Vancouver Island in the Pacific, and from Quebec, Nova Scotia and Newfoundland in the Atlantic. (W. R. Martin, 1989, p. 1)

From these locations in time we can establish the various phases of whaling history, arranged one after another from the past to the present. The contrast we are working on here is between *sequence* in time (as managed by temporal conjunctions) and *setting* in time (as managed by thematic circumstances of location in time). *Sequence* manages time as a series of naturally unfolding everyday events; *setting* chunks time into clumps of composite activities. Where this chunking is generalized, across historians, then the phases may be conventionalized and named (e.g., the Middle Ages, WWII, the Cold War; note in passing the use of uppercase letters to reinforce the technicality, which in turn affords acronyms for very famous chunks). The critical factor here has to do with packaging time—moving from a series of events to phases, which can then be further compartmentalized through naming—giving us a more technical, "thing-ised" history. This represents a move from more typically spoken to more typically written discourse.

Autobiographical recount resembles personal recount in being written in the first person, but manages a longer time line in a similar way to historical recounts. Biographical recount is closely related, although written in the third person rather than first. Text 5 foregrounds pivotal phases of Captain Cook's life by using Theme predication (*it was then that* ... , *it was when he was employed on the charting of the Newfoundland coast and the estuary of the St Lawrence River that* ...).

[5] <u>On 3 November 1726</u>, in Marton-in-Cleveland, an agricultural village hidden amidst the scenic beauty of the Yorkshire Dales in the rural acres of the North Riding, James and Grace Cook brought their week-old son to the parish church of St Cuthbert for baptism. <u>When the boy grew to adolescence</u> he was apprenticed to a grocer in the

nearby fishing village of Staithes. It was there that he felt the first call of the sea—a passion which never left him. He was not prepared to spend his life as a grocer and within eighteen months he moved down the coast to Whitby where he signed on as a deck hand on a Whitby collier.

Cook's progress in the merchant navy was steady but not spectacular. At the age of 26 he was offered his first ship and it was then, for reasons best known to himself, that he took the decisive step in his life and gave up the opportunity of advancement to join the Royal Navy as an able seaman. His talents and hard-won knowledge soon gained him recognition in the Navy. He obtained his master's certificate in 1757 after serving under Hugh Palliser during the blockade of the French ports and he served in Canada during the siege and the capture of Quebec. It was when he was employed on the charting of the Newfoundland coast and the estuary of the St Lawrence River that he met an army surveyor called Samuel Holland. Within a very short time Cook had mastered the surveying and map-making techniques which Holland taught him. (Aughton, 1999, pp. 6–7)

ABSTRACTION

To fully appreciate the compartmentalization of time factor just introduced, we need to look more closely at the language responsible for turning activity into things (Halliday, 1998). For example, *the Long March* is a nominal group as far as grammar is concerned; this phase of the Chinese Revolution is construed as a thing. But semantically we know, as mature readers, that it refers to an activity, involving thousands of soldiers marching from the south to the north of China. The grammar of *the Long March* is in a sense out of step with its meaning. Why does the historian prefer two levels of meaning, in tension with one another, where one meaning might do?

Consider the following excerpt from Mandela's autobiographical recount, toward the very end as he sums up his life in relation to the meaning of freedom (Martin, 1999b):

[6] I was not born with a hunger to be free. I was born free—free in every way that I could know. Free to run in the fields near my mother's hut, free to swim in the clear stream that ran through my village, free to roast mealies under the stars and ride the broad backs of slow-moving bulls. As long as I obeyed my father and abided by the customs of my tribe, I was not troubled by the laws of man or God.

It was only when I began to learn that my boyhood freedom was an illusion, when I discovered as a young man that my freedom had already been taken from me, that I began to hunger for it. At first, as a student, I wanted freedom only for myself, the transitory freedoms of being able to stay out at night, read what I pleased and go where I chose. Later, as a young man in Johannesburg, I yearned for the basic and honourable freedoms of achieving my potential, of earning my keep, of marrying and having a family—the freedom not to be obstructed in a lawful life.

But then I slowly saw that not only was I not free, but my brothers and sisters were not free. I saw that it was not just my freedom that was curtailed, but the freedom of everyone who looked like I did. That is when I joined the African National Congress, and that is when the hunger for my own freedom became the greater hunger for the freedom of my people. It was this desire for the freedom of my people to live their lives with dignity and self-respect that animated my life, that transformed a frightened young man into a bold one, that drove a law-abiding attorney to become a criminal, that turned a family-loving husband into a man without a home, that forced a life-loving man to live like a monk. I am no more virtuous or self-sacrificing than the next man, but I found that I could not even enjoy the poor and limited freedoms I was allowed when I knew my people were not free. Freedom is indivisible; the chains on any one of my people were the chains on all of them, the chains on all of my people were the chains on me ... (Mandela, 1995, p. 750)[3]

"When I was a child, I spake as a child"[4] or however that line goes. So when recounting his childhood, Mandela uses language in which grammar and semantics match up. Participants are realized as nouns, qualities as adjectives, processes as verbs, assessments as modal verbs, and logical connections as conjunctions, as laid out in Table 5.1. The discourse is relatively concrete.

Then *born free* becomes *boyhood freedom*, and the recount shifts to a more abstract discourse with recurring tension between meaning and wording. Meanings of all kinds drift in the direction of the noun, as we see in Table 5.2.

Even causal relations that might otherwise have been realized as connections between clauses are realized inside the clause as nominalized Agents that act on other nominalizations—as with the transforming Theme-predicated Agent below:

It was this desire for the freedom of my people to live their lives with dignity and self-respect that animated my life, ...

Halliday (1994) refers to this skewed coding of meaning in grammar as "grammatical metaphor," because there are two meanings instead of one (the grammatical one and the semantic one) and the grammatical meaning in some sense symbolizes the semantic one. Halliday (1998) summarizes the pay-off of this skewed coding for the evolution of scientific discourse. The pay-off for Mandela is that alongside the meaning potential of the adjective (as in paragraph 1), he now has in addition the meaning potential of the noun to construe his changing conception of freedom (see Martin, 1999b for details). The abstract discourse extends his meaning potential in just the ways he needs to make sense of his life. We'll return to look at the pay-off for historians in general in more detail further in the chapter.

A crude map of this interstratal tension is presented in Fig. 5.1, which alongside the drift toward nominalization allows for verbal realizations of logical connections.

CAUSE

Historians and history teachers typically try to do more than chronicle the past—they try to explain it. It's not just a matter of when things happened, but why they happened as they did. For a text that foregrounds causal as opposed to tempo-

---

[3]From *A Long Walk to Freedom* by Nelson Mandela. Copyright © 1994 by Nelson Rolihlahla Mandela. By permission of Little, Brown, and Company (Inc.).

[4]Arriving in Manly, a beach suburb in metropolitan Sydney, I once recited (based on a sign that greeted visitors) "Seven miles from Sydney and a thousand miles from care." My daughter Phoebe, then 4 years old, said "Where's Care?" Now 12, she gets the joke when I tell the story (cf. Halliday, 1993).

TABLE 5.1

Congruent Realizations

participant as Thing *(noun)*

I, fields, hut, stream, village, mealies, stars, bulls, father ...

quality as Epithet *(adjective)*

free, clear, broad

process as Process *(verb)*

was born, to run, to swim, to roast, rise, obeyed ...

assessment as Finite *(modal verb)*

could

logical relation as Textual Theme *(conjunction)*

as long as

TABLE 5.2

Incongruent Realizations

process as Thing *(noun)*

this desire	cf. I desired freedom
hatred	cf. They hated the prisoner

quality as Thing *(noun)*

a hunger to be free	cf. I was hungry to be free
dignity	cf. They were dignified
narrow-mindedness	cf. They were narrow-minded
humanity	cf. They were humane

assessment as Thing *(noun)*

achieving my potential	cf. I achieved what I could
truth	cf. It wasn't true
responsibilities	cf. I must act

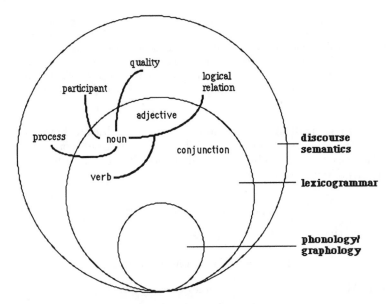

FIG. 5.1   Tension across meaning and wording in abstract discourse.

ral connections, consider Text 7, here, which exemplifies historical account as opposed to recount (not simply one event after another but one event giving rise to
another). Causal connections have been underlined.

[7] … As it turned out however, there was a last minute rush. There were no doubt
particular reasons for this. But a general reason was that developments at home and
abroad had changed the political landscape. At home, China had moved on from New
Democracy to full-blooded socialism; abroad, Khrushchev had denounced Stalin and
his "cult of personality" and proposed new strategies for the international communist
movement.

In China, "socialist transformation" was set off by Mao's victory in a dispute between
himself and most of the rest of the party's leadership over the right way to react to a cri-
sis in agriculture. In 1953, the government found that it was short of grain to feed the
urban population. A system of compulsory procurement, under which private transactions in grain were forbidden in rural markets until the agents of the state, often mill-
ers, had bought up fixed quotas of grain at low prices, was therefore introduced. This
change relieved the situation in towns. But, in the absence of any rapid growth in output, it produced severe shortages in the countryside. Mao's response was to demand
the rapid collectivisation of agriculture—the replacement of privately owned farms by
agricultural-producer cooperatives, to begin with of a kind in which members would
be remunerated in part for their contributions of land, draught animals and tools, but
quite soon at a "higher stage," where members would be rewarded only for their labour.

It was Mao's belief that collectivisation would lead to increased output, through the
achievement of economies of scale from the creation of larger farms, and also make it

easier for the government to procure the grain it needed to feed the country's urban population. But he was influenced at least as much by his fear that the pattern of ownership created by land reform would soon produce a high degree of economic and social polarisation in the countryside—that the richer peasants would accumulate more land and other assets, that the poorer peasants would be forced to sell or mortgage their land and that the leveling effects of land reform would therefore be undone. (Evans, 1993, pp. 126–128)

Note that these highlighted connections are typically realized within rather than between clauses in abstract history of this kind. The only causal conjunctions deployed are *therefore* and *to*; elsewhere we find nouns like *reason*, verbs such as *lead to*, and prepositions like *for*:

Congruently realized causal connection:

CONJUNCTION	therefore

Incongruently realized causal connections:

NOMINAL	Reason/s, effects, response
VERBAL	Make, lead to
PREPOSITIONAL	For, through, from, (in the absence of[5])

Note in particular the tightly packed chain of causally connected nominalizations in *collectivization would lead to increased output, through the achievement of economies of scale from the creation of larger farms*. However, by focusing exclusively on these explicit lexicalizations of cause, we are not doing justice to the causation motif permeating the entire recount. One further aspect of this is the agentive role of leaders like Krushchev and Mao in commanding change.

- verbal cause (sayers commanding abstractions)
  Khrushchev had ... *proposed* new strategies ...
  Mao's response was to *demand* the rapid collectivization of agriculture ...

Another is the agentive effect of abstractions on abstractions, realized across a range of effective material processes:

- material cause (abstractions affecting abstractions)
  developments at home and abroad had *changed* the political landscape
  In China, "socialist transformation" was *set off* by Mao's victory ...

---

[5]Arguably a lexicalised preposition here, although one derived of course by recoding a quality as a thing.

This change *relieved* the situation in towns.
it (this change) *produced* severe shortages in the countryside
that the pattern of ownership *created* by land reform ...
that the pattern of ownership ... would soon *produce* a high degree of
    economic and social polarization in the countryside

Clause structures of both kinds make available a very large range of processes for developing a fine grained explanation of why things happened as they did. Alongside the very limited range of causal meanings afforded by conjunctions (Halliday, 1994; Martin, 1992), we have available the open system lexis of material and verbal processes—which gives historians the resources they need to delicately explain how one thing (and I mean "thing") led to another.

Although this expansion of resources may be subtle and essential, it also has the effect of making explanations less accessible to critique. Consider for example Australia's current Prime Minister refusing to apologize on behalf of the nation for the stolen generations:

> [8] The Prime Minister acknowledges and thanks you for your support for his personal apology to indigenous people affected by past practices of separating indigenous children from their families. However, the government does not support an official national apology. Such an apology could imply that present generations are in some way responsible and accountable for the actions of earlier generations, actions that were sanctioned by the laws of the time, and that were believed to be in the best interests of the children concerned. (Senator Herron writing on behalf of the Prime Minister, John Howard, to Father Brennan in late 1997.)

And here's an example of what this text might have sounded like if causality were realized between rather than within clauses (as we might unpack the PM's position for an 8-year-old):

> [8'] The Prime Minister received your message and he thanks you because you supported him because he apologized personally to indigenous people because government officials took their children away from them. But the government will not apologize officially on behalf of the nation, because if it does, then people might argue that indigenous people can blame present generations and make them explain why government officials took their children away; but they took them away because the laws of the time approved and allowed them to take them away, and the government thought the children would benefit more if the officials took them away than if they left them with their families.

Note that at certain points in our translation we have had to fill in material that was not made explicit in Senator Herron's reply—for example, who was it that took the children away (government officials) and who might hold current generations responsible (indigenous people)? And this highlights the way in which nominalized language allows writers to manipulate agency. In Text 8' there are nine Agents, all but one of them people acting on other people (Agents underlined below):

because you supported him

because government officials took their children away from them.

that indigenous people can blame present generations

and indigenous people make them explain

why government officials took their children away;

but they took them away

and the laws of the time allowed them to take them away,

if the officials took them away

than if they left them with their families.

In Text 8, on the other hand there are only four Agents, none of them specific individuals (Agents underlined below):

... affected by past practices of separating indigenous children from their families.

the government does not support ...

Such an apology could imply ...

... were sanctioned by the laws of the time

Alongside this, nominalized language also enables writers to reframe arguments in their own terms. In Text 8' for example, there are 18 ranking clauses to argue with; the Mood elements of these clauses (Subject and Finite) are listed in Table 5.3.

In Text 8, on the other hand, there are only four ranking clauses[6] to dispute. The first two of these are in effect performatives (acknowledging and thanking), so there is nothing to challenge. This leaves two clauses, one having to do with the government not supporting an apology and the other with what such an apology could imply, as we see in Table 5.4.

This shifts the debate away from the facts of the matter (who did what to whom and who will hold whom accountable as in Text 8') and over to the abstract legal niceties of whether or not an apology will lead to claims for compensation, which is what the government is really worried about. At this point in Australian history, leadership meant not having to say you're sorry.

Before leaving the motif of explanation, we need to consider genres that are both permeated with abstract causal motifs of this kind (like historical accounts) and are in addition globally structured around phases of cause and effect—consequential and factorial explanations. These are the genres required when the

---

[6]The clause following *imply* is taken as an embedded fact, not a projection, in this analysis: *Such an apology could imply [[that present generations are in some way responsible and accountable for the actions of earlier generations, actions that were sanctioned by the laws of the time, and that were believed to be in the best interests of the children concerned]].*

TABLE 5.3

Mood Elements in Text 8'

Ranking Clause	Finite	Subject
The Prime Minister received ...	did	he?
and he thanks ...	does	he?
because you supported ...	did	I?
because he apologized ...	did	he?
because government officials took ...	did	they?
But the government will not ...	won't	it?
because if it does ...	might	it?
then people might argue ...	might	they?
that indigenous people can blame ...	could	they?
and indigenous people make ...	would	they?
why government officials took ...	did	they?
but they took ...	did	they?
because the laws of the time approved ...	did	they?
and the laws of the time allowed ...	did	they?
and the government thought ...	did	it?
The children would ...	would	they?
If the officials took ...	did	they?
Than if they left ...	did	they?

reductive linearity of the grand narrative (Lyotard, 1984) construed by historical recounts and accounts is broken down to focus on simultaneous causes or effects. Complex causes and effects are always around of course, if we choose to look at them; but in grand narratives they are elided and submerged, to give a naturalized trajectory of inevitability to mainstream readings of the past.

Consequential explanations consider multiple effects of some event; factorial explanations consider multiple factors leading to some event. These are two of the

TABLE 5.4

Mood Elements in Text 8

Ranking Clause	Finite	Subject
The Prime Minister acknowledges ...	does	he?
and (he) thanks ...	does	he?
However, the government does not ...	doesn't	it?
Such an apology could ...	could	it?

genres favored by secondary-school examiners in Australia where students regularly encounter questions like *What were the effects of the Treaty of Versailles?* or *What were the causes of WWI?* How many of us have escaped old chestnuts such as these? Text 9 exemplifies this concern with simultaneous causes and effects. First Buggy, the secondary-school historian, describes three effects of the Long March, which can be simultaneously read as three factors in the eventual Communist victory. Buggy then includes a reprise by Mao, who renders his explanation in more lexically metaphorical language.

[9] How Did the Long March Contribute to the Eventual Communist Victory?

First of all, it established the leadership of Mao Zedong. Although Mao was challenged by the leader of the Fourth Route army, Zhang Guotao, the prestige Mao acquired during the Long March assured his dominance. Mao's leadership also brought an end to the dominance of the Soviet Union in the party and made Chinese Communism more independent.

The Long March forged a tightly knit army that drew strength from its sufferings. The survivors formed the tough nucleus of the New Red Army which developed at Yunan. The policy of going north to fight the Japanese also stimulated high morale in the Red Army and appealed to patriots throughout China.

As it passed through twelve provinces the Red Army brought the message of Communism to hundreds of millions of peasants, who would otherwise have never heard of Communism.

In a report delivered a few months after the completion of the march in December 1935, Mao Zedong summed up the achievement.

We say that the Long March is the first of its kind ever recorded in history, that it is a manifesto, an agitation corps and a seeding machine ... It proclaims to the world that the Red Army is an army of heroes and that the imperialists and their jackals, Chiang Kai-shek and his like are perfect nonentities ... It declares to approximately two hundred million people of eleven provinces that only the road of the Red Army leads to their Liberation. Without the Long March how could the broad masses have known so quickly that there were such great ideas in the world as are upheld by the Red Army?

The Long March is also a seeding machine, it has sown many seeds in eleven provinces which will sprout, grow leaves, blossom into flowers, bear fruit and yield a crop in the future.

To sum up, the Long March ended with our victory and the enemy's defeat. (Buggy, 1988, p. 240)

Below we come back to a discussion of the organization of global explanatory structures of this kind; Martin (1996) approaches this kind of organization from the perspectives of both analysis and synthesis.

As with accounts, and perhaps even more so, factorial and consequential explanations are permeated with the clause-internal causal motifs outlined above. Drawing on Halliday's (1994) ergative analysis of the English clause, we can outline in Table 5.5 this motif for Text 9, where abstract Agents recurrently affect abstract Mediums. Note in passing the range of material processes deployed to relate causes and effects.

VALUE

Beyond chronicling then there is explaining; and beyond explaining there is interpretation—because saying why things happened as they did necessarily involves a stance—an evaluative orientation to what is going on. This raises the issue of subjectivity and objectivity in history, and how texts present themselves along this cline. Coffin (1997) suggests a three-term stance system, involving "recorder," "interpreter" and "adjudicator" positions (cf. Iedema, Feez, & White, 1994; White, 1997 on media discourse). In recorder stance, texts present themselves as factual chronicles and avoid inscribing attitude. Text 10 exemplifies this voice, which maintains its "objectivity" in the face of heart-wrenching experiences.

[10] "The Journey of Healing"

Yesterday I went into the library and we talked about Aboriginal people. When they were little someone took them to another place. When they grew up they couldn't find their families. [Year 1, Vietnamese student]

For interpreter stance, texts focus explicitly on judgements of behavior; for historians, the whimsy of fortune, along with the abilities and courage of protagonists are favorite themes. Adjudicator stance is rarer, and involves historians making moral judgements about truthfulness and ethics.

Recorder voice	No judgement (more "objective")
⇕	
Interpreter voice	Judgements of luck, ability, courage
⇕	
Adjudicator voice	Moral judgements (more "subjective")

TABLE 5.5

Reasoning (written grammar, i.e. abstractions causing abstractions)

Agent [abstraction]	Process [caused]	Medium [abstraction]
the Long March	contributed to	the eventual Communist victory
it [= the Long March]	established	the leadership of Mao Zedong.
the prestige Mao acquired	assured	his dominance.
Mao's leadership	brought an end to	the dominance of the Soviet ...
" "	made	Communism ... independent.
the Long March	forged	a tightly knit army
{that [= the army]}	drew	strength from its sufferings.
The survivors	formed	the tough nucleus of the ... Army ...
The policy of going north	stimulated	high morale ...
{The Red Army}	brought	... Communism to ... peasants

Part of the rhetoric of history is shifting from one stance to another as the past unfolds. Three excerpts from a feature article by Manne (1999) show him moving from objective recording, through the interpretation of William Craig's abilities, and on to adjudication of governmental morality and truthfulness. The article begins objectively, but culminates subjectively as Manne positions his reading of the past in relation to ongoing political debate.

recording (no explicit judgements):

[11a] "No Mercy for Nellie Bliss"

The story begins with a letter sent on February 17, 1903, to the police in Townsville. It was written by the Northern Protector of Aboriginals in Queensland, the notable anthropologist, Dr Walter E. Roth, who was shortly to become Chief Protector in Queensland, and later the sole royal commissioner into the conditions of Aborigines in the north of Western Australia. Historians may eventually come to see him as the architect of the policy of Aboriginal child removal in Australia.

[later] <u>interpreting</u> (judging abilities):

[11b] Craig followed his telegram with a letter. He had listened to Nellie Bliss with <u>genuine attentiveness</u>. He <u>was able to</u> put to the Home Secretary, <u>in a morally and le-gally persuasive language</u>, the kind of case he now knew Nellie herself would have put before the court if she had <u>been able to</u> speak English or ... pay for a barrister ...

[finally] <u>adjudicating</u> (judging morality, truthfulness):

[11c] We have, in recent times, been told flatly that this policy was driven by a con-cern for the best interests of the children. We have been told, too, that the policy <u>ac-corded with the moral standards</u> of the time. No-one, however, who follows this story—who witnesses the grief of Nellie Bliss, the terror of Walter, the arrogance of Dr Walter Roth and the astonished <u>indignation</u> of William Craig—could seriously come out believing that what we have been told is *true*. (Manne, 1999, p. 11)

Outside the media, adjudicator stance is rare. In the discipline of history itself it is perhaps felt to be unscholarly; beyond this, taking up a moral position will tend to narrow one's readership down to those who share your point of view. Solidarity is very much at risk. Interpreter stance is not as volatile, and a great deal of history discourse seems to be concerned with deploying recorder stance to convince read-ers of the plausibility of interpretations. Text 12 is another example from Buggy (1988), which starts with an interpretation that is then carefully substantiated with objective recording and incorporation of primary sources.

[12] The Breakout: 16 October to 25 November

This most successful phase of the Long March owes a great deal to the diplomatic skills of Zhou Enlai and to the bravery of the rearguard.

Knowing that the south-west sector of the encircling army was manned by troops from Guangdong province, Zhou began negotiations with the Guangdong warlord, Chen Jitang. Chen was concerned that a Guomindang victory over the Communists would enable Chiang Kaishek to threaten his own independence. Chen agreed to help the Communists with communications equipment and medical supplies and to allow the Red Army to pass through his lines.

Between 21 October and 13 November the Long Marchers slipped quietly through the first, second and third lines of the encircling enemy. Meanwhile the effective resis-tance of the tiny rearguard lulled the Guomindang army into thinking that they had trapped the entire Communist army. By the time the Guomindang leaders realized what was happening, the Red Army had three weeks' start on them. The marching columns, which often stretched over 80 kilometres, were made up of young peasant boys from south-eastern China. Fifty-four per cent were under the age of 24. Zhu De had left a vivid description of these young soldiers:

They were lean and hungry men, many of them in their middle and late teens ... most were illiterate. Each man wore a long sausage like a pouch ... filled with enough rice to last two or three days.

By mid-November life became more difficult for the Long Marchers. One veteran recalls:

When hard pressed by enemy forces we marched in the daytime and at such times the bombers pounded us. We would scatter and lie down; get up and march then scatter and lie down again, hour after hour. Our dead and wounded were many and our medical workers had a very hard time. The peasants always helped us and offered to take our sick, our wounded and exhausted. Each man left behind was given some money, ammunition and his rifle and told to organize and lead the peasants in partisan warfare when he recovered.

When entering new areas the Red Army established a pattern which was sustained throughout the Long March:

> We always confiscated the property of the landlords and militarist officials, kept enough food for ourselves and distributed the rest to poor peasants and urban poor … We also held great mass meetings. Our dramatic corps played and sang for the people and our political workers wrote slogans and distributed copies of the Soviet Constitution … If we stayed in a place for even one night we taught the peasants to write six characters: "Destroy the Tuhao" (landlord) and "Divide the Land." (Buggy, 1988, p. 225)

Actually, evaluation interacts with abstraction and explanation here in a very typical copatterning of resources. The initial part of the text, which does the interpreting, is also the most nominalized part of the text; and the text that follows is in one sense an argument for the interpretation. As the text unfolds, it presents itself as more objective and more concrete, and this a good reason for agreeing with Buggy's interpretation of the reasons for the success of this phase of the Long March:

level of abstraction 1 (interpreter stance):

> This most successful phase of the Long March owes a great deal to the diplomatic skills of Zhou Enlai and to the bravery of the rearguard.

The next part of the text documents Zhou Enlai's diplomacy and, subsequently, the bravery of the rearguard. This passage contains a number of grammatical metaphors (underlined below), but is not as grammatically metaphorical as the introduction. The text uses this middling level of abstraction to spell out the events that form the basis for the historian's evaluation of the reasons for the success of this phase of the Long March.

level of abstraction 2 (recorder stance):

> Knowing that the south-west sector of the encircling army was manned by troops from Guangdong province, Zhou began negotiations with the Guangdong warlord, Chen Jitang. Chen was concerned that a Guomindang victory over the Communists would enable Chiang Kaishek to threaten his own independence. Chen agreed to help the Communists with communications equipment and medical supplies and to allow the Red Army to pass through his lines.
>
> Between 21 October and 13 November the Long Marchers slipped quietly through the first, second and third lines of the encircling enemy. Meanwhile the effective resistance of the tiny rearguard lulled the Guomindang army

> into thinking that they had trapped the entire Communist army. By the time the Guomindang leaders realized what was happening, the Red Army had three weeks' start on them. The marching columns, which often stretched over 80 kilometres, were made up of young peasant boys from south-eastern China. Fifty-four per cent were under the age of 24. Zhu De had left a vivid description of these young soldiers:

Finally the text moves to primary source material by way of providing evidence for the preceding interpretation, drawing on diary records of those actually involved in the fighting:

> When hard pressed by enemy forces we marched in the daytime and at such times the bombers pounded us. We would scatter and lie down; get up and march then scatter and lie down again, hour after hour. Our dead and wounded were many and our medical workers had a very hard time. The peasants always helped us and offered to take our sick, our wounded and ex-hausted. Each man left behind was given some money, ammunition and his rifle and told to organize and lead the peasants in partisan warfare when he recovered.

level of abstraction 3 (exemplified through recorder stance):
The interplay of primary and secondary sources is an important aspect of history teaching in Australian secondary schools. Textbooks like Buggy's, for example, include substantial sections comprised of primary materials (both texts and images) on the basis of which students are taught to make history. Unlike some textbooks, Buggy demonstrates how to integrate primary with secondary material as part of the rhetoric of evaluation, abstraction and explanation just reviewed.

ARGUING

This brings us to persuasion, where the rhetoric of demonstration exemplified in Texts 11 and 12 above is not enough—because the judgement to hand is simply too contentious (a volatile adjudication perhaps) not to be argued for. So once again we have to move beyond recounts and accounts to texts that are globally structured—but this time as arguments rather than explanations. Note that the motivation for moving to global reasoning this time round is more interpersonal than ideational; it has to do with forming community around shared values. With factorial and consequential explanations on the other hand the motivation for global structure was more ideational; there it had to do with acknowledging the complexity of the causal relations (i.e., multiple causes and effects).

This brings us to the genres of argument—exposition and discussion, which may focus either on a macro-proposition (why readers should believe something) or on a macro-proposal (why readers should do something). We'll focus on macro-propositions here; for discussion of hortatory arguments see Martin 1985, 1995a). Text 13 exemplifies exposition, which in this case tries to justify the controversial Thesis that war can be a good thing. It presents two Arguments in favor of the thesis (development of manufacturing and research) and then closes with a Reiteration of the benefits of war (a lesson that politicians round the world have learned all too well).

[13]

Thesis: (a) Wars are costly exercises. (b) They cause death and destruction (c) and put resources to nonproductive uses (d) but they also promote industrial and economic change. (e) This benefit does not mean that war is a good thing, but that it sometimes brings useful developments.

Argument 1: (f) The Second World War further encouraged the restructuring of the Australian economy towards a manufacturing basis. (g) Between 1937 and 1945 the value of industrial production almost doubled. (h) This increase was faster than otherwise would have occurred. (i) The momentum maintained in the post-war years (j) and by 1954–1955 the value of manufacturing output was three times that of 1944–1945. (k) The enlargement of Australia's steel-making capacity, and of chemicals, rubber, metal goods and motor vehicles all owed something to the demands of war. (l) The war had acted as something of a hot-house for technological progress and economic change.

Argument 2: (m) The war had also revealed inadequacies in Australia's scientific and research capabilities. (n) After the war strenuous efforts were made to improve these. (o) The Australian National University was established with an emphasis on research. (p) The government gave its support to the advancement of science in many areas, including agricultural production.

Reiteration: (q) Though it is difficult to disentangle the effects of war from other influences, (r) it is clear that future generations not only enjoyed the security and peace won by their forefathers but also the benefits of war-time economic expansion. (Simmelhaig & Spenceley, 1984, p. 121)

Note that in Text 13 the causal relation of reason to belief is not strongly scaffolded (cf. Text 14 below). Working with students learning to write exposition in primary school, we have tended to be much more explicit:

I think (war is a good thing) for two <u>reasons</u> ...
<u>Firstly</u> ...
<u>Secondly</u> ...
<u>In conclusion</u> (there's a lot of benefit to war).

But for Text 13, understanding the reasoning means recognizing the genre and the causal configuration of its staging.

Having said this, it's important to note that the rhetoric of abstraction and evaluation introduced previously is still present here, in an even more elaborated form. Martin (1992, 1993a) noted that Halliday's analysis of Theme and New in English clause structure resonates with similar patterns at higher levels of text organization. Hyper-Themes (the topic sentence of traditional school rhetoric) for example can be used to predict patterns of Theme selection in the clause just as Hyper-News can be used to sum up News; Hyper-Themes may themselves be predicted by Macro-Themes (introductory paragraphs) just as Hyper-News may be consolidated as Macro-News (summary paragraphs); and so on for as many layers of prediction and accumulation as required to punctuate a discourse's information flow. A crude rendering of this hierarchy of periodicity is offered as Fig. 5.2.

The second paragraph of Text 13 exemplifies this "sandwich" texture, with clauses g–k elaborating f (Hyper-Theme) before being summed up as l (Hyper-New).

(f) The Second World War further encouraged the restructuring of the Australian economy towards a manufacturing basis.

(g) Between 1937 and 1945 the value of industrial production almost doubled. (h) This increase was faster than otherwise would have occurred. (i) The momentum was maintained in the post-war years (j) and by 1954–1955 the value of manufacturing output was three times that of 1944–1945. (k) The enlargement of Australia's steel-making capacity, and of chemicals, rubber, metal goods and motor vehicles all owed something to the demands of war.

(l) The war had acted as something of a hot-house for technological progress and economic change.

Paragraph three has a Hyper-Theme (m–n), but not a Hyper-New—reflecting the fact that writers differ in their predilection for predicting or accumulating or both. I suspect that the more a writer writes to a detailed plan, the more likely it is that there will be layers of prediction forecasting where the text is going; writers who don't know what they are going to say until they say it tend to favor periodic accumulation.

Moving on from the "Hyper-" to the "Macro-" level, Text 13 as a whole is an expository sandwich, with Thesis as Macro-Theme and Reiteration as Macro-New:

(a) Wars are costly exercises. (b) They cause death and destruction (c) and put resources to nonproductive uses (d) but they also promote industrial and economic change. (e) This benefit does not mean that war is a good thing, but that it sometimes brings useful developments.

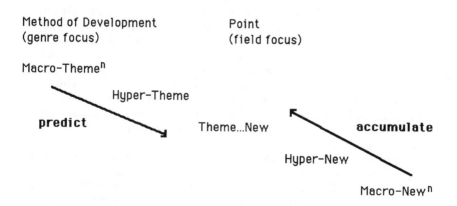

FIG. 5.2   Waves of abstraction (i.e., layers of Theme and New).

(f) The Second World War further encouraged the restructuring of the Australian economy towards a manufacturing basis ...

(m) The war had also revealed inadequacies in Australia's scientific and research capabilities....

(q) Though it is difficult to disentangle the effects of war from other influences, (r) it is clear that future generations not only enjoyed the security and peace won by their forefathers but also the benefits of war-time economic expansion.

To read this argumentative rhetoric we have to recognize the layers of prediction and accumulation, which can be challenging because all layers in discourse of this kind are fairly nominalized—it's degrees of abstraction that matter and effective readers are apparently fine-tuned to these. And Text 13 does deal with concrete examples in paragraphs 2 and 3 following the Hyper-Themes. Beyond this, readers also have to recognize the key evaluation that is triggering the arguments—at issue here are the positive, not the negative effects, of war, although both are introduced in Text 13's Macro-Theme. The sandwich rhetoric is critical here, because it is _useful_ developments that is picked up in the Reiteration as _the benefits_ of war-time economic expansion. Another key indicator is the use of lexical metaphor to flag key evaluations, typically as Hyper-Theme or Hyper-New, as we see in these examples from the texts we've been looking at:

[4] The global picture, then, was a mining operation ... (Hyper-New)

[6] the chains on any one of my people were the chains on all of them, the chains on all of my people were the chains on me ... (Hyper-New)

[9] the Long March is the first of its kind ever recorded in history, [that] it is a manifesto, an agitation corps and a seeding machine ... (Hyper-Theme)

[13] The war had acted as something of a hot-house for technological progress and economic change ... (Hyper-New)

So to the rhetoric of evaluation, grammatical metaphor, and explanation established previously, we can now add hierarchy of periodicity and lexical metaphor. The interplay of these factors is what gives history discourse its distinctive character.

This is a lot to learn, especially in education sectors where teachers and students do not share a metalanguage for talking about discourse, and where pedagogic principles are influenced by the "progressive" ideology that direct teaching is an impediment to learning (cf. Martin, 1998). Text 14 shows an 11/12-year-old from a nonmainstream ESL background working into the discussion genre, where more than one side of an issue is presented and adjudicated. From the perspective of traditional school grammar, there is of course much to proscribe in such a text, which does not consistently deploy English grammar, and sometimes uses spoken English where it does. But following Australian initiatives to introduce factual writing in primary school (cf. Cope & Kalantzis, 1993; Hasan & Williams, 1996), the basic scaffolding for the discussion genre is there—ready for the grammatical metaphor and evaluation of mature argument to develop. Whether it does or not is of course a matter for epigenesis—will the students in question find themselves in the kind of learning environment that will trigger the ontogenesis? What are the triggers? Who will enable them? What do we do with students who arrive at university without this rhetoric in place? For relevant Australian secondary school materials see Brook, Coffin, & Humphrey, 1996; Coffin, 1996.

[14] Currently the year 6 have being discussion whether or not should there be war. Here are some reasons why war should happen. It's possible many people think war should happen because it could wipe out a whole lot of populations so many other people could have more food to eat. Sometimes we may have war because to end an argument or to reach a better solution. It can be seen that people need to show patriotism for a nation.

But on the other hand if war happens many innocent people get killed, that includes young people that may one day be our future leaders. Furthermore, if one country fights the rest of the other countries gets involved and many people suffer. One other important reason is the cost of weapons and many other feel is a waste which could be spent on the starved and homeless people.

My point of view after looking at both sides is war should not happen because government are the ones that makes the decision so they should be the ones that fight each other.

MAPPING HISTORIES

At this point it is perhaps appropriate to develop an overview of the discourses of modernity we have been reviewing to portray history as we've known it. A summary outline is presented as Table 5.6, organized by genre and annotated with genre staging, some informal description of the function of each genre and some notes on key linguistic features (Coffin, 1997; Martin, 1999a). The outline has been arranged as a kind of learner pathway, beginning with the personal recount genres familiar to most students from their oral culture. It then develops through the autobiographical, biographical, and historical recounts that deal with longer stretches of phased activity. At this point the pathway moves from texts construing time (recounts) to those construing cause (accounts, explanations, and arguments)—a major move accompanied by a significant increase in grammatical metaphor, as signaled by the thicker boundary line. The next step takes us from linear grand narratives to texts organized around multiple causes and effects (explanations), and from there to texts organized around multiple arguments (expositions and discussions).

Although the genres are bounded by solid lines separating categories (with the thicker lines representing major developments), it is perhaps better to read the pathway as a cline (technically a genre topology; Martin, 1997)—because it is not unusual to find texts that straddle the borders (e.g., recounts with some causal links or accounts with temporal ones). And how one views a genre may in any case be a matter of reading position. Text 9, for example, might be read by some as an exposition presenting arguments as to why the Long March was a success, (rather

TABLE 5.6

Genres of History—A Learner Pathway

Genre [staging]	Informal Description	Key Linguistic Features (Halliday 1994, Martin 1992)
Personal recount [Orientation ^ Record]	Agnate to story genres; what happened to me	Sequence in time; 1st person; specific participants
Autobiographical recount [Orientation ^ Record]	Borderline—agnate to story & factual genres; story of my life [oral history]	Setting in time; 1st person; specific participants
Biographical recount [Orientation ^ Record]	Story of someone else's life	Setting in time; 3rd person (specific); other specific & generic participants
Historical recount [Background ^ Record]	Establishing the time line of the grand narrative	Setting in time; 3rd person; mainly generic participants (but specific great 'men')
Historical account [Background ^ Account]	Naturalizing linearization rendering the grand narrative inevitable	Incongruent external causal unfolding; 3rd person; mainly generic participants; prosodic judgement
Factorial explanation [Outcome ^ Factors]	Complexifying notion of what leads on to/from what	Internal organization of factors; factors externally linked to outcome; 3rd person; mainly generic participants
Consequential explanation [Input ^ Consequences]	Complexifying notion of what leads on to/from what; hypothetical variant—if x, then these outcomes	Internal organization of factors; consequences externally linked to input; 3rd person; mainly generic participants
Exposition—one sided; promote [Thesis ^ Arguments]	Problematic interpretation that needs justifying	Internal conjunction keying on thesis
Challenge[5]—one sided; rebut [Position ^ Rebuttal]	Someone else's problematic interpretation that needs demolishing	Internal conjunction keying on thesis

continued on next page

TABLE 5.6   *(continued)*

Genres of History—A Learner Pathway

Genre [staging]	Informal Description	Key Linguistic Features (Halliday 1994, Martin 1992)
Discussion—multi-sided; adjudicate [Issue ^ Sides ^ Resolution]	More than one interpretation considered	Internal conjunction keying on thesis; + internal organization of points of view
Post-colonial discourse [Foucault; Lyotard]	Avoiding reductive temporal & causal linearization into grand narrative/effacing voices of the 'other' …	Replace naturalizing time/cause explanation with 'spatial' discursive formation realizing episteme

Note. For reasons of space the challenge genre has not been illustrated here; it constitutes a counter argument to a prevailing thesis (a rebuttal).

than an explanation); Text 13 on the other hand might be read by others as an explanation of the consequences of war (rather than an exposition)—and in either case, subjectivity may be coloring the readings (communist vs nationalist, capitalist vs environmentalist respectively). This is a controversial area; my own position is that modernist texts do indeed naturalize a reading position, but that readers can read against the grain of a discourse if they are able and so choose. When treating Text 9 as explanation and Text 13 as exposition, I am arguing that these are the genres the configurations of meaning in these texts work to naturalize.

In constructing this learner pathway we were influenced by what is generally known as a spiral curriculum, which starts where students are and guides them forward through successive zones of proximal development toward explicit discourse goals (Coffin, 1997; Martin, 1998; Rothery, 1989, 1996). The pathway is constructed on linguistic principles, as inspired by Halliday's (1993) notion of a language-based theory of learning. Our feeling was that genres that foreground features of written rather than spoken discourse, especially grammatical metaphor, and that unfold rhetorically rather than chronologically will be harder for students to learn—harder still for nonmainstream students whose coding orientation does not equip them to learn written discourse by osmosis (without it being taught) in school. This is not to say that genres further along the pathway cannot be taught without working through every step along the way; but it is to suggest that skipping steps will mean that extra work has to be done to familiarize students with the discourse resources that they may thus have missed.

It may be useful at this point to unpack a little of the linguistic reasoning involved in these contingencies. The key genres of modernist history are restated in Table 5.7, in groups reflecting the stronger boundaries in Table 5.6. Above and below these genres six key factors differentiating them from one another are outlined. Using Halliday's (e.g., 1994) notion of interpersonal, ideational, and textual mean-

TABLE 5.7

Factors Underpinning Learner Pathway for History Genres

History Topology

1	prosodic appraisal		periodic appraisal		thesis appraisal
2	proposition				proposition/ proposal
3	tell	record	explain		
			reveal	probe	argue
	Auto/ biographical recount [later]	historical recount [in/during]	historical account [external cause, incongruent]	factorial & consequential explanation [internal cause]	exposition/ challenge
					discussion
4	individual focus	group (+ hero) focus			
5	text time = field time			text time ≠ field time	
6	episodic unfolding in time		causal unfolding	internal unfolding	

ing, the pathway can be unpacked, factor by factor, as follows (' ... ' represents a boundary from the table):

1. interpersonal meaning: ongoing reaction to what went on (prosodic appraisal) ... clusters of evaluation of what went on (periodic appraisal) ... formulate thesis around appraisal of what went on (thesis appraisal)
2. interpersonal meaning: give information (proposition) ... justify an interpretation about what happened or what should be (proposition/ proposal)
3. ideational meaning: tell what happened to an individual (tell) ... record what happened to groups (record) ... explain what led on to what (reveal) ... probe a set of factors leading to or from some event (probe) ... present arguments around an interpretation of what happened (argue)
4. textual meaning: largely specific reference (individual focus) ... largely generic reference, except for great "men" (group + "hero" focus)

5. textual meaning: relatively congruent (text time follows field time) …
relatively grammatically metaphorical (text time differs from field
time)
6. textual meaning: external temporal (episodic unfolding in time) … external metaphorical consequential (causal unfolding) … internal[7] conjunctive organization (internal (rhetorical) unfolding)

MORE TO HISTORY

There's more to history than has met our eye. More genres—for example report
and description (as discussed in Martin, 1993a). More discourse—the whole issue
of primary and secondary sources has scarcely been touched on (Brook et al.,
1996), which in turn raises the issue of more modalities—because primary sources
typically include images that have to be viewed (Kress & van Leeuwen, 1996;
Lemke, 1998). And more text—because the genres reviewed here are typically
configured into macro-genres as textbooks and student projects (Martin, 1995b, in
press). Chapter 9 of Buggy (1988), for example, is a macro-recount of the Long
March that unfolds as follows:

[Outline]

Introduction

The Breakout: 16 October to 25 November

Battle of Xiang River: 25 November to 3 December

The Capture of Zunyi: January 1935

Zunyi Conference: 15–18 January 1935

The Golden Sands River Crossing: 29 April to 8 May

The Luding Bridge Crossing: 29 May 1935

The Great Snowy Mountains: July 1935

The High Grasslands: August 1935

Lazikou Pass: 16 September

How did the Long March Contribute to the Eventual Communist Victory?

---

[7]For internal versus external conjunction see Martin 1992, 1993a.

[[The Long March Legend and Reality = 16 pp scaffolded primary sources]]

Why did the Long March Succeed?

[Structured Question, Problems and Issues, Role Play, Empathy Exercises]

[Bibliography]

Alongside an Outline, Bibliography and interactive sections (Structured Question etc.), and 16 pages of primary sources, it consists of 10 historical recounts unfolding serially through time (including Text 12 shown previously), a consequential explanation (Text 9 shown previously) and one factorial explanation. In Buggy's chapter these genres are clearly separated into discrete sections. In other textbooks boundaries may not be so clearly marked, nor even so clear. Readers have to learn to navigate the change of gears, including cases where transitions involve one genre phasing gradually out of another. To this we have to add a concern with so-called "genre-mixing," a misnomer if ever there was one—because to mix genres we have to have genres to mix, and this implies recognizable typologies. Perhaps more appropriate here is the notion of mixed texts, drawing on more than one genre, in various ways. Martin (2002) considers renovation, hybridization, multimodality, and macro generic assemblages in secondary school geography—all very different ways of 'combining' genres. Other possibilities include embedding, where one genre functions as a stage in another (Martin, 1995b), and contextual metaphor, where one genre stands in for another (e.g., children's stories as scientific explanations; Martin, 1990; 1997). The range of variation[8] reflects the diversity of social factors at play; to study change we need a rich model of multifunctional texts, not a reductive one.

By way of closing I make two points. First, from the perspective of functional linguistics, the key to understanding the texture of the advanced literacy needed for secondary and postsecondary schools is grammatical metaphor[9]—the process whereby language expands its meaning potential by cooking meaning twice. This is the process that brings the meaning potential of the entire grammar to bear on meaning of any kind, however allocated to specific functional regions (noun, verb, modal, adjective, conjunction) in everyday life. This expanded meaning

---

[8]The range of variation will come as no surprise to functional grammarians, who deal regularly with renovation (*Don't disappear that overhead!*), blends (*It is stocky, muscled body, short legs and massive chest make the jaguar a powerful and efficient hunter.*), multimodality (*3 of them went POW!*), clause complexing (*Yes, but Anna will probably always be a bit shorter than you, 'cos Anna's Mummy and Daddy are much shorter than Mummy and Daddy, so Anna will probably never be as tall as you even when she's grown up.*), embedding (*Factors [favorable to the development of the true tropical rainforest] are annual rainfall amounts in excess of 1500mm.*) and grammatical metaphor (*The effects of industrialization and the need of more land due to the growth of population seriously affected wildlife and still is today*); (Halliday, 1994; Matthiessen, 1995; Martin, Matthiessen, & Painter, 1997).

[9]For ideational metaphor see especially Halliday and Martin (1993); Halliday (1998), Martin (1992), chapter 6; interpersonal metaphor hasn't been in focus here, but is explored in Halliday (1994); Martin (1995a).

potential is what modernity has used to construct its uncommon sense disciplines and institutions, and what postmodernity in its turn has subsumed to reconstrue these disciplines and institutions as discourses that co-articulate (with attendant modalities such as image, sound, and action) our social semiotic life. The move from primary to secondary schooling in the western world symbolizes ontogenetic readiness as far as this expanded meaning potential is concerned (Halliday, 1993). Where students end up depends on how they take up the potential. Modernity deployed a distribution of this potential that squandered the human resources we now need to remake our postcolonial world.

Second, power and status—again, from the perspective of functional linguistics, it is important not to reduce access to the discourses outlined for history here to a question of status. Sure they sound good, and those controlling can sound literate and learned as they choose. But the key point here is not that these discourses have prestige—because the reason they have acquired prestige is that they privilege. They give controllers the meaning potential to intervene across a range of sites, as they so choose, which would otherwise be closed—to enact bureaucracy for example, or build technology—to manage the tools modernity has used to annihilate so many languages and cultures, and to so severely damage our biosphere—the tools to salvage these as we so choose. The status comes from the power, not the other way round.

I'm not saying everyday language isn't powerful; it's after all the tool we use for dealing with our lovers, family, and friends. It matters there. And Archie Roach, for example, took this discourse, combined it with a flair for musical composition and singing, and helped move a people—along a road to reconciliation they might not otherwise have stumbled along. But it is important to keep in mind he had Paul Kelly[10] producing him, Mushroom Records to distribute him, print and electronic media to project him, popular culture to consume him ... and those enabling discourses are far from the everyday discourse Archie Roach sings. A stolen child, but he got off skid row; an inspiring story, but not many are let off. Perhaps one lesson we can take from this is that the power of multimodal discourse may turn out to be a useful complement to the ever more abstract postmodern discourse we draw on to deconstruct modernity. It can be better grounded in the materiality of our social world, which is where change ultimately has to happen—perhaps it is an essential tool for enacting critique, as we generate constructive accounts of what we want to happen in our world. Our privilege, to use and distribute, as we so choose.

REFERENCES

Atkinson, D. (1999). *Scientific discourse in sociohistorical context: The Philosophical transactions of the Royal Society of London, 1675–1975*. Mahwah, NJ: Lawrence Erlbaum Associates.
Aughton, P. (1999). *Endeavour*. Moreton-in-March: The Windrush Press.

---

[10]Kelly is one of Australia's most respected singer/songwriters in the troubadour tradition, who has been very active producing music by indigenous artists—one of Australia's most important "Shamrock Abs."

Bazerman, C. (1988). *Shaping written knowledge: The genre and activity of the experimental article in science*. Madison: University of Wisconsin Press.

Brook, R., Coffin, C., & Humphrey, S. (1996). *Australian identity: A unit of work for junior secondary history*. Sydney, Australia: Metropolitan East Disadvantaged Schools Program. (State Equity Centre, Bridge & Swanson St., Erskineville, NSW, Australia).

Buggy, T (1988). *The Long Revolution: A history of modern China*. Sydney, Australia: Shakespeare Head Press.

Coffin, C. (1996). *Exploring literacy in school history*. Sydney, Australia: Metropolitan East Disadvantaged Schools Program.

Coffin, C. (1997). Constructing and giving value to the past: An investigation into secondary school history. In F. Christie & J. R. Martin (Eds.), *Genre and institutions: Social processes in the workplace and school* (pp. 196–230). London: Cassell.

Cope, W., & Kalantzis, M. (Eds.). (1993). *The powers of literacy: A genre approach to teaching literacy*. Pittsburgh, PA: University of Pittsburgh Press.

Eggins, S., Wignell, P., & Martin, J. R. (1993). The discourse of history: distancing the recoverable past. In M. Ghadessy (Ed.), *Register Analysis: Theory and practice*, (pp. 75–109). London: Pinter.

Evans, R. (1993). *Deng Xiaoping and the making of modern China* (rev. ed.). London: Penguin.

Halliday, M. A. K. (1993). Towards a language-based theory of learning. *Linguistics and Education, 5*, 93–116.

Halliday, M. A. K. (1994). *An introduction to functional grammar*. London: Edward Arnold.

Halliday, M. A. K. (1998). Things and relations: Regrammaticising experience as technical knowledge. In J. R. Martin & R. Veel (Eds.), *Reading science: Critical and functional perspectives on discourses of science* (pp. 185–235). London: Routledge.

Halliday, M. A. K., & Martin, J. R. (1993). *Writing science: Literacy as discursive power*. London: Falmer.

Hardy, F. (1968). *The unlucky Australians*. Melbourne, Australia: Thomas Nelson.

Hasan, R., & Williams, G. (Eds.). (1996). *Literacy in society*. London: Longman.

Human Rights and Equal Opportunity Commission. *Bringing Them Home: National inquiry into the separation of Aboriginal and Torres Strait Islander children from their families*. (1997). Sydney, Australia: Author.

Iedema, R., Feez. S., & White, P. (1994). *Media literacy (Write it Right Literacy in Industry Project: Stage Two)*. Sydney, Australia: Metropolitan East Disadvantaged Schools Program. (State Equity Centre, Bridge & Swanson St., Erskineville, NSW, Australia).

Kress, G., & van Leeuwen, T. (1996). *Reading images: The grammar of visual design*. London: Routledge.

Lemke, J. (1990). *Talking science: Language, learning, and values*. Norwood, NJ: Ablex.

Lemke, J. (1998). Multiplying meaning: Visual and verbal semiotics in scientific text. In J. R. Martin & R. Veel (Eds.), *Reading science: Critical and functional perspectives on discourses of science* (pp. 87–113). London: Routledge.

Lyotard, J. (1984). *The postmodern condition*. Minneapolis: University of Minnesota Press.

Mandela, N. (1995). *Long walk to freedom: The autobiography of Nelson Mandela*. London: Abacus.

Manne, R. (1999, May 26). No mercy for Nellie Bliss. *Sydney Morning Herald*, p. 11.

Martin, J. R. (1985). *Factual writing: Exploring and challenging social reality*. Geelong, Vic., Australia: Deakin University Press.

Martin, J. R. (1990). Literacy in science: Learning to handle text as technology. In F. Christie (Ed.), *Literacy for a changing world*, (pp. 79–117). Melbourne: Australian Council for Educational Research (Fresh Look at the Basics). (Republished in Halliday & Martin, 162–202.)

Martin, J. R. (1992). *English text: System and structure*. Amsterdam: Benjamins.

Martin, J. R. (1993a). Life as a noun. In M. A. K. Halliday & J. R. Martin (Eds.), *Writing science: Literacy as discursive power*, (pp. 221–267). London: Falmer.

Martin, J. R. (1993b). Technology, bureaucracy and schooling: Discursive resources and control. *Cultural Dynamics* 6(1), 84–130.

Martin, J. R. (1995a). Interpersonal meaning, persuasion and public discourse: Packing semiotic punch. *Australian Journal of Linguistics* 15(1), 33–67.

Martin, J. R. (1995b). Text and clause: Fractal resonance. *Text* 15(1), 5–42.

Martin, J. R. (1996). Waves of abstraction: Organising exposition. In T. Miller (Ed.), *The Journal of TESOL France 2.2: Functional Approaches to Written Text: Classroom applications* (pp. 87–104). Paris: TESOL France & U.S. Information Service.

Martin, J. R. (1997). Analysing genre: Functional parameters. In F. Christie & J. R. Martin (Eds.), *Genre and institutions: Social processes in the workplace and school* (pp. 3–39). London: Cassell.

Martin, J. R. (1998). Mentoring semogenesis: 'Genre-based' literacy pedagogy. In F. Christie (Ed.), *Pedagogy and the shaping of consciousness: Linguistic and social processes*, (pp. 123–155). London: Cassell.

Martin, J. R. (1999a). A context for genre: Modeling social processes in functional linguistics. In R. Stainton & J. Devilliers (Eds.), *Communication in linguistics*, (pp. 1–41). Toronto, CA: GREF (Collection Theoria).

Martin, J. R. (1999b). Grace: the logogenesis of freedom. *Discourse Studies* 1(1), 31–58.

Martin, J. R. (2000a). Grammar meets genre: Reflections on the 'Sydney School.' *Arts: the Journal of the Sydney University Arts Association, 22*, 47–95.

Martin, J. R. (2000b). Design and practice: Enacting functional linguistics in Australia. *Annual Review of Applied Linguistics 20*, 116–126.

Martin, J. R. (2002). From little things big things grow: Ecogenesis in school geography. In R. Coe, L. Lingard & T. Teslenko (Eds.), *The rhetoric and ideology of genre: Strategies for stability and change*. Cresskill, NJ: Hampton Press.

Martin, J. R., Matthiessen, C. M. I. M., & Painter, C. (1997). *Working with Functional Grammar*. London: Edward Arnold.

Martin, J. R., & Plum, G. (1997). Construing experience: Some story genres. *Journal of Narrative and Life History 7, 1*(4), 299–308.

Martin, J. R., & Veel, R. (Eds.). (1998). *Reading science: Critical and functional perspectives on discourses of science*. London: Routledge.

Martin, W. R. (1989). Innovative fisheries management: International whaling. In A. T. Bielak (Ed.), *Innovative fisheries management initiatives* (pp. 1–4). Ottawa: Canadian Wildlife Federation.

Matthiessen, C. M. I. M. (1995). *Lexicogrammatical cartography: English systems*. Tokyo: International Language Sciences Publishers.

Morgan, W. (1997). *Critical Literacy in the classroom: The art of the possible*. London: Routledge.

Muspratt, S., Luke, A., & Freebody, P. (Eds.). (1997). *Constructing critical literacies: Teaching and learning textual practice*. Sydney, Australia: Allen & Unwin. (Also Hampton Press).

Myers, G. (1990). *Writing biology*. Madison: University of Wisconsin Press.

Ogborn, J., Kress, G., Martins, I., & McGillicuddy, K. (1996). *Explaining science in the classroom*. Buckingham, UK: Open University Press.

Rafael, V. (1988). *Contracting colonialism: Translation and Christian conversion in Tagalog society under early Spanish rule*. Manila, Phillipines: Ateneo de Manila University Press.

Roach, A. (1990). Took the children away. *Charcoal Lane*. Sydney, Australia: Mushroom Records (Produced by P. Kelly & S. Connolly).

Rose, D. B. (1991). *Hidden histories: Black stories from Victoria Rover Downs, Humbert River, and Wave Hill Stations*. Canberra, Australia: Aboriginal Studies Press.

Rothery, J. (1989). Learning about language. In R. Hasan & J. R. Martin (Eds.), *Language development: Learning language, learning culture* (pp. 199–256). Norwood, NJ: Ablex.

Rothery, J. (1996). Making changes: Developing an educational linguistics. In R. Hasan & G. Williams (Eds.), *Literacy in society* (pp. 86–123). London: Longman.

Simmelhaig, H., & Spenceley, G. F. R. (1984). *For Australia's sake*. Melbourne, Australia: Nelson.

Swales, J. M. (1990). *Genre analysis: English in academic and research settings*. Cambridge, UK: Cambridge University Press.

Veel, R., & Coffin, C. (1996). Learning to think like an historian: The language of secondary school history. In R. Hasan & G. Williams (Eds.), *Literacy in society* (pp. 191–231). London: Longman.

Wallace, J., & Louden, W. (2002). *Dilemmas of science teaching: Perceptions on problems of practice*. London: Routledge Falmer.

Walton, C. (1996). *Critical social literacies*. Darwin, Australia: Northern Territory University Press.

White, P. (1997). Death, disruption and the moral order: The narrative impulse in mass 'hard news' reporting. In F. Christie & J. R. Martin (Eds.), *Genre and institutions: Social processes in the workplace and school* (pp. 101–133). London, UK: Cassell.

6

Challenges of the Science
Register for ESL Students:
Errors and Meaning-Making

Mary J. Schleppegrell
University of California, Davis

This chapter presents an analysis of second-language writing, showing how English as a Second Language (ESL) students deploy the meaning-making resources of English in their science lab reports in ways that differ from the choices made by a native speaker of English, with different results in terms of the overall shape and voice of the texts that they produce. Analyzing the texts of native speakers helps us identify the grammatical resources that enable writers to create a text of a particular type. With this knowledge, we can look at second-language writers' texts to see where the students may need to develop lexico-grammatical and discourse-structuring resources that are functional for a particular task.

The lab report is a commonly-assigned genre in science and technical courses. A genre is a culturally recognizable text type that unfolds through a series of stages. Each discipline has its own genres that are recontextualized in academic assignments. A study of 10 undergraduate courses in natural science and engineering (Braine, 1989) found that 85% of the assignments required students to report on a specified participatory experience such as a laboratory experiment. Such assignments not only assess students' performance in the laboratories, but also prepare them for the real-life writing tasks they will perform when they leave the university.

Constructing particular instances of a genre calls for the coherent presentation of meanings at the clause level. This means that a focus on genre necessarily requires attention to register elements. Halliday (1978, 1994) defines register in terms of the lexical and grammatical choices that construe particular contexts of situation. He proposes that there are three kinds of meanings expressed in every clause: the "ideational," "interpersonal," and "textual." Grammatical choices in the systems that realize each of these metafunctions actively construct the situational context, made up of the three variables "field" (what is happening); "tenor" (who is participating); and "mode" (the means or channel through which the text is realized). For example, field is construed through ideational grammatical choices—the lexical items and logical connectors that tell us what is going on. Tenor is construed through interpersonal grammatical choices such as mood (whether statements, questions, or demands), intonation (in speech), and modality and other attitudinal markers. Mode is construed through choices from the textual component of the grammar that structure information, including cohesive devices, clause-combining strategies, and theme structure (Halliday, 1994).

The register features required for academic assignments differ in significant ways from the registers of ordinary spoken interaction, making it necessary for even those students whose English is already well developed for everyday tasks to expand their linguistic repertoires and learn to be more precise in their linguistic formulations to meet the demands of school-based tasks (Schleppegrell, 2001). Although all students face this challenge, nonnative speakers are at a particular disadvantage, because they may have both limited resources in English and less experience with the genre and register expected in the assignments they are given. That means that their attempts to tackle new genres with new register expectations may not only miss the mark in terms of genre and register choices, but also inevitably result in clause formations that depart from native speaker norms ("errors").

The language of each discipline has evolved in ways that enable the construal of the kinds of meanings that the discipline requires. Engaging in the discourses of different disciplines requires that students draw on the register features that help them simultaneously realize ideational, interpersonal, and textual meanings in appropriate ways, construing the field, tenor, and mode anticipated by the genre assigned. Different register choices are more or less appropriate, or more or less effective, in the realization of particular stages of each genre. By analyzing the ways of using language that are valued in different disciplines, we can illuminate the key issues that face teachers and students in gaining control of disciplinary knowledge. Science discourse has been an especially productive arena for research in the framework of Halliday's Systematic Functional Linguistics (SFL) (e.g., Lemke, 1990; McNamara, 1989; Unsworth, 1999; and the articles in Halliday & Martin, 1993; Martin & Veel, 1998). An SFL analysis, then, can reveal how each student's linguistic resources need to evolve and develop in order to make the kinds of meanings that writing an effective lab report requires.

The Task and Texts

The reports analyzed here were written in an upper-division Chemical Engineering course. The course has as a goal that students will "develop skills in communication by using experimental results as the basis for the preparation of written and oral reports" (course syllabus). Assignment guidelines tell students that "the purpose of the written report is to provide a summary of techniques used in the experiment and to present and evaluate the results and compare them with results of established theories and/or literature values" (course syllabus). According to an instructor for the course, students who have graduated and entered the profession report that this is the most valuable course in the engineering curriculum because of the writing demands that prepare them for the professional work context.

This chapter analyzes the reports of three ESL students on one of the assigned experiments. Another report on the same experiment, written by a native speaker of English, also is referred to throughout this chapter. This *model* report was characterized by the instructor as a good example of what is expected for this task. The three reports by second-language students, on the other hand, were characterized by their instructors as examples of writing that are weak and difficult to respond to.[1] In using the native speaker report as a model, it is not intended that this report be seen as ideal in any way.[2] This model report itself contains linguistic infelicities as well as errors of content, but as the instructors consider it to be a good example of what they value, it enables us to recognize the range and variety of resources that this native speaker has drawn on for this task, demonstrating the richness available in the systems of English for construing the kinds of meanings expected in an advanced literacy task of this type.[3]

Students are given a course syllabus that specifies that each laboratory report should have seven major divisions: Abstract, Introduction, Theory, Experimental method, Results, Discussion, and Conclusions. Within each section students are expected to accomplish certain moves (Swales, 1990); for example, in the introduction, to "explain the background and importance of the work, the goals of the work, why it was done, and how it related to published work" (course syllabus). All of the reports analyzed here demonstrate the genre conventions specified by the syllabus in terms of the section headings. How and whether the different moves are realized varies, however. Content understanding is obviously involved in whether or not a student realizes the required moves, but linguistic abilities also clearly constrain the presentation of content knowledge for the ESL students.

The model report states the purpose of this particular experiment, where the students are using Stefan diffusion tubes to determine the diffusion coefficients for three solvents in air, in (a):[4]

(a) The purpose of this study is to measure the diffusion coefficients for the vapors of three volatile compounds, acetone, ethanol, and n-hexane, in air. To accomplish this, the method first developed by Stefan will be used—the displacement of the liquid-air interface as a function of time will be followed. By varying the temperature and comparing the results to those found in the literature, we hope to obtain information to assess the accuracy of the Stefan method for these three compounds under a given set of experimental conditions. Analysis of the data should suggest areas

---

[1]An instructor of one of the sections of this course, who interacts with second-language students on a regular basis, describes them as falling into the same distribution of strong and weak students as native English speakers, but notes that second-language students often get lower grades in this course because of the writing requirements.

[2]In using the term "model," it is also important to stress that this report did not serve in any way as a model for the other students.

[3]It is undoubtedly true that a different native speaker would have drawn on a different set of grammatical resources. But by identifying the implications of the model report writer's choices for expressing the meanings called for by this assignment, we can see the grammatical systems that are at issue for all students.

[4]Students' writing is presented as in their texts, but with obvious spelling errors corrected.

where the underling assumptions of this method may fail and therefore place limits on their application.[5]

This assignment requires the students to do a number of things, including introducing the assumptions and equations they will use in the experiment and discussing their results in terms of the assumptions and theory they adopt. Each of the students responds to the assignment in her own way, as we would expect. The students' experimental results varied, raising different issues for each to address in her report. But we can look at the success with which the students accomplish the task by examining how they handle the demands of the genre and register. In particular, the analysis focuses on the presentation of assumptions for the experiment as well as the students' discussion of how those assumptions are justified or called into question by the results of the experiment. This analysis provides insights into how grammar and discourse structuring choices construe the kinds of meanings that are appropriate for this disciplinary task.

Theory Section: Presenting Ideas

The purpose of the Theory section is to "state the basis needed to interpret the data obtained in the experiment" (course syllabus). Students are told to include "a precise statement of the assumptions, governing equations, and appropriate initial or boundary conditions" (course syllabus). In the model report, the Theory section has four long paragraphs in which the writer introduces the assumptions of the experiment and presents the equations she will use to calculate her results, explaining the relevance of the particular equation to the stated assumptions. The ESL writers present much less elaborated texts. The most expansive of the ESL students, Writer 3, writes only two long paragraphs. Writer 2 does not write any paragraphs, but just uses single sentences to introduce a series of equations. Writer 1 begins with one paragraph that states all the assumptions of the report, and then uses single sentences to introduce equations. None of the ESL students is able to engage in the nuanced discussion of the assumptions and their relationship to the equations that the writer of the model report presents.

It is not knowledge about the expectations for the lab report genre that is the problem, nor is it a question of not knowing which assumptions need to be stated. The ESL students generally know the assumptions that need to be stated and that the Theory section is the appropriate place in the report for stating the assumptions. What the ESL students need is knowledge of the functional value of the grammatical and lexical choices that would enable them to state the assumptions in ways that strengthen their authority and the cohesiveness of their texts, construing the interpersonal and textual meanings that are functional for these purposes. We can see how they are limited in this regard by analyzing a key move in this section, the stating of assumptions, and the language that they draw on for this move.

---

[5]As we can see from this paragraph, even the native speaker of English makes some mistakes. The word *underling* goes overlooked and unmarked, but the instructor circles *their* in the last sentence and writes *its?*

The partial text of the Theory section of the model report is given in (b), with the statements of assumptions in italics:

(b) For the analysis, these systems *will be considered* binary. Air *will be treated* as a singular compound. The error introduced by this simplification *is assumed to be* negligible (cites two sources).... The subscript A will be used to represent the diffusing vapor, while B, *the assumed* stagnant air.... When eq. (1) is combined with the species continuity equation, *assuming* no chemical reaction, temperature (T) and Pressure (*P) held constant, and the diffusion process *considered* one dimensional (z direction), (equation) Eq. (3) results. Here *it was also assumed* that $N_A > N_B$. *This assumption* depends on B having negligible solubility in A. The accumulation term can be neglected *if one assumes* a quasi-steady state condition. An order of magnitude analysis will show that *this is a valid assumption when* (equation) ... *Assuming* eq. (4) holds, the solution of eq. (3) with the following boundary conditions, (equation), leads to an equation which can be rearranged with some algebra to read (equation). Here, right at the liquid-gas interface, the gas-phase concentration of A expressed as mole fraction is x_{A0}. This *is taken to be* the gas-phase concentration of A corresponding to equilibrium with the liquid at the interface, provided that A and B form an ideal gas mixture (cite).... Equation (6) has been modified from the original *with the assumptions* of ideal gas and M_A on the same order of magnitude as M_B....

Stating assumptions can be grammatically complex, calling for construction of long clauses with embedding and linking of clauses through hypotaxis. Even the model report shows the difficulty of this in terms of grammatical structure, as we see in (c), a statement marked "awkward" by the instructor:

(c) The subscript A will be used to represent the diffusing vapor, while B, the assumed stagnant air.

Presumably it is the ellipsis in the second clause that the instructor finds awkward. But this sentence also gives us an indication of the variety of grammatical resources that this student is able to draw on in presenting her assumptions and justifying them. This flexibility is less available to the ESL students.

As we see in (b), the model report uses a variety of verbs, including *consider, treat, assume,* and *is taken to be,* in the clauses where assumptions are presented, demonstrating the range of lexical resources she draws on for this purpose. In addition, she is able to use these lexical resources in a variety of ways, enabling her to use different clause types and giving her flexibility in the construction of the text.

The ESL students, on the other hand, do not demonstrate this range of resources for this task, and so have more difficulty presenting and justifying their assumptions. The ESL reports have no lexical variation in the way they present assumptions, using only the word *assume* in one of its forms to state the assumptions. And in using *assume,* they do not have control of the range of forms this lexeme can take, limiting their flexibility in the construction of their texts.

It is instructive to compare how the model report writer uses *assume* with how the ESL writers use it. Table 6.1 presents the various functions that the notion *assume* takes in this section of the model report, where *assume* occurs in a variety of word classes, including verbal, nominal, and adjectival, and performs a variety of

TABLE 6.1

Ways *Assume* Is Used in the Model Report

Clause or Phrase with assume	Grammatical Role and Function
If one *assumes* Y X is *assumed* to be	*Assume* as mental process in active or passive construction; most congruent use, presenting *assume* as a process.
When X, *assuming* Y, Z results	*Assume* as mental process in nonfinite construction; introduces a paratactic clause extending the conditions being specified.
The *assumed* stagnant air	*Assume* as postdeictic prenominal modifier (Halliday 1994, p.183); presents the notion *assume* as a quality.
This *assumption* depends on X	*Assume* as noun; enables the mental process to be presented as a clause participant. Here deictic *this* links cohesively with the previous clause.

clause functions, as predicator (finite and nonfinite), modifier, subject, complement, and object of a preposition.

Drawing on this variety of ways of presenting the same lexical meaning, the
writer is able to manipulate text structure and interpersonal voice in ways that enable her to project an authoritative stance and present a well-organized statement.
This gives her a flexibility that enables her to construct a text that links from clause
to clause in cohesive ways, elaborating on the set of assumptions she adopts for the
experiment. By using various forms of *assume*, the model report writer is able to create texture in her report that puts given information in the background and highlights what is new. For example, consider these sentences from (b):

(b) Here *it was* also *assumed* that $N_A > N_B$. *This assumption* depends on B having negligible solubility in A.

Here $N_A > N_B$ is presented in the first clause as new information with *assume* used as
a passive verb; a construction that allows the new information to be highlighted at
the end of the clause. In the following clause, use of the nominal form *this assumption* as subject enables the writer to begin the clause with this given information
and go on to qualify the assumption appropriately. In using the nominal form, the
writer is able to use *assumption* in a variety of positions in her clauses; for example,
in sentence complements (*this is a valid assumption when*) and in prepositional
phrases (*with the assumptions of Y*).

This writer is using the resources of grammatical metaphor (Halliday, 1998; Halliday & Martin, 1993). Halliday proposes the term "grammatical metaphor" to describe a process by which two layers of meaning result from grammatical choices (Halliday 1994, 1998). Congruently, in a clause, *things* are expressed as nouns, *happenings* are expressed as verbs, *circumstances* are expressed as adverbs or prepositional phrases, and relations between elements are expressed as conjunctions. With grammatical metaphor, the choice of elements for these grammatical categories is *incongruent*, as other categories are used. By drawing on incongruent forms, an academic writer is able to realize the same kind of meaning at different points in the clause, drawing on a wider range of options for text construction and development by construing a process as a clause participant, as with *this assumption*, or as a quality, as in *the assumed* stagnant air.

The nonfinite clauses with *assuming* also enable her to structure her text. For example,

(d) When eq. (1) is combined with the species continuity equation, *assuming* no chemical reaction, ...

This choice enables her to insert further assumptions into her text, where appropriate, as in (d). She can also use the nonfinite clause as the starting point for her next statement, introducing as background an assumption that is a condition for the next equation she will present, as in (e):

(e) *Assuming* eq. (4) holds, the solution of eq. (3) with the following boundary conditions, (equation), leads to an equation which can be rearranged with some algebra to read (equation).

Being able to use *assume* in a range of ways, the student has the option of using the nonfinite, adjectival, and nominal forms for a variety of sentence functions. By controlling the resources that enable her to use the notion *assume* in grammatically different ways, she is able to bring texture to her report, managing the flow of information effectively as she develops her discussion. In addition, she projects an authoritative interpersonal stance by adopting impersonal ways of presenting her assumptions that draw on passive and nonfinite verbal forms.

The resources that the model report writer draws on are much more extensive than those that the ESL students draw on for the same task, as the ESL writers use only a small subset of the structures that the model report writer uses. Whereas the model report draws on all of the forms of *assume* in Table 6.1, the ESL students are more limited, each using only two different forms.

In general, the ESL students strive for the most economical presentation of their assumptions, using a more limited set of lexical and grammatical resources, but each ESL writer adopts different strategies for this task. Writer 2 is the least successful in terms of content, including only two of the key assumptions, which she presents in one sentence, constructed as a set of related conditional clauses:

(f) Assuming the diffusion is one-dimensional and the flux of species A is much greater than the flux of species B (equation), then Eq (1) takes the following form: (equation)

No further statements about assumptions are made in this section. Although (f) is *error free* in terms of surface form, the writer has not ventured to attempt the presentation of explanation or elaboration, as the model report does, and fails to include all the assumptions that are relevant.

Writer 1 and Writer 3 have more difficulty grammatically, but also present more assumptions. Writer 1 compensates for the grammatical difficulty by listing all her assumptions in one long sentence introduced by an imperative *assume*:

(g) Assume the diffusion occurs at quasi-steady state; and the concentration is zero at the top of diffusion tube, none reaction, slip condition (flat velocity profile), one dimensional diffusion, the experiment was carry out under constant pressure.

By choosing an imperative verb form, the writer is able to list the various assumptions one after another, without regard for syntactic categories or clause linkage. This writer shows that she has considered the assumptions needed for this experiment, presenting the appropriate disciplinary knowledge, but the limited range of grammatical resources she is able to draw on puts her at a great disadvantage, as we will see, when she needs to engage in discussion of her experimental results.

In some cases, the ESL writers assert or presume what the writer of the model report states explicitly as an assumption, avoiding explanation and elaboration. For example, one assumption of the experiment is that air will be treated as a compound, so that the systems under study can be treated as binary. We can see that the model report is explicit about this in the first sentence of (b): *For the analysis, these systems will be considered binary.* In contrast, none of the ESL students presents this as an explicit assumption. Writer 1 does not address it at all. Writer 2 presents the *binariness* as given, introducing this notion as a modifier in the noun phrase that begins her theory section:

(h) For a binary mixture system, the diffusive flux is given by Fick's law: (equation)

Using yet a different strategy, Writer 3 asserts the *binariness* early in her paper, in the Introduction:

(i) The Stefan diffusion is binary system, one of the components, in the liquid state, is placed in the bottom of a vertical tube, the second component, a gas is passed over the top of the tube.

So the binary nature of the system, presented as an explicit assumption by the native speaker (*these systems will be considered binary*), is presented as presumed by Writer 2 (*For a binary system mixture ...*) and is presented as an assertion by Writer 3 (*the Stefan diffusion process is binary mixture ...*). The ESL students do not introduce this information in a step-by-step fashion through a series of clauses that introduce, define, and situate this assumption in a framework that provides a clear view of their understanding, as the model report does.

It is not that the ESL students do not present the relevant assumptions. Of the six major assumptions for this experiment that are stated in the model report, (that the systems are binary, the air is stagnant, there is no chemical reaction, temperature and pressure are held constant, the diffusion is one-dimensional, and the experiment is quasi-steady state), Writer 3 mentions all of these and Writer 1 mentions all but one. Only Writer 2 fails to address the appropriate field-specific material here, mentioning only two of the key assumptions. So in terms of addressing the core content of this section of the report, two of the writers are dealing with the major points, and one is falling short. But without a full range of grammatical resources, even the ESL writers who mention the key assumptions fail to bring together the presentation of content and simultaneous evaluative comment on that content that characterizes the model report as she mentions the negligible error that the assumptions might introduce, or the factors that the assumptions depend on [see (b)].

Writer 3, the most prolific of the ESL writers, does attempt to do more than just list her assumptions, but her clause-level problems with grammar and lexis often make the statements infelicitous. For example:

(j) An important analysis of Stefan diffusion tube is assumed that the diffusion process occurred at a quasi-steady state.

Control over the transitivity structure for *assume* is one aspect of the grammatical difficulty displayed in (j). We see in the model report that the passive construction, attempted by this writer, requires a structure like *It is assumed that ...* or *X is assumed to occur. ...* (j) is a hybrid that is neither of these, requiring the reader to identify how the parts of the clause relate to each other. The writer also attempts to introduce evaluation here (*important*), but is unable to integrate the evaluation effectively with the presentation of the assumption. So while the quasi-steady state assumption is introduced from a content point of view, the writer's grammatical choices do not effectively construe the simultaneous evaluation that the writer attempts.

This problem of lack of control of grammatical resources becomes more evident when the meanings to be communicated require a more complex interaction of ideational, interpersonal, and textual resources. Although in the Theory section of the report, the presentation of assumptions comes across fairly clearly even with weak control over the academic register features, when we turn to the Discussion section of the report, we see that the students face much greater challenges.

Discussion Section: Evaluating Results

The Discussion section demonstrates the complexity of the grammar that is needed to achieve the purposes of these reports. This section is the one most important part of the report, accounting for 20 out of 100 possible points (as compared with the Theory section, which is worth 5 points). The Discussion section is described as "an evaluation of the results, including an assessment of reliability and precision (error analysis), and a statement of what the results mean" (course syllabus).[6] When the

---

[6]An Appendix to the syllabus lists the criteria for evaluation of these sections of the report as follows: For the *Theory* section: Key theoretical results summarized, Significant equations needed for analysis of data; Assumptions stated; Adequate references; No derivations. For the *Discussion* section: Hard, quantitative statements; Positive statements of what results mean; Critical comparison with theory and literature results; Assessment of how well goals were met; Realistic evaluation of reliability and precision of results; lack of or overemphasis on error analysis.

students need to foreground interpersonal and textual meanings, or to employ interpersonal or textual resources to express, clarify, or elaborate their disciplinary knowledge, they face much greater obstacles in making their points clearly. This section shows how students' use of modality and verb tense compromise their interpersonal meaning, and how their clause-combining choices result in a lack of development of their texts. We will also see how attempting to draw on ideational resources without the interpersonal and textual features that enable ideational meanings results in texts that are incoherent except to the knowledgeable reader.

Other research has also highlighted the difficulties that the discussion section of lab reports presents (Dudley-Evans, 1986; Jacoby, Leech, & Holten, 1995). Students cannot provide evaluation, assessment, and statements of what their results mean without drawing on the interpersonal resources of the grammar, and textual resources are also needed to simultaneously structure the ideational and interpersonal meanings in relevant ways that enable the cohesive presentation of these meanings. In stating assumptions in the Theory section, a minimal listing that draws on the basic technical lexis may suffice, although poorly. In the elaborated and evaluative tasks that the Discussion section requires, however, students need to foreground textual and interpersonal resources in order to engage in the kind of nuanced evaluation that scientists typically use (Hunston, 1993). This is the kind of writing that students need to learn in order to write science in ways that will earn them the respect of the scientific community.

It is not easy to compare these four reports in terms of how well they evaluate their results, because the experiments themselves had different outcomes, and so the issues that the students need to address are different. Presumably, however, each student needs to engage in elaborated explanation, and here again we see differences between the model report and two of the ESL reports in the length of the texts they write. The model report has seven paragraphs that raise questions about the validity of the assumptions and suggest ways to compensate for uncertainties. Two of the ESL students write much less. As in other sections of her report, Writer 1 writes the least, only one paragraph that focuses on potential sources of error. Writer 2 writes four paragraphs, discussing assumptions that could have caused discrepancies in her results. Writer 3, as in the Theory section, is the most expansive of the ESL writers, writing six paragraphs that summarize her results, show how her assumptions were justified, and discuss issues of error and procedures that might have compromised the results. So here again we see that two of the ESL students use a strategy of writing little, and the student who makes a serious attempt to engage in an evaluative discussion has difficulty drawing on grammatical resources that are effective for this task.

Modality, as a resource for infusing a text with meanings of probability, necessity, and other evaluative assessments, can be an effective means of realizing interpersonal meanings. But modal verbs are problematic for ESL students, as their semantic and pragmatic meanings are highly variable and are also influenced by cultural norms (Hinkel, 1995). We see this in Writer 2's report as she discusses assumptions that could cause discrepancies in the results, drawing heavily on modal verbs as a resource, as in (k):

(k) There were a lot of assumptions associated with this experiment which *could* cause some discrepancy in the final results. It was assumed that the temperature at the interface was the temperature of the liquid and this *may not be* the case. This assumption *could* have some effect on the final result because as stated earlier, the diffusion coefficient is a function of the temperature. It was also assumed that air is an ideal gas and single species, and that *may be not* case because air is mixture of different species. This also *may* affect the final results. (emphasis added)

The modality of (k) is a modality of possibility used to provide assessment. But her verb-tense choices are infelicitous, as the modality of possibility that she intends, suggesting what might have affected her particular results, requires present perfect constructions (*could have caused; may not have been; could have had*, etc.). This is the verb-tense choice that, together with her modal choices, would present the situated meanings relevant to reporting on the specifics of her experiment. Because she chooses instead the present modal constructions, the evaluation she intends is realized instead as uncertainty, an interpersonal stance that lacks authoritativeness.

Verb-tense choices are also problematic for Writer 1. (l) is the full text of her discussion section, presented in just one paragraph. After her first two sentences that introduce the general point she is going to make, she shifts to present tense for the rest of the paragraph, as we see in (l):

(l) The experiment may work well for ideal gases, but the compound we used is not ideal gases. There some errors when we analyzed it under ideal gases law. The higher the dipole moment of the molecules and larger the molecular weight molecules have the greater error encounter because there is greater interaction between the particles. Hexane has the error within 6% while Acetone have error of 164%. Acetone and Methanol are highly polar compounds compare to hexane. Acetone have higher error because molecular weight of Acetone is greater than Methanol. Methanol has 17% error compare with 164% error of Acetone. The diffusivity is higher when the temperature is raise because the molecules have higher kinetic energy so they are travel faster and diffuse faster. The error also associate with the assumption that the distance from the reference mark to the tube is 3.96855 cm, because those dimension haven't been recorded. The none slip condition is also played an importance role in the error.

Her use of present tense construes a generic context, presenting her results as if they are timeless generalizations rather than a report of her specific results in this instance. This is in contrast with the writer of the model report, who regularly shifts between the present tense that realizes timeless meanings and the past tense forms that present the results of her particular experiment, as we see in (m):

(m) A large molecular size is expected to retard the compound's rate of diffusion. N-Hexane was the largest compound investigated and it produced the smallest calculated D_{AB} value, as was expected.

Here the model report writer provides the guiding generalization in a clause with present tense, but then shifts to past tense to give her specific results. This enables her to present an authoritative interpersonal stance as she moves from the general to the specific.

Writer 1's paragraph is also problematic from a textual point of view, as she is clearly unable to marshal the resources she needs to engage in the kind of discussion that is called for in this section. As Dudley-Evans (1986) and Jacoby et al. (1995) point out, the discussion section of a lab report requires "effective blending of selection, ordering, citation, summary, paraphrase, description, reporting, evaluation, critique, argument, and persuasion" (Jacoby et al., 1995, p. 358). Without control over the grammar needed to accomplish these moves, Writer 1 makes a series of assertions that go unexplored. She tries to accomplish four major moves in this paragraph. She concedes that the experiment may work well for ideal gases; however, she didn't use ideal gases, and that led to some error. She sets up some conditions for error, and presents her results for hexane, acetone, and methanol, explaining how they conform to the predictions. She brings in another condition related to diffusion, but it is unclear how this links with what she has said previously. Finally, she mentions one other assumption (the nonslip condition) that could have contributed to the error. As in her Theory section, where she just listed the assumptions of the experiment, here, too, she presents a series of issues but does not engage in the kind of discussion that is called for at this stage. Only the point about the effect of molecular weight is expanded. Of course we do not know to what extent this reflects a lack of knowledge, but her lack of control over the grammatical resources that are functional for this move clearly contributes to the lack of discussion of the points that she does raise.

One symptom of the difficulty she has with this mode is in the clause-combining strategies she uses. (l)' highlights these:

(l)' The experiment may work well for ideal gases,

but the compound we used is not ideal gases.

There some errors

when we analyzed it under ideal gases law.

The higher the dipole moment of the molecules and larger the molecular weight molecules have the greater error encounter

because there is greater interaction between the particles.

Hexane has the error within 6%

while Acetone have error of 164% ...

Acetone have higher error

because molecular weight of Acetone is greater than Methanol ... The diffusivity is higher when the temperature is raise

because the molecules have higher kinetic energy

so they are travel faster and diffuse faster.

The error also associate with the assumption that the distance from the reference mark to the tube is 3.96855 cm,

because those dimension haven't been recorded ...

From the conjunctive links highlighted in (l)', we can see that the writer uses *but, when, because, while,* and *so* to link finite clauses. This pattern of linking with conjunctions is typical of spoken discourse, and is a strategy that ESL writers often draw on, using conjunctions for a variety of interactional and text-linking functions that may even appear illogical when presented in formal written English (Schleppegrell, 1996). Writer 1 lacks control of the grammatical metaphor necessary for doing this kind of writing, where control over different ways of presenting the same meanings would enable her to organize her discussion in ways that would highlight her main points.

We saw that the model report writer is able to draw on the resources of grammatical metaphor in her Theory section. In her Discussion section, too, she is able to present information in a variety of grammatical constructions that give her flexibility and authoritativeness in constructing her text. For example, the model report writer presents the point about the relationship between the diffusion values and the increase in temperature using a typical construction of scientific English (Halliday, 1998), where a verb links two expanded noun phrases or a noun phrase and a prepositional phrase:

(n) The increasing D_{AB} values for increasing temperatures in acetone demonstrate the expected temperature dependence of D_{AB}. The smaller diffusivity expected for larger compounds was demonstrated by the smaller D_{AB} generated for n-hexane.

In (n), the writer uses two clauses, corresponding to the two sentences, each with complex noun phrases (*The increasing D_{AB} values for increasing temperatures in acetone; the expected temperature dependence of D_{AB}; The smaller diffusivity expected for larger compounds; the smaller D_{AB} generated for n-hexane*) linked in each sentence with the verb *demonstrate*; once in active and once in passive voice. This enables her to present a lot of information in two clauses that are densely-packed with information. Writer 1, on the other hand, uses four finite clauses in one sentence to explain the relationship between temperature and the diffusion values, which she asserts rather than presumes in the nominal forms that the model writer uses:

(o) The diffusivity is higher *when* the temperature is raise *because* the molecules have higher kinetic energy *so* they are travel faster and diffuse faster.

By using grammatically metaphorical forms, the model writer presents the notion that *The diffusivity is higher when the temperature is raise* as *The increasing D_{AB} values for increasing temperatures*. This results in a text that is closer to the discourse expectations for this genre than the oral-like constructions of (o).

We have seen that Writers 1 and 2 present very limited discussions of the assumptions and results of their experiments, adopting a strategy of saying little, perhaps to avoid the linguistic problems that they would face in more extensive discussion. Writer 3, on the other hand, as in the Theory section, adopts a different strategy. She engages in the discussion that is needed at this point in the report, but in doing so, reveals very significant difficulties in constructing the kind of English text that is needed to make the complex points that she wants to make.

Writer 3 has some notion of the grammatical resources that would be functional for this task, drawing on the expanded noun phrases and embedded clauses that enable the construction of an argument of this kind, but she is unable to marshal the grammatical resources needed to link these linguistic elements in ways that realize the meanings she intends. So the attempt to accomplish a task for which the writer has limited interpersonal and textual resources also limits her ability to realize her intended ideational meanings.

Her limited grammatical resources put her presentation of disciplinary knowledge at risk, as at times the complexity of what she is trying to say is in advance of the grammatical resources she can draw on to say it. For example, she says:

(p) *Lee and Wilke indicated that the change in liquid-gas interface typically did not as temperature drop associated with the mixing vapors never exceeded 0.1 K.* As a result, the changing of temperature in the diffusing vapor due to reversed thermal diffusion was negligible. (italics added)

Writer 3 is using elements of the academic register, including academic and technical lexis (*indicated, associated with, exceeded*), and nominalized forms (*change, temperature drop*), but she is using them as in spoken interaction, where a series of clauses can be chained together without the logical relationships being made precise. In written academic English this approach is not successful. Readers outside the field typically find the italicized sentence of (p) impossible to process meaningfully. However, an instructor for this course, on having this sentence pointed out as difficult to interpret, responded that the student was making a very important point, one that few students address. The instructor commented that the student is "doing some real thinking here," and suggested that the italicized sentence might be paraphrased in this way:

(q) According to Lee and Wilke, the temperature at the liquid-gas interface is within 0.1 K of the temperature at the vapor phase.

When we compare (p) and (q) grammatically, we can see how the student and the instructor construe the similar meaning in different ways. Table 6.2 makes this comparison. The participants (represented typically by nouns), and the processes (represented typically by verbs) in each clause, when looked at together, construe the same meanings in both the instructor's and the student's versions, focusing on the *temperature, interface*, and *vapors*. But the way that the processes and participants are presented and the way that the student makes logical connections leave her meanings unclear. The student tries to convey the logical relationships through causal links: *no change in the liquid-gas interface because (as) the temperature drop never exceeded 0.1K; the temperature drop is caused by (associated with) mixing vapors.*

The instructor's version, on the other hand, draws on technical terms that subsume the processes mentioned by the student so that the processes can be pre-

TABLE 6.2

Comparison of Student's Sentence With Instructor's Version

Student's Version [first sentence in (p)]:	Instructor's Version [(q)]:
Lee and Wilke indicated that the change in liquid-gas interface typically did not as temperature drop associated with the mixing vapors never exceeded 0.1 K.	According to Lee and Wilke, the temperature at the liquid-gas interface is within 0.1 K of the temperature at the vapor phase.
Grammatical Choices: Sentence consisting of a finite projecting clause (*Lee and Wilke indicated*), followed by two clauses linked with a causal *as*.	Grammatical Choices: Sentence consisting of a nonfinite clause of projection (*According to Lee and Wilke*), followed by a clause with a relational process (*is within*).
Participants: the change, liquid-gas interface, temperature drop, vapors, 0.1 K.	Participants: temperature, liquid-gas interface, 0.1 K, vapor phase
Processes: not change, mixing, not exceed	Processes: is
Logical Relationships: causal (*as*; *associated with*)	Logical Relationships: spatio-temporal (*at, within*; *at*)

sented as participants; for example, *vapor phase* incorporates the *mixing* process. The *change, drop,* and *mixing* that the student construes as participants are construed by the instructor prepositionally with *within* and *at.* This realizes the logical relationship between the nominalized clause participants as *is within,* with the comparison of temperatures realized through the prepositional phrases with *at.* The instructor draws on the resources of grammatical metaphor to present the process of *mixing vapors* as a technical term, *vapor phase,* enabling the whole point to be presented in one clause with a verb that construes the relationship between the two temperatures metaphorically as a spatio-temporal one. The student, on the other hand, is struggling to find the way to present the relationship between two complex processes, the change in temperature at one point compared with the change in temperature at another point, and lacks both the technical terms and the grammatical means of construing the relationship.

The broader organization of Writer 3's text is also problematic. She elaborates her discussion of each issue, but has difficulty highlighting her points of analysis. (r) is an example paragraph:

(r) Analysis of the data in this experiment illustrated that the experimental diffusion coefficients of Methanol and n-Hexane agreed with the Chapman Enskog diffusion coefficient with the different of 5% and 4% for the 30°C experiment, of 6% and 1% for the 37°C experiment respectively. These experimental diffusion coefficients satisfy the property of diffusion coefficients of species increasing as the temperature increasing. The results of the two experiments for the two compounds agreed with Chapman-Enskog values, but these results did not agreed with Yaws' correlation values, with the percent difference of 39% and 31% at 30°C and 101300 Pa, and 31% and 29% at 37°C and 101300 Pa respectively (Table 4). So different methods gave different diffusion coefficients. The diffusion coefficient of Acetone as function of temperature was shown on the Figure 4 in the previous section. The experimental diffusion coefficients of Methanol and n-Hexane in 45°C experiment and Acetone's coefficients in 30°C, 37°C, and 45°C experiments had very large percent different with theoretical values with the average percent difference were above 30%. In general, the difference between the experimental and the theoretical values were within and without the error bound limit.

Here the student is attempting a move that the other ESL students do not even attempt, but that is required by the assignment, the comparison of experimental and theoretical values for the coefficients. Although the model report found that the experimental and theoretical results were similar, Writer 3 did not get this result, so she has to engage in a complex explanation, as we see in (r) above. Her difficulties can be seen throughout the paragraph. She does not provide an overall statement of her point that highlights the fact that her results agreed with one set of theoretical values, but not the other, until the middle of her paragraph, where she says that different methods gave different diffusion coefficients. Such a statement at the beginning of the paragraph (a "Hyper-Theme" (Martin, 1992, chap. 5, this volume)) would enable the scaffolding of the discourse that is needed here.

Because the results agreed with one of her theoretical models and not the other, she needs to make this contrastive meaning and identify where the differences are most important. She uses *but* to make the contrast, and *so* to draw her conclusions, but depends on the statements of difference between her values and the theoretical values to make her points, never explicitly making the judgement that would seem to be required here. Here we see how textual meanings are at risk for this student. She does not draw on the resources that would make her reasoning clear, leaving to the reader the work of drawing the appropriate conclusions from her results, as the only indications of reasoning are the *but* and *so*. In contrast, the model report writer draws on an elaborate set of grammatical resources to present results that were counter to expectations, as in (s):

(s) One would expect the compounds with the highest vapor pressure to produce the least accurate calculated values for D_{AB}. The assumptions made in the derivation rely on a flat velocity profile with diffusion being the major component of the velocity of A up the tube. This would not be the case if the vapor pressure approached the total pressure of the system. Given the error bounds on the calculations, it is not possible to draw any firm conclusions about this from the data. Acetone at 45°C had the highest vapor pressure investigated, 509 mmHg, and yet gave a calculated value within 4.09% of the literature.

In (s), the model writer uses extensive resources for modality (*one would expect; this would not be the case, given the error bounds, it is not possible*) and use of passive voice to construe an interpersonal stance of objectivity and measured judgement. These resources are beyond the capability of Writer 3. Instead of drawing on the resources of modality and tense shifts to give her writing interpersonal meaning and texture, she structures (r) primarily as a simple reporting of her results, using no modality and primarily simple past tense.

In addition, when Writer 3 tries to draw a conclusion to her paragraph at (r), she fails to make the logical connections that would realize the meanings she intends, and her infelicitous discourse marking results in an illogical last sentence. She says *In general, the difference between the experimental and the theoretical values were within and without the error bound limit.* The instructor comments in the margin at this point in the paper that the differences can't be both *within and without* the *error bound limit.* In other words, the student seems to have made an illogical statement. But a closer reading of this student's work, and in particular the way this student uses the term *in general,* leads to another interpretation. She also uses the expression *in general* at another point in her report, in her Abstract:

(t) In general, the diffusion coefficient of n-Hexane, Methanol, and Acetone were determined of 0.05203+/–0.00023cm2/sec, 0.09651+/–0.00008 cm2/sec, and 0.073795+/–0.00007 cm2/sec at 303 K and 101300 Pa respectively.

Here she is presenting the results of her experiment, and *in general* also seems an illogical choice to introduce the sentence. But if we understand that this expression seems to function for her with a meaning that we could paraphrase as *to give a general overview,* both uses of *in general* can be seen as relevant to what she is doing at those points in the report. In the last sentence of (r), the student is using *in general* to introduce a distinction that will be developed in the next paragraphs of her report, as she discusses both those differences that were within the error bounds and those that were not. This student has great difficulty drawing on the language needed to make these points, and the textual meaning is particularly difficult to negotiate in making linkages and indicating the method of development she is adopting.

Martin (1996) suggests that grammatical choices that enable the scaffolding of an argument help to make an academic text more effective. For ESL writers, such scaffolding is a challenge. They need to use grammatical metaphor in order to construe meanings in ways that structure a text so that the discussion unfolds logically and authoritatively, and to expand their introductions and conclusions so that they preface and sum up more effectively. In addition, they need a good understanding of the meanings of discourse-organizational markers that structure and scaffold their texts.

Summary

With richer and more diverse grammatical and lexical resources at her disposal, the writer of the model report elaborates and extends the points she makes at each stage. The ESL students, on the other hand, for the most part use the linguistic strategies they have available to them to make the points they want to make as succinctly as possible, at the risk of presenting incomplete information and inadequate discussion.

These writers' choices in the areas of modality, verb tense, discourse organization, conjunction, and clause-combining strategies all contribute to the realization of a register that may even obscure the meanings they intend. Although disciplinary knowledge can be conveyed through technical lexis and is often understood by a knowledgeable reader even when it is presented without the effective use of the interpersonal and textual resources of the grammar, without those resources, reports are less authoritative and the method of development is often obscured.

We have focused here on the presentation of theory and discussion of results in these reports, but these are not the only functional moves that were difficult for ESL students. Other problematic areas include comparing, referring to tables and graphs, providing a list of equipment, stating a causal relationship, and stating findings of the range of error. In these and other functional moves, students need assistance in learning not only how to present their ideas, but also how to do this with an authoritative stance and with information structured in ways that are expected and appropriate for the various academic tasks they are undertaking.

SECOND LANGUAGE ERRORS

We have focused on the lexical and grammatical resources that these students are drawing on to write their reports, but these reports also show another feature of ESL writing, the errors that are typical of second language students. Second language students' writing in English typically has mistakes in word choice, tense, verb form, article use, clause structure, and other grammatical, lexical, and discourse-organizational categories. Identifying grammatical errors is an almost irresistible impulse for the academic reader of ESL writing, as they are typically salient and distracting. For example, let's look at the first sentences that an instructor would encounter in reading these reports; the beginning of each of the abstracts:

(u) Writer 1: The diffusivity of different solvents at different temperatures are determine by using the Stefan Diffusion Tube experiment.

(v) Writer 2: In this experiment, diffusion coefficients of three volatile vapors and its dependence on temperature was measured.

(w) Writer 3: Diffusion coefficient of a specific chemical is an important value that really need to know for the application in chemical engineering and industry such as mass transfer and heat transfer problems.

From the very first words of the reports, the problems with English are apparent. In reading Writer 1, for example, an instructor might mark the verb form error *determine;* and in reading Writer 2, might mark (at least) the agreement problems with *its* and *was.* Writer 3 needs an article at the beginning of the sentence, a subject for the *that* clause [adding a subject may also mean a change in verb agreement (*that one really needs to know? that scientists really need to know?*)], and *the application* might be changed to *applications.*

Analyzing the reports in this way gives us the list of ESL errors in each report displayed in Table 6.3, based on traditional ways of counting ESL errors.[7] As Table 6.3 shows, the three ESL reports present different error profiles, but all of these students make numerous sentence-level errors in English that interfere with the meanings they intend to present. The words-per-error calculation shows that in the most error-ridden report, by Writer 1, an error of the types listed occurs about every nine words. The most accurate writer, Writer 2, makes an error about every 21 words. A holistic reading of the reports confirms that these writers have difficulty controlling the English language well enough to present clear, comprehensible prose.

However, these students are operating at a very advanced level in English, and their errors are most frequent in areas of the grammar that are known to pose great

TABLE 6.3

ESL Errors in Lab Reports

	Writer 1 1002 words	Writer 2 1376 words	Writer 3 3114 words
Error Type			
Sentence fragments	2	2	4
Count/mass noun & article	35	22	89
Word choice/ word class	30	14	63
Verb form/verb tense	29	13	37
Subject/verb agreement	12	5	9
Complementation/ modification	1	8	19
Comparison	3	1	14
Totals	112	65	235
Words/error	8.9	21.2	13.3

(Model report: 2693 words)

---

[7]Counting ESL errors is notoriously difficult, due to ambiguities in interpretation and the difficulty of associating errors with particular lexical items. These errors were independently identified by three coders to provide reliability, with discrepancies resolved through discussion.

difficulty to the nonnative writer. These students understand the structure of the English sentence, as we see from the few fragment errors. The most frequent errors, for all of these writers, are in using articles, count/mass nouns, and plural marking, systems of English noun phrase grammar that are notoriously difficult for language learners to master. Word-choice and word-class errors are another very difficult area, including choice of preposition and formation of derivational alternatives. Verb-form and verb-tense errors, which require facility with finite and nonfinite clauses and knowledge about the functions that verb-tense shifts perform in different types of texts, are also problematic for second-language writers. Developing control over these grammatical and lexical systems takes time for second language learners and presents new challenges in each domain and discipline.

As we can see in Table 6.3, the length of the students' reports varies considerably, with the model report and one of the ESL students' reports both more than twice as long as the other two ESL reports. A lack of elaboration is often mentioned as a feature of ESL writing (Silva, 1993), and although this is a feature of two of these reports, we also have an example here of an ESL writer who writes at greater length than the model.

This is relevant to the kinds of errors the students make, too, as the types of errors reflect what the students are doing or failing to do in these reports. For example, as Table 6.3 shows, Writer 2 and Writer 3 make complementation/ modification errors with greater frequency than Writer 1, and Writer 3 makes comparison errors with much greater frequency than Writer 1 and Writer 2. Comparison and complementation/modification errors come from problems in constructing complex sentences with clause embeddings and incorporation of nonfinite clauses. As we have seen, this is the kind of clause structure that is functional for constructing an elaborated discussion. Writer 3, writing the longest report, attempts to draw comparisons and engage in discussion in ways that Writer 1 and Writer 2 do not. So the greater frequency of these types of errors indicates that Writer 3 is doing things with language that are important for this task, but that call for grammatical resources she has not yet mastered.

The limitations of the writers in terms of grammatical resources are strikingly apparent when they attempt to do a complex task for which their language is not yet well developed enough. As we have seen, Writer 3's attempt to engage in the more elaborated explanation that is required for this report stands in contrast to the strategy that Writer 1 and Writer 2 follow. Writer 1 and Writer 2 adopt a strategy of saying little, resulting in fewer errors of the kinds that occur when the writer risks engaging in more complex explanation. Writer 3, on the other hand, follows the model report in trying to do what is required for the report, engaging in elaborated explanation, and in so doing, makes many errors in the complex constructions required for the kind of clause structure that uses pre- or postmodification, complementation, or comparison. Development means more errors, and when few errors occur, the writer may be using too cautious an approach. Attempting more complex explanation results in more surface errors, as attention needed to monitor the errors is used to focus on making the scientific meanings.

When we focus on only the surface errors in this way, we are accepting the overall structure and tone of the text and are attending only to *cleaning up* the grammatical forms. This takes our focus off the structure of the texts and whether the student has effectively presented the meanings that are most important for accomplishing this advanced literacy task. The problem with this approach is that, in many instances, correcting errors is not enough to make the text effective. For example, Writer 3's first sentence, at (w), is not made felicitous through the correction of the surface errors suggested above. Even with the surface errors corrected, the sentence does not make an effective opening to the report. Most important, the student fails to meet the demands of the genre here, as it is inappropriate to begin the abstract with a statement about the significance of the experiment. But semantic problems are also evident. For example, the expression *a specific chemical* is indefinite, where a generic expression, as in (u) (*different solvents*) or (v), *volatile vapors*, may be more appropriate. Finally, the expression *important value that really need to know* construes an interpersonal stance that resounds of informal oral interaction in a way that comes across as unsophisticated and lacking authoritativeness. The positive appraisal of the value of this experiment that the student attempts to convey is undermined by the grammatical choices.

Just responding to discrete ESL errors is not enough to bring students' writing in line with the more academic register that they need to adopt to be successful in this task. Correcting the grammatical errors on an item-by-item basis fails to get at the real issues for these writers, because *errors* in choices that affect interpersonal and textual meanings often are not identified through a sentence-level focus, as they do not appear problematic except in the context of a whole text. Even if every surface error were corrected, these students would still not be presenting lab reports that have the authoritative voice and clear method of development that characterize the model report.

Every subject matter instructor faces the task of responding to disciplinary writing that shows ESL features. ESL students do the best they can to present their written assignments in the clearest English that they can produce. Unfortunately, for many of these students, this English does not meet the standard that many instructors expect of students at this level of education. Even the native speaker has difficulty with the complex and unfamiliar language needed for these lab reports. The instructor makes marginal notes criticizing her for failing to make key points or for lack of clarity in presentation. On the other hand, she is praised when she raises issues that the instructor evaluates positively. The ESL students get less feedback that focuses on meaning and content. It is apparent that the instructors are quite distracted by the ESL features of the papers, as some papers have no comments on content at all, even where it is clear that the papers are weak or lacking. Instead, some instructors mark only the grammatical errors, so what the student gets back is a paper covered with corrections. Where meaning breaks down, typically instructors respond with "unclear" or "awkward" in marginal comments. We know from other research how discouraging such responses can be (e.g., Zamel, 1998). In the context of schooling, the reader's (e.g., instructor's) response to writing has a major influence on the developing writer. Depending on how the instructor responds to the student report, a student may be encouraged to adopt a strategy of saying little but trying to say it grammatically; or, on the other hand, of saying all that she has to say at the risk of making many grammatical errors. Unfortunately, many students adopt the former strategy, as errors can lead to judgements about ESL writers that are often expressed in cognitive, not linguistic, terms, and students can be judged as disorganized thinkers because of their grammatical difficulties.

It is important to keep in mind that these students are able to perform at a high level on these writing assignments in spite of the many grammatical and discourse errors they make. Many of the errors can be easily read over, and a sympathetic reader can make the corrections and not lose sight of the intended meanings. As we saw above, sentences that are difficult to parse from a linguistic point of view can be clear to a knowledgeable reader. Readers with subject-matter knowledge are able to connect with the disciplinary knowledge that the students present, even where they do not express that knowledge in clearly comprehensible academic English. Just as *mistakes* in spoken English are often overlooked by participants in the interaction, readers can also bring subject-matter knowledge that enables them to ignore linguistic infelicities. This shows how important context can be in making a text meaningful.

But even if a knowledgeable reader can make out the possibly intended meanings, students are expected to write texts that can be understood outside of the contexts of their creation; even by readers who may not be as attuned to the potential meanings as course instructors. This means that ESL students need to learn to adopt the register features that give their work the authoritativeness and textual structure that realize the meanings expected in standard academic English. Academic registers have evolved in the way they have because they are functional for their purposes (see Halliday, 1993 for a discussion of the evolution of the register of science), and if students do not draw on appropriate register features, they fail to achieve the purposes of the text.

Developing writing ability is a long-term, ongoing process in which students confront new difficulties and new hurdles with each new genre at each new level of learning. At the university, as we work with second-language writers who are still developing their linguistic resources, it is important to focus on the negotiation of meaning that we know facilitates second-language development. To improve their writing, these students need assistance drawing on the appropriate grammatical elements that present the meanings they intend as they use language in meaningful contexts. Instructors need to engage students in interactive coconstruction of meaning and model appropriate and effective ways of realizing intended meanings at the clause level.

CONCLUSION

Presentation of disciplinary knowledge is at risk for ESL writers without the full range of resources of the grammar. ESL students have a more limited set of options at their command than does the native speaker of English for responding to the demands of the laboratory report assignment. Yet in their writing in the disciplines, ESL students are expected to present field-based knowledge even without the full range of grammatical resources that are needed to meet the instructor's genre expectations. As students who lack a range of grammatical resources focus on presenting disciplinary knowledge in their writing assignments, their infelicitous grammatical choices sometimes present a stance that may be inappropriate or create a text that lacks cohesion or fails to represent intended meanings.

Second-language writers typically depend heavily on resources for ideational meaning, using technical lexis and foregrounding the concepts they want to present. In so doing, they may realize interpersonal and textual meanings that are contrary to their intentions, conveying attitudes that they do not intend to convey, or presenting information in ways that lack cohesion. Problems that students may have in presenting an appropriate voice or in developing an effective text are difficult to identify by looking at discrete errors, but inevitably affect the overall impression that the writing creates. When infelicitous interpersonal meanings are interpreted as intentional, students can be seen as lacking confidence, on the one hand, or taking too strong a stance, on the other. Infelicitous textual meanings can be interpreted as disorganized thinking or problems in conceptualizing. Such moral and cognitive evaluations of students' writing are inappropriate when the issues involved are ones of texturing writing so that it conveys the meanings that the writer intends.

This chapter has demonstrated how genre-based language demands can be identified through a functional linguistic perspective that helps us focus on how students can be helped to gain control of the grammatical resources for making academic meanings. A clearer view of the strategies that ESL writers are adopting to cope with the demands of their writing assignments can give us insights regarding how best to negotiate meaning and provide assistance that can help them present their disciplinary knowledge. Assignments such as this lab report can be exploited for textual analysis and then used as the basis for productive practice following focus on form. Students can learn the ways that ideational, interpersonal, and textual meanings are simultaneously realized by the grammatical and lexical choices they make.

Universities are currently enrolling increasing numbers of students who do not speak English as a native language. These students typically qualify for the university through the normal admissions process, presenting secondary school grades and standardized test scores that make them competitive with other applicants. At the university, they are expected to complete the same tasks at the same level as their native speaker peers, although their English language skills may be less developed. The level of expectations for their performance rises as they face increasingly difficult linguistic tasks at each stage and in each new course and discipline. Educational institutions have a responsibility for helping students develop the linguistic resources they need to accomplish such tasks. Second-language writers need instruction that helps them gain a greater awareness about language structure and its role in construing various disciplinary contexts and genres.

REFERENCES

Braine, G. (1989). Writing in science and technology: An analysis of assignments from ten undergraduate courses. *English for specific purposes, 8,* 3–15.

Dudley-Evans, T. (1986). Genre analysis: An investigation of the introduction and discussion sections of MSc dissertations. In M. Coulthard (Ed.), *Talking about text* (pp. 128–145). Birmingham, UK: English Language Research.

Halliday, M. A. K. (1978). *Language as social semiotic.* London: Edward Arnold.

Halliday, M. A. K. (1993). The construction of knowledge and value in the grammar of scientific discourse: Charles Darwin's *The origin of the species*. In M. A. K. Halliday & J. R. Martin (Eds.), *Writing science: Literacy and discursive power* (pp. 86–105). Pittsburgh, PA: University of Pittsburgh Press.

Halliday, M. A. K. (1994). *An introduction to functional grammar* (2nd ed.). London: Edward Arnold.

Halliday, M. A. K. (1998). Things and relations: Regrammaticising experience as technical knowledge. In J. R. Martin & R. Veel (Eds.), *Reading science: Critical and functional perspectives on discourses of science* (pp. 185–235). London: Routledge.

Halliday, M. A. K., & Martin, J. R. (Eds.). (1993). *Writing science: Literacy and discursive power*. Pittsburgh, PA: University of Pittsburgh Press.

Hinkel, E. (1995). The use of modal verbs as a reflection of cultural values. *TESOL Quarterly, 29*(2), 325–341.

Hunston, S. (1993). Evaluation and ideology in scientific writing. In M. Ghadessy (Ed.), *Register analysis: Theory and practice* (pp. 57–73). London: Pinter.

Jacoby, S., Leech, D., & Holten, C. (1995). A genre-based developmental writing course for undergraduate ESL science majors. In D. Belcher & G. Braine (Eds.), *Academic writing in a second language: Essays on research and pedagogy* (pp. 351–374). Norwood, NJ: Ablex.

Lemke, J. (1990). *Talking science: Language, learning, and values*. Norwood, NJ: Ablex.

Martin, J. R. (1992). *English text*. Philadelphia, PA: John Benjamins.

Martin, J. R. (1996). Waves of abstraction: Organizing exposition. *The Journal of TESOL France, 3*(1), 87–104.

Martin, J. R., & Veel, R. (Eds.). (1998). *Reading science: Critical and functional perspectives on discourses of science*. London: Routledge.

McNamara, J. (1989). The writing in science and history project: The research questions and implications for teachers. In F. Christie (Ed.), *Writing in schools* (pp. 24–35). Geelong, Victoria, Australia: Deakin University Press.

Schleppegrell, M. J. (1996). Conjunction in spoken English and ESL writing. *Applied Linguistics, 17*(3), 271–285.

Schleppegrell, M. J. (2001). Linguistic features of the language of schooling. *Linguistics and Education, 12*(4), 431–459.

Silva, T. (1993). Toward an understanding of the distinct nature of L2 writing: The ESL research and its implications. *TESOL Quarterly, 27*(4), 657–677.

Swales, J. M. (1990). *Genre analysis: English in academic and research settings*. Cambridge, UK: Cambridge University Press.

Unsworth, L. (1999). Developing critical understanding of the specialized language of school science and history texts: A functional grammatical perspective. *Journal of Adolescent and Adult Literacy, 42*(7), 508–521.

Zamel, V. (1998). Strangers in academia: The experiences of faculty and ESL students across the curriculum. In V. Zamel & R. Spack (Eds.), *Negotiating academic literacies: Teaching and learning across languages and cultures* (pp. 249–264). Mahwah, NJ: Lawrence Erlbaum Associates.

7

On the Use of Selected Grammatical Features in Academic Writing

Marianne Celce-Murcia
University of California, Los Angeles

The usefulness (or lack thereof) of explicit grammar instruction in learners' acquisition of a second or foreign language has long been a topic of debate in applied linguistics. Krashen (1982)—and those agreeing with him—have argued that explicit grammar instruction is of little or no consequence in facilitating second-language acquisition. From Krashen's perspective, knowledge of grammar only helps learners to monitor their production (time permitting). He and his supporters further argue that extensive exposure to comprehensible input in the target language is the best means of promoting second-language acquisition.

Other applied linguists, including this author, have long opposed the position held by Krashen and his followers (e.g., McLaughlin, 1987; Rutherford & Sharwood Smith, 1988; Ellis, 1997; & Odlin, 1994). To demonstrate the role and value of explicit grammar instruction, these applied linguists have argued against Krashen's position using both a cognitive account of the second-language acquisition process and the results of research carried out in communicative language classrooms. They have proposed that raising the students' conscious awareness of how to use grammatical resources accurately and appropriately is important for language acquisition in general and for the development of advanced literacy skills in adolescent and adult learners in particular.

However, many professionals interested in grammar and convinced of the value of explicit grammar instruction (linguists, grammarians, writers of composition handbooks or style books, language teachers, language textbook writers, etc.) still tend to view "grammar" primarily as a sentence-level phenomenon. Such a perspective is outmoded and has had negative consequences for the way in which grammar is described and taught. An exclusively sentence-based view of grammar is also inconsistent with the notion of communicative competence (Hymes, 1972), which—according to Canale (1983)—consists of at least four interdependent competencies:

- linguistic/grammatical competence (i.e., control of syntax and morphology)
- sociolinguistic competence (i.e., knowing which lexicogrammatical form to choose given the topic, the social setting, and one's interlocutor[s])
- discourse competence (i.e., knowing how to put sentence-level propositions into sequence to form coherent, connected text)
- strategic competence (i.e., knowing how to negotiate assistance/clarification, etc. when one's lack of competence in any above area impedes communication)

Moreover, because the notion of communicative competence is at the core of communicative language teaching, it is clearly important that we move beyond the sentence level in our conceptions of grammar and begin to better understand the relationship between (a) the morphological and syntactic aspects of linguistic competence and (b) the social and pragmatic aspects of discourse competence (Celce-Murcia & Olshtain, 2000). Grammar is an essential component not only of communicative competence but also of advanced literacy, a claim that is strongly supported by the samples of second-language writing that I cite in this chapter.

Functional linguists such as Givón (1979), Halliday (1994), Ochs, Schegloff, and Thompson (1996) have long argued that few rules of grammar are context-free and that texts and contexts that account for more than the sentence level are a necessary part of any descriptively adequate account of language use. Unfortunately, this perspective has not yet become the norm in language pedagogy. The grammar instruction that learners of English as a second or foreign language require if they are to achieve advanced literacy skills must be discourse-based and discourse-grounded so that learners acquire not only the forms but also the meanings and uses of the target grammatical structures (Celce-Murcia & Larsen-Freeman, 1999).

One of the earliest accounts of some discourse-level grammatical features in English was offered by Halliday and Hasan (1976), who accounted for ties of reference, substitution/ellipsis, conjunction, and lexical cohesion that crossed sentence boundaries and made texts cohesive. This inventory has been expanded somewhat in Halliday and Hasan (1989), Cook (1989), McCarthy (1991), and the work of others to include additional cohesive devices such as the sequencing of tenses, use of parallel structure, and so on. This chapter discusses three discourse-level grammatical features, including one type of grammatical cohesive device, contrastive logical connectors. The other two example structures show us that even choices in verb morphology and selection of a special sentence structure can be highly discourse-sensitive.

THREE GRAMMATICAL FEATURES
PROBLEMATIC FOR ESL WRITERS

The three grammatical features that I have chosen to target in this chapter represent the three different levels at which grammar interacts with text in written academic English: the phrasal/morphological level, the sentential level, and the supra sentential level. The phrasal-level feature is voice: active, passive, and the often ignored middle or ergative voice. The sentence-level feature is the existential construction beginning with *there*, and the supra sentential feature is a set of commonly used contrastive logical connectors. Each feature will be discussed in turn below, and the three grammatical case studies will be followed by a consideration of outcomes and suggestions for further research.

Voice

I begin the body of my chapter with the most tentative findings—from an in-progress research project on voice: active, passive, and middle (or ergative). This three-voice potential for a special class of English verbs was pointed out over 30 years ago when Fillmore (1968) wrote about change-of-state verbs like *break* that display a three-way distinction with respect to voice:

Active/transitive voice: John broke the window.

Passive voice: The window was broken by John.

Middle/ergative voice: The window broke.

While *break* is not a verb that is particularly frequent in most academic writing, many other change-of-state verbs with three possible voices regularly occur in academic discourse, e.g., *open, close, increase, decrease, change, move, grow, develop, improve, reverse,* among others. The problem is that most nonnative speakers have never developed any awareness of how to use the middle/ergative voice for the many verbs that can take this option in English. They tell me they operate with a two-step heuristic when making decisions about what voice to use in their sentences—obviously an oversimplification:

- If the subject is an agent or causal instrument, use the active voice: (e.g., John/the stone broke the window.)
- If the subject is inanimate, use the passive voice: (e.g., The window was broken (by John/with the stone).)

What makes this problem especially challenging is that other than Zobl (1989) and Yip (1995), there have been very few studies even suggesting that this three-way voice distinction might pose a problem for nonnative speakers of English who are trying to achieve advanced literacy. Both Zobl and Yip point out that "overpassivation" occurs in the writing of many ESL/EFL learners because they have not acquired any awareness of how to use the middle/ergative voice in English. Vongpumivitch (1999) has begun to do research in this area as part of her doctoral studies in our program. She is a native speaker of Thai and perceives as problematic her inability to use the middle voice in her academic writing in the ways that native speakers do. Using the Brown University Corpus of written English (see Francis & Kučera, 1982), Vongpumivitch looked at the relative frequencies of active, passive, and middle voice for four English verbs: *increase, decrease, open,* and *close.* Table 7.1 summarizes her findings:

> For all three verbs with an adequate number of tokens—*decrease* had too few and the percentages for this verb are thus somewhat suspect—the most frequent voice was active, followed by middle voice, with passive voice having the lowest frequency.

When is the middle voice used? With the verbs *increase* and *decrease* it tends to be used when the inanimate subject is something that is objectively or subjectively measurable (rather than an animate agent/dynamic instrument subject—both of which favor active voice—or a patient subject—for the passive voice). Vongpumivitch found that these two verbs take middle voice with subjects like *volume, temperature, number of, the rate, the size, sales, average, population, cost,* and so on. For the verbs *open* and *close* the inanimate subjects of middle-voice verbs were things that literally or figuratively open or close such as *door, locker, refrigerator, window, eyes, mouth, umbrella, parachute, movie, film, play, restaurant, nightclub, trial, conference, stock exchange.* Across the genres of the Brown corpus Vongpumivitch found that *increase* and *decrease* occur most frequently in all three voices in the learned documents (i.e., academic writing). *Open* and *close* had a much more even distribution across genres, with the various fiction subgenres showing a contrast between active and middle voice but virtually no use of the passive voice.

Vongpumivitch (1999) concludes that active voice occurs when there are explicit subject agents/instruments and explicit object patients. However, the reasons for choosing between passive voice and middle voice are not yet completely clear. She is doing further research with additional verbs and a larger database to try to find a good explanation. Thus, this is very much work in progress. Yet I was compelled to discuss this topic because ESL/EFL learning problems in this area have been largely ignored to date and because my own foreign graduate students have clearly been struggling with voice in their academic writing. For example: (My error data come from two native speakers of Japanese)

TABLE 7.1

Voice Frequencies of Selected Verbs

Verb	# of Tokens	Active	Passive	Middle
increase	245	44.23%	14.74%	40.38%
decrease	26	20.83%	8.33%	70.83%
open	360	57.06%	12.94%	30.00%
close	123	60.23%	15.91%	23.88%

Over the period of the study the learners' VOT values for /p, t, k/ were decreased.

This is clearly a statement where the middle or ergative voice (i.e., VOT values for /p, t, k/ decreased) would be preferred over the passive by native speakers because VOT *values* are something measurable. Another Japanese speaker writes:

The results clearly show that error repair rates were varied depending on the type of feedback given to learners at different grade levels.

In this case, also, the middle voice (i.e, error repair rates varied) would be preferred over the passive voice by native English speakers because the subject noun phrase *error repair rates* is once again a measurable entity rather than a patient being acted on by an agent or instrument.

These errors—and many others like them—confirm the observations and findings of Zobl (1989) and Yip (1995), who predicted that overpassivation would be the type of error made by advanced learners who had not yet mastered the use of middle voice in their academic English writing. The results also suggest that Vongpumivitch's more complete findings will provide us with useful descriptive information for developing more explicit discourse-grounded pedagogy when teaching voice. Given the current state of pedagogy on voice (it treats only the distinction between active and passive) and the types of errors many of my ESL/EFL graduate students continue to make in their writing, I conclude that further information on the use of middle voice—in contrast to active or passive voice—is urgently needed.

Existential 'There' Constructions

In English composition instruction for native speakers, writers are usually advised to avoid the existential *there* construction so that their prose will not be weak and wordy (e.g., Baker, 1979; Heath Handbook, 1986). In ESL/EFL instruction, use of sentences with existential *there* subjects are typically taught with reference to what is visible in the physical environment; the presentation is usually sentence-level with little or no consideration given to the discourse function of the structure:

There is a book on the table.

There are two red pencils on the desk.

In analyzing a sizeable corpus of written and spoken English, Lloyd-Jones (1987) found that such explicitly locative uses of the existential *there* construction accounted for only about 10% of all her tokens. What, then, are the typical functions of this construction in written discourse?

Ahlers (1991), a former graduate student, encouraged by the work of Lloyd-Jones and also that of Huckin and Pesante (1988), assembled a database of expository written English. She found that of the 100 tokens of existential *there* randomly selected for close analysis, only one was a sentence-level token like the two previous examples—a finding that more or less confirmed what Huckin and Pesante had reported.

The most frequent discourse function of the existential *there* construction in Ahlers' corpus was its use in presenting a major topic or subtopic for subsequent development, as in the following excerpt from a biology textbook (all examples of the target construction are underlined).

MODES OF NATURAL SELECTION

<u>There are</u> three major modes of natural selection, as shown in Fig. 35.4 and defined by the following list:

1. *Stabilizing selection* favors intermediate forms of a trait and operates against extreme forms; hence the frequencies of alleles representing the extreme forms decrease.

2. *Directional selection* shifts the phenotypic character of the population as a whole, either in response to a directional change in the environment or in response to a new environment; hence the allelic frequencies underlying the range of phenotypes move in a steady, consistent direction.

3. *Disruptive selection* favors extreme forms of a trait and operates against intermediate forms; hence the frequencies of alleles representing the extreme forms increase. (Starr & Taggart, 1989, p. 547)

The above excerpt follows a deductive presentation and reasoning style. Another important but somewhat less frequent pattern that Ahlers found was the reverse of the first pattern (i.e., inductive organization where the details and specifics come first with the existential *there* construction occurring at the end of the discourse episode), often stating an important generalization. This is what occurs in the following excerpt from an economics textbook:

The establishment of a uniform price of a good in the international market is illustrated in Fig. 6.2. In the left half of the Figure, we have the US demand for and supply of the commodity in question; on the right are the UK demand and supply schedules for the same commodity. With no foreign trade of the good, the US equilibrium price would be OP, with the quantity OM exchanged; and in the UK the equilibrium price would be OP' and the quantity OM'. But with trade—and with neither costs of transportation nor tariffs or other restrictions on trade—then the US and the UK become a consolidated market. In this larger single market, <u>there is</u> an equilibrium price at which total (US plus UK) quantity demanded is equal to total quantity supplied (Alchain & Allen, 1972, p. 740).

This type of rhetorical development also occurs relatively frequently in social science research articles that test a null hypothesis. After a presentation of numbers reflecting nonsignificant results, the author(s) often state a conclusion, in paragraph-final position, with some statement such as:

... There were no significant differences between the control group and the experimental group.

The one other discourse function of some importance that Ahlers found for existential *there* sentences was a more local listing function where very specific items on a list are often marked by existential *there*. Such examples appear in a segment from the same economics text I cited previously (Alchain & Allen, 1972):

We have illustrated a case of complete factor-price equalization consistent with our assumptions. But we would never satisfy all of the assumptions required to achieve full factor-price equalization—and in some instances none of them—in the real world. These assumptions include:

1. There are only two productive factors, labor and capital, each of which is "homogeneous" throughout the world.

2. A given commodity has a single production function.

3. There are only two commodities, both produced with constant returns to scale. [note: this list has five more items—two with *there* constructions and three without.] (p. 751)

At the time that Ahlers carried out her study (1991), the only ESL/EFL textbook she could find that taught the existential *there* construction in a manner consistent with the uses she had found in her analysis of academic writing was Byrd and Benson (1989). All the other sources she examined presented the construction strictly at the sentence level, a practice that gives learners an extremely limited and incomplete picture of how this construction functions in written discourse. Looking at more current publications, I have found only one other recent ESL textbook with some discourse-level exercises comparable to Byrd and Benson (i.e., Frodesen & Eyring (1997, pp. 230–232) for the topic-introducing function, the first of the three functions mentioned above). I also found two style manuals (Beene & Vande Kopple (1992) and Williams (2000)) addressed primarily to native English speakers, with some good observations on when and why to use—or not use—existential *there* in expository writing. However, such discourse-level presentations are still the exception rather than the rule in ESL/EFL textbooks and style manuals.

Sasaki (1990) carried out a study in Japan with Japanese learners of English who were attending a postsecondary university entrance exam preparation course. These learners first completed a free writing task (describing facts they had received in list form about Taro's school), and then they did a controlled writing task. On the free writing task many of the learners avoided the existential *there* construction, which does not exist in Japanese but which would be the preferred form in English for writing a description of Taro's school (using the listing function discussed earlier):

e.g., There are 27 students in Taro's school.

Only the learners with the highest level of proficiency in Sasaki's study produced the above construction on the free writing task and then only part of the time. The controlled writing task demonstrated that virtually all the learners were able to produce the target construction when doing a highly controlled task. On the free writing task, however, those learners with the lowest proficiency hardly ever produced the above construction. Instead, they produced a variety of other constructions when attempting to express propositions like the one above, some of which were grammatical in English, but many of which were not:

*Taro's school is/are twenty seven students.

Taro's school has twenty seven students.

*Taro's school has student in twenty seven.

*Students of Taro's school is 27.

Twenty seven students are in Taro's school.

This appears to be a case of avoidance (Schachter, 1974), which means that learners who are not secure about how and when to use the existential *there* construction will simply resort to other grammatical means to convey their message.

To test whether such avoidance might also apply to more advanced second language learners using academic English at the graduate level, I compared three PhD dissertation proposals: one was written by a native speaker of English; the other two were by native speakers of Japanese, one of whom (the advanced learner) had markedly better English proficiency than the other (the intermediate learner). Both native Japanese speakers were much more advanced than most of the learners in Sasaki's study. The native English speaker wrote 44 pages of double-spaced text in 14 point font and used the existential *there* construction 15 times (one instance was in a quote). The native speaker of Japanese described as an advanced English user wrote 39 pages of double-spaced text in 12 point font and used the existential *there* construction 33 times (four instances were in quotes). Both writers displayed extremely similar patterns of use in that they both used two thirds of their existential *there* sentences in their reviews of the literature (10 for the English speaker and 22 for the advanced Japanese speaker, whose proposal had a longer literature review than that of the native speaker).

The other native speaker of Japanese, who has intermediate-level proficiency, provided an extremely interesting contrast. This student wrote 30 pages of double-spaced text in 12 point font without using one single token of the existential *there* structure. I identified several places, particularly in the review of the literature, where native English speakers would very likely have used an existential *there* construction. Here is one such example:

INTERMEDIATE ESL WRITER:

"Lastly, Chaudron discusses four problems with feedback to justify the usefulness of the set of types and features in Chaudron (1977). The four problems (Chaudron 1988:145, 149) are as follows:" (the four problems are listed)

SUGGESTED REFORMULATION:

Lastly, there are four problems concerning feedback that justify the usefulness of the set of types and features first proposed in Chaudron (1977) and discussed again in Chaudron (1988: 145, 149): (the four problems are listed)

My reformulation not only uses the existential *there* construction to introduce the list of problems the author wishes to mention, it also allows me to focus the discourse on teacher feedback, the topic of the proposal, rather than on Chaudron, one of the applied linguists who has published research on teacher feedback.

Although further study is needed, even this limited analysis demonstrates that the tendencies reported in Sasaki (1990) can also be found more generally in learners' writing in English. Whereas the native and highly advanced English writers both employed the existential *there* construction in rhetorically appropriate and parallel manners, the intermediate English user did not write one single token of this construction. It is possible to write in English without using the existential *there* construction, yet its complete absence is likely to make for awkward prose in spots. The intermediate-level student is not comfortable using this construction and does not, in fact, seem to have any sense of when and why to use it in written English.

Contrastive Logical Connectors.

After considering Halliday's division of logical connectors (also referred to as conjunctive adverbials) into categories such as (1) additive, (2) contrastive, (3) causal, and (4) temporal (Halliday & Hasan, 1976), Williams (1996) concludes that such global groupings for connectors can mislead language learners. Instead, based on at least 50 contextualized written tokens for each connector analyzed, Williams proposes that it is semantically more accurate to say that these logical connectors call attention to propositional frames that are encoded in the text. This is also in line with what Blakemore (1989) suggests. In other words, most logical connectors seem to imply a unique propositional frame such that if one uses the wrong connector, the cohesion and coherence of the text is impaired.

Williams (1996) describes the meanings of more than 30 logical connectors. In this chapter, however, I focus only on summarizing his findings for four contrastive logical connectors because it has been my experience that these connectors are particularly difficult for nonnative speakers to master and distinguish (similar information on contrastive logical connectors based on Williams (1996) is also provided in Celce-Murcia and Larsen-Freeman (1999, pp. 532–533).

For the logical connector *in/by contrast*, the propositional frame can be stated as:

X (a) in/by contrast Y (b)

The frame specifies that two different subjects or topics differ in at least one respect. Thus we can say:

South Carolina is mild in the winter. In contrast, South Dakota is frigid.

Here we are contrasting the winter temperatures in South Carolina with those in South Dakota—contrasting mild temperatures with frigid temperatures. However, we cannot use *in/by contrast* in the following context because the required frame elements are not present:

> Calvin wanted to fly to the moon. *In contrast, he didn't know how.

Here there are not two different subjects that differ (note that *however* would be acceptable here because, as we will see, *however* is acceptable in a wide range of contrastive propositional frames).

An example of *in contrast* taken from academic writing follows:

> Low income sections of urban areas, often called the inner city, have a special range of problems that reduce the income-earning potential of their residents. The labor markets in the inner city are segmented into 'primary' and 'secondary' jobs, which provide very different levels of income and occupational status ...

> For example, primary labor market jobs are characterized by good wages, upgrading opportunities, on-the-job training, and fringe benefits. In contrast, secondary labor markets are characterized by jobs with low wages, little or no on-the-job training, few opportunities for upgrading, and few fringe benefits. (Anderson, 1979, p. 42).

In this passage the author uses *in contrast* to introduce the point about secondary labor markets, the second topic that has different levels of income and occupational status from the primary labor markets that constituted the first topic; such a contrast satisfies the propositional frame that is called for when using *in contrast*.

Often confused with *in/by contrast* by native and nonnative speakers alike, the logical connector *on the other hand* has a propositional frame that specifies it is only necessary to have a single subject or topic, which is then compared with reference to two contrasting qualities:

> X (a) on the other hand X (b).

Often the contrasting qualities are of the "good/bad" type:

> Minnesota is bitterly cold in the winter. On the other hand, it is one of the more scenic states. (i.e, Minnesota is bad in one way, but good in another).

Note that subjects (or topics) need not be lexically identical; a good paraphrase relationship is sufficient. In the following example *real estate sales* is a topic paraphrasable as *people buying homes*:

> Real estate sales can be a thrilling business to be in. On the other hand, people aren't buying homes today the way they did last year. (i.e., Real estate sales are good in one way but bad in another, so it might not make the perfect business career.)

In academic written discourse *on the other hand* occurs in texts such as the following:

The direct programs have also been flawed by not being tuned to specific market conditions. In markets characterized by a surplus of quality units, and hence lower prices per unit of housing service for low quality dwellings than for higher quality and newer units, subsidies for new construction are a very costly way to provide minimal standard housing, compared to upgrading the existing stock. On the other hand, in markets where low quality housing is in short supply relative to the demand for it, new units make economic sense. (De Leeuw, Schnare, & Struyk, 1979, p. 170).

In the above excerpt the presumed unifying topic is *specific market conditions*; two examples of which are then described. However, would also be plausible to substitute *in/by contrast* for *on the other hand* because the text is dense and the arguments are complex, such that one could view the two markets as two different topics with two different consequences. Thus, there are cases where, depending on the writer's perspective and degree of abstraction, either *in/by contrast* or *on the other hand* would be acceptable.

The logical connector *on the contrary* is rather different from the two preceding ones. It links a proposition, stated as a negative, with a contradiction of the proposition, in that order:

The Yankees didn't win. On the contrary, they lost.

In fact, the assumption that the second proposition after *on the contrary* will contradict the first negative one is so strong that this may well be the only contrastive logical connector that can stand alone without having an overt following clause or proposition:

The Yankees didn't win. On the contrary!

A propositional frame such as the following makes explicit the implied contradiction that is signaled by this logical connector:

X (negative proposition); on the contrary, Y (contradiction of X)

In academic writing we find excerpts such as the following with this connector:

I have analyzed the arguments for the accepted view and found them unconvincing. In this article I offer a different view, based on new insights into how cultural change comes about. According to this view, the spread of the Indo-European languages did not require conquest. On the contrary, it was likely to have been a peaceful diffusion linked to the spread of agriculture from its origins in Anatolia and the Near East … (Renfrew, 1989, p. 106)

Nonnative speakers of English have been observed to use *on the contrary* in frames that are more appropriate for *in/by contrast* or *on the other hand*, or vice versa, because they have not yet internalized the frames associated with each of these logical connectors. They seem to feel that one contrastive logical connector will more or less substitute for another. This fuzzy and incomplete understanding of the meaning of

each connector results in errors such as the following one, which was produced by a
native speaker of Japanese pursuing graduate studies at my university:

> ... Lightbown and Spada (1990) showed that learners who received error corrections
> performed better on some corrected sentences than those that did not. White
> (1991), White, Spada, Lightbown, & Ranta (1991), Spada & Lightbown (1993) also
> showed the positive effect of corrective feedback in developing second language pro-
> ficiency in classroom interaction. *On the contrary, other studies examined the ef-
> fect of corrective feedback in an experimental environment and found that the effect
> of corrective feedback is much more limited ...

In this environment *in/by contrast* is clearly more suitable than *on the contrary* if
we apply the propositional frame proposed by Williams, which requires a negative
in the proposition before on the contrary. I have checked this with several native
speakers of English by leaving the connector blank and asking which of the two
connectors is best. The preference for *in/by contrast* was unanimous. To demonstrate that this is a persistent error in the writing of this PhD candidate, I cite a similar example from another paper he wrote recently:

> For example, a teacher might provide feedback for a student's error in an utterance
> elicited by the teacher in a question-answer sequence. *On the contrary, if a student
> asks a question with an error in the utterance, but whose approximate meaning is un-
> derstood by the teacher, the teacher will answer instead of correcting the student's
> question....

In this discourse context, either *in/by contrast* or *on the other hand* would be favored
over *on the contrary* by native English speakers. The negation that satisfies the
frame for *on the contrary* to occur is not present here.

Note once again that in both of the above excerpts with second language errors—as well as in all the preceding text excerpts that illustrate use of contrastive
logical connectors—*however* is acceptable. The logical connector *however* has no
specific propositional frame, according to Williams (1996). It may be used almost
anywhere to draw the reader's attention to a difference. We have seen earlier that
this can be a difference between expectation and reality, between a problem and
lack of a solution, or between contrasting qualities of one or more subjects/topics.
It can also be used in cases such as the following, which would not allow any of the
three semantically more explicit contrastive connectors described previously (i.e.,
on the contrary, in/by contrast, on the other hand):

- certainty versus uncertainty:
  We may go to Hawaii, or we may go to California. However, we have to
  find a way to escape the snow this winter.
- topic shift:
  I lost $20,000 in Las Vegas last weekend. However, let's talk about
  something else.

For nonnative speakers one possible solution is to use only *however* when a
contrastive logical connector is needed. This is certainly not the best solution be-

cause native speakers use a variety of logical connectors in their academic English writing; most style manuals agree that a degree of lexical variety is required for effective writing in English. Learners should thus be concerned with mastering the logical connectors most typically used in the academic writing of their particular discipline for both reading and writing purposes. In all likelihood, more than one contrastive logical connector will be used, although academic discourse communities seem to have describable preferences for using certain logical connectors rather than others (Jiang, 1983). This makes discipline-specific language learning particularly relevant to the acquisition of this feature of advanced literacy—and undoubtedly many other features as well.

CONCLUSION

The three preceding descriptions of grammatical structures functioning in academic discourse illustrate a point that has become increasingly clear to me and many of my graduate students during the past several years: We need to reanalyze virtually all of English grammar at the discourse level in order to be able to teach our students *rules* of grammar that will serve them when they read and write English for academic purposes. Sentence-level knowledge and production of a structure are but elementary prerequisites to knowing how to use or interpret a structure in written discourse. When to use the structure and for what purpose one might use it constitute critical knowledge for learners wishing to acquire advanced literacy skills. Our reference grammars and teaching materials must begin to supply teachers and learners with this kind of discourse-embedded grammatical information. However, this will happen only if a sufficient number of relevant data-based studies are carried out with their findings subsequently disseminated to the proper audiences.

ACKNOWLEDGMENTS

The author wishes to acknowledge her use of the data samples, counts, and analyses from the work of current and former graduate students Ahlers (1991), Vongpumivitch (1999), Williams (1996), Lloyd-Jones (1987) and Sasaki (1990). Without their research this study would not have been possible. She thanks Howard Williams for useful feedback on an earlier draft, Dzidra Rodins for help with the predicate calculus, Amy Seo for work-study support, and Christine Holten for several relevant references. Any errors and omissions in this chapter rest solely with the author.

REFERENCES

Ahlers, E. A. (1991). *A discourse analysis of non-referential 'there' in academic writing*. Unpublished master's thesis in teaching English as a second language, University of California, Los Angeles.
Alchain, A., & Allen, W. (1972). *University Economics, 3rd edition. Belmont, CA: Wadsworth Publishing Company.*

Anderson, B. E. (1979). Improving the employability of the unemployed. In H. J. Bryce (Ed.), *Revitalizing cities* (pp. 39–60). Lexington, MA: Lexington Books.

Baker, S. (1979). *The practical stylist.* (2nd ed.). New York: Thomas Y. Crowell.

Beene, L., & Vande Kopple, W. (1992). *The riverside handbook.* New York: Houghton Mifflin.

Blakemore, D. (1989). Denial and contrast: A relevance theoretic analysis of *but. Linguistics and Philosophy, 12,* 15–37.

Byrd, P., & Benson, B. (1989). *Improving the grammar of written English: The handbook.* Belmont, CA: Wadsworth Publishing Company.

Canale, M. (1983). From communicative competence to communicative language pedagogy. In J. Richards & R. Schmidt (Eds.), *Language and Communication* (pp. 2–27). London: Longman.

Celce-Murcia, M., & Olshtain, E. (2000). *Discourse and context in language teaching.* New York: Cambridge University Press.

Celce-Murcia, M., & Larsen-Freeman, D., with Williams, H. (1999). *The grammar book: An ESL/EFL teacher's course* (2nd ed.). Boston, MA: Heinle & Heinle.

Cook, G. (1989). *Discourse analysis.* Oxford, UK: Oxford University Press.

DeLeeuw, F., Schnare, A., & Struyk, R. (1979). Housing. In W. Gorham & N. Glazer (Eds.), *The urban predicament* (pp. 119–178). Washington, DC: Urban Institute.

Ellis, R. (1997). Second language research and language teaching. Oxford: Oxford University Press.

Fillmore, C. J. (1968). The case for case. In E. Bach & R. Harms (Eds.), *Universals in linguistic theory* (pp. 1–90). New York: Holt, Rinehart, & Winston.

Francis, W. N., & Kučera, H. (1982). *Frequency analysis of English usage.* Boston: Houghton Mifflin.

Frodesen, J., & Eyring, J. (1997). *Grammar dimensions book 4* (2nd ed.) Boston: Heinle & Heinle.

Givón, T. (Ed.). (1979). *Syntax and semantics: Discourse and syntax* (Vol. 12). New York: Academic Press.

Halliday, M. A. K., (1994). *Introduction to functional grammar* (2nd ed.). London: Edward Arnold.

Halliday, M. A. K., & Hasan, R. (1976). *Cohesion in English.* London: Longman.

Halliday, M. A. K., & Hasan, R. (1989). *Language, context, and text: A socio-semiotic perspective.* Oxford, UK: Oxford University Press.

Heath Handbook (1986). Boston: Heath Publishing.

Huckin, T., & Pesante, L. (1988). Existential *there. Written communication, 5*(3), 368–391.

Hymes, D. (1972). On communicative competence. In J. B. Pride & J. Holmes (Eds.), *Sociolinguistics: Selected reading* (pp. 269–293). Harmondsworth, UK: Penguin.

Jiang, M. S. (1983). *Towards an understanding of the logical connectors because, since, as, and for.* Unpublished master's thesis in teaching English as a second language, University of California, Los Angeles.

Krashen, S. D. (1982). *Principles and practice in second language acquisition.* Oxford, UK: Pergamon Press.

Lloyd-Jones, M. (1987). *A contextual analysis of non-referential there in American English.* Unpublished master's thesis in teaching English as a second language, University of California, Los Angeles.

McCarthy, M. (1991). *Discourse analysis for language teachers.* Cambridge, UK: Cambridge University Press.

McLaughlin, B. (1987). *Theories of second language acquisition.* London: Edward Arnold.

Ochs, E., Schegloff, E., & Thompson, S. (Eds.). (1996). *Interaction and grammar.* Cambridge, UK: Cambridge University Press.

Odlin, T. (Ed.). (1994). Perspectives on pedagogical grammar. New York: Cambridge University Press.

Renfrew, C. (1989, October). The origins of Indo-European languages. *Scientific American*, 106–114.

Rutherford, W. E., & Sharwood Smith, M. (Eds.). (1988). *Grammar and second language teaching: A book of readings*. New York: Harper & Row.

Sasaki, M. (1990). Topic prominence in Japanese EFL students' existential constructions. *Language Learning, 40*(3), 337–368.

Schachter, J. (1974). An error in error analysis. *Language Learning, 24*(2), 205–214.

Starr, C., & Taggart, R. (1989). *Biology, the unity and diversity of life*. (5th ed.) Belmont, CA: Wadsworth Publishing Company.

Vongpumivitch, V. (1999). *A corpus analysis of five change-of-state verbs*. Unpublished term project for Applied Linguistics and TESL 274, Spring Quarter, University of California, Los Angeles.

Williams, H. (1996). *An analysis of English conjunctive adverbial expressions*. Unpublished doctoral dissertation in Applied Linguistics, University of California, Los Angeles.

Williams, J. (2000). *Style: Ten lessons in clarity and grace* (6th ed.). New York: Longman.

Yip, V. (1995). *Interlanguage and learnability: From Chinese to English*. Amsterdam/Philadelphia: John Benjamins.

Zobl, H. (1989). Canonical typological structures and ergativity in English L2 Acquisition. In S. Gass & J. Schachter (Eds.), *Linguistic Aspects of Second Language Acquisition* (pp. 203–221). Cambridge, UK: Cambridge University Press.

8

Literacies, Identities, and Discourses

James Paul Gee
University of Wisconsin, Madison

One of the central themes of the so-called New Literacy Studies (see Barton, 1994; Gee, 1996, 2000; and Street, 1995, for programmatic statements) is this: If you want to ask questions about literacy, don't look at reading and writing in themselves, but as they are embedded within specific social practices. In a narrow sense, reading and writing are technologies, and like all technologies they have no effects in and of themselves, but only specific (and different) effects as they mediate different activities within different social practices.

However, reading and writing do not just mediate activities within social practices. They also always mediate different socially and historically situated *identities* (e.g., a cutting-edge physicist; an urban street gang member; a first-grader in a skill-and-drill classroom; a radical feminist, etc.) within different social practices. And it is here that issues of success or failure in schools and other sorts of institutions are most strongly located. As technologies, reading and writing require no great intelligence to master—or at least such mastery is open to a quite broad band of intelligences. But as they define identity-relevant positions in social space, reading and writing can be dangerous and risky endeavors, indeed.

Something of a paradox arises here. If we look at reading and writing as devices for defining identity-relevant positions in social space, then it is clear that they almost always do this alongside oral language, as well. That is, there is, very often, no good reason to make a primary distinction between written language and oral language. And why stop with language (oral or written)? What about all the other devices—the nonverbal symbol systems, images, objects, artifacts, tools, and technologies—with which we come to mean some things and not others as we inhabit identity-relevant social positions? So, if we want to study literacy, we are led inevitably to the full array of semiotic resources with which people mean and be (Kress, 1997).

None of this is really the least bit novel any more. It is simply one construal of a New Literacies Studies perspective. I want here to sketch one approach to language and literacy along these lines. My eye is on the question of why certain *kinds of people* struggle with certain kinds of literacy, but I will first have to lay out a good bit of apparatus, much of which may seem tangential to literacy. Indeed, that is part of my point: We can only understand success and failure in regard to literacy from a perspective in which literacy (at least, in a narrow sense) itself is not foregrounded.

After developing this apparatus, I demonstrate some of its implications by sketching out two specific examples. One example involves an oral interaction between a graduate student and a professor as they (attempt to) interact within the "Discourse" (see further on for a discussion of this notion) of graduate study in a research-based university. The other is an example of writing where history is addressing public policy issues (specifically, what should be taught in the schools). Here I want to stress how form and function are married in a quite specific way within specific Discourses.

DISCOURSES

Oral and written language exist always and only inside what I call "big D" "Discourses" (Gee, 1996, 1999; I reserve the word "discourse," with a small "d," for "language in use"). A Discourse is composed of distinctive ways of "being and doing" that allow people to enact and/or recognize a specific and distinctive socially-situated identity (e.g., being-doing an *appropriate* first-grader in Ms. Smith's progressive classroom; an *appropriate* sort of U.S. generative linguist; or an *appropriate* sort of Los Angeles Latino teenage street-gang member, etc.). The ways of being-doing a Discourse involve distinctive ways of using (oral and/or written) language, other symbol systems, thinking, believing, valuing, acting, interacting, gesturing, and dressing. They involve, as well, distinctive ways of coordinating and getting coordinated by other people, symbols, objects, tools, technologies, places, and times of various sorts (Latour, 1999).

Discourses are not units or tight boxes with neat boundaries. Rather they are *ways of recognizing and getting recognized* as certain sorts of *whos* doing certain sorts of *whats* (Wieder & Pratt, 1990). All recognition processes involve satisfying a variety of constraints in probabilistic and sometimes partial ways. One and the same *performance* can get recognized in multiple ways, in partial ways, in contradictory ways, in disputed ways, in negotiable ways, and so on and so forth through all the multiplicities and problematics that work on postmodernism has made so popular.

Although there are an endless array of Discourses in the world, nearly every human being, except under extraordinary conditions, acquires an initial Discourse within whatever constitutes his or her primary socializing unit early in life. Early in life, we all learn a culturally distinctive way of being an *everyday person*, that is a nonspecialized, nonprofessional person. We can call this our "primary Discourse." Our primary Discourse gives us our initial and often enduring sense of self and sets the foundations of our culturally specific vernacular language (our everyday language), the language in which we speak and act as everyday (nonspecialized) people.

As a person grows up, lots of interesting things can happen to his or her primary Discourse. Primary Discourses can change, hybridize with other Discourses, and they can even die. In any case, for the vast majority of us, our primary Discourse, through all its transformations, serves us throughout life as what I call our "life world Discourse" (Habermas, 1984). Our life world Discourse is the way that we use language, feel and think, act and interact, and so forth, in order to be an every-day (nonspecialized) person. In our pluralistic world there is much adjustment and negotiation as people seek to meet in the terrain of the life world, given that life worlds are culturally distinctive (i.e., different groups of people have different ways of being-doing *everyday people*).

All the Discourses we acquire later in life, beyond our primary Discourse, we ac-quire within a more public sphere than our initial socializing group. We can call these "secondary Discourses." They are acquired within institutions that are part and parcel of wider communities, whether these be religious groups, community organizations, schools, businesses, or governments.

As we are being socialized early in life, secondary Discourses very often play an interesting role. Primary Discourses work out, over time, alignments and alle-giances with and against other Discourses, alignments and allegiances that shape them as they, in turn, shape these other Discourses. One way that many social groups achieve an alignment with secondary Discourses they value is *by incorporat-ing certain aspects of the practices of these secondary Discourses into the early (primary Discourse) socialization of their children.*

For example, some African American families incorporate aspects of practices and values that are part of African American churches into their primary Discourse (Daniel & Smitherman, 1990), as my family incorporated aspects of practices and values of a very traditional Catholicism into our primary Discourse. This is an ex-tremely important mechanism in terms of which bits and pieces of a valued commu-nity or public identity (to be more fully practiced later in the child's life) are incorporated as part and parcel of the child's private, home-based, life world identity.

Social groups that are deeply affiliated with formal schooling often incorporate into the socialization of their children practices that resonate with later school-based secondary Discourses (e.g., see Rogoff & Toma, 1997). For example, their children, from an early age, are encouraged (and coached) at dinner time to tell stories in quite expository ways that are rather like little essays. Or, parents in-teract with their children over books in ways that encourage a great deal of labeling and the answering of a variety of different types of questions, as well as the forming of intertextual relationships between books and between books and the world.

I refer to the processes by which families incorporate aspects of valued second-ary-Discourse practices into their primary Discourses as "filtering" (Gee, 1996). Filtering is used as a way to facilitate children's later success in valued secondary Discourses. None of what I have said about filtering is particularly novel—in fact, it is a well-studied phenomenon. However, the point I want to stress is this: *Filtering functions not primarily to give children certain skills, but, rather, to give them certain val-ues, attitudes, motivations, ways of interacting, and perspectives, all of which are more important than mere skills for successful later entry into specific secondary Discourses "for real" (skills follow from such matters).*

When we are concerned with the acquisition of Discourses in high school, col-leges, and workplaces, there is another aspect of filtering that becomes relevant: *Filtering early in life can facilitate the acquisition of specific Discourses later that them-*

selves, in turn, facilitate the acquisition of yet other related Discourses, creating a chain of filtering relationships. The person who seems effortlessly successful at an elite college has often benefitted from having entered a chain of Discourses each of which has facilitated the acquisition of the next. This (beyond the equally important issue of conflict between primary/life world Discourses and specific secondary Discourses) is why early home experiences and experiences in the early years of school still have important implications for people later in life.

SOCIAL LANGUAGES

There is no such thing as language (e.g., English) or literacy (e.g., reading or writing) *in general.* People do not learn *English.* Rather, they learn a specific "social language" (variety or register of English) fit to certain social purposes and not to others. They don't learn to *read* or *write,* they learn to read or write *something* (some type of text) written in a specific social language used in specific ways by specific groups of people for specific purposes. Everyone is a native speaker of a number of different social languages and a nonnative speaker of lots of other social languages. And nearly everyone is literate in respect to some sorts of texts and related social practices and illiterate in regard to lots of others.

There are a great many different social languages, for example, the language of medicine, literature, street gangs, sociology, law, rap, or informal dinner-time talk among friends (who may belong to distinctive cultures or social groups). To know any specific social language is to know *how its characteristic design resources are combined to enact specific socially-situated identities and social activities.* To know a particular social language is either to be able to *do* a particular identity or to be able to recognize such an identity, when we do not want to or cannot actively participate.

Let me give two examples, longer versions of which I have used elsewhere (Gee, 1996, 1999). First, a young woman, Jane, telling the same story to her parents and to her boy friend, says to her parents at dinner: "Well, when I thought about it, I don't know, it seemed to me that Gregory should be considered the most offensive character," but later to her boyfriend she says: "What an ass that guy was, you know, her boyfriend." In the first case, she uses distinctive lexical and grammatical resources to enact "a dutiful and intelligent daughter having dinner with her proud parents" and in the other case to enact "a girl friend being intimate with her boy friend." Note, by the way, that the particular labels I use here are neither important, nor to be taken too seriously. Such labels need not be (and usually are not) used by people overtly and, if they are, they are usually part of the negotiatory and contestatory nature of social languages and Discourses. The point is just that people must have some, however tentative, unspoken, and problematic, idea of *who is doing what.*

Second, to take an example from Myers (1992), consider a biologist writing in a professional science journal who writes: "Experiments show that *Heliconius* butterflies are less likely to oviposit on host plants that possess eggs or egg-like structures," but who writes about the same topic in a popular science magazine as follows: "*Heliconius* butterflies lay their eggs on *Passiflora* vines." The first passage uses distinctive lexical and grammatical resources to enact "a professional adaptationist biologist of a certain type engaged in managing uncertainty through the manipulation of theory and experiment" (see Myers, 1992), the second passage uses distinctive lexical and grammatical resources to enact "a highly trained observer looking at animals and plants in nature."

Why am I using the term "social language," rather than, say, "register?" Why am I repeating, for the umpteenth time, that language always (simultaneously) constructs and reflects specific socioculturally defined and meaningful contexts? Because I want to stress the connections between the "grammar" of a social language and the work of recognizing and enacting socially situated identities. Other people studying the same phenomenon of contextually situated language often have other (although equally important) interests. I am interested in socially situated identities.

So let me take a moment and say what I mean by the "grammar" of a social language. There are two different types of "grammars" relevant to social languages. The first type of grammar is just grammar in the traditional sense of things like nouns and verbs, subjects and objects, phrases and clauses, and so forth. The other—less studied, but more important—grammar is the *rules* by which grammatical units like nouns and verbs, subjects and objects, phrases and clauses, as well as various sorts of discourse features, are used to create patterns that signal or index characteristic *whos-doing-whats-within-Discourses*. That is, we speakers and writers design our oral or written utterances to have patterns in them in virtue of which interpreters can attribute situated identities and specific activities to us and our utterances. I call this second type of grammar "d/Discourse grammar."

These patterns—grammar in the sense of d/Discourse grammar—I hasten to add, are not fancy devices of postmodern theory. They have been referred to in various ways by various sorts of linguists for a long time. They have sometimes been called, among other things, "collocational patterns." This means that various sorts of grammatical devices "co-locate" with each other. The patterns I am trying to name here are "co-relations" (correlations) among many grammatical devices, from different levels of the traditional grammar of nouns and verbs, subjects and objects, phrases and clauses (as well as discourse features, which I cannot exemplify here because the examples I present here are so short). These correlations, in turn, also co-relate to (coordinate with) nonlanguage stuff (i.e., ways of thinking-believing-valuing-acting-interacting, etc., with various other people, tools, and technologies) to constitute (for historical, i.e., *conventional* reasons) *whos-doing-whats-within-Discourses*.

For example, in Jane's utterance to her boyfriend, *What an ass that guy was, you know, her boyfriend*, note how informal terms like "ass" and "guy," the vague reference *that guy*, the informal parenthetical device *you know*, and the informal syntactic device of right dislocation (i.e., letting the phrase "her boyfriend" hang out at the end of the sentence) all pattern together to signal that this utterance is an informal social language used to achieve solidarity. Of course, as we add more specific grammatical features across longer stretches of talk, take into consideration the content of the language, and correlate both of these with nonlanguage stuff, we will converge more and more specifically onto a distinctive social language used by a distinctive group of people for distinctive purposes.

Or note how the following sentence from the professional science article I cited from Myers' work above patterns together different sorts of grammatical resources: "These egg-mimics are an unambiguous example of a plant trait evolved in response to a host-restricted group of insect herbivores." Here things like nominalizations and compounds that name entities in terms of the role they play in a theory and not directly in nature (e.g., *these egg-mimics, plant trait, host-restricted group of insect herbivores,* and the whole phrase *an unambiguous example of ...*), copulative verbs (*are*), reduced relative clauses (*plant trait evolved ...*), seriated prepositions (*of ... in ... to ... of*), and complex embedding (the phrases within phrases in *an unambiguous example of ...*) hang together to signal that this (written) utterance is a distinctive professional social language. Again, as we add more features, consider content, and correlate nonlanguage stuff, we will narrow down to a quite specific social language used by a quite specific group of biologists (or adaptationists of a certain type).

SITUATED MEANINGS

Words and phrases, in use, have, not general meanings, but "situated meanings" (or "assembled meanings"). Words and phrases are associated with different situated meanings in different contexts, in different social languages, and in different Discourses. For example, consider what happens in your head when I say, "The coffee spilled, get a mop" versus "The coffee spilled, get a broom" versus "The coffee spilled, can you restack it." In each case, you actively assemble a different situated meaning for coffee (as liquid, grains, or containers).

The concepts or meanings (or representations) with which words are associated are *assembled*, out of diverse features, on the spot, in terms of the contexts and Discourses within which they are being used (Barsalou, 1992; Clark, 1997). Different contexts and different Discourses trigger different assemblies. Sometimes these assemblies are fairly routine and automatic, thanks to having been done more or less in the same way on many past occasions; other times they require new work to come up with novel assemblies for new contexts or new Discourses.

Let me develop a bit more what I mean by saying that concepts or meanings are assembled on the spot (and for the spot, so to speak). In the context of a life world Discourse, if we are asked a question like *How far does the light go?* while staring at a lamp, we are likely to answer: *Not far, only as far as I can see the light illuminate an area near the light source.* In this case, we assemble a meaning for *light* that is something like *illuminated region.*

In the context of physical science, on the other hand, we would answer the question quite differently and assemble a different meaning. In the case of physics, there are a number of different assemblies that could be associated with *light*, one of which is *rays* (lines of light) that travel indefinitely far and that can reflect off of surfaces. In terms of this assembly, we would answer our question: *The light travels forever unless it reflects off a surface.*

Of course, there are other assemblies for *light* in yet other Discourses. For example, in the context of theater, *light* is associated with assemblies dealing with things like *lighting effects.* Furthermore, new assemblies do and can arise as Discourses change and interact or as new situations arise.

Situated meanings are, crucially, *rooted in embodied experience*—one has to see the meaning as a pattern extracted from the concrete data of experience (Barsalou, 1999). To do so one must have had lots of practice with experiences that trigger the pattern. Situated meanings are not definitions. If one can not situate the meaning of a word or phrase, then one has only a verbal or definitional meaning for the word or phrase. Such verbal meanings, although they can facilitate passing certain sorts of tests, are of limited value when language has to be put to use within activities.

The experiences in which situated meanings are rooted are ones we have had as embodied perceivers of the material world and as participants of various and sundry social practices, including rhetorical practices. Consider, for example, the following case of a high school student's first and second draft of a paper on "Albinism" (the two drafts were separated by a good deal of work on the part of the teacher):

First Draft:
Then to let people know there are different types of Albinism, I will tell and explain all this.

Second Draft:
Finally, to let people know there are different types of Albinism, I will name and describe several.

In the first case, the student appears to have formed situated meanings for *tell* and *explain* that have to do with telling a story and explicating the *big picture* (*all this*) through that story. This is, of course, an activity the student has experienced a great many times, including in his life world. Unfortunately, in the sort of academic writing in which the student was engaged, the phrase *different types of Albinism* requires its meaning to be situated in a quite different way, one inconsistent with how the student has situated the meanings of *tell* and *explain*.

If one has experienced *the activity of classifying in academic Discourses* of certain types, one would not be tempted to use *tell* and *explain* as this student has done (note that *tell* and *explain* have other situated meanings in terms of which they could occur with the phrase *different types of Albinism*—for example, a teacher could write on a student essay: "You first need to tell your readers what the different types of Albinism are and then to explain how these types are distinguished").

On the other hand, one can readily situate more appropriate meanings for *name* and *describe* consistent with the appropriate situated meaning for *different types of Albinism* (although one can situate wrong ones for *name* and *describe*, as well, of course, as in: *Scientists name different types of Albinism differently*). To do this one needs *to have experienced certain sorts of acts of classification within certain sorts of Discourses.*

I should note, as well, in passing, that even the student's second version is not quite right in terms of many academic Discourses' ways with classifying (*people* is wrong, and *name* is just a bit off—something like: *There are different types of Albinism. Below I list several of these and describe them* would have been yet better). This example, simple as it is, tells us how subtle a process situating meaning can be.

So when anyone is trying to speak/write or listen/read within a given social language within a given Discourse, the crucial question becomes, *what sorts of experiences (if any) has this person had that can anchor the situated meanings of words and phrases of this social language?* Otherwise, one is stuck with a merely general and verbal understanding (the sort that, alas, is often nonetheless rewarded in school).

SITUATED MEANINGS AND DISCOURSE MODELS

Having argued that the meanings of words are not general concepts, we can now ask why we have the feeling that words are associated with something more general? Part of the answer is simply the fact that the single word exists, and we are misled by this fact to think that a single, general meaning exists.

But, another part of the answer is that for any word each of us has access to parts (or sometimes all) of an "explanatory theory" or, better, a "Discourse model" associated with the word, which need not be and usually is not wholly conscious (D'Andrade & Strauss, 1992; Holland & Quinn, 1987; Strauss & Quinn, 1997—these sources use the terms "cultural model" or "cultural schema," rather than "Discourse model"). Discourse models are narratives, schemas, images, or (partial) theories that explain why and how certain things are connected or pattern together. Discourse models are simplified pictures of the world (they deal with what is taken as typical) as seen from the perspective of a particular Discourse.

As an example, let us return to light again and consider the notion of *light* in the life world and in physics. First of all, for most people, their everyday (life world) Discourse models associated with *light* are not the same as the models associated with *light* in physics. In most people's life worlds, there are Discourse models connected to *light* that associate it with images of light filling and giving access to, even creating, spaces, an opposition to darkness, and a variety of other images. Of course, different social groups add distinctive elements to their Discourse models of light. Having not studied the matter closely, I cannot really say what sorts of discrete life world Discourse models exist within and across societies in regard to light, although the matter is certainly open to empirical study.

On the other hand, the Discourse model of light in physics is the specialized theory of electromagnetic radiation, a *big theory* composed of many subparts (smaller models relevant to light in different ways). This theory and its subparts are more overt and articulated than most life world Discourse models. The theory and its subparts attempt to relate together several different situated meanings with which light is associated in physics: situated meanings such as light as a bundle of waves of different wave lengths; light as particles (photons) with various special (e.g., quantum like) properties; light as a beam that can be directed in various ways and for various purposes (e.g., lasers); light as colors that can mix in various fashions, and more.

It is important, too, to realize that the Discourse models that relate and help make larger sense of situated meanings are, in most domains, shared and distributed. We usually know only parts of a Discourse model (or a theory in science), but we can cooperate with other people who know other parts to act as a team that knows and can do more than any individual in the team. Furthermore, in many cases, parts of our Discourse models reside in various tools and technologies, including, of course, books (e.g., different parts of certain sorts of middle-class Discourse models of children, child development, and parenting reside in parents' and children's minds, but also in a bevy of *how to* and popular psychology books, magazines, and videos). We cooperate with such tools and technologies, as well as other people, to know and do more than we can do on our own.

And what is the *bite* of talk of Discourse models? In the absence of situated meanings, Discourse models are inert—good only for mouthing *common sense* (from some Discourse's perspective) or writing down theories on tests. Despite this fact, classrooms very often give learners pieces of theory without any situated meanings for the words in the theory. On the other hand, in the absence of Discourse models, situated meanings fail to hang together and they lack any generality. In hands on activities, learners can gain some situated meanings, but without the theory those meanings don't make any more general coherent sense.

THE KEY QUESTION

Having gotten this far, I can now state the key question that interests me about literacy: Why is it so hard to successfully acquire a new Discourse (with its concomitant oral and written social languages) when one has come to the acquisition of that Discourse as what I will call an "authentic beginner"? By the term "authentic beginner" I mean to single out those people who come to the acquisition of a Discourse—whether this involves learning to read in Ms. Smith's progressive first-grade classroom, learning to write essays in a typical *Freshman English Discourse*, or learning to be-do a graduate student in a particular discipline—without the sorts of background, previous practice, skills, values, and motivations that more advantaged learners have acquired through filtering and chains of filtering. These more advantaged learners may look like they are beginners, but they are actually "false beginners" who have had an important head start on the acquisition of the Discourse (and the identity it entails).

This is, of course, a huge question and I can hardly address it here in any really substantive way. What I can do is suggest some crucial parameters involved in the question, concentrating on those that, perhaps, seem to have less to do with literacy *proper* than other, more studied parameters. The apparatus I have developed thus far is meant to give us one way (there are other equally good ways) to talk about these parameters. I proceed here by considering a specific example.

A FIRST EXAMPLE

I want now to develop a specific example to accomplish two things: First, I demonstrate the workings of social languages, situated meanings, Discourse models, Discourses, and identities in a concrete case; second, I point out that rather subtle aspects of being (identity), doing (acting), and speaking can undermine a person's performance in a Discourse, aspects that have little to do with grammar or even language as these are traditionally construed. The implication of this last point is, of course, that language teachers need to teach more than grammar or even language. They need to teach Discourses, as well, or, better put, they need to scaffold their students through active reflection on and in Discourses and their social practices.

I once had a doctoral student from Korea in my office whose doctoral advisor had *dropped* her. She wanted me to take her on as a doctoral student, although it was clear to both of us that her prior work had not been evaluated all that highly by her previous advisor. However, that work had been carried out in an area that was both notoriously difficult and not really all that relevant to what the student, in fact, wanted to do for her thesis. It was clear, as well, that she would need a good deal of further training in my area (discourse analysis) before she could start her thesis work in earnest. In the course of our discussion about her past work and her future prospects, when I was showing some reluctance to take her on as a student, the student said the following:

It is your job to help me, I need to learn.

This utterance is, of course, in impeccable English. It was, nonetheless, couched in a social language that I did not expect, one that, in turn, communicated to me a Discourse model, situated meanings, and an identity I did not expect. This encounter made me more consciously aware of the social language, Discourse models, situated meanings, and identity I expected of a doctoral student in this sort of encounter in a research-based university. This kind of mismatch in expectations can have very real consequences, and, indeed, did for this student who had already been turned down by all other relevant possible advisors (unbeknownst to me at the time).

After several conversations with this student, it seemed to me that one of the Discourse models she was operating with was a distinctive model of faculty–student relationships. The Discourse model I attributed to her was something like this:

Discourse Model:
A faculty member (who is in a *helping* profession) is morally obligated, in virtue of the definition of the position and job he or she holds, to give aid to a student (who is in the role of a client or patient, in a sense) who is having problems and who needs help learning, just so long as the student wants to work hard. It does not matter how much time or how much effort this will require from the faculty member. In return, the student will give the faculty member deference, respect, loyalty, thanks, and certain forms of assistance.

I have no idea whether this Discourse model is connected in any way to Korean culture, nor does it matter in the least, for my purposes here. And, indeed, in some settings (e.g., in many elementary schools), lots of U.S. teachers do, in fact, operate by something much like this model. Unfortunately, this model is not one with which many doctoral advisors at research universities operate. Many of them, at least in my experience, operate with a Discourse model something like the following:

Discourse Model:
A faculty member is willing to give a good deal of time and effort to doctoral students who are near their thesis work only when they have shown they can *make it*, produce good work, and become a *credit* to the faculty member, thereby justifying the effort that the faculty member puts into the student (and takes away from his or her own research).

The Korean student enacted a socially situated identity not connected to this Discourse model: the identity of a needy, problem-plagued, suppliant. In fact, her Discourse model implied that the needier students were, the more obligated the faculty member was to help them (provided they were willing to keep working hard). This is, I believe, just the identity that is guaranteed, in many doctoral programs in U.S. research universities, to get you no advisor or, indeed, to lose one you already have. The identity this student needed to enact, at least if she was to match my initial expectations, was that of a self-motivated, advanced graduate student with goals that no longer fit her previous advisor, but with growing interests and potential strengths and skills in my area.

Finally, the student's socially situated identity and her Discourse led me to attribute specific situated meanings to her words. In turn, of course, these situated meanings helped create the identity and Discourse model I have discussed. These things—identity, Discourse models, and situated meanings—are all reflexively related. Each of these both creates and reflects—at one and the same time—all the others. They are a package deal and that's why *one has to get the whole package right*.

For example, in the student's utterance, within its overall context, the word *help* took on the situated mean, here and now, of something like *charitable assistance*. I had been expecting a situated meaning more like *professional guidance*, as it might have had she said: "With your help, I believe I can write a really good thesis." Or, to take another example, the student's word *need*. In this context, it took on the situated meaning of *neediness* in the sense of something like: "my ability to learn is inadequate without a good deal of effort on your part," when I would have expected a situated meaning more like "good, but still able to be supplemented," as it might have had she said: "Though I have a pretty good background in linguistics, I need you to help me develop it further to do a really good thesis."

Now someone is bound, at this point, to ask, perhaps in exasperation, "But what's this got to do with literacy? How well did this student write?" Of course, I want to suggest that for students like this one, learning language and literacy ought to be about learning social languages and Discourse models within Discourses, not just about oral or written English per se. And Discourses always involve multiple ways of acting-interacting-speaking-writing-listening-reading-thinking-believing-valuing-feeling with others at the right times and in the right places so as to get recognized as enacting an appropriate socially situated identity. It's a package deal—it does you no good to get bits and pieces of the Discourse right, you have to get the whole thing right.

The fact that the Korean student did not seem to understand the social language, situated meanings, and Discourse models required for her to be-and-do an advanced graduate student seeking a thesis advisor certainly led me to suspect that she did not understand the sorts of related social languages, situated meanings, and Discourse models required for diverse writing tasks in the Discourse in which she was seeking my mentorship. Reading her work (as well as reading new work she wrote at my request) simply bore that out. The grammatical errors in her writing were a minor matter. Her failure to situate (customize) meaning in terms of the sorts of experiences, conversations, texts, and Discourse models that instantiate the Discourses she was attempting to write within was the problem. In fact, ironically, perhaps, her words, phrases, and sentences had only the sorts of general and canned meanings that have traditionally been thought, incorrectly, to be what meaning is all about.

POLITICAL COMPLICATIONS

Discourses are inherently and irredeemably political and so is the process of acquiring them. They are political in three ways: First, internal to a Discourse there are almost always hierarchical positions (e.g., doctoral advisor—thesis advisee). Second, Discourse are partly defined in relationships of alignment and conflict with other Discourses (e.g., the Discourse of being-and-doing a certain sort of middle-class child is more compatible with the forms of language, practices, and values of early school-based Discourses than is the Discourse of being-and-doing a child in some non-middle-class homes and in the homes of some non-Anglo ethnic groups). Third, Discourses are harder to acquire and often tension-filled for many of those who have come to their acquisition as what I referred to earlier as "authentic beginners." Such people are often marginalized by the Discourse they are attempting to acquire as they are compared to more advantaged "false beginners," that is, people who have already gained a good deal of practice, in earlier related Discourses, with skills and identities relevant to the new Discourse.

There is no doubt that issues of power, culture, and gender were at play in the example I have just sketched. In fact, the moment-to-moment outcomes of such interactions are often over determined in the sense that issues of status, culture, and gender (and often class) are operating simultaneously and sometimes in alignment with each other. But the issue I want to concentrate on here is that this (quite bright) student had spent years as a graduate student in the United States and still did not know how to navigate in the Discourse in ways that ensured she would move from being a peripheral participant in it to becoming a central participant (Lave & Wenger, 1991).

This was, of course, not her *fault*. She was failed by the institution she was in, although she was, of course, also a participant in that failure. There are a good many reasons for this sort of failure—most of them having to do with institutional priorities connected to status and power that I cannot discuss here—but such failures also operate because people within academic institutions are often blind to how much there is beyond reading and writing involved in the successful acquisition of an academic Discourse. They are blind to how many, often subtle, aspects of *being-doing-valuing-feeling with language and other semiotic resources, moment-by-moment, within social interactions* are also crucially involved.

Finally, let me say, too, that the points I have made about this example are not meant to be about foreign graduate students only and per se. They are meant to apply to all types of authentic beginners, whether these be first graders learning to read or college students seeking access to academic Discourses. As I said previously, by "authentic beginners" I mean people, whether children or adults, who have come to learning sites of any sort *without* the sorts of early preparation, pre-alignment in terms of cultural values, and sociocultural resources that more advantaged learners at those sites possess.

ANOTHER EXAMPLE

I now close this paper with a brief discussion of situated meanings and Discourse models at work in the sorts of written language one would typically find in college. I argue that the same tools I have discussed earlier apply here, as well. More specifically, I argue that language form relates to function not just in a general sense, but in quite local and specific ways tied to the nature of particular Discourses and their associated Discourse models.

Consider, in this regard, then, the following sentences from Paul Gagnon's book *Democracy's Untold Story: What World History Textbooks Neglect* (1987, pp. 65–71):

> Also secure, by 1689, was the principle of representative government, as tested against the two criteria for valid constitutions proposed in the previous chapter. As to the first criterion, there was a genuine balance of power in English society, expressing itself in the Whig and Tory parties. *As narrowly confined to the privileged classes as these were*, they nonetheless represented different factions and tendencies. Elections meant real choice among separate, contending parties and personalities.

In his book, sponsored by the American Federation of Teachers, the Education Excellence Network, and Freedom House, Gagnon speaks to what he thinks ought to be the *essential plot* of Western history as taught in schools. Gagnon's work has played an important role in the debate over national and state history standards in schools, a debate essentially about what ought to count as history in schools. In fact, Gagnon helped write several of the drafts of the Massachusetts history standards. Although the passage above is from a book written in 1987, the issues it deals with, and the ways in which it deals with them, are still current in terms of contemporary debates about history in the schools.

Consider the sentence: "As narrowly confined to the privileged classes as these were, they nonetheless represented different factions and tendencies." The underlined "as" clause is a nonfinite clause that has several typical functions in English. For example, it states background information, that is, information that is not directly asserted, but is treated as taken-for-granted (assumed) background information in terms of which the information foregrounded in the main clause ("they nonetheless represented different factions and tendencies") can be understood and evaluated. This background clause also functions as a concession, that is, it concedes a problem or issue that might affect how one evaluates the information in the main clause. The clause has several other functions, as well.

However, this rather general linking of form and function—although important—is not really enough to render this sentence, and the passage it is in, fully senseful for a reader. To render the sentence and the passage fully senseful, the reader needs to understand the specific functions this sentence is serving here and now in this text. And to do this, the reader needs to understand how this sentence functions not just in the text, but within the Discourse the text is a part of.

Gagnon's use of "As narrowly confined to the privileged classes as these were" as a backgrounded, concessive clause allows him to treat the fact that the Whig and Tory parties were confined "to the privileged classes" as background, taken-for-granted information, despite the fact that some other historians might see this *as a focal piece of information* that actually destroys the claim made in his main clause ("they nonetheless represented different factions and tendencies"). Gagnon is writing from within a specific Discourse model common to certain kinds of historians (and not others). This model runs something like this: Democracy unfolded in a single linear historical process in terms of which Western societies moved from having less of it to having more of it and in terms of which the struggles of earlier groups (like the elite Whigs and Tories) were contributors to the struggles of later (often less elite) groups (like women and African Americans). In terms of this model, the way in which Gagnon has matched form and function in his sentence, backgrounding certain information through the *as* clause and foregrounding other information in his main clause, appears natural and unproblematic.

When a reader understands and accepts this Discourse model, he or she is guided to situate the meanings of words like *representative government*, *elections*, and (elsewhere in Gagnon's text) *democracy* in quite specific ways. The reader is guided or encouraged to construct situated meanings for *representative government* and *democracy* in terms of which a legislative body is *representative* despite the fact that most people are unrepresented by it, and a nation is a *democracy* despite the fact that most people are not allowed to vote. Many schooled readers have so often situated meanings for these sorts of words along just these lines that they seem perfectly natural, even automatic. But, from the point of view of other Discourse models, even within history, such situated meanings can come to seem absurd and rendered much less automatic.

For example, there are other sorts of historians who operate with other sorts of Discourse models than Gagnon does. Some historians operate with Discourse models in terms of which the Whigs and Tories, far from being ancestors for women and African Americans in the democratic struggle, are part and parcel of the forces that have oppressed and opposed them. They were not harbingers for the democracy, such as it is, that women and African Americans have achieved, but forces that historically helped delay and forestall it. For these historians, history is not one continuous story of ever-increasing democracy. Rather, it is a set of discontinuous struggles—some moving toward greater democracy, some away from it—between *haves* and *have nots*, struggles that problematize the notion of democracy in 17th century England and even in the contemporary United States. In terms of these alternative Discourse models, much of Gagnon's text takes on situated meanings in terms of which it seems, at points, contradictory.

Let me mention that part of the texture of history as an academic Discourse is the competition and contestation between these two sorts of Discourse models (and others). Furthermore, it may very well be the case that these models are not *empirical* in the sense that *facts* could determine that one of them is *true* and the other *false*. The models really represent different ways of seeing the world, different perspectives that background and foreground events in the past in different ways.

It is unfortunate, however, that too often texts like Gagnon's are used in debates about public policy (e.g., what to teach in the schools) by a public that is unaware of contending Discourse models (even within the Discourse of academic history) and unaware of how automatically they have situated meanings for words like "democracy" that may, from other perspectives, appear paradoxical. Of course, this is where critical literacy comes into play. When we juxtapose different Discourse models and different ways of situating meanings within and across Discourses we can destabilize automatic processes and get people to reflect overtly on meaning making and the sociopolitical functioning of Discourses in society.

Now my point is just this: One cannot understand Gagnon's grammar, nor his larger meanings, if one does not know how to situate the meanings of his words, phrases, and grammatical choices within specific Discourse models connected to the values and interests of specific Discourses. Otherwise, one has only a verbal understanding of Gagnon's text. Readers can only situate the meanings of Gagnon's words and phrases if they have had experiences with reading texts like Gagnon's as part and parcel of interactions with a variety of texts and other people within and across a variety of aligned and competing Discourses (e.g., academic history, school history, and public policy Discourses). They can situate his meanings, too, only if they are willing (and able) to engage in the sort of identity work and transformations that this activity of situating requires.

And here we must acknowledge that some types of readers, and not other types, will find it repugnant to situate Gagnon's meanings in the ways in which his text invites readers to do. These readers—provided they have acquired a Discourse that allows them to do so—can resist Gagnon's text by situating his words and phrases within a different Discourse, one which may bring out paradoxes and contradictions in his text.

Just as I argued earlier, when discussing the Korean student, that teaching language ought to be about teaching meaning making within Discourses, so, here, too, my argument is the same. To teach anyone to read Gagnon's text—or texts like it—one would have to teach them how Discourse models and situated meanings work within specific Discourses. Teaching grammar, even in the sense of general form-function mappings, is not sufficient. One has to teach how grammatical forms relate to very specific functions within very specific Discourses.

CONCLUSION

There is a deep paradox at work in schools in relation to Discourses. At virtually every level of schooling, it is often difficult to know just what Discourse or Discourses are at stake. Actually, in any classroom, multiple Discourses are simultaneously at stake. Students can be successful or not, and in different ways, in regard to each of these and in terms of their complex relations to each other.

In an overly simplified way, we can say that there are often three sorts of Discourses present in any classroom. First, there is almost always some form of "sorting Discourse" (or more than one). The sorting Discourse recruits students' ways with words, beliefs, values, knowledge, information, deeds, other people, objects, tools, places, and times to sort them into evaluative categories of a great variety (e.g., good student, good reader, good at math; poor student, disabled reader, not good at math, LD).

Second, there are ways of being an "acceptable" kind of student in a particular classroom, program, or school. A given teacher, program, or school builds (consciously or not, coherently or not) a specific culture of which learners become (more or less) members. I call this an "in-house Discourse" (and, again, there may be more than one). Such Discourses position the student as a certain sort of learner, knower, and person engaged in certain sorts of ways (and not others) with words, beliefs, values, knowledge, information, deeds, other people, objects, tools, and places. This Discourse may or may not be closely related to the sorting Discourse, although, of course, it nearly always contracts some relationship with it.

Third, learners may be required to master some set of social practices, in depth, that have integral connections, in words, deeds, and identity formation, to related social practices outside school. For example, a learner may learn some part of science in such a way that the learner can use this knowledge to understand deep conceptual connections and engage in problem solving in ways that resemble, in some substantive (however partial) way, how these things work in a science-based Discourse outside of school. Or, to take another sort of example, a learner in a social studies class may engage in specific forms of community activism connected to the practices and identities of local community activists of certain sorts. I call these "exterior Discourses," allowing for the fact that they are often, in reality, classroom simulations of outside Discourses. In exterior Discourses, the learner *walks the walk* and *talks the talk*, in some important respects, of a Discourse whose main home is not in the school. Exterior Discourses can, of course, fit more or less well or poorly with the sorting Discourse or the in-house Discourse.

One and the same fact, concept, object, tool, or practice can be part of each of these Discourses and, thus, play a different role in each case. For example, a hands-on science-like activity could be fodder for the sorting Discourse, a framework for the in-house Discourse, or an element of an exterior Discourse. It may have a different role or meaning in each case. We cannot tell which role it is playing unless we look at the whole context it is in.

It is, of course, a mainstay of the "hidden curriculum" literature that in schools very often exterior Discourses do not exist (Varenne & McDermott, 1998). Rather, what is called "science," "math," or "history" usually amounts only to some form of *doing school* that is simply in the service of (is simply the material for) the sorting Discourse(s) and/or the in-house Discourse(s). Indeed, in many colleges and universities, Freshman Writing has become an in-house Discourse all its own with few substantive ties to other Discourses at play elsewhere in the college or university.

It would take another chapter, of greater length than this one, to deal with the complexity of Discourses in schools. What I want to suggest in this chapter is only this: For authentic beginners and the faculty who deal with them, it is crucial to place the issue of Discourses at the forefront of education. Such learners need to gain meta-awareness about how specific Discourses work and how Discourses work across schools, colleges, and universities, as well as society as a whole. They need also to gain embodied experiences within Discourses that can offer them new and valued identities. In the end, however, perhaps this is what schooling should be about for everyone.

REFERENCES

Barsalou, L. W. (1992). *Cognitive psychology: An overview for cognitive scientists*. Hillsdale, NJ: Lawrence Erlbaum Associates.

Barsalou, L. W. (1999). Language comprehension: Archival memory or preparation for situated action. *Discourse Processes, 28*, 61–80.

Barton, D. (1994). *Literacy: An introduction to the ecology of written language*. Oxford, UK: Blackwell.

Clark, A. (1997). *Being there: Putting brain, body, and world together again.* Cambridge, MA: MIT Press.

D'Andrade, R., & Strauss, C. (Eds.). (1992). *Human motives and cultural models.* Cambridge, UK: Cambridge University Press.

Daniel, J. L., & Smitherman, G. (1990). How I got over: Communication dynamics in the Black community. In D. Carbaugh, (Ed.), *Cultural communication and intercultural contact* (pp. 27–44). Hillsdale, NJ: Lawrence Erlbaum Associates.

Gagnon, P. (1987). *Democracy's untold story: What world history textbooks neglect.* Washington, DC: American Federation of Teachers.

Gee, J. P. (1996). *Social linguistics and literacies: Ideology in Discourses* (2nd ed.). London: Taylor & Francis.

Gee, J. P. (1999). *An introduction to discourse analysis: Theory and method.* London: Routledge.

Gee, J. P. (2000). The new literacy studies: From "socially situated" to the work of the social. In D. Barton, M. Hamilton, & R. Ivanic, (Eds.), *Situated literacies: Reading and writing in context* (pp. 180–196). London: Routledge.

Habermas, J. (1984). *Theory of communicative action, Vol. 1,* (T. McCarthy, trans.). London: Heinemann.

Holland, D., & Quinn, N. (Eds). (1987). *Cultural models in language and thought.* Cambridge, UK: Cambridge University Press.

Kress, G. (1997). *Before writing: Rethinking paths into literacy.* London: Routledge.

Latour, B. (1999). *Pandora's hope: Essays on the reality of science studies.* Cambridge, MA: Harvard University Press.

Lave, J., & Wenger, E. (1991). *Situated learning: Legitimate peripheral participation.* Cambridge, UK: Cambridge University Press.

Myers, G. (1992). *Writing biology: Texts in the social construction of scientific knowledge.* Madison: University of Wisconsin Press.

Rogoff, B., & Toma, C. (1997). Shared thinking: Cultural and institutional variations. *Discourse Processes, 23,* 471–497.

Strauss, C., & Quinn, N. (1997). *A cognitive theory of cultural meaning.* Cambridge, UK: Cambridge University Press

Street, B. (1995). *Social literacies: Critical approaches to literacy in development, ethnography and education.* London: Longman.

Varenne, H., & McDermott, R. (1998). *Successful failure: The school America builds.* Boulder, CO: Westview.

Wieder, D. L., & Pratt, S. (1990). On being a recognizable Indian among Indians. In D. Carbaugh, (Ed.), *Cultural communication and intercultural contact,* (pp. 45–64). Hillsdale, NJ: Lawrence Erlbaum Associates.

9

African American
Language and Literacy

John Baugh
Stanford University

Tremendous misunderstanding still surrounds issues of language and literacy among African Americans. This chapter describes the ways that the situation of African Americans differs from that of other immigrants to the United States and highlights the consequences of those differences for the literacy skills development of African American students. It then describes the ways that African American vernacular English differs from standard English and the implications of these differences for literacy development. Finally, it suggests ways that we can adopt a pedagogy that is mindful of the linguistic skills students bring to school at the same time that it helps them move toward achievement of advanced literacy.

THE UNIQUE LINGUISTIC HERITAGE OF AFRICAN SLAVE DESCENDANTS IN THE UNITED STATES

As is the case with every racial and ethnic group in the United States, African Americans are highly diverse, and defy monolithic classification in racial or linguistic terms.[1] However, the first people of African descent to arrive in the Americas did so as slaves, and not as immigrants in search of freedom, wealth, and

---

[1]For example, advances in DNA technology remind us that women of African descent often bore the children of their owners, thereby mixing the races since the inception of slavery. It is futile to attempt to provide a biological definition of African American identity; for the purpose of this discussion, we focus on those people of African descent who self-identify as "African American." In some cases such self-identified African Americans are naturalized citizens who emigrated to this country more recently; whereas others—who are the major object of this discussion—can trace all or part of their ancestry to enslaved Africans in America.

enhanced opportunities. Slaves, as property, were not *free* to exercise the common liberties of other citizens in the postcolonial birth of the United States. At that time it was illegal to teach a slave how to read or write. Even after President Lincoln's *Emancipation Proclamation*, ex-slaves did not gain access to good schools or the high levels of literacy that such schools typically instill. The lingering shadow of racial segregation forces us to seek new ways to overcome the problem of low levels of literacy among African American students.

African American slave descendants have a unique linguistic heritage. Although they were in contact with different European languages, including French, Spanish, and Portuguese, people of African descent in North and South America share common linguistic attributes that gave rise to the Black English trial in 1979 (see Smitherman, 1981), and the Ebonics[2] controversy of 1997 (see Baugh, 1999, 2000; Rickford & Rickford, 2000). Whereas the typical European immigrants may have arrived in the United States with very little money and no knowledge of English, they did so with other speakers of their indigenous mother tongues, and typically formed communities where they continued to speak those languages. For slave descendents, on the other hand, the situation was quite different.

Whenever possible, slave traders would isolate slaves by language in an attempt to restrict uprisings. This prevented African Americans from using their native tongues, forcing them to adopt the language of the slave owners. Because slaves were overtly denied access to literacy and formal education, their English acquisition was impeded by capricious racial and legal obstacles that reinforced the subordination of enslaved Africans and their posterity. Negative stereotypes about slaves were then reinforced by negative stereotypes about their speech. This speech was further misrepresented in vaudeville, movies, television, advertising, and cartoons that indoctrinated those who saw them with the message that blacks, speaking nonstandard English, were simply less intelligent than whites.

These negative images persist today, and it is on this uneven linguistic landscape that teachers seek to nurture literacy. The combination of impoverished education and a devalued linguistic heritage that was reinforced through slavery and racial segregation set the wheels in motion that resulted in the Ebonics controversy and other attempts to increase standard English proficiency and literacy among

---

[2]Psychologist Robert Williams coined the term "Ebonics," defining it as "the linguistic and paralinguistic cues that on a concentric continuum represent the communicative competence of the West African, Caribbean, and United States slave descendant of African origin. It includes the various idioms, patois, argots, idiolects and social dialects of black people, especially those that have been forced to adapt to colonial circumstances" (Williams 1975, p. 5). This original definition of Ebonics concentrates not on English, or the United States; rather, it is a term that refers to the linguistic consequences of the African slave trade. The original definition of Ebonics also applies to the Caribbean and West Africa, although Ebonics speakers in Haiti or Brazil do not share the same language as African slave descendants who reside in the United States. However, because events in Oakland catapulted Ebonics onto the world stage, the vast majority of people around the world, including many linguists, have come to equate Ebonics with the speech of Black Americans.

students of African descent.[3] Many people would like to ignore the unique linguistic legacy of the African slave trade throughout North and South America in the name of asserting that today all are equal. People of African descent are expected to follow the path of other immigrants in adopting the dominant language (and dialect) of the nation where they live.

In an effort to support Oakland educators, and to enlist linguistic expertise, linguists of considerable stature began to embrace the term "Ebonics," but they did so based on Oakland's definition, not that originally proposed by Williams in 1975 (see O'Neil, 1998). As a result, the available literature is divided with respect to the definition of Ebonics.

Ogbu's (1978) distinction between voluntary and involuntary immigration is very relevant to this matter, because those whose ancestors came to the United States voluntarily did so with access to schooling and a desire to master English. But involuntary immigrants, in this instance African slaves, were denied access to their mother tongues and to schools. They learned English through pidginization and creolization rather than through a gradual bilingual transition to English, as did other immigrants.

Pidginization, which results in the birth of a new language born of contact between two or more mutually unintelligible parent languages, took place throughout the world, accompanying the African slave trade. The British, Dutch, Portuguese, and Spanish, and many Africans themselves were merchants of human cargo, and the linguistic consequences of slavery uprooted Africans from their native speech communities into a foreign linguistic context where their native language was not understood.

When the children of these slaves first heard languages, they were often the pidgin languages spoken by their parents and others who interacted with slaves. As a result, the pidgin was transformed into a Creole. Creolization is the evolutionary process whereby a pidgin (which has no native speakers) becomes a creole language as it becomes the first language of the children of the pidgin speakers. There remains considerable controversy over a host of historical, political, and linguistic details surrounding the linguistic legacy of slavery. These controversies, in turn, resonate among scholars who seek ways to improve educational prospects for African American students.

AFRICAN AMERICAN LANGUAGE: A DIALECT OR SEPARATE LANGUAGE?

Even linguists have not always valued African American vernacular as a cohesive linguistic system with its own integrity and structure. Because the language of slaves

---

[3]The Oakland, California, Unified School District's Board of Education endorsed a resolution in 1997 declaring that "African-American people, and their children, are from home environments in which a language other than the English language is dominant ... " (see Baugh, 2000, p. 39). Oakland's board stated that their primary motivation was to improve the education of the vast majority of African American students who were having considerable difficulty with school. Some journalists speculated that Oakland's board was planning to seek bilingual education funding; funding that is provided to students who are not native speakers of English. Although some African Americans, for example, Haitian Americans, in many instances have learned English as a second language, this is not the case for the majority of African Americans.

was devalued, so too was the study of their speech. Why would language scholars be concerned with *bad speech* or other *corrupt* forms of the language? In addition, European languages had established writing traditions whereas the African languages—with an oral tradition—did not; thereby also causing some to devalue these languages. But studies of Black speech by language scholars in the 1960s and 1970s exposed the lack of a linguistic basis for the negative stereotypes associated with this dialect and demonstrated the logical coherence of vernacular African American English (AAE; e.g., Bailey, 1965, 1966; Dillard, 1972; Fasold, 1972; Labov, 1969, 1972; Smitherman, 1978; Wolfram, 1969). Since 1972, linguists have referred to Black speech as "Black English" or "African American English." The misconceptions of nonlinguists about African American language behavior (i.e., in speech and writing) have been identified and dismantled by linguists, but much misunderstanding still exists within the educational community and the community at large.

Whereas dominant dialects, typically spoken by affluent and well educated members of a speech community, are often equated with *correct* or *proper* speech in provincial folk mythology, linguists recognize that nonstandard dialects are also fully formed linguistic systems that serve their speakers well in their lives and communities. Linguists contrast *standard* dialects and *nonstandard* dialects, and reject the notion that some dialects are *bad English*. The antonyms in Table 9.1 illustrate the contrast between the linguistic and folk notions.

Linguists consistently use *nonstandard English* rather than the derogatory folk terminology, because African American English is a coherent dialect; it is not flawed either logically or grammatically.

The unique linguistic history of the manner in which slaves and their descendants learned English has raised important questions about the classification of dialects and languages, as well as about the social, racial, and geographic parameters that determine where a dialect ends and a language begins. The vast majority of African Americans speak English, albeit through a broad range of socially stratified dialects spread across urban and rural communities. The extent to which their speech conforms to standard American English, or is dissimilar from standard dialects of American English will vary based on a host of personal, circumstantial, and historical variables that are both obvious and inherently complex.

TABLE 9.1

Contrasting Terminology for English Dialects

Preferred Linguistic Terminology

Standard English	←—→	*Nonstandard English*

Folk terms for standard and nonstandard English

Correct English	←—→	Incorrect English
Proper English	←—→	Improper English
Good English	←—→	Bad English

The vast majority of African Americans have learned English natively, but they span a broad range of regional, social, and educational dialects. Despite this considerable diversity, many similarities exist among speakers of vernacular African American English across the United States. For example, the use of habitual *be* as in *They be happy*, has been attested in urban and rural African American speakers across the nation.

Those who would like to know more about AAE phonological features, such as the use of /f/ for /th/ in word-final position (as in "boof" for "booth"), or zero usage of final consonants in consonant clusters (as in "lif" for "lift" or "las" for "last") should consult Wolfram (1994) and Bailey and Thomas (1998). Such features have been shown to be dialect differences in pronunciation that are equivalent to other phonological differences in dialects that are typically referred to as different "accents."

Grammatical differences, beyond the "*be*" example previously cited, are described more fully by Rickford (1999), including evidence pertaining to *done, been*, and Preterite Had + Verb-ed structures such as *Bob had kicked the ball* instead of *Bob kicked the ball* or *He had went home* instead of *He went home*. These linguistic details are significant for many reasons. They not only reveal the precise differences between dominant linguistic norms, they confirm potential (and authentic) sources of linguistic confusion and interference for many African American students who encounter academic difficulty in school.

But these differences are not significant enough to account for the failure of many African American students to develop advanced literacy skills. Speaking a nonstandard dialect is not the primary reason for these students' difficulties in school. In many countries, children who speak nonstandard dialects are very successful in attaining high levels of advanced literacy in the standard dialect. In the United States, however, because of the unique history of African Americans, there is little understanding of the linguistic and educational issues that face these students, and they are often stigmatized for speaking nonstandard English, which is all too often made the primary reason for their failure at school.

OVERCOMING LINGUISTIC BARRIERS IN BIDIALECTAL AFRICAN AMERICAN COMMUNITIES

The vast majority of U.S. citizens and residents do not understand the plight of African American students who are unsuccessful in school. Based on survey after survey across the country, the vast majority of people lay the blame for educational failure at the feet of the student, and perhaps their parents (or guardians). The linguistic issues are rarely addressed.

Extensive evidence confirms that many African Americans, urban and rural, speak nonstandard vernacular dialects of English that are stigmatized by the larger society, and often by the educational system. Teachers today seldom have linguistic training or adequate resources to understand the language issues that would prepare them to fully cultivate their students' language and literacy skills. Educational policies need to address the educational inequalities that were originally born of slavery, and further incubated through racial segregation and poverty. Linguistic barriers have been recognized as one of the largest hurdles confronting the typical African

American student and leading to academic failure. Indeed, this was the primary jus-tification for the Oakland School Board's African American Task Force to pursue Ebonics (see Baugh, 2000; Rickford & Rickford, 2000; Smitherman, 2000). Any educational policy that builds on the notion that a dominant dialect is syn-onymous with the *proper* or *correct* dialect is misguided at its outset. But the general public, and many educators, do not understand what a nonstandard dialect is. Fur-thermore, the educational implications of students speaking nonstandard dialects are still very controversial. Some strive to eradicate the nonstandard dialect; oth-ers urge that we value the dialects students bring to school and build on them as we help students gain literacy skills.

In testimony before the U.S. Senate in 1997, Labov described the situation as follows:

> There are two major points of view taken by educators. One view is that any recogni-tion of a nonstandard language as a legitimate means of expression will only confuse children, and reinforce their tendency to use it instead of standard English. The other is that children learn most rapidly in their home language, and that they can benefit in both motivation and achievement by getting a head start in learning to read and write in this way. Both of these are honestly held and deserve a fair hearing. (Labov, 1997)

Unfortunately, neither of these views adequately addresses the issue of how ad-vanced levels of literacy can be achieved by speakers of AAE. Most of the work in this area has focused on emergent literacy, learning in the early years; for example, through the use of dialect readers (Labov, 1994; Rickford & Rickford, 1995).

One way to address this is to focus on students' abilities to shift their style of speech. All speakers modify their speech according to the situations they are par-ticipating in (Ervin-Tripp, 1972; Giles & Powesland, 1975). My earliest work on African American language (Baugh, 1983) studied the ways in which these speak-ers modified their speech to suit their immediate situation. Inspired greatly by the work of Ferguson (1959) and Brown and Gilman (1960), I was seeking to identify those linguistic elements that appeared to be within the conscious control of vari-ous African American adults; that is, depending on the relative formality of any given speech event. For example, most African Americans that I interviewed were more likely to use African American English in the presence of familiar acquain-tances regardless of race, and their speech was much more formal when they were meeting someone for the first time. This was most evident in terms of phonological and morphological variation; the more intimate the relationship, the more vernac-ular features of AAE appeared. Less familiar relationships were often marked by striking phonological, morphological, and grammatical movement toward stan-dard English norms.

This kind of adjustment according to situation is not the same as the code-mix-ing and code-switching that occurs in bilingual communities. Switching between two (often mutually unintelligible) languages is not the same as shifting between two (often highly intelligible) dialects. Under many circumstances, African Amer-ican students will become bidialectal; that is, they will acquire the skill to shift be-tween their home vernacular and standard English with relative ease and considerable proficiency. But motivating students to make these style shifts is not easy. Many minority students seek to avoid behavior that they consider to be *White*, and language is included among these perceptions (see Fordham & Ogbu, 1986).

Students can be encouraged to adopt new styles or registers in their speaking and writing, however, if they see the value of such linguistic skill. Delpit (1995) suggests some ideas for working with students who speak nonstandard English, including comparing features of the dialects, encouraging students to translate or style shift between dialects, and conducting activities in which standard English is called for, where students need to play roles using standard English. To those who argue that we should not interfere with students' dialects at all, Delpit (1998) argues that teaching academic discourse to African American students is both possible and necessary.

Kutz (1986) also addresses the controversy about using students' language versus initiating them into academic discourse by arguing that although students have the right to their own language, teachers need to focus on helping them develop proficiency with academic discourse. She calls for a middle ground based on what we know about style-shifting, comparing learning a new dialect to learning a new language. She suggests, for example, that writing courses focus on helping students learn to ask questions as experts in a discipline would. She criticizes a focus on error instead of on the growth of the writer, and suggests that teachers need to understand that features will occur in students' writing that reflect neither the source nor the target language. With a conceptual framework that sees student writing as a stage in a developmental process, we can understand their errors as developmental, systematic, rule-governed, predictable, and transitional, and can focus beyond the errors on the whole language production.

We need to focus on the writing development of African American students who are working to achieve advanced literacy. Studies of writing such as Whiteman (1981) demonstrate that all speakers of nonstandard dialects show dialect features in their writing, but that developmental factors also play a role. Students need opportunities to develop advanced writing skills through engagement in motivating tasks that are relevant to their purposes in learning.

Linguistic differences are but the tip of a substantially larger iceberg where differences in the allocation of educational resources, glaring differences in class sizes, and the variable quality of school teachers all contribute substantially to a student's overall academic performance. Rather than continue the practice of chastising African American students for speaking differently than members of the majority culture, educators (and their African American students) are more likely to meet with success if they adopt a pedagogy that is motivational and mindful of the language and culture that students bring with them to school. Rather than attempt to eliminate all traces of African American vernacular, they should help students learn and acquire knowledge of the grammatical differences between standard English and nonstandard vernacular African American English. In much the same manner that we do not demand that representatives of Congress abandon their regional accents in pursuit of their professional careers, so too would it be wrong to demand that African American students cleanse all ethnic traces of their speech in their quest to gain standard English proficiency. The ultimate goal is to enhance the communication and educational prospects for all students, regardless of their background or the languages that they bring to school.

REFERENCES

Bailey, B. (1965). "Toward a new perspective in Negro English dialectology." *American Speech 40,* 171–177.

Bailey, B. (1966). *Jamaican Creole syntax.* London: Cambridge University Press.

Bailey, G., & Thomas, E. (1998). Some aspects of African American English phonology. In S. Mufwene, J. Rickford, G. Bailey, & J. Baugh (Eds.), *African American English, structure, history, and use,* (pp. 227–244). London: Routledge.

Baugh, J. (1983). *Black street speech: Its history, structure and survival.* Austin: University of Texas Press.

Baugh, J. (1999). *Out of the mouths of slaves: African American English and educational malpractice.* Austin: University of Texas Press.

Baugh, J. (2000). *Beyond Ebonics: Linguistic pride and racial prejudice.* New York: Oxford University Press.

Brown, R., & Gilman, A. (1960). The pronouns of power and solidarity. In T. A. Sebeok (Ed.), *Style in language* (pp. 253–276). Cambridge, MA: MIT Press.

Delpit, L. (1995). *Other people's children: Cultural conflict in the classroom.* New York: The New Press.

Delpit, L. (1998). The politics of teaching literate discourse. In V. Zamel & R. Spack (Eds.), *Negotiating academic literacies: Teaching and learning across languages and cultures,* (pp. 207–218). Mahwah, NJ: Lawrence Erlbaum Associates.

Dillard, J. L. (1972). *Black English.* New York: Random House.

Ervin-Tripp, S. (1972). On sociolinguistic rules: Alternation and co-occurrence. In J. J. Gumperz & D. Hymes (Eds.), *Directions in sociolinguistics: The ethnography of communication,* (pp. 213–250). New York: Holt, Rinehart and Winston.

Fasold, R. (1972). *Tense and the form 'be' in Black English.* Washington, DC: Center for Applied Linguistics.

Ferguson, C. (1959). Diglossia. *Word, 15,* 325–340.

Fordham, S., & Ogbu, J. (1986). Black students' school success: Coping with the burden of 'Acting White.' *The Urban Review, 8*(3), 176–206.

Giles, H., & Powesland, P. (1975). *Speech styles and social evaluation.* New York: Academic Press.

Kutz, E. (1986). Between students' language and academic discourse: Interlanguage as middle ground. *College English, 48*(4), 385–396.

Labov, W. (1969). The logic of nonstandard English. In J. Alatis (Ed.), *Georgetown Monographs on Language and Linguistics* (Vol. 22, pp. 1–31). Washington, DC: Georgetown University Press.

Labov, W. (1972). *Language in the inner-city: Studies in the Black English vernacular.* Philadelphia: University of Pennsylvania Press.

Labov, W. (1994). Can reading failure be reversed: A linguistic approach to the question. In V. Gadsen & D. Wagner (Eds.), *Literacy among African American youths* (pp. 39–68). Cresskill, NJ: Hampton Press.

Labov, W. (1997). U.S. senate testimony: *Ebonics Hearings.* January 23. Honorable Arlen Specter presiding.

Ogbu, J. (1978). *Minority education and caste.* New York: Academic Press.

O'Neil, W. (1998). If Ebonics isn't a language, then tell me, what is? In T. Perry & L. Delpit (Eds.), *The real Ebonics debate: Power, language, and the education of African American children* (pp. 38–48). Boston: Beacon Press.

Rickford, John. (1999). *African American vernacular English: Features, evolution, educational implications.* Oxford: Blackwell.

Rickford, J., & Rickford, A. (1995). Dialect readers revisited. *Linguistics and Education,* 7(2), 107–128.

Rickford, J. R., & Rickford, R. J. (2000). *Spoken soul: The story of Black English.* New York: John Wiley and Sons.

Smitherman, G. (1978). *Talkin' and testifyin': The language of Black America.* Boston: Houghton Mifflin Co.

Smitherman, G. (Ed.). (1981). Black English and the education of black children and youth: *Proceedings of the National Invitational Symposium on the King decision.* Detroit, MI: Wayne State University Press.

Smitherman, G. (2000). *Talkin' that talk: Language, culture, and education in African America.* London: Routledge.

Whiteman, M. F. (1981). Dialect influence in writing. In M. F. Whiteman (Ed.), *Writing: variation in writing: Functional and linguistic-cultural differences.* Hillsdale, NJ: Lawrence Erlbaum Associates.

Williams, R. (1975). *Ebonics: The true language of Black folks.* St. Louis, MO: Robert Williams and Associates.

Wolfram, W. (1969). *A sociolinguistic description of Detroit Negro speech.* Washington, DC: Center for Applied Linguistics.

Wolfram, W. (1994). The phonology of a sociocultural variety: The case of African American Vernacular English. In J. E. Bernthal & N. W. Bankson (Eds.), *Child phonology: Characteristics, assessment, and intervention with special populations,* (pp. 227–244). New York: Thieme Medical Publishers.

10

Enhancing the Critical Edge of (L2) Teacher-Education: Some Issues in Advanced Literacy

Vai Ramanathan
University of California, Davis

A thought collective exists wherever two or more people are actually exchanging thoughts. He is a poor observer who does not notice that a stimulating conversation between two persons soon creates a condition in which each utters thoughts he would not have been able to produce either by himself or in different company. A special mood arises, which would not otherwise affect either partner of the conversation but almost always returns whenever these persons meet again. Prolonged duration of this state produces from common understanding and mutual misunderstanding, a thought structure [Denkgebilde] that belongs to neither of them alone but nevertheless is not at all without meaning. Who is its carrier and who its originator? It is neither more nor less than the collective of [two] persons. If a third person joins in, a new collective arises. The previous mood will dissolve and with it the special creative force of the former [small] collective. (Fleck, 1981, p. 44).

Primarily concerned with how power operates at various levels of schooling, critical pedagogy and critical language awareness (Fairclough, 1992) have been, thus far, oriented toward disseminating issues related to the "political economy of schooling, the state and education, the representation of texts, and the construction of student subjectivity" (McLaren, 1989, p. 159). While critical pedagogists have been varied in their points of focus (Aronowitz & Giroux, 1993; Auerbach, 1996; Benesch, 1991; Giroux, 1992), with interests ranging from the libertarian to the radical and the liberationist (McLaren, 1989), they seem to be allied in their commitment to certain objectives, namely to empower the powerless and to find ways of addressing and transforming social inequalities in the schooling world. Research in this domain has been both theoretical and practical, with the former favoring ways of conceptualizing schooling, education, and self-awareness (Aronowitz & Giroux, 1993), and the latter being oriented toward critical ethnographies (e.g., Canagarajah, 1993).

Partially in the realm of critical pedagogy, the focus of this chapter is in an area of advanced literacy—namely the metacognitive development of second language (L2) teachers in training—with the general aim being to empower these teachers to transform their worlds by encouraging in them a heightened meta-awareness. For the purposes of the present discussion, I use the phrase "advanced literacy" to mean two things. First, a relatively obvious reading of it, namely what people do with reading and writing at tertiary levels of schooling and beyond. Secondly, and more relevantly as far as the present chapter is concerned, this phrase refers to the ability to be questioning and critical—to be meta-aware, in other words—about the different disciplinary components that teachers are being socialized into as they go through their professional training. (Thus, the notions "advanced literacy," "critical pedagogy," and meta-awareness are all inextricably linked.) While a degree of meta-awareness is assumed in the general process of empowerment (after all, one cannot address problems in one's existing condition unless one has reflected on them and recognized one's own participation in the conditions), meta-awareness in itself has not fully developed as a distinct mode of operation in the general area of teacher-education (especially in realms such as L2 teacher-education). Having would-be teachers engage in critical reflection, questioning and analysis of the various components that make up their professional worlds—the programs they are enrolled in and the larger disciplines—is a first step in this direction.

These worlds can be seen to be "thought collectives" (Fleck, 1981) of the sort that Fleck describes in the quote heading this chapter. Although the quote implies that a thought collective is relatively small and transient—involving two people—in this chapter, I use the term to refer to a relatively stable disciplinary community that holds people with shared interests, goals, ideas, and events together (Ramanathan & Kaplan, 2000) with visible and invisible ties. It is easy to see, for instance, how two ESL practitioners, complete strangers to each other, can connect (at a TESOL conference for example) because of a shared "thought structure" that belongs to everybody in the discipline. This sharedness occurs because numerous connections within the thought collective (TC) are being held in place, including relations between researchers, teachers, genres, texts, teaching practices, events, activities, and lectures. As the quote says, prolonged duration of such sharedness produces from "common understanding and mutual misunderstanding a thought structure" that belongs to nobody and everybody at once. Having potential teachers identify, reflect on, and question the various components that make up their thought collectives as well as their own individual contribution toward the stability of these components affords them a critical and multidimensional view that would otherwise not be possible. Such self-conscious reflection on the very components they are engaged in and being socialized into ultimately heightens their meta-awareness.

The suggested ways in which this can be achieved are intended to contribute to and promote debate about issues in teacher education and do not aim at providing definitive solutions. Neither are these suggestions intended to seem too *theoretical* (as opposed to the generally practical nature of teacher-education programs). On the contrary, they are to be seen as ways in which a critical edge can be built into all spheres of individual programs, including the practical realm. Such a stance is in keeping with the idea that it is not enough that we have teachers-in-training become literate by "picking up the tools of the trade," but that they should be able to talk critically about what is involved in picking up these "tools" as they are in the process of doing so (Blanton, 1998; Heath, 1985). The overall awareness that such literacy is likely to engender is of the sort that will enhance their professional astuteness, making them questioning and thoughtful of their practices and contributions, regardless of the contexts they find themselves in (including K–12 settings, community colleges, intensive English programs, composition programs, refugee institutions, EFL and ESL cultural contexts). Clearly such meta-awareness cannot be gauged by numerical, conventional measures of assessment without running the risk of such measures seeming arbitrary and imposed. Notional and fuzzy, it is perhaps best to think of and address this concept in terms of how teachers could be encouraged to make the kind of professional judgments that Dewey talks about:

> [To gauge] the relative indicative or signifying values of the various features of the perplexing situation; to know what to let go of as of no account; what to eliminate as irrelevant; what to retain as conducive to the outcome; what to emphasize as a clew to the difficulty. This power in ordinary matters we call *knack, tact, cleverness*; in more important affairs, *insight, discernment* (Dewey, cited in Simpson & Jackson, 1997:1998, authors' emphasis).

Among teachers, the development of such judgments is believed to partially grow with articulated reflection on one's teaching practices,[1] and within the realm of teaching English as a second language (TESOL), for instance, this point has been developed and made accessible by Richards and Lockhart (1994). While this chapter also promotes, as Richards and Lockhart do, the idea that teachers contemplate their practices, beliefs, and assumptions,[2] it seeks to go a step beyond by encouraging teachers to critically meditate on and question (1) the discipline's social practices (2) and their individual participation in these practices. I argue that one way of heightening this awareness is by making teachers conscious—through active reflection and questioning—of how their TCs function as activity systems with cognitions distributed across various components. Although I draw on specific contexts within the Applied Linguistics/TESOL worlds as illustrations—because these are the worlds I know best—the larger points I am making are applicable to

---

[1]Such reflection is supposed to foster the Deweyan characteristics of open-mindedness (the ability to suspend judgement, to consider alternative view points), responsibility (the ownership of consequences for actions), and whole heartedness (feelings of commitment to continuous professional development) (Vacca, Vacca, & Bruneau, 1997).

[2]For a comprehensive review on encouraging reflective practice among L1 teachers, see Vacca et. al (1997). Van Maanen (1977) discusses three kinds of teacher-reflection: technical reflection, which encourages teachers to address day-to-day problems in their classrooms, practical reflection, which includes thinking of long-term educational goals, and critical reflection, which encourages thinking about ethical dimensions of teaching.

teacher education at all educational levels. I first discuss previous research in critical pedagogy and TESOL teacher-education, and then address some key tenets of
theories of "activity systems," "distributed cognitions," and "situated learning" and
examine related concepts such as "discourse communities" (e.g., Swales, 1998),
and Discourses (Gee, 1991, chap. 8, this volume), explaining how thought collectives are different from these related terms. I then discuss some avenues by which
self-conscious reflection on the various components that make up the TCs can be
heightened, and conclude with a discussion of the general importance of
meta-awareness in the realm of (L2) teacher education.

CRITICAL PEDAGOGY, TEACHER-EDUCATION, AND TESOL

In this section I address some ways in which recent research in critical pedagogy
has focused on rethinking the role of the teacher. This constitutes a partial context
against which the premises of the current chapter can be located. Giroux (1992, p.
31) maintains that educators at all levels of schooling need to be seen as "intellec-
tuals," "who as mediators, legitimators, and producers of ideas and social practices,
perform a pedagogical function that is eminently political in nature," and recognize it as such. Viewing and constructing a teacher as an "intellectual" is empowering in that we see him/her as a person who has the courage to question authority
and who refuses to act counter to his/her experience or judgment. Such teachers
are more likely to try out "parallel pedagogies" (Shor & Freire, 1987, p. 44), concurrent with those they are expected to follow toward liberating themselves and
their students from traditional, restrictive schooling structures. They are able to
make the pedagogical political and vice-versa, a feature that Giroux (1992) maintains ultimately makes for new forms of culture, alternative social practices, new
modes of communication, and a practical vision for the future.

Issues related to teacher education cover a range of domains, including
reconceptualizing teacher-training programs (Freeman & Johnson, 1998), having
potential teachers trace their evolution through diary entries they keep (Bailey &
Nunan, 1996), encouraging reflective practice (Nunan, 1992; Richards & Lockhart, 1994; Bailey, Curtis, & Nunan, 1998), and advocating "dialogic inquiry"
(Schleppegrell, 1997) so that teachers develop a richer knowledge base about their
students' backgrounds, motivations, and learning strategies. The focus, on the
whole, has tended to be on areas such as modifying current TESOL programs and
reevaluating the position and role of the potential teacher in the ESL classroom.
Freeman and Johnson (1998, p. 399) maintain that current TESOL programs
heavily emphasize "discrete amounts of knowledge usually in the form of theories
and methods ..." and advocate evolving programs whose core focus is on "the activity of teaching itself ... on the teacher who does it, the contexts in which it is
done, and the pedagogy by which it is done" (1998, p. 397). In other words, they
advocate a position wherein the teacher-as-learner is the center, where the
teacher's prior knowledge, rationalizations, decisions, immediate contexts, and
the schooling environments are all recognized as crucial components of a
teacher-education program. Freeman (1996, p. 222) examines how teachers' classroom practices are influenced by their participation in a teacher-education pro-

gram: how over time, their "local language becomes more critical as they cast their experiences in terms of the discourse they are being socialized into and as they rename and negotiate what they do in their teaching." Similar to Freeman's study is one by Richards, Ho, and Giblin (1996) wherein they studied how five trainee teachers responded to a short teacher-training (RSA) program. They found that teachers interpret the program they are in in significantly different ways from each other as they attempt to deconstruct their experiences in light of their "beliefs and assumptions about themselves, about teachers, about teaching, and about learners" (Richards et al., 1996, p. 258).

Several other studies on the growth and development of L2 teachers exist as well (e.g., Burton, 1998; Campbell, 1996; Clair, 1998; Flowerdew, 1998; Golombek, 1998; Johnson, 1996; Nunan, 1996; Shamim, 1996). Although many of them draw on suggestions and theories articulated by L1 critical education theorists (c.f. Aronowitz & Giroux, 1993; Gee, 1997), none of them addresses the need for potential teachers to be meta-aware of the socialization process that inducts them into their disciplines. While Richards and Lockhart (1994) advocate this position to some degree—by encouraging teachers to reflect on their teaching goals, for instance—they do not encourage critical reflection and questioning in terms of the teacher's role in relation to the discipline.

Although reflection on one's teaching goals is built into heightening meta-awareness, it is crucial to go a step beyond and encourage would-be teachers to frequently reflect on, address, and question their teaching goals in relation to larger disciplinary concerns, including ways in which genres operate in various realms of their disciplines, how their professional goals are tied to the goals of the disciplines, how debates in the disciplines percolate down to the smaller contexts of their individual classrooms, how they contribute to text-types and genres remaining stable or changing in their disciplines, and how "basic facts" and "truths" in their disciplines can, from another disciplinary point of view, be regarded as highly questionable. This chapter is about heightening teachers' meta-awareness so that they begin talking and thinking about how their individual disciplines function and are sustained and how they contribute to that functioning and sustenance, and ways in which this can be incorporated into existing curricula.

"DISCOURSE COMMUNITIES" AND "DISCOURSES"

Two terms that bear similarity to TCs are "discourse communities" and "Discourses." The term "discourse community" has been much debated and discussed in the last decade (Berkenkotter & Huckin, 1995; Miller, 1994; Ramanathan & Kaplan, 2000; Swales, 1998; Van Nostrand, 1994) with varying nuanced definitions and interpretations being offered. Although this section does not offer a comprehensive review of previous explanations of this term (see Swales, 1998 for a relatively full review), I would like to mention some key definitions because these are subsumed in the general understanding of thought collectives as presented in this chapter. Each of the following definitions of discourse community (partially based one Swales, 1998) centers around a different focal point.

A Discourse Community With a Focus on Texts

James Porter (1992), who offered a poststructuralist definition of the term, maintains that "the term discourse community is useful for describing a space that was unacknowledged.... What was before largely scene, unnoticed background, becomes foreground" (1992, p. 84). He defines the term as:

> A discourse community is a local and temporary constraining system, *defined by a body of texts* (my emphasis) (or more generally, practices) that are unified by a common focus. A discourse community is a *textual system* (my emphasis) with stated and unstated conventions, a vital history, mechanisms for wielding power, institutional hierarchies, vested interests, and so on. Thus, a *discourse* community cuts across sociological or institutional boundaries (original emphasis). (1992, p. 106)

Among the advantages that Porter mentions for this definition is that it focuses directly on texts in terms of "rhetorical principles of operation" (Porter, 1992, p. 88) (and is thus, closely allied to rhetoric as a discipline).[3] Texts—their composition, reproduction and dissemination—are key points of emphasis in this interpretation of the term.

A Discourse Community With a Focus on Groups

Moving away from texts as a central feature, Killingsworth and Gilbertson (1992) stress that groups of readers and writers comprise discourse communities. They make a distinction between *local versus global* discourse communities, where groups of readers and writers in the former typically "work together in companies, colleges, departments, neighborhoods, government agencies or other groups defined by specific demographic features," (1992, p. 162) while those in the latter are defined exclusively by a commitment to particular kinds of action and discourse, regardless of where and with whom they work. They fine-tune their definition with other distinctions: that "local communities ... may monitor membership by physical surveillance (corporate badges, parking stickers, correct dress ...)" whereas "membership in global communities tends to be regulated exclusively by discourse-governed criteria (writing style, publication in certain journals ...)" (1992, p. 169). As Swales (1998, p. 201) points out, the two types of discourse communities can come into conflict "as they compete for the loyalties of individual members of both."

A Discourse Community With a Focus on Place

The idea of place discourse communities (Swales, 1998) appears to be closely tied to "communities of practice" (Hanks, 1996; Lave & Wenger, 1991) in that it ori-

---

[3]The other advantages of this interpretation of discourse community that Porter mentions include: (1) its tolerance for a high degree of ambiguity, (2) its ability to take a historical view of communities (3) and its ability to see communities not as "nice neat packages," but as "messy, ill defined and unstable" (Porter, 1992, p. 88).

ents the term around a "project site" (Bizzell, 1992; Swales, 1998). The following definition captures this aspect of the term:

> A community of practice is an aggregate of people who come together around mutual engagement in an endeavor. Ways of doing things, ways of talking, beliefs, values, power relations—in short, practices—emerge in the course of this mutual endeavor ... (Eckart & McConnell-Ginet, 1992, p. 464, cited in Swales, 1998, p. 202).

Echoes of the idea of site/place being its own community can be seen in Lave and Wenger's definition (1991) of "legitimate peripheral participation," which addresses the issue of how newcomers to a group get initiated into the group's practices. They draw attention to the point "that learners inevitably participate in communities of practitioners and that the mastery of knowledge and skill requires newcomers to move toward full participation in the sociocultural practice of a community" (1991, p. 29).

The key difference between the two terms "thought collectives" and "discourse communities" is one of focus. Thought collectives *center around the development of thoughts and professional cognitions of people who participate in them*, so that texts, sites, and groups—key foci in the definitions of discourse communities—are seen to emerge from the collective cognitions. None of the above definitions of discourse community focus on the (development of) thoughts and cognitions of participants, and it is precisely this latent point that this chapter highlights.

Gee's notion of "Discourses" is another term with which the notion of TCs overlaps. Gee used the term "Discourse" to mean:

> ... a socially accepted association among ways of using language, of thinking, feeling, believing, valuing, and of acting that can be used to identify oneself as a member of a socially meaningful group or "social network," or to signal (that one is playing) a socially meaningful "role." (1991, p. 143)

Clearly, Gee's use of the term is an all-encompassing one, where someone's Discourse is that person's "identity-kit which comes complete with the appropriate costume and instructions on how to act, talk and often write, so as to take on a particular social role that others will recognize" (Gee, 1990, p. 142). Gee focuses on the entire individual to address how all of the various subdiscourses make up his/her being. The notion of TC, on the other hand, with its focus on the collective cognitions of participants in a community, isolates the sociocognitive realm for closer examination. Although acknowledging that our cognitions are embedded in our social lives, it singles this area out for scrutiny by making the sociocognitive the primary site of attention. As with the term "discourse community," the difference between Discourse(s) and thought collective(s) is one of focus.

TESOL THOUGHT COLLECTIVES AS ACTIVITY SYSTEMS WITH DISTRIBUTED COGNITIONS AND SITUATED LEARNING

Aspects of three related theories—of activity systems, distributed cognitions and situated learning—can explain how TCs function and how the meta-awareness of second-language teachers can be heightened. Rather than see one theory as superior to the other two (in terms of scope, its explanatory power and comprehensiveness), I amalgamate features of all three because each affords specific insights into how to conceptualize and understand TCs. What follows is a partial summary of these theories and does not aim to be comprehensive (for fuller reviews, see Cole, Engestrom & Vasquez, 1997; Lave & Wenger, 1991; Nardi, 1996).

Activity Systems

The basic unit of analysis in activity theory is an activity. This theory maintains that constituents of an activity—subject, object, actions—change as conditions and contexts change. Nardi (1996) believes that the notion of mediation is key in activity theory because artifacts—signs, instruments, language, machines—mediate activity and are "created by people to control their own behavior" (1996, p. 75). Artifacts are seen as situated, historical, and sometimes persistent structures that cut across time and space and that mediate between the human and the world; thus, it is the relationship between the user and artifact that is central to this theory. Context, then, for proponents of this view, is activity itself and vice-versa. "People consciously and deliberately generate contexts (activities) in part through their own objects; hence context is not just 'out there'" (Nardi, 1996, p. 76), but integral to people's relationships with the world.

Distributed Cognitions and Situated Learning

Often used together, these constructs are located in a body of research that explores the situated character of human understanding and communication and takes as its focal point the relationship between learning and the social situations in which it occurs. Lave and Wenger (1991), key proponents of this theory, maintain that learning takes place in a participation framework and not in any individual's mind, and is distributed among coparticipants. The central defining characteristic of such situated learning is *legitimate peripheral participation*, which as we saw earlier, refers to the process by which learners get initiated into a community of practitioners, moving eventually toward becoming full participants in the community. Cognitions, then, are located in the system. The focus is on the coordination between individuals, artifacts and the communities they are part of—to see these units as part of a whole, with each informing the other's identity—and not on singling out particular units (activities or artifacts for instance, as the activity theorists do) by which to interpret learning. Learning, from this perspective, involves the whole person; "it implies becoming a full participant, a member, a kind of person" (Lave & Wenger, 1991, p. 53).

Keeping the above points in mind, let us turn to discussing how TESOL TCs function as activity systems with distributed cognitions. Fleck (1981, p. 48) defines a thought-collective as a community wherein

> thoughts pass from one individual to another, each time a little transformed, for each individual can attach to them somewhat different associations. Strictly speaking, the

receiver never understands the thought exactly in the way that the transmitter intended it to be understood. After a series of such encounters, practically nothing is left of the original content. Whose thought is it that continues to circulate? It is one that obviously belongs not to any single individual but to the collective. Whether an individual construes it as truth or error, understands it correctly or not, a set of findings meanders throughout the community, becoming polished, transformed, reinforced, or attenuated while influencing other findings, concept formation, opinions, and habits of thought.

Implied in this quote is the idea that a thought collective is a bidirectional sociocognitive construct that allows us to view participation in it as partially constitutive of participant behavior, responses, and general orientation to the world. Although Fleck describes a "thought-collective" as two people exchanging thoughts, I use the term to refer to certain bonds that hold the "thoughts"/cognitions (construed broadly) of teacher-education programs and the larger disciplines together. Potential teachers have their cognitions and thought-processes shaped by a variety of components in the programs, including hallway chats, student–teacher conferences, people, events, and social practices, all of which in turn shape the nature, philosophy, and general direction of the program. The larger TESOL discipline can be seen to be a larger concentric circle, reflecting—on a more macro scale—social practices similar to those of an average MA-TESOL program, for instance. Participation in both TCs—including attending classes, fulfilling assignments, doing presentations, publishing in ESL-related journals, presenting at conferences, participating in TESOL-related administrative tasks—reinforces a bidirectional relationship with the program and discipline partially shaping the cognitions of TESOLers and vice-versa.

The issue of where cognitions reside—whether in an individual's head or in the context—is of particular importance in this discussion. Vygotsky (1962), who can be viewed as an early activity theorist, outlines ways in which tools and symbols mediate between an individual and the context, thus shaping and distributing individual and collective cognitions. Although the term "distribution" connotes a "spreading across" or "stretching over" (Cole & Wertsch, 1996), thus implying the lack of a single locus or fixed point, it also implies, as Salomon (1993) points out, a sharing—"sharing authority, language, experiences, tasks, and a cultural heritage" (1993, p. 11), all features that characterize a thought-collective. Bateson (1972, p. 459, cited in Cole et al., 1997, p. 13) offers the following scenario to capture the intertwined nature of one's mental makeup, the environment, and the tools one uses to achieve one's ends:

> Suppose I am a blind man, and I use a stick. I go tap, tap, tap. Where do I start? Is my mental system bounded at the hand of the stick? Is it bounded by my skin? Does it start halfway up the stick? Does it start at the tip of the stick?

Cognition, as the above scenario implies, does not have specific boundaries and starting/ending points, but is distributed across a range of components including the stick and the activities that the blind man is involved in with the stick. Cole et al. (1997) argue that answers to the questions in the quote above change depending on how one thinks of the event.

When the man sits down to eat his lunch, the stick's relation to mind totally changes, and it is forks and knives, not sticks that become relevant. In short, the ways in which mind is distributed depends crucially on the tools through which one interacts with the world, and these in turn depend on one's goals. The combination of goals, tools, and setting ... constitutes simultaneously the context of behavior and the ways in which cognition gets distributed in that context. (Cole et al., 1997, p. 13).

Clearly then, activity, tools, and events and the complex interaction between them influence local cognitions and one's mental behavior.[4] In the previous quote, the forks and knives serve as tools/mediators that link the person organically and intimately to the world, and are more than just filters or channels through which experience gets embodied and consciousness formed. In this sense, one's cognitions are not mentalistic, abstract states in one's head, but states of being that constantly get negotiated depending partially on the local constraints, available tools (the availability and perhaps preference to eat with forks and knives as opposed to chopsticks or one's fingers, for example), and the prevailing social practices of one's thought-collective at a given time.

In the light of the present discussion, then, TESOL thought collectives can be seen as activity systems whose cognitions are distributed across a variety of discipline-specific tools and activities including particular texts, genres, writing practices, teaching styles and orientations, jargon terms and research practices (Ramanathan & Kaplan, 2000), components that together orient the participants' thought styles and cognitions in particular directions. These are the components with and through which (potential) teachers mediate their TCs that cumulatively exert a "force" (Fleck, 1981, p. 42) on their thinking. By inviting and sometimes mandating participation in its numerous and varied social practices, a TC can thus be seen to shape its participants' sociocognitive behavior.

HEIGHTENING THE METACOGNITIVE SKILLS OF TEACHERS

I turn now to addressing how the meta-awareness of teachers can be heightened. Although many of these features are addressed by teacher education programs, they are typically done so implicitly (Ramanathan & Kaplan, 2000). Conscious and active reflection by would-be teachers on the functioning of their TCs is crucial if we wish to develop them into critical pedagogues. As language educators we

---

[4]Also crucial to keep in mind is the role that sociocultural practices play in shaping mental behavior. Whereas culture can, on the one hand, be seen as a uniform, patterned ensemble of beliefs, values, symbols, and tools that people share, it is also very heterogeneous, given how locally circumscribed it is by local constraints and interactions. Marcus (1998), for example, based on his exploration of how knowledge is distributed across persons, generations, occupations, classes, religions, and institutions, maintains that culture is necessarily a distributed phenomenon, and has to be understood as such. This tension between patterning and heterogeneity in "cultures" plays itself out in interesting ways in certain kinds of thought-collectives—specifically discipline-oriented communities—which can be seen as microcosmic cultural entities that are at once stable and uniform with specific rules, as well as dynamic structures that make room for heterogeneity and difference (Ramanathan & Kaplan, 1999).

need to systematically build such awareness into our classes and programs. Presented below are four ways in which this can be achieved.

Making Teachers Aware of How Their Thought Collectives Function as Activity Systems

One way of alerting potential teachers to how their TCs are activity systems of which they are an integral part is by getting them to articulate ways in which they are sutured into the TCs, connecting everyday actions and goals. Enabling them to see how their everyday participation in the TCs is tied to their personal goals, which in turn are tied to the (goals of) the TCs, is important if they are to discern their location—amidst the location and roles of other components—in the TC.

Also important is getting them to recognize how the "tools" they use—including those they use in their classrooms: textbooks, curricular materials, syllabi—achieve with varying success the goals they set for themselves (or the courses they are teaching). Activity theory posits that "objects" and "tools" (Nardi, 1996) are used to target particular "goals," that actions are conscious (one has a goal in mind) and that different actions may be undertaken to meet the same goal (with some actions being more *fruitful* than others). As Leont'ev (cited in Nardi, 1996, p. 74) said:

> a person may have the object of obtaining food, but to do so he must carry out actions not immediately directed at obtaining food.... His goal may be to make a hunting weapon. Does he subsequently use the weapon he made, or does he pass it on to someone else and receive a portion of the total catch? In both cases, that which energizes his activity and that to which his action is directed do not [necessarily have to] coincide.

In other words, there need not be a direct, one-to-one relationship between actions and goals in an activity system. A variety of seemingly unrelated, indirect actions can cumulatively percolate toward achieving directly or indirectly related goals. Having potential teachers identify some ways in which this occurs in their TCs—how their everyday actions of attending classes and completing their assignments are tied to their larger goals of becoming EFL/ESL teachers, that the tools (assignments, readings, presentations, theses) they use toward reaching their goals may or may not be direct mediators between themselves and their TESOL worlds, is important for their sense of location in their TCs. Like the stick or the fork, the tools that teachers use influence their cognitions and are partially influenced by a range of factors including local constraints, the availability and choice at the time, and the general preference of choosing one tool over other available tools. For instance, an MA-TESOL student-teacher, may, in a program that offers a choice between comprehensive exams and a thesis, decide to do a thesis. Seeing that successful completion of one of these tools is required for graduation, and that enrolled students typically want to graduate, these tools are directly tied to student goals. The extra work a student might do, on the other hand—tutoring an ESL child in her spare time, when it is not a requirement for her program—would be an example of a tool that is indirectly tied to her MA-TESOL degree (but that enhances her abilities as an ESL teacher).

Also important is heightening the awareness of potential teachers of how choice is built into their everyday actions. Making potential teachers, for instance, critically aware of how they *automatically* choose to address their written class assignments in standard English—as opposed to using colloquialisms or the vernacular—is likely to raise important issues that all (of us) teachers need to address: that we are making a definite choice when using this variety in an academic setting, that we recognize that it yields better *results* than a nonstandard variety, that we are aware that power is unevenly assigned to different language varieties, how (we as) teachers play a role in perpetuating this unequal distribution by upholding the worth of one *appropriate* variety (Fairclough, 1992), what can be done in small or not-so-small ways to address inequalities. Providing arenas where potential L2 teachers can consciously make such connections and critically reflect on how their small, automatic, choices in the everyday activities of their TC index a variety of nuances about themselves, and how these automatic choices orient them toward using particular tools is crucial to enhancing their overall meta-awareness.

Equally important is connecting actions and cognitions, heightening teachers' awareness of how particular events and actions perpetuate certain kinds of cognitions in their TCs. Sensitizing them to understand how their participation in various *activities* of their thought collective—including classes, meetings, student conferences, writing term papers, taking exams—ultimately stabilizes and perpetuates particular *modes of thought* is crucial. If, for example, the general thrust of a particular MA-TESOL program is more on intercultural relations in EFL contexts than on teaching methodology, and the classes, curricular materials, and the general orientation of the program leans in this direction, then the cognitions of the enrolled TESOLers are likely to be more heightened in this area. Getting potential teachers to become aware of how their cognitions are thus locally shaped by prevailing and dominant modes of thought available in their current environment will ultimately help them to see how different cognitions and modes of thought make their way into the larger discipline. It will provide them with a clearer sense of how the collective leaning of groups of scholars toward one research area can contribute to the flowering of specific modes of thought, how various theories of second-language development, for instance, are formed, stabilized, or discarded, and how their involvement and participation in their respective TESOL programs ultimately contributes to keeping particular cognitions in the larger discipline in place. Such awareness is likely to reduce the gap between themselves and the theories *out there*, and will allow them to see connections between themselves and the seemingly free-floating cognitions in their TCs.

Having Teachers Recognize How the Activities They Are Engaged in Constitute the Context, and How Cognition Gets Distributed Across Various Components in Their TCs

Activity theory proposes that the activity itself is the context: "What takes place in an activity system composed of objects, actions, and operation, is the context" (Nardi, 1996, p. 76). Thus, context is not relegated to features/phenomena external to the individual but is regarded as internal to the person as well. This take on context introduces a unity, an inseparability of thought and activity, where action and thinking are not mutually exclusive. Cognition is seen as distributed across individuals participating in activities and in the tools and artifacts they use when engaged in particular activities. According to Flor and Hutchins (1991), distributed cognition:

> is a new branch of cognitive science devoted to the study of: the representation of knowledge both inside the heads of individuals and in the world ... ; the propagation of knowledge between different individuals and artifacts ... ; the transformations which external structures undergo when operated on by individuals and artifacts ... By studying cognitive phenomena in this fashion it is hoped that an understanding of how intelligence is manifested at the systems level, as opposed to the individual cognitive level, will be obtained. (Flor & Hutchins, 1991, cited in Nardi, 1996, p. 77)

In other words, distributed cognition views its minimal unit of analysis as comprising agents, activities, and tools, among other components. Because the system is not relative to an individual but to a distributed collection of interacting people and artifacts, we cannot understand how a system achieves its goals without understanding the coordinated efforts of all the individual agents and their respective tools (Nardi, 1996). Heightening the awareness of potential teachers to how cognition gets distributed across various components in an MA-TESOL TC, (including reading, writing, discussing, seminar, practicum, and assignment practices) and how this distribution is intimately tied to the goals of the TC (namely to produce informed, effective, self-reflective teachers of English) will enable them to see how they and their TC move globally toward their respective goals. It will also allow them to see how cognition gets spread out across several and varied components in the discipline at large, with some clusters of components evolving their own subdiscourses (Gee, 1991) within the TC.

Take for example the area of second-language writing: having L2 writing teachers articulate their participation with particular debates in the field (in both TCs—their immediate teacher-education programs and the larger discipline) through the classes they teach and the papers they present at conferences will help them see more tangibly how various positions/cognitions regarding debates get distributed across clusters of peoples. An example of such a debate in L2 writing is the current one on the extent to which the cultural background of the student is relevant to writing instruction (Raimes & Zamel, 1997; Ramanathan & Atkinson, 1999; Ramanathan & Kaplan, 1996a, 1996b, 1997; Spack, 1997), or a more recent debate regarding feedback on grammar (Ferris, 1999; Truscott, 1999). Getting potential L2 teachers to position themselves—both in the realms of theory and practice—in debates such as these allows them to link various aspects of their individual participation to these debates; it also allows them to see how various components of the debate get acted on, responded to, and carried further. Such multifaceted awareness affords them a more global vision of the field and their position in it.

Having Potential Teachers Recognize "Persistent and Evolving Structures" in Their TCs and Having Them Reflect on Their (Individual and Collective) Roles in the Stability and Growth of These Structures

Along with heightening their awareness of how cognitions get distributed in their TCs, it is also important to make enrolled teachers conscious of the relatively "persistent/stable structures" (Nardi, 1996) of their TCs. By "persistent" structures, I refer to certain ways of talking, including jargon terms, particular artifacts, institutions, tools, disciplinary values, textual forms/genres, registers, components that are reasonably stable and not likely to change quickly. Alerting potential teachers to how various cognitions get rooted in these persistent components and how both cognitions and components are encased in and constitutive of a range of social practices is important if they are to engage in metatalk. Making them aware of how various persistent social practices in TCs keep particular written genres stable (how the social practice of having them write reader's notes, for example, for particular readings in the seminars they take keeps the genre of "readers notes" persistent and stable in the TC), or how the practice of submitting and reviewing abstracts (Kaplan et al., 1994) partially sustains the genre of (well written) abstracts in the TCs is crucial. Equally important is getting them to see how disciplinary changes do occur over time (e.g., that changes in social practices/conventions in the scientific discourse community have led to changes in scientific writing; Atkinson, 1998; Huckin, 1987). Having them recognize how key textual components—abstracts, proposals, term papers, textbooks, readings, and assignments—are, thus, relatively *persistent* tools/text-types in their TCs, that even slight changes in these tools can have a ripple effect on the general orientation and ecology of the TC, affords them a more holistic vision of the relative (im)movables in their TCs.

Encouraging them to reflect on how they coconstruct the different texts they engage in (Wells, 1999) entails getting them to recognize when particular "situation-types" demand specific textual forms. They do this based on their knowledge of "regular patterns of co-occurrence that exist between particular semiotic properties of the situation and particular choices from the semantic resources that make up the culture's linguistic meaning potential (register) and of the way in which these choices are sequentially deployed in the staged organization of the event (genre)" (Wells, 1999, p. 48). Heightening meta-awareness of such issues is necessary if we want potential L2 teachers to not be constrained by persistent structures, including those that constitute stereotypical *class lessons*, but feel empowered to strike out in relevant, but different directions that entail rethinking/reconceiving some of the persistent structures they contend with.

Particular kinds of speech/talk in the TC can be classified under "persistent structures" as well. Wells (1996) details ways that certain kinds of responses made by teachers to student contributions do/do not enhance student performance:

> Continually to choose the "evaluate" option—whether accepting or rejecting—does much to create a situational context in which right answers will be given priority by students. By contrast, frequently choosing the "extend" option creates a different context—one which emphasizes the collaborative construction of meaning, both in

the setting of goals to be aimed for and in the construction of "common knowledge." And the choice of the options which call upon students to justify, explain and exemplify creates another context—one which encourages students critically to examine and evaluate the answers that they make to the questions that interest them and which simultaneously provides an opportunity for their apprenticeship into these "genres of power." (Lemke, 1989, cited by Wells, 1996, p. 97).

Having potential teachers become self-conscious about the types of feedback/follow-up they offer their students, and/or alerting them to ways that changes in their utterances can make a difference in the relative success of student performance is important if they are to see how "persistent" and rooted their kind of talk is. As Wells points out, in much of the research in the human sciences, the emphasis has been on investigating how "activity systems" determine ways that "actions" are operationalized. Concentrating on teacher-talk "invites us to consider the converse relationship—how changing the 'operations' by means of which an 'action' is carried out can ultimately change the 'activity system' in which the 'action' is embedded" (Wells, 1996, p. 97). It is partially in these small ways that teachers can effect changes in education (Fairclough, 1992); by making them self-conscious and meta-aware of specific features of their talk, they can transform the "persistent," sometimes negative features of their speech toward kinds that will elicit better student responses.

Making potential teachers aware of how they can analyze their TC from a variety of angles (from the individual to the broadest disciplinary levels) and ways in which the picture changes depending on the perspective taken (Russell, 1995, p. 56) can only enhance their sense of all viewpoints being perspectival. Getting them to see, for instance, that an anthropological take on TESOL as a discipline would in all likelihood have serious reservations about the spread of English language literacy across the world, given the slow erosion of local, indigenous languages it might engender (Pennycook, 1994) will afford them insight into how views external to the thought collective might be diametrically opposed to the TC's goals. In other words, alerting them to (the possibility of) such views would be a first step in their recognizing that what they regard as "immovables" in the TC can, from another disciplinary point of view, be seen as relatively "movable" and questionable.

Having Teachers Articulate Explicit Connections Between Texts, Various Domains of Reference, and Various Teaching-Learning Contexts

Alerting potential teachers to the general notion of intertextuality and how contexts always harken back to other previous or concurrent ones, and ways in which such connections get played out in the various domains of their teacher-education existence is crucial if they are to understand the general web of interconnectedness that they are in and that they help create. As Lemke (1995, p. 10) points out, "Each community and every subcommunity within it has its own system of intertextuality: its own set of important or valued texts, its own preferred discourses, and particularly its own habits of deciding which texts should be read in the context of which others, and why, and how." Encouraging potential teachers to articulate, among other things, how a "text is not an autonomous or unified object, but a set of relations with other texts" (Leitch, 1983; cited in Porter, 1986, p. 35) and getting them to establish the numerous ways in which their current texts evidence traces of other texts is central to their schema building. It is also central to their overall understanding of how they contribute to the system of intertextuality that glues the TCs together (Lemke, 1995).

One way of encouraging this awareness is by having them recreate the partial context of a debate in the field based on assigned readings (for example, the "universality" of the communicative approach to L2 language teaching, and some problems when transplanting it across cultures; (Holliday, 1994) to make them sensitive to particular positions taken in related texts. Such an exercise can alert them to ways that texts/readings draw on prior texts for much of their meaning. Likewise, having them juxtapose texts from different Discourses (examining the rhetorical patterns of texts from different disciplines or different cultures) or juxtaposing texts from different historical stages of a Discourse (Gee, 1997) (such as examining features of scientific writing from the 18th century versus current scientific articles) or even texts of different authors writing on similar issues (Cazden, 1989) will encourage them to make explicit connections between their intertextual storehouses and domains of reference, thus fostering a level of meta-awareness about textual forms that would otherwise be absent.

Encouraging teachers to make explicit inter(con)textual connections between what and how they learn to what and how they teach is crucial to their seeing the constant interplay between theory, practice, and their individual evolution as teachers and learners. Having them articulate ways in which their experiences with a particular language teaching method does/does not comport with what they are reading about, or how their peer-reviewing workshops in their writing classrooms do/do not connect meaningfully with their course readings regarding the same will give them opportunities to critically position themselves vis-a-vis their experiences in the classroom and what they read. Articulating such connections will heighten their *orientational* dimension (Lemke, 1995, p. 11) by making them conscious of how they orient their still evolving views and meanings to particular audiences while recognizing that these views are located within a "system of different viewpoints available in the community [read TC] toward our topic" (Lemke, 1995, p. 11). What potential teachers draw from their readings and how these readings get translated into what they do in the classroom when teaching index value preferences and stances that commit them to (or disassociate them from) the politics of their TCs. Making them meta-aware of this bi-directional relationship between theory and practice, between what they read and how they act, between their personal orientations and the larger dynamics of their TCs is crucial if they are to grasp how "orientational meaning situates us in the realm of textual politics" (Lemke, 1995, p. 11).

MOVING INTO THE LARGER PICTURE

Gee (1999, p. 16) maintains that entry and acceptance into a community (read TC) depends to a large extent on the degree to which the novice has learned the community's "social language," thereby developing recognizable social identities. He characterizes the term "social language" as follows:

> ... a social language offers speakers or writers distinctive grammatical resources with which they can "design" their oral and written "utterances" to accomplish two inter-related things: a) to get recognized by others (and themselves) as enacting a specific socially situated *identity* (that is, to "come off" as a particular "kind of person") and b) to get recognized by others (and themselves) as engaged in a specific *activity*.

Clearly the socialization that teacher-education programs offer is oriented toward potential teachers developing their "social languages" to where they become identifiable and full participants in the TCs. These social languages emerge from and are embedded in specific social practices. Not only is it crucial that potential teachers pick up this social language in their socialization through their individual programs, but it is equally important that they develop a meta-awareness about it and all that it implies for their individual development and growth. It is important to have acquired the rules of the trade before encouraging meta-awareness about them—indeed Martin (chap. 5, this volume) argues that learners need to deal with discourses as discourses before they can be critical of them. But it is also important to keep in mind that adult learners have already acquired a great many of the required discourses before they come to a teacher-education program. Indeed, their admission into a teacher-education program is contingent on their already being partially proficient in the relevant discourses necessary for successful completion of the program.

The kind of meta-awareness that I am promoting in this chapter is similar to Lemke's proposition on reflection on "praxis" (1995), namely adopting a self-reflexive and self-critical attitude that encourages reflection and analysis on the practices of a community including those relating to texts, genres, social practices, and one's own individual participation in their creation and sustenance. It includes getting teachers to view their TC worlds as activity systems that have and reproduce local ideologies that seem "naturalized" or "commonsensical" because they are held in place, in part, because of their individual participation in the various social practices of the collective. Such awareness is crucial if we want them to recognize that the "common sense [or natural] in its ideological dimension is itself an *effect of power*" (Fairclough, 1989, p. 92, author's emphasis), that sometimes a "naturalized type tends to be perceived not as that of a particular grouping within the institution but as simply that of the institution itself." Such an approach would help all teachers to go beyond the series of oppositions that seem endemic to teacher-education (qualitative vs. quantitative research methods, sociolinguistic vs. cognitive approaches to language learning, communicative language teaching vs. traditional, older methods) toward developing a more nuanced, comprehensive, critical theory of practice (Bordieu, 1991) wherein they address, for instance, how such oppositions get created and reinforced in the first place.

This kind of meta-awareness can emerge only through deliberate and frequent questioning and analysis of ways in which the various and intricate aspects of socialization shape the potential teachers' identities as well as ways in which these teachers make meaning of these (con)texts. As Lemke maintains, "it is not the texts as objects, nor the speech as verbal text, that makes meaning, but our activity in interacting with these, producing and interpreting them, that makes meaning. [Con]Texts do not have meaning; meanings are relations we make through practices in which we are never the sole participant, never the sole originator of the practice" (1995, pp. 158–159). Certainly, Fleck's definition of thought collective complements this view: "common understanding and mutual misunderstanding" produce a set of relations and meanings, "a thought structure [Denkgebilde]" that belongs simultaneously to nobody in particular and everybody in general. Getting potential teachers to fully comprehend this fact; making them meta-aware of the different ways in which their TCs sustain, produce, and evolve meanings within and between their various components will inevitably alert them to some/all of the issues just discussed—how all texts harken back to other texts, how the activities they are engaged in are a result of local, and not-so-local cognitions in their TCs, how their TCs have persistent structures that anchor various and distributed cognitions. Building a degree of meta-awareness into every course that enrolled L2 teachers take—where they self-consciously focus on and question the various components of their socialization process and their individual participation and contribution—will ultimately allow them to view their TCs as "dynamic open systems" (Lemke, 1995, p. 162) whose general balance and (in)stability is partially in their hands. It will allow them to acknowledge and question the phenomenon of naturalization in their TCs that has as one of its layers a "commonsensical" approach that needs to be to peeled to reveal its second layer, an essence (Fairclough, 1989, p. 92). Cognizant of and as participants in a collective that makes room for and encourages such peeling and revealing, they ultimately are able to understand that they can (collectively or individually) respond to and change their TCs; that were it not for them, the TCs would not exist. Such awareness can only be empowering.

REFERENCES

Auerbach, E. (1996). Adult ESL/literacy from the community—to the community: A guidebook for participatory literacy training. Mahwah, NJ: Lawrence Erlbaum Associates.

Aronowitz, S., & Giroux, H. (1993). Education under siege. Westport, CT: Bergin and Garvey.

Atkinson, D. (1998). Scientific discourse in sociohistorical context: The philosophical transactions of the Royal Society of London, 1675–1975. Mahwah, NJ: Lawrence Erlbaum Associates.

Bailey, K., Curtis, A., & Nunan, D. (1998). Undeniable insights: The collaborative use of three professional development practices. TESOL Quarterly, 32(3), 546–556.

Bailey, K., & Nunan, D. (1996). Voices from the language classroom: Qualitative research in second language education. NY: Cambridge University Press.

Bateson, G. (1972). Steps to the Ecology of Mind. (2nd ed.). New York: Ballantine Books.

Benesch, S. (Ed.). (1991). ESL in America: Myths and possibilities. Portsmouth, NH: Boynton/Cook Publishers.

Berkenkotter, C., & Huckin. T. (1995). Genre knowledge in disciplinary communication: cognition/culture/power. Hillsdale, NJ: Lawrence Erlbaum Associates.

Bizzell, P. (1992). Academic discourse and critical consciousness. Pittsburgh, PA: University of Pittsburgh Press.

Blanton, L. (1998). Discourse, artifacts, and the Ozarks: Understanding academic literacy. In V. Zamel & R. Spack (Eds.), *Negotiating academic literacies*, (pp. 219–325). Mahwah, NJ: Lawrence Erlbaum Associates.

Bordieu, P. (1991). *Language and symbolic power.* Cambridge, MA: Harvard University Press.

Burton, J. (1998). A cross-case analysis of teacher-involvement in TESOL research. *TESOL Quarterly, 32*(3), 397–446.

Campbell, C. (1996). Socializing with the teachers and prior language learning experience: A diary study. In K. Bailey & D. Nunan (Eds.), *Voices from the Language Classroom*, (pp. 201–223). Cambridge, UK: Cambridge University Press.

Canagarajah, S. (1993). Critical ethnography of a Sri Lankan classroom: Ambiguities in student opposition to reproduction through TESOL. *TESOL Quarterly, 27*, 601–626.

Cazden, C. (1989). Contributions of the Bakhtin Circle to Communicative Competence. *Applied Linguistics, 10*(2),116–127.

Clair, N. (1998). Teacher study groups: Persistent questions in a promising approach. *TESOL Quarterly, 32*(3), 465–492.

Cole, M., Engestrom, Y., & Vasquez, O. (1997). Introduction. In M. Cole, Y. Engestrom, & O. Vasquez (Eds.), *Mind, culture, and activity* (pp. 1–21). Cambridge, UK: Cambridge University Press.

Cole, M., & Wertsch, J. (1996). *Contemporary implications of Vygotsky and Luria.* Worcester, MA: Clark University Press.

Eckert, P., & McConnell-Ginet, S. (1992). Think practically and look locally: Language and gender as community-based practice. *Annual Review of Anthropology, 21*, 461–490.

Fairclough, N. (1989). *Language and power.* London, UK: Longman.

Fairclough, N. (1992). *Critical language awareness.* New York: Longman.

Ferris, D. (1999). The case for grammar correction in L2 writing classes: A response to Truscott. *Journal of Second Language Writing, 8*(1), 1–11.

Fleck, L. (1981). *Genesis and development of a scientific fact.* Chicago: University of Chicago Press.

Flor, N., & Hutchins, E. (1991). Analyzing distributed cognition in software teams: A case study of team programming during perfective software maintenance. In J. Koenemann-Belliveau, T. G. Moher, & S. P. Robertson (Eds.), *Proceedings of the fourth annual workshop on empirical studies of programmers*, (pp. 36–59). Norwood, NJ: Ablex.

Flowerdew, J. (1998). Language learning experience in L2 teacher education. *TESOL Quarterly, 32*(3), 529–536.

Freeman, D. (1996). Renaming experience/reconstructing practice: Developing new understandings of teaching. In D. Freeman & J. Richards (Eds.), *Teacher learning in language teaching* (pp. 221–241). Cambridge, UK: Cambridge University Press.

Freeman, D., & Johnson, K. (1998). Reconceptualizing the knowledge-base of language teacher education. *TESOL Quarterly, 32*(3), 417.

Gee, J. (1991). *Social linguistics and literatus: Ideologies in discourses.* Philadelphia, PA: Falmer Press.

Gee, J. (1997). Meanings in Discourses: Coordinating and being coordinated. In S. Muspratt, A. Luke, & P. Freebody (Eds.), *Constructing critical literatus: Teaching and learning textual practice* (pp. 273–302). Cresskill, NJ: Hampton Press.

Gee, J. (1999). *Learning language as a matter of learning social languages within discourses.* Paper presented at the College Composition and Communication Conference, Atlanta, GA.

Giroux, H. (1992). *Border crossings: Cultural workers and the politics of education.* New York: Routledge.

Golombek. P. (1998). A study of language teachers' personal practical knowledge. *TESOL Quarterly, 32*(3), 447–464.

Hanks, W. (1996). *Language and communicative practices.* Boulder, CO: Westview Press.

Heath, S. B. (1985). Literacy or literate skills: Considerations of ESL/EFL learners. In P. Larson, E. Judd, & D. Messerschidt (Eds.), *On TESOL 84* (pp. 15–28). Washington, DC: TESOL.

Holliday, A. (1994). *Appropriate methodology in context.* Cambridge, UK: Cambridge University Press.

Huckin, T. (1987). *Surprise value in scientific discourse.* Paper presented at College Composition Communication Conference, Atlanta, GA.

Johnson, K. (1996). The role of theory in L2 teacher education. *TESOL Quarterly, 30,* 765–771.

Kaplan, R. B., Cantor, S., Hagstrom, C., Kamhi-Stein, L., Shiotani, Y., & Zimmerman, C. (1994). On abstract writing. *Text, 14*(3), 401–426.

Killingsworth, K. J., & Palmer, J. S. (1988). *Ecospeak: Rhetoric and environmental politics in America.* Carbondale: Southern Illinois Press.

Lave, J., & Wenger, E. (1991). *Situated learning.* Cambridge, UK: Cambridge University Press.

Leitch, V. (1983). *Deconstructive criticism.* Ithaca, NY: Cornell University Press.

Lemke, J. (1995). *Textual politics: Discourses and social dynamics.* Bristol, PA: Taylor and Francis.

Lemke, J. (1989). *Using language in the classroom.* Oxford, UK: Oxford University Press.

Marcus, G. (1998). *Ethnography through thick and thin.* Princeton, NJ: Princeton University Press.

McLaren, P. (1989). *Life in schools.* New York: Longman.

Miller, C. (1994). Rhetorical community: The cultural basis of genre. In A. Freedman & P. Medway (Eds.), *Genre and the new rhetoric* (pp. 67–78). London: Taylor and Francis.

Nardi, B. (Ed). (1996). *Context and consciousness: Activity theory and human-computer interaction.* Cambridge, MA: MIT Press.

Nunan, D. (1996). Hidden voices: Inside's perspectives on classroom. In K. Bailey & D. Nunan (Eds.), *Voices in the language classroom* (pp. 41–56). Cambridge, UK: Cambridge University Press.

Pennycook, A. (1994). *The cultural politics of English as an international language.* New York: Longman.

Porter, J. (1986). Intertextuality and the discourse community. *Rhetoric Review, 5,* 34–47.

Porter, J. (1992). *Audience rhetoric: An archeological composition of the discourse community.* Englewood Cliffs, NJ: Prentice Hall.

Raimes, A., & Zamel, V. (1997). Response to Ramanathan and Kaplan. *Journal of Second Language Writing, 6,* 79–81.

Ramanathan, V., & Atkinson, A. (1999). Individualism, academic writing and ESL writers. *Journal of Second Language Writing, 8*(1), 45–75.

Ramanathan, V., & Kaplan, R. B. (1996a). Audience and voice in current composition textbooks: Implications for L2 student-writers. *Journal of Second Language Writing, 5,* 21–34.

Ramanathan, V., & Kaplan, R. B. (1996b). Some problematic "channels" in the teaching of critical thinking in current L1 composition text-books: Implications for L2 student-writers. *Issues in Applied Linguistics, 7,* 225–249.

Ramanathan, V., & Kaplan, R. B. (1997). Response to Raimes and Zamel. *Journal of Second Language Writing, 6,* 83–88.

Ramanathan, V., & Kaplan, R. B. (2000). Genres, authors, discourse communities: Theory & application for L2 writing instructors. *Journal of Second Language Writing, 9*(2), 171–191.

Richards, J., & Lockhart, C. (1996). *Reflective teaching in second language classrooms.* New York: Cambridge University Press.

Richards, J., Ho, B., & Giblin, K. (1996). Learning how to teach in the RSA cert. In D. Freeman & J. Richards (Eds.), *Teacher learning and language teaching* (pp. 242–259). Cambridge, UK: Cambridge University Press.

Russell, D. (1995). *Activity theory and its implications for writing.* Mahwah, NJ: Lawrence Erlbaum Associates.

Salomon, G. (Ed.). (1993). *Distributed cognitions.* Cambridge, UK: Cambridge University Press.

Schleppegrell, M. (1997). Teacher research through dialogic inquiry. *Canadian Modern Language Review, 54*(1), 68–83.

Shamim, F. (1996). In or out of the action zone: Location as a feature of interaction in large ESL classes in Pakistan. In K. Bailey & D. Nunan (Eds.), *Voices in the language classroom* (pp. 123–144). Cambridge, UK: Cambridge University Press.

Shor, I., & Freire, P. (1987). *A pedagogy for liberation.* South Hadley, MA: Bergin and Garvey Publishers.

Spack, R. (1997). The rhetorical construction of multilingual students. *TESOL Quarterly, 31,* 765–774.

Swales, J. (1998). *Other floors, other voices.* Mahwah, NJ: Lawrence Erlbaum Associates.

Truscott, J. (1999). The case for "The case against grammar correction in L2 writing classes": A response to Ferris. *Journal of Second Language Writing, 8*(2),111–122.

Vacca, R., Vacca, J., & Bruneau, B. (1997). Teachers reflecting on practice. In J. Flood, S. Brice Heath, & D. Lapp (Eds.), *Handbook of Research on teaching literacy through the communicative and visual arts* (pp. 445–450). New York: Simon & Schuster, Macmillan.

van Maanen, M. (1977). Linking ways of knowing with ways of being practical. *Curriculum Inquiry, 6,* 205–228.

Van Nostrand, A. D. (1994). A genre map of R & D knowledge production for the U.S. Department of Defense. In A. Freedman & P. Medway (Eds.), *Genre and the new rhetoric* (pp. 133–145). London: Taylor and Francis.

Wells, G. (1996). Using the tool-kit of discourse in the activity of teaching and learning. *Mind, Culture, Activity, 3*(2), 74–101.

Wells, G. (1999). *Dialogic Inquiry.* Cambridge, UK: Cambridge University Press.

11

Some Key Factors Affecting English Learners' Development of Advanced Literacy[1]

Robin Scarcella

University of California, Irvine

In earlier papers (Scarcella 1996, 1999), I argued that much of the second language (L2) research has been inappropriately applied to classroom instruction. Researchers who synthesized studies on adult L2 students were telling public school teachers to reduce the amount of English language instruction that they gave their students in Grades K through 12. They held that English language development occurred in natural stages over time through the learner's exposure to English and that instruction was not necessary. As a result of such advice, I argued, a significant number of students were languishing in California public schools. I suggested that much of the L2 research underlying the advice was outdated or applied incorrectly and that California's diverse immigrant populations had suffered as a result.

By any measure, many students have not fared well in California's public schools. In 1995 a special report of the California Special Education Reading Task Force reported that roughly 35% of all children in the state had reading difficulties (CA Dept. of Ed., 1995). In a study undertaken by the U.S. Education Department, the National Assessment of Educational Progress (1999), students at the 4th, 8th, and 12th grades completed narrative, informative, and persuasive writing assignments as part of the National Writing Assessment. California students scored below the national averages, even scoring below students in Texas and New York, states that have comparable numbers of students from low socioeconomic levels

[1]I am grateful to Lily Wong Fillmore and Russell Rumberger for detailed comments on previous drafts. Special thanks are also due to Mary Schleppegrell for her careful editorial comments and suggestions. Errors in content are my own.

and, like California, have large numbers of nonnative English speakers. About 56% of the California students who were tested demonstrated only basic skills—defined as imperfect mastery of grammar, vocabulary, and spelling. These students were able to communicate their ideas, but only informally and with poor English proficiency. Their writing was full of grammar and spelling errors. Some 24% could not even communicate their ideas comprehensibly, lacking control of even the basic, commonly occurring features of English vocabulary and grammar. Deficiencies in writing proficiency were most apparent among the students who came from low socioeconomic backgrounds. Many of these students were English learners (ELs), that is, nonnative speakers of English.

Inadequate writing skills become apparent when ELs enter institutes of higher education. This is the case at the University of California at Irvine (UCI). In 1999, over 60% of the UCI freshmen who took the Subject A Exam, a freshman composition test, failed it. In the academic year 1999–2000, approximately 300 ELs out of 1,700 entering freshmen were required to take specially designed English courses for L2 learners at UCI. Despite these students' many years in the United States (on average, about 8 years), excellent high school grade-point-averages (above 3.5, in the upper 12% of their high school graduating classes) and high scores on the Scholastic Aptitude Test (well above 1000), their English language problems prevented them from achieving success in freshmen writing courses, and they were required to take specially designed English language courses to address their language difficulties.

Wong Fillmore and Snow (1999) provide a more comprehensive picture of how poorly California's college students are doing in English, describing students' English abilities at the 22 campuses of the California State University system in these words:

> All entering freshmen have to take a placement test in English and math. The failure rate of the English placement test across the 22 campuses in 1998 was 47%; at one campus, it was 85%. Students who fail the test are required to take and pass remedial English courses which focus on helping them acquire the language and literacy skills required for university level work.

The language difficulties of California's ELs are serious and teachers, often lacking adequate knowledge and teaching skills (Gándara, 1997), are poorly prepared to help them. The guidance that these teachers receive in workshops and in-services does little to prepare them to address their students' language needs.

FEATURES OF ADVANCED LITERACY

Having previously examined research and programs based on the research as well as the inadequate results, I propose a new approach to studying ELs' linguistic needs. The first step is to recognize the diversity of these needs and to begin to identify key factors contributing to student success and failure in the acquisition of advanced English literacy. I use the expression "advanced English literacy" to refer to knowledge of the multiple, interrelated competencies related to reading, writing, speaking, and listening. (For discussions of the diverse aspects of this proficiency, see Biber, 1986, 1988; Halliday, 1994; Halliday & Hasan, 1989; Halliday &

Martin, 1993.) The linguistic and metacognitive competencies associated with advanced literacy enable learners to do the following:

* Summarize texts, using linguistic cues to interpret and infer the writer's intention and messages;
* Analyze texts, assessing the writer's use of language for rhetorical and aesthetic purposes, and to express perspective, mood, etc.;
* Extract meaning and information from texts, and relate it to other ideas and information;
* Evaluate evidence and arguments presented in texts, and relate it to other ideas and information;
* Evaluate evidence and arguments presented in texts, and critique the logic of the arguments made in them;
* Recognize and analyze textual conventions used in various genres for special effect, to trigger background knowledge, or for perlocutionary effect;
* Recognize ungrammatical and infelicitous usage in written language, and make necessary corrections to texts in grammar, punctuation, and capitalization;
* Use grammatical devices for combining sentences into concise and more effective ones, and use various devices to combine sentences into coherent and cohesive texts;
* Compose and write an extended, reasoned text that is well developed and supported with evidence and details;
* Interpret word problems—recognizing that in such texts, ordinary words may have quite specialized meaning—for example, that *share equally among them* means to divide a whole into equal parts; and
* Extract precise information from a written text and devise an appropriate strategy for solving problems based on the information provided in the text. (Wong Fillmore & Snow, 1999)

Note that the view of literacy taken here is broad, involving decoding as well as higher-order thinking—conceptualizing, inferring, inventing, and testing. It entails oral communication skills as well as reading and writing abilities (see, for example, August & Hakuta, 1997; Wong Fillmore & Snow, 1999.) Advanced literacy involves knowledge of grammar, vocabulary, pragmatics, metalinguistic knowledge and strategies. Such components are often considered integral to communicative competence (Canale & Swain, 1980; Celce-Murcia, 1995; Scarcella, Andersen & Krashen, 1990).

Grammar is a key component of advanced literacy (Celce-Murcia, 1991). This knowledge enables students to produce situationally appropriate, grammatically accurate utterances, and to accomplish the goals listed previously. For example, learners with advanced proficiency in grammar know that the word *assuming* is used before conditional clauses: *Assuming X is true, then Y* ... (Schleppegrell, chap.

6, this volume). Modal auxiliaries, including *will/would, can/could, may/might, should, must, have to,* and *ought to* are particularly important in advanced English literacy, as they express certainty, uncertainty, necessity, and possibility. Students with advanced English proficiency not only know the meanings and functions of the modal auxiliaries but also their correct use in indicating appropriate time frames (present, past, and future). Knowledge of verb + preposition combinations (fixed expressions such as *I disagree with you* and *He discriminates against her*) is also characteristic of advanced English literacy. An important part of advanced English literacy is the ability to substitute pronouns for noun phrases and use pronouns clearly and consistently. Passive structures to foreground actions and background the agents of these actions (*The book was written by Shakespeare*) and ergative structures (*The rate decreased*) are also characteristic of advanced English proficiency, as are conditionals (*If you were to add X, you would get Y*) (for a more detailed description of this knowledge, see Schleppegrell & Colombi, 1997; see also the chapters by Celce-Murcia, chap. 7, and Schleppegrell, chap. 6, this volume.) Learners who have not acquired sufficient knowledge of English grammar make errors that, at best, brand them as nonnative and, at worst, stigmatize them as uneducated and prevent them from communicating effectively in academic situations.

Vocabulary is another key component of an advanced literacy (see, for example, Hatch & Brown, 1995). Lexical knowledge enables learners to extract accurate information from texts, to interpret word problems and to analyze words for rhetorical effect. It also enables learners to recognize and correct their own infelicitous uses of words, to use words for rhetorical and stylistic purposes, and to utilize lexical devices to combine sentences into cohesive texts. Knowledge of vocabulary includes not only the forms and meanings of words but also the grammatical features that govern the use of words. For instance, the word *criterion* has an irregular plural form *criteria,* the adjective *impotent* is generally used to describe people, not countries, the verb *sanction* is generally transitive and requires an object (*He would not sanction her behavior*), and the noun *conservation* is generally followed by a prepositional phrase that begins with the preposition *of* (as in *conservation of energy*).

Pragmatics is another important part of advanced literacy. Pragmatic knowledge enables learners to produce such complicated genres as expository essays, research papers, abstracts, and dissertations (see, e.g., Swales, 1990; Zamel & Spack, 1999). It enables learners to write text that is appropriate with respect to such situational features as the channel (whether written or oral), the genre (whether a poem, a narrative, or an expository essay), the topic discussed, the interests and needs of their readers, and the purposes of their texts. It enables learners to determine when to suggest that citations counter other citations, whether to provide background knowledge pertaining to citations, how much background information to provide, how to logically arrange citations, and how to integrate them effectively into their texts (McCarthy Young & Leinhardt, 1998). It enables learners to "compose and write an extended, reasoned text which is well-developed and supported with evidence and detail" (Wong Fillmore & Snow, 1999).

Other components of advanced English literacy are also important. Students who have advanced literacy use metalinguistic abilities and higher-order thinking skills to critique their own writing. They have a wide array of metacognitive and linguistic strategies that enable them to make sense of difficult texts. In addition, they have acquired culturally and situationally appropriate attitudes, beliefs, and values that enable them to communicate effectively in a variety of settings (see, for example, Gee, chap. 8, this volume).

FACTORS CONTRIBUTING TO SUCCESSFUL ADVANCED LITERACY DEVELOPMENT

English learners have varying degrees of success in acquiring the linguistic and cognitive features of advanced English literacy. Recall that 20% of California students did well on the National Assessment of Writing and 65% passed standardized reading exams; undoubtedly, a small but significant number of ELs are among these students. Because succeeding on these exams requires advanced literacy, we can consider these students successful language learners. A review of recent research suggests a number of factors that contribute to the EL's successful acquisition of advanced literacy: advanced literacy in a first language (Bialystok, 1997; Cummins, 1979; 1984; Durgunoglu, Nagy, & Hancin-Bhutt, 1993; Hornberger, 1989; Krashen, 1993); strong basic oral English upon entering school in the early grades (August & Hakuta, 1997; Snow, Burns, & Griffin, 1998); opportunities for interaction with speakers of standard English (Wong Fillmore & Snow, 1999); basic reading ability (August & Hakuta, 1997; Krashen, 1993; Snow, Burns, & Griffin, 1998); input via written text (Wong Fillmore & Snow, 1999); attention to form (August & Hakuta, 1997; Snow, Burns, & Griffin, 1998; Swain & Lapkin, 1990); and excellent English instruction, including (especially) instruction in reading.

In the discussion that follows, I review these factors and argue that the most important factor contributing to advanced literacy in English is effective English language instruction. Successful ELs develop advanced English literacy through appropriate instruction at critical junctions in their language learning. Although some successful learners have had advantages such as having advanced literacy in their first languages and multiple opportunities to interact with speakers of Standard English, all successful learners have received effective English language instruction.

Advanced Literacy in the First Language

One important factor contributing to advanced literacy in English by ELs is advanced literacy in the first language. Many learners who are highly successful in acquiring advanced English literacy are not young learners, but older learners who begin their schooling in the United States after the fourth grade. These learners have gained advanced literacy in their first languages through their schooling.

Learners who are highly literate in their first languages are often able to pick up oral English fairly quickly, developing competence in vocabulary, grammar, and pragmatics. When conversing in English, they are already familiar with many similar speech situations; they know how to use extralinguistic information to make sense of speech, and they know the importance of listening for cues like *ya know what?* They are able to predict what is said and they are often able to fill in the gaps when they lack the linguistic resources to understand their addressees (Shaw, 1992; Wong Fillmore, 1991b).

Just as these successful learners acquire the basic proficiency needed to communicate orally in English, so too they acquire the basic proficiency needed to read in English. Their ability to read in their first languages helps them to access basic types of reading materials in their second (Bialystok, 1997; Cummins, 1979; Durgunoglu, Nagy, & Hancin-Bhutt, 1993; Hornberger, 1989; Krashen, 1993; for a review, see Fitzgerald, 1995). They are adept at using comprehension skills when reading in their first languages—focusing on unknown words, making inferences, and using prior knowledge. They apply these strategies when they read in English. They know what to expect when they read the types of elementary genres that they encounter in the lower grades. For example, they are already familiar with how children's story books are organized and where important details in these books are found. Their knowledge of their first languages enables these older learners to quickly master an elementary school entry-level English.

When given adequate instruction, within a year these learners are often able to develop good phonological competence, word reading skills, reading fluency, and reading comprehension strategies. Because these successful learners develop strong beginning reading skills early on, many are able to read children's books effortlessly and enjoy reading (Krashen, 1993). Often they read both inside and outside of class, and their reading helps them to advance their general English proficiency, to improve their reading proficiency, and to increase their background knowledge. By the time these learners are introduced to academic reading, most are able to access it fairly well with appropriate instructional support.

Just as the learners' knowledge of their first languages helps them to access basic reading materials, it also helps them to access more advanced, academic ones. These learners have already studied such academic subjects as science, social studies, literature, and mathematics in the upper elementary, middle school, and/or high school grades. They are able to predict the placement of important information in these texts, and they have already been exposed to the ways different academic texts are organized. They have already encountered many academic genres in their first languages and they are comfortable with these same genres in English. Their superior knowledge of subject matter and extensive background knowledge help them to make sense of the English that they hear and read and to acquire advanced English literacy fairly rapidly (Krashen, 1993). This is especially the case when they are given instruction that builds on their knowledge (Wong Fillmore & Snow, 1999).

Through their reading as well as their interactions with others, their English skills improve. With appropriate instruction, they are able to achieve advanced English literacy. This literacy enables them to interact in academic settings, allowing them passage into "the community of the educated" (Lemke, chap. 2, this volume). Most of the successful learners are recent arrivals to the United States who have begun their schooling in American public schools after the fourth grade (so that they have acquired a high level of proficiency in their first languages) but before the 10th grade (so that they still have enough time to obtain adequate exposure to the features of advanced English literacy and sufficient and appropriate language instruction). Sometimes these successful learners are given the additional advantage of being held back in school for one or two grades. With language instruction, they often make rapid progress in the beginning stages of English language development, eventually attain age-appropriate advanced English literacy, and go on to succeed in institutes of higher education.

It should be noted that students with literacy in their first languages generally, but not always, do better acquiring advanced English literacy than students without literacy in their first languages. Much depends on how much and what type of educational experience they had at the time of immigration. Age at the time of immigration is also a major factor, as is the level at which the learners were reading prior to immigrating. If they arrived in the United States before they had the opportunity to study academic subjects, they probably will not have acquired much advanced literacy in their first languages. Much depends on other individual factors: for example, whether or not these students find it easy or desirable to interact with speakers of Standard English (SESs); whether or not SESs deign to interact with the ELs; whether or not the ELs are motivated to read; and so on. It is also important to mention that many students acquire advanced literacy in English even when they have lost their first languages. At the University of California, for example, thousands of California's immigrant students are losing their first languages while simultaneously acquiring advanced English literacy. Advanced literacy in a first language is, then, helpful, but it is neither sufficient nor required for the development of advanced English literacy. Some students who have advanced literacy in their first languages may fail to thrive due to poor instruction in reading and in English generally.

Strong Basic Oral English Proficiency

Another important factor contributing to the development of advanced literacy is basic oral English proficiency. Knowledge of English phonology, vocabulary, grammar, and pragmatics that is sufficient for communicating needs in informal situations, often acquired incidentally by listening to others communicate, by interacting in English, or through their preschool experiences, helps ELs interact with SESs, which in turn enables them to develop their oral English proficiency fairly rapidly. The development of the learners' oral proficiency is facilitated when SESs provide them with exposure to standard English and opportunities to use this English. However, even those ELs who do not have opportunities to communicate with SESs are often able to gain English literacy skills relatively easily with appropriate instruction if they have sufficient built-up competence in English. Their knowledge of English vocabulary, morphology, syntax, and the pragmatics of basic conversations provides them with a foundation for learning the more complex features of English associated with advanced literacy.

When ELs with strong oral English proficiency enter school, they may or may not have the preliteracy experiences of their native English-speaking peers. For instance, in their homes, they may not necessarily have been encouraged to tell simple children's stories, to participate in language games, or to narrate stories illustrated in picture books. However, the absence of preliteracy experiences does not prevent successful learners from learning how to read, if they arrive in the United States in early childhood and begin their schooling in the lower grades. Especially if they attend well-funded schools where they receive excellent instruction, by the time these students reach high school, they have the advanced English literacy needed to compete well with native English speakers.

It is worth noting that instruction is key to developing these students' English abilities. If teachers do not design lessons that build on the students' previous knowledge of English, their English usually does not develop. Even when these children enter school with quite a lot of English and interact frequently with SESs, it is likely that they will fail to develop advanced English literacy without appropriate instruction.

Interaction With SESs

An additional factor contributing to advanced English literacy is interaction with SESs. Such interaction provides ELs with exposure to standard English and provides them with the practice and feedback required to develop phonology, lexicon, morphology, syntax, and pragmatics. It also contributes to their knowledge of the world. Their increased proficiency in English and background knowledge provides them with a strong foundation for the acquisition of advanced literacy.

Wong Fillmore and Snow (1999) explain that many ELs are unable to obtain sufficient exposure to English input because they attend schools with many learners lacking English proficiency. English learners who find themselves surrounded by other learners who have not acquired the accurate use of everyday English do not acquire academic English without considerable instructional intervention. These learners end up making little or no progress learning English, or they learn English from one another (Wong Fillmore, 1982; 1991a) and end up acquiring "learnerese," a variety of English that deviates greatly from standard English. They are not language learners who are still in the process of acquiring the linguistic features of English; they have developed a stable, nonstandard variety of English.

English learners who are surrounded by peers who do not use Standard English require English instruction in order to acquire even a low level proficiency in Standard English. The key word here is "require." Without this instruction, it is improbable that they will ever acquire advanced levels of proficiency in Standard English. They will become socialized to use the varieties valued in their communities (Moll, 1998; Moll & Greenberg, 1990). Although they will become competent language users within these communities (Gutierrez, Baquedano-Lopez & Turner, 1997), these varieties will not provide them with the advanced English language skills that they need to excel in academic communities in the United States (Langer, 1991; see also Rogoff, 1990).

However, even students who interact with SESs on a daily basis may not acquire advanced literacy without instruction. This is because students rarely use the linguistic forms that characterize advanced literacy in their daily communication. There are large differences between the informal English used in everyday interaction and the more formal English literacy required in academic settings. Interactional opportunities with SESs may have less effect on learning to read and write well and acquiring the features associated with advanced literacy than it has for learning a target-like version of spoken English.

Basic Reading Ability

Reading serves as both a factor that affects language development and an outcome factor that develops as the result of such factors as instruction and motivation. It is through their reading of basic texts that ELs build up their store of cultural and background knowledge and competence in phonology, lexicon, morphology, syntax, and pragmatics. Their increased proficiency in English and background knowledge provides them with a strong foundation for the acquisition of advanced literacy. It improves their general English proficiency and this in turn enables them to improve their reading. They are then able to advance their English proficiency through instruction.

Once these learners find reading easy, they often read extensively. Their reading then contributes to their knowledge of specific school subjects and leads to continuous linguistic growth which further facilitates their interaction with SESs. By the time they graduate from high school, they are proficient enough in academic English to continue to acquire it through their reading, interactions, and instructional activities in academic situations.

Learners who cannot read in their first languages do not have the advantage of being able to transfer knowledge of reading and academic language from their first languages into English. They also have an additional disadvantage when they begin their schooling with insufficient oral English proficiency to communicate well in ordinary situations. Without sensitivity to English sounds and sufficient knowledge of English vocabulary, grammar, and pragmatics, they have difficulty learning to access even the most basic types of English reading materials on their own. Their lack of oral proficiency prevents them from acquiring decoding skills, orthography skills, word knowledge, and comprehension skills easily.

Those who fail to learn to read in the early grades cannot gain advanced literacy without intensive instruction. The reading materials in the upper grades are so beyond their proficiency levels that it is impossible for them to access them. These learners require preliteracy experiences and language instruction designed to quickly take them from the beginning proficiency level to the intermediate level. If these learners' previous schooling has been poor, they also require excellent content instruction designed to build their background knowledge. Without this instruction, they will continue to have difficulty understanding their reading.

Unfortunately, the instruction that these learners receive is often inadequate, neither developing their general English proficiency nor their content knowledge sufficiently. As a result, these learners do not gain the skills to access reading or only the skills to access reading very poorly. Their inability to read undermines their ability to develop their English. Without intensive instructional intervention, it is not possible for these students to develop advanced levels of literacy in English. They lack the basic building blocks—general English proficiency, which includes reading ability, that is needed to acquire it. Their vocabulary is highly restricted and their grammatical proficiency is limited.

Although difficult to determine precisely, the number of unsuccessful students of this type is large. Recall that 24% of California students who took the National Writing Assessment lacked even the basic English skills to convey their thoughts comprehensibly. Struggling EL readers were undoubtedly a significant portion of this group. What is particularly troubling about ELs who are unable to read is that their English proficiency is so far below what is required to participate in academic situations that there is little possibility of their ever participating effectively in them. Their failure to read has dire consequences: "It is the most likely reason that children drop out of school, are retained or referred to special education. Poor reading skills also greatly limit postsecondary school and work options" (CA Dept. of Ed., 1995, p. v).

Those who only have acquired a beginning or an intermediate level of English proficiency will not be able to engage in the academic situations that lead to further enhancement of their English without considerable instruction.[2]

The state of California recognizes the need to help children develop basic reading skills. Students who are having difficulty reading are obtaining increased teacher-guided instruction, receiving extra homework, covering more material, and attending additional summer classes. Already the reading scores of elementary school children in California have shown limited improvement. When these intensive efforts to improve basic reading instruction are supplemented with other instructional activities that develop advanced English proficiency, these efforts may help these students acquire advanced literacy.

Input Via Written Text

Clearly written text provides essential input for advanced literacy development. It is perhaps the most dependable source of academic English input ELs can have (Wong Fillmore, undated). However, not all reading material is good input for developing advanced literacy. Simplified input that does not represent the types of literate texts proficient users of the language read will not help learners obtain the language proficiency needed for advanced literacy. Good input comes from authentic, unsimplified literature and textbooks. It is primarily through these texts that ELs acquire the specific kinds of background information and language that they need to develop advanced literacy. However, not even all literature and academic texts necessarily contribute to the learners' development of advanced literacy. Good input for the development of advanced literacy is well-formed, coherent and cohesive, interesting, and engaging. Moreover, it contains the features of advanced literacy. Good input for the development of advanced literacy need not be long. As Wong Fillmore (undated) points out, even short, unsimplified academic or literature texts can expose ELs to the vocabulary, grammar, and pragmatics of advanced English literacy. What is important is that ELs receive sufficient exposure to these types of texts on a continual basis.

Despite ELs' exposure to good input, they still may fail to acquire advanced literacy. Both native and nonnative English speakers need help at times assessing

---

[2]Reading would help ELs to acquire an English proficiency beyond the beginning level (August & Hakuta, 1997; Snow, Burns, & Griffin, 1998; Wong Fillmore & Snow, 1999). However, to read they have to have more than a beginning proficiency in English. They must have mastered enough English to make sense of the reading (Fitzgerald, 1995; Goldenberg, 1996).

their texts. Most English learners often find it difficult to use texts as input for literacy development without instructional guidance. Wong Fillmore (undated) argues that teachers can assist ELs in acquiring advanced literacy through their reading by helping them make sense of their texts; focusing their attention on the ways in which authors use language; discussing the meaning and interpretation of words, phrases, and sentences in the texts; and helping students understand the linguistic features that indicate relationships. Teachers can hold learners accountable for learning the language as well as the content that they encounter in their texts and ensure that their students use the words, phrases, sentences, and organizational patterns used in their texts. In short, teachers can teach ELs how to analyze texts themselves so that they will attend to the language features of the texts on their own and understand how language is put together to achieve meaning and rhetorical effect. When learners are able to analyze text on their own, they are able to increase the amount of input that they process and that therefore advances their development of literacy. If they can routinely attend to the features of literature and academic texts outside of their classrooms by themselves, they become capable of developing advanced literacy on their own.

Attention to Form

Attention to form constitutes another important factor contributing to EL's success in acquiring advanced literacy. Learners who attend to the linguistic features of their texts are more likely to acquire these features and practice using them in their own communication. Learners can rely on many strategies that foster their ability to attend to form, including routinely analyzing texts for relationships, organization, word meanings, specific uses of words and idioms, and rhetorical effect. When they read, learners who attend to form ask themselves questions concerning the credibility of the author and the logic of the arguments presented. When they write, they use editing strategies to correct their vocabulary and grammar mistakes and they use revising strategies to improve their content and organization. Learners who attend to language forms are aware of the complexities of advanced uses of the language and often seek instructional support to acquire these uses. They pay attention to their teachers' instructional feedback on their language use and use this feedback to improve their English.

Most learners, however, do not attend to language forms. In fact, some learners rely on strategies that prevent them from attending to these forms. Such strategies may actually deter their English language development, as they enable reading without attending to the language features of their texts, and often help learners read only poorly and with inaccurate understanding. These strategies include:

- reading for the gist rather than attending to the linguistic features of texts;
- reading for specific pieces of information (such as numbers, dates, and names) rather than reading materials carefully and analytically;
- using previous knowledge about the content of the material to guess the meaning of the text without reading it;

- figuring out the gist of the reading material from their teachers' oral summaries or previews of the material rather than actually reading the material; and
- accessing information from the reading by only attending to key discourse features (such as titles, headings, and subheadings) or visuals (including graphs, pictures, and illustrations).

The bulk of California's ELs who have difficulty acquiring advanced literacy skills are probably those who do not attend to language forms. They know how to read basic materials, but they lack the proficiency to access advanced reading materials accurately because of strategies that undermine their efforts. These students have not acquired advanced English literacy and their reading and writing scores on statewide and national tests decline in the upper grades.

Strategies that enable learners to communicate informally without much English proficiency also prevent learners from attending to language forms. Many learners at all grade levels begin school with strategies that enable them to communicate inaccurately in informal contexts (Hammond, 1988). These strategies enable them to learn a lot of common English words from their communities and local media—including movies, videos, television, CDs, and the radio and they learn to rely on these words to stretch their ability to communicate. Their oral proficiency, when augmented with even a little instruction, helps them to learn to read basic types of material. However, they read without carefully attending to the language forms.

These ELs often develop beginning reading skills early on, and through these skills, as well as through their instruction and their interactions with others, they make rapid gains in improving their general English proficiency. Unfortunately, their rapid gains do not help them to develop more advanced literacy. Because these learners are quickly able to function in many informal English settings and to accomplish many daily communicative goals successfully, albeit inaccurately, they come to believe that they have acquired enough English to succeed in their schooling. This is especially the case when their teachers do not give them corrective feedback on their English or cushion them by giving them high grades on their written assignments when, in fact, their writing on these assignments is very poor.

Reading does not usually help learners who do not attend to linguistic forms to acquire advanced literacy in English. This is because the students rely on strategies that undermine their ability to acquire English. Teachers often believe that this group of students requires little instruction because superficially the learners seem to make adequate progress acquiring English. The fact that they picked up early school-based literacy so quickly and have gained a track record for doing well in the early grades gives their teachers the false impression that the students do not need intensive instructional support.

There is little relation between the teachers' beliefs and the students' actual skills. The teachers often assume that students can already use words and sentence structures precisely and accurately when, in fact, they cannot. In their schools, the students read academic materials, write scholarly papers, and participate in intellectual discussions. However, they do all this without the requisite competence; they are unable to access their reading accurately, to write their papers competently, or to participate in academic interactions successfully. They do not receive adequate instruction or feedback that tells them that they lack the English proficiency needed to carry out academic tasks. They do not have sufficient competence to access academic English reading material. They are able to decode this material, but reading academic reading material requires more than mere decoding skills. It requires the pragmatic, grammatical, lexical, and metalinguistic abilities of advanced English. The students' inability to read academic texts accurately undermines their ability to acquire advanced proficiency in English. Their reading does little to enhance their knowledge of academic vocabulary, grammar, or pragmatics.

Unsuccessful learners who rely on strategies to read without attending carefully to the language features of their reading are often able to complete the same academic tasks that the more successful types of ELs complete. However, the completion of these tasks does not lead these less successful learners to improve their English (Scarcella, 1999). They practice using everyday English imperfectly. But imperfect practice does not lead to the development of advanced English proficiency.[3] The linguistic forms that these learners use when they complete school tasks are inappropriate, as Wong Fillmore and Snow (1999) put it, "characteristic of vernacular English, varieties of nonstandard English and Learnerese." Largely as a result of the ELs' regular completion of academic tasks, lack of input from SESs, and inappropriate instructional intervention, these forms stabilize, becoming a more or less permanent part of the ELs' linguistic repertoires. The students are naive. They believe that they access academic reading materials in the same ways as their more successful peers, but in reality they do not. They are incapable of interpreting academic texts accurately and using advanced features of English precisely and accurately.

For learners who do not attend to language forms, reading—when not supplemented with intensive, specialized instructional intervention—does not lead to the development of advanced proficiency in English. These learners often go on to college where they encounter academic obstacles. (Recall my previous description of ELs enrolled at UCI and Wong Fillmore and Snow's [1999] description of the students enrolled in California's state university system.) This is a growing population of students, many of whom are included in what is sometimes called *Generation 1.5* (Harklau, Losey, & Siegal, 1999). Regardless of the grade in which they begin their schooling, without considerable instruction, they do not develop the advanced English proficiency needed to complete academic tasks effectively.

There are, of course, some learners who, despite their inattention to language forms, are able to acquire academic literacy subconsciously on their own through their own personal reading. However, the results of standardized exams suggests that the number of these learners, whether native or nonnative, is small.

DISCUSSION

Clearly, the list of factors previously described is incomplete. Other factors leading to success and failure in acquiring advanced English literacy can be discerned. Un-

---

[3]For these learners, only perfect practice leads to perfection.

doubtedly, such factors as motivation, attitude, anxiety, and community, and societal variables all affect the literacy development of ELs (Gardner, Tremblay, & Masgoret, 1997; Oxford, 1996). There is tremendous individual variation in the development of advanced English literacy. The factors interact, contributing to this variation. Also, literacy development rarely proceeds so linearly or stabilizes so completely as I may have inferred. Diverse aspects of language are acquired differentially. Some aspects are acquired quickly while others are acquired slowly if, indeed, they are ever acquired. There is considerable backsliding when it comes to literacy development. Some factors may affect the acquisition of some features of academic literacy, but not others.

Despite these drawbacks, the factors described above explain the results of major language exams taken by ELs in California as well as other reports (see, for example, Snow et al., 1998; and Wong Fillmore & Snow, 1999). At a time when many are groping to explain the educational difficulties of ELs, the factors provide some preliminary explanations. They explain why some learners acquire advanced levels of proficiency in English while others do not and why some learners never learn to read while others are able to read basic reading materials but are unable to read academic ones proficiently.

Unsuccessful ELs could be successful. Just because students do not have strong oral proficiency when they enter school or access to SESs need not result in their failure to develop advanced English literacy. The major factor distinguishing them from successful learners is instruction. Like successful learners, unsuccessful ones could receive age-appropriate instruction that would help them acquire English. For example, before learning to read, they could receive instruction that develops their sensitivity to English sounds and rhythms. They could also be given instruction focused on developing receptive and expressive vocabulary, grammar, and pragmatics. They could be taught how to use multiple linguistic and nonlinguistic cues to figure out the precise meanings of words. They could be motivated to read widely—for general information and for pleasure. Their teachers could increase the amount of exposure they receive to Standard English by reading to them out loud, focusing the learners' attention on specific features of English, and getting them to use these features in their own writing and speech. When learning to read academic texts, students could be given increased exposure to academic texts and opportunities to use these texts. They could be taught to avoid relying on those strategies (such as reading for the gist) that undermine their ability to improve their English and they could be taught those strategies (such as attending to specific grammatical features) that help them improve their English. The linguistic components could be made salient for them (see, for instance, Celce-Murcia, 1991; Lightbown & Spada, 1990; Swain, 1985, 1989; and Wong Fillmore, 1985). They could be given instructional feedback in age-appropriate and culturally responsive ways (Ferris, 1995, 1997). And they could be required to use this feedback to improve their English.

Learners who do not receive instruction when they need it can still attain success with sustained intensive, specialized instruction at a later time. However, it takes an exhaustive effort on the part of learners to acquire advanced English proficiency when they lack general English proficiency. English learners are best served when their teachers provide instruction—including corrective feedback—when it is needed.

Unquestionably, such factors as academic literacy in a first language, strong oral proficiency in English, input via appropriate written texts, and opportunities to interact with SESs contribute to success in the mastery of the English required for academic learning and literacy. However, instruction is crucial. Less successful learners require much more intensive English instruction of a more specialized nature than successful learners. In addition, those learners who receive little exposure to standard English in their communities may also require a different type of instruction in which teachers provide them with greater exposure to standard English inside the classroom, instruction that draws their attention more explicitly to the features of this variety of English, instructional activities that require them to use the features of standard English accurately, explicit instruction that builds their knowledge of the ways in which words, as well as grammatical and pragmatic features, are used in English, editing exercises, and instructional feedback tailored specifically to develop standard English.

Although instructional support for English language development is frequently inadequate, given the wrong-headed advice many teachers have received from L2 researchers and theorists, it may be somewhat less costly for students who enter California classrooms with prior L1 educational experience or basic English proficiency than for those who lack either. This is an argument that supports the notion that successful learners have had previous schooling of an academic nature in their native languages before immigrating to the United States. It is also an argument in support of teaching English to children during their preschool years.

Nevertheless, all ELs require instruction to master advanced English literacy. The number of ELs who lack advanced English literacy is increasing. Despite the heavy emphasis on beginning reading skills in California schools, many of the state's ELs will continue to fare poorly if their teachers fail to provide them with instruction that advances their literacy. An intensive effort will need to be made to teach advanced English literacy that matches the intensive effort that is presently being made to teach basic reading in the lower grades.

Previous research was inappropriately applied and led to ineffective teaching programs and dismal results. It overlooked key factors that lead to advanced levels of English literacy, such as proficiency in a first language, enough oral competence in English to access beginning-level, grade-appropriate reading, basic reading proficiency, interaction with SESs, input via written texts, attention to form, and effective instruction.

CONCLUSION

The main point of this chapter is this: In order to acquire advanced literacy in English, the overwhelming majority of ELs require carefully delivered instruction. Without this instruction, ELs may learn to access print and read basic materials, but they will never gain the proficiency in English that they need to access more advanced texts. This is primarily because there are large and significant differences between the kind of English literacy needed to participate in ordinary, everyday situations and to accomplish daily communicative goals and the kind of English literacy needed to participate in academic situations and to accomplish the academic goals discussed earlier. Advanced language proficiency requires instruction, whether in the first language or in the second. There is some transferability (as the successful learners demonstrate), but even then, instructional help with the lexical, grammatical, pragmatic, and metacognitive features of advanced English is necessary. In fact, appropriate instruction is required for everyone including most speakers of Standard English. The ones who need it less are children who have been exposed to a lot of text-based language (by virtue of having much read to them by parents) or extended discourse in the form of academic conversations, whether in English or in any other language. Children do not get exposure to this type of language through their everyday social interactions with others, whether or not these others speak Standard English. The primary sources are adults or older learners in the context of talking about materials that use lexical features, grammatical devices, and pragmatic features that are typical of extended, reasoned talk about complex materials. The bottom line here is instruction: Instruction that focuses on language itself and on metacognitive strategies for dealing with the written word.

In concluding, I echo my previous warning. It is important to evaluate critically the findings of previous L2 research and to question the direct application of research on adults and international students to the schooling of language minority children. This earlier research suggests that instruction plays only a minimal role in the advanced literacy development of English learners. However, to acquire advanced literacy, the English learners in California's schools do not need less instruction; most need more.

REFERENCES

August, D., & Hakuta, K. (Eds.). (1997). *Improving schooling for language minority children: A research agenda*. Washington DC: National Academy Press.
Bialystok, E. (1997). Effects of bilingualism on children's emerging concepts of print. *Developmental Psychology, 33*(3), 429–40.
Biber, D. (1986). Spoken and written textual dimensions in English: Resolving the contradictory findings. *Language, 62,* 384–414.
Biber, D. (1988). *Variation across speech and writing*. Cambridge, UK: Cambridge University Press.
California State Department of Education. (1995). *Every child a reader*: The Report of the California Reading Task Force, Sacramento. Author.
Canale, M., & Swain, M. (1980). Theoretical bases of communicative approaches to second language teaching and testing. *Applied Linguistics 1,* 1–47.
Celce-Murcia, M. (1991). Grammar pedagogy in second and foreign language teaching. *TESOL Quarterly, 25*(3), 459–480.
Celce-Murcia, M. (1995). Communicative competence: A pedagogically motivated model with content specifications, *Issues in Applied Linguistics, 6*(2), 5–35.
Cummins, J. (1979). Linguistic interdependence and the educational development of bilingual children. *Review of Educational Research, 49*(2), 222–251.
Cummins, J. (1984). *Bilingualism and special education: Issues on assessment and pedagogy*. Clevedon, Avon: Multilingual Matters.
Durgunoglu, A., Nagy, W. E., & Hancin-Bhatt, B. J. (1993). Cross-language transfer of phonological awareness. *Journal of Educational Psychology, 85*(3), 453–465.

Ferris, D. R. (1995). Can advanced ESL students be taught to correct their most serious and frequent errors? *CATESOL Journal, 8*(1), 41–62.

Ferris, D. R. (1997). The influence of teacher commentary on student revision. *TESOL Quarterly, 31,* 315–339.

Fitzgerald, J. (1995). English-as-a-second-language learners' cognitive reading processes: A review of research in the United States. *Review of Educational Research, 65,* 145–152.

Gándara, P. (1997). *Review of research in instruction of limited English proficient students.* University of California Linguistic Minority Research Institute. Educational Policy Center, Davis. (http://www.lmrinet.ucsb.edu/lexecsum/execsum3.html)

Gardner, R. C., Tremblay, P. F., & Masgoret, A. M. (1997). Towards a full model of second language learning: An empirical investigation. *The Modern Language Journal, 81,* 344–362.

Goldenberg, C. (1996). The education of language minority students: Where are we and where do we need to go? *The Elementary School Journal, 96*(3), 353–361.

Gutiérrez, K., Baquedano-López, P., & Turner, M. G. (1997). Putting language back into language arts: When the radical middle meets the third space, *Language Arts, 74*(5), 368–378.

Halliday, M. A. K. (1994). *Introduction to functional grammar* (2nd ed.). London: Edward Arnold.

Halliday, M. A. K., & Hasan, R. (1989). *Language, context and text: A socio-semiotic perspective.* Oxford, UK: Oxford University Press.

Halliday, M. A. K., & Martin, J. R. (Eds.). (1993). *Writing science: Literacy and discursive power.* Pittsburgh, PA: University of Pittsburgh Press.

Hammond, R. (1988). Accuracy versus communicative competency: The acquisition of grammar in the second-language classroom. *Hispania, 71,* 408–417.

Harklau, L., Losey, K., & Siegal, M. (Eds.). (1999). *Generation 1.5 meets college composition.* Mahwah, NJ: Lawrence Erlbaum Associates.

Hatch, E., & Brown, C. (1995). *Vocabulary, semantics, and language education.* New York, NY: Cambridge University Press.

Hornberger, N. (1989). Continua of biliteracy. *Review of Educational Research, 59*(3), 271–296.

Krashen, S. D. (1993). *The power of reading.* New York, NY: Libraries Unlimited.

Langer, J. (1991). Literacy and schooling: A sociocognitive perspective. In E. H. Hiebert (Ed.), *Literacy for a diverse society* (pp. 9–27). New York, NY: Columbia University, Teachers College Press.

Lightbown, P., & Spada, N. (1990). Focus-on-form and corrective feedback in communicative language teaching: Effects on second language learning, *Studies in Second Language Acquisition, 12,* 429–447.

McCarthy Young, K., & Leinhardt, G. (1998). Writing from primary documents: A way of knowing in history. *Written Communication, 15*(1), 25–68.

Moll, L. (1998, February). *Funds of knowledge for teaching: A new approach to culture in education.* Keynote address delivered to the Illinois State Board of Education. Twenty-first Annual Statewide Conference for Teachers of Linguistically and Culturally Diverse Students.

Moll, L., & Greenberg, J. (1990). Creating zones of possibilities: Combining social contexts for instruction. In L. C. Moll (Ed.), *Vygotsky and education* (pp. 319–348). Cambridge, UK: Cambridge University Press.

National Assessment of Educational Progress. (1999). *NAEP 1998 Writing Report Card.* NCES No. 1999464. Release date: Sept. 28, 1999. (http://nccs.ed.gov/pubsearch/pubsinfo.asp?pubid=1999464)

Oxford, R. (1996). *Language learning motivation: Pathways to the new century.* (Tech. Rep. No. 11.) Honolulu, University of Hawaii Press.

Rogoff, B. (1990). *Apprenticeship in thinking: Cognitive development in social context*. New York, NY: Oxford University Press.

Scarcella, R. (1996). Secondary education, second language research, and academic English. *CATESOL Journal, 9*(1), 129–151.

Scarcella, R. (1999). *Balancing approaches to English learner instruction. Balancing Instruction for English Language Learners*. English Literature and Reading Project Conference. Sacramento: California State Department of Education.

Scarcella, R., Andersen, E., & Krashen, S. (Eds.). (1990). *Developing communicative competence in a second language*. New York, NY: Harper and Row.

Schleppegrell, M. J., & Colombi, M. C. (1997). Text organization by bilingual writers: Clause structure as a reflection of discourse structure. *Written Communication, 14*(4), 481–503.

Shaw, P. (1992). Variation and universality in communicative competence: Coseriu's model, *TESOL Quarterly, 26*(1), 9–25.

Snow, C., Burns, S., & Griffin, P. (Eds.). (1998). *Preventing reading difficulties in young children*. Washington DC: National Academy Press.

Swain, M. (1985). Communicative competence: Some roles of comprehensible input and comprehensible output in its development. In S. Gass & C. Madden (Eds.), *Input in second language acquisition* (pp. 235–53). Rowley, MA: Newbury House.

Swain, M. (1989). Manipulating and complementing content teaching to maximize second language learning. *TESOL Canada Journal, 6*, 68–83.

Swain, M., & Lapkin, S. (1990). Aspects of the sociolinguistic performance of early and late immersion students. In R. C. Scarcella, E. S. Andersen, & S. D. Krashen (Eds.), *Developing communicative competence in a second language* (pp. 41–54). New York, NY: Harper & Row.

Swales, J. (1990). *Genre analysis: English in academic and research settings*. Cambridge, UK: Cambridge University Press.

Wong Fillmore, L. (1982). Instructional language as linguistic input: Second Language Learning in Classrooms. In L. C. Wilkinson (Ed.), *Communication in the classroom* (pp. 283–294). New York, NY: Academic Press.

Wong Fillmore, L. (1985). When does teacher talk work as input? In S. M. Gass & C. Madden (Eds.), *Input in second language acquisition* (pp. 17–50). Rowley, MA: Newbury House Publishers.

Wong Fillmore, L. (1991a). Second language learning in children: A model of language learning in social context. In E. Bialystok (Ed.), *Language Processing by Bilingual Children* (pp. 49–69). New York, NY: Cambridge University Press.

Wong Fillmore, L. (1991b). When learning a second language means losing the first. *Early Childhood Research Quarterly, 6*, 323–346.

Wong Fillmore, L. (Undated). *The importance of background knowledge in second language-learning*. Scott Foresman. Educator, 2. (http://www.scottforesman.com/sfaw/teacher/educator2educator/ltintlwf.html)

Wong Fillmore, L., & Snow, C. (1999). *What educators—especially teachers—need to know about language: The bare minimum*. Unpublished paper. (http://www.cal.org/ericcll/teachers/teachers.pdf)

Zamel, V., & Spack, R. (Eds.). (1999). *Negotiating academic literacies: Teaching and learning across languages and cultures*. Mahwah, NJ: Lawrence Erlbaum Associates.

12

Writing to Learn: Science in the Upper-Elementary Bilingual Classroom

Barbara J. Merino
University of California, Davis
Lorie Hammond
California State University, Sacramento

This study describes how upper elementary school science teachers who work with bilingual students facilitate the learning of scientific concepts and skills through writing. The project described here, the Bilingual Integrated Curriculum Project (BICOMP), uses a thematic approach in which a series of science inquiry lessons are scaffolded and then integrated with other areas of the curriculum. Writing figures as an important component of the curriculum and is used in a variety of ways. Focusing in particular on the lab reports of fifth-grade bilingual students, we show how the emergent stages of advanced literacy can be scaffolded and guided by the activities and resources provided by the teacher.

ACADEMIC LANGUAGE

Although many community and family influences affect the achievement of English Language Learners (ELLs), it is widely acknowledged that many Spanish-speaking children have difficulty succeeding in school because of a failure to develop advanced literacy skills in what has been termed "academic English." Academic English has been broadly defined as the English skills necessary to participate in academic tasks in the classroom (see Scarcella, chap. 11, this volume). A

227

variety of models have been proposed to explain the role of academic language proficiency in educational attainment. Some, like Cummins (1981; 1999) have focused on the cognitive load and degree of context students manipulate as they respond to academic tasks. Some researchers have focused on a close analysis of the language used in specific disciplines, considering academic English as a compilation of many subregisters such as the language of mathematics, for example (Crandall, Dale, Rhodes, & Spanos, 1989).

Canale and Swain (1980), in a widely discussed model, propose four key areas to consider: grammatical competence (encompassing lexical, syntactic and phonological knowledge in an integrated whole), sociolinguistic knowledge (knowing which lexico-grammatical form to choose given the topic, the social setting and the interlocutor), discourse competence (knowing how to put sentence-level propositions in sequence to form coherent text), and strategic competence (knowing how to negotiate clarification when lack of competence impedes communication). This model implies that unique aspects of language proficiency are tapped by each knowledge type and gives a broader perspective from which to view academic English. Delpit (1995), among others, argues that members of minority communities are often not privy to the rules of a variety of tasks typical of academic settings and need to be taught these rules overtly. Teachers then may be helped by an accessible analysis that outlines the unique features of the discourse skills of academic English in specific tasks.

Recently a *standards* movement has evolved across the United States as a catalyst for educational reform in all areas of the curriculum. National professional organizations as well as federal and state governments have joined the fray in articulating standards within each discipline, including language arts and specifically language development for the population of English language learners (California State Board of Education, 1999). The standards are understandably broad but on the whole tend to give greater emphasis to narrative language, neglecting informative, and persuasive language. The principal organization promoting English as a second language (TESOL) has recently published its own national standards (1997) and does target among its goals "to use English to achieve academically in all content areas," further specifying that students are expected to "use English to interact in the classroom and to obtain, process, construct and provide subject matter information in spoken and written form" … as well as to "use appropriate learning strategies to construct and apply knowledge." Although these standards do more to overtly delineate the areas of academic English teachers must address, the specifics are only broadly outlined through sample scenarios to illustrate the goals. Standards offer some advantage to teachers and policy makers in providing a more systematic template to organize instruction and assessment. However, standards that neglect areas of discourse that are important can further undermine teachers' efforts to address the development of discourse skills students need to survive in a rigorous instructional program.

DISCOURSE SKILLS IN SCIENCE

The development of discourse skills in science among monolingual learners has been the object of active inquiry over the past 20 years (Grabe & Kaplan, 1996; Swales,

1990). With English language learners, studies of writing have focused on the older learner, usually at the university level, investigating, for example, the process of composing (Raimes, 1985) and revising (Ventola & Mauranen, 1991). Very little research has been done on the experience of Spanish speakers writing in English. Bilingual children's writing has been looked at largely from the perspective of the narrative (Edelsky, 1986; Swain, 1975). This emphasis is understandable, given the stress schools give to narratives in both reading and writing throughout the elementary years. In a recent study of a dual immersion school, for example, Dubcovsky (1999) reported a focus on reading and writing narratives and very limited opportunities for the development of expository text in bilingual classes even at the point of exit at sixth grade. Because science is perhaps one of the most neglected areas of the curriculum for bilingual learners, it is not surprising that studies that target the development of writing abilities in science in this population are scarce indeed.

Genre has been broadly defined by Grabe and Kaplan (1996, p. 206) as "discourse types that have identifiable formal properties, identifiable purposes, and a complete structure (i.e., a beginning, a middle and an end)." Educators bring their own take on the term, viewing it at times quite broadly as Tomkins does when she considers genre "a category of literature" or "discourse of any type, spoken or written" (1998, p. 370). In this study, we adopt the perspective of Saville-Troike (1982, p. 34), who defines genre as "a type of communicative event" and who advocates an informant-oriented approach to its investigation, stating that "the units used for segmenting, ordering, and discovering data should be those of the group, and not *a priori* categories of the investigator."

"Task" has been defined by Swales (1990, p. 76) as:

> One of a set of differentiated, sequenceable goal-directed activities drawing upon a range of cognitive and communicative procedures relatable to the acquisition of pre-genre and genre skills appropriate to a foreseen or emerging sociorhetorical situation.

This study describes discourse skills needed for tasks and genres related to science experimentation that can be targeted for development at the upper elementary level to help students develop academic language and advanced literacy.

A review of methods books used in the preparation of teachers of science at the elementary level reveals limited discussion of the discourse skills to be developed through science instruction. Victor (1985) outlines three methods of evaluation at the elementary school level: essay tests, objective tests, and written reports, describing as a prevailing practice the use of objective tests and written reports. He endorses a greater use of essay questions that are well focused and target one phenomenon from multiple perspectives. Most essay questions call for "explanation, description or identification" (Victor, 1985, p. 232), with explanations the most frequently targeted discourse act. Victor also suggests teaching use of quotations to avoid plagiarism. Regarding reports, he cautions teachers to insure that a report has a purpose, a beginning, a middle, and an end. These broad directives offer very little support for how teachers can develop the discourse of science.

Many science methods texts for the elementary school focus on reports that tap written resources rather than reports on an experiment. This practice is, in part, the result of the challenge of conducting experiments in the classroom and the further challenge of writing about them. Within constructivist science, where independent inquiry is promoted as a core principle, the discourse of reporting findings, the explanation of a phenomenon based on an experiment, is more overtly taught but still to a limited degree. Even in more recent methods books that are identified as constructivist, for example, in Bentley, Ebert, & Ebert (2000), the tendency is to focus on investigation reports or inquiry reports without providing much scaffolding for teachers on how to develop the discourse peculiar to scientific writing. The tasks that are targeted are presented as isolated pieces: brainstorming concepts, writing questions, making written summaries of a lecture or text material. For the most part then, a focus on writing about science experiments has been evolving very slowly in science education (but see, e.g., Merino & Hammond, 1995). Koch (1996) provides a structure for stories in science based on a series of questions. For example, *Expressing prior knowledge* is cued by the question: What do I know about ...?

Recent secondary-level texts present high expectations for writing lab reports, but this is relatively speaking, a new phenomenon. Thus Collete and Chiappetta (1986, p. 80) in their text designed for middle- and secondary-student teachers, mention reports only in passing, in fact issuing a cautionary note about the overuse of reporting data: "If students devote too much time and effort in recording and reporting data, they may develop an unfavorable attitude toward the laboratory." In fact, they suggest that "labeling a diagram" may be sufficient in some cases, although they do encourage giving students ample opportunity to draw their own conclusions and state them in their own words. More recently some methods textbooks and schools themselves have taken a more proactive stance on developing the discourse skills unique to science. For example, Baker and Piburn (1997) dedicate a whole chapter to language and science in their methods text designed for middle- and secondary-school classrooms. The lab report is not taught overtly, but components of it are addressed indirectly, for example, by requiring students to write reflections about their preconceptions and reconcile them with evidence.

The lab report as a genre varies extensively in its application in grades K through 12 education in the United States. Nonetheless, the elements outlined in lab reports are usually based on the expectations of the written reports that will figure in high stakes events such as science fairs. Some school districts, particularly those that give prominence to science fairs and expect most of their students to attend university, have developed structured rubrics to evaluate the elements of a lab report, providing rich detail on what students must supply for each element: hypothesis, procedure, and so on. On the whole, however, writing tends to be emphasized as ways of personalizing science, promoting scientific discourse as an aid to learning, and a way of connecting students' lives to science.

TEACHING THE LAB REPORT

The Sheltered Constructivist Approach (Coughran, Hoskins, & Merino, 1986; Merino & Hammond, 1998) seeks to integrate science with other areas of the curriculum by focusing on a series of themes, such as "weather", in science as well as in art, literature, and math. A concept, such as "uses of weather knowledge," is explored in a week of science lessons and the same theme is integrated into lessons from other areas of the curriculum. The BICOMP program uses a communicative approach that allows students to reflect on their understanding of a science concept, participate in hands-on activities to explore the concept, reflect on their acquired knowledge, and follow-up with an inquiry activity shaped by their own interests. The approach is labeled "sheltered constructivism" because students first participate in activities under the guidance of the teacher, who contextualizes tasks by using communicative techniques and the students' first language. Students then spin off to further activities that build on questions they want to pursue in science and other areas. Spin-off activities in literature and art use resources from a variety of cultural groups.

The students we report on here are in fifth-grade bilingual programs in which Spanish and English alternate as the medium of instruction on a day-by-day basis. Science is taught three times a week, using a preview–review model that enables students not yet fluent with the language of the day to access key concepts. Several techniques were used by the teachers in this study to scaffold the texts. For many of the tasks, BICOMP already provided a visual model, giving some guidance as to the format. Teachers often provided an example themselves as they participated in the activity or showed a student example to provide ideas about how students could respond. Models from the media or literature were also used, such as a video account of a tornado in a weather forecast, for example.

We examine here students' performance in writing science lab notes and reports on experiments. Mini modules on each concept focused on the need to maintain careful records to understand what happens, to report to others so that other scientists could repeat the experiment and to keep a record for future use. The need to act like a scientist, recording faithfully and in detail what transpires in the science lessons is the most important macro feature of lab reports. Students' texts are considered in terms of conceptual development from micro understandings in the context of specific experiments, (the hot air made the balloon blow up) to macro understandings, which imply a higher degree of generalization (when air is heated, it expands).

INFORMAL LAB NOTES

In this section, we discuss students' responses on informal lab notes that stimulate recall of the science experience at the end of the day or at the beginning of the science lesson on the following day. We can demonstrate this task with the responses of two fifth-grade students. John is a student with a monolingual English background, who, in the words of his teacher, "does very well academically,—verbal—a leader." He provides a complete description of the experiment in a text that is consistently well formed.

John - Entry 1 (early Fall)
We took a thermometer off a card, then we stuck it in a cup of ice and watched the liquid in it go down. Then we took a cup filled with warm water and watched it rise up.

A variety of cohesive ties are used. The action is presented in chronological and logical order. *Then* as a temporal cohesive device is featured twice, nicely scaffolding the sequence of events. The additive *and* is used in well designed parallel structures in the laying out the sequence of events. John displays his discourse competence in writing up a brief but complete and cohesive account of the experiment. John's response is not perfect, as he does not say that the thermometer needs to be placed in the cup filled with warm water, but he generally adheres to the teacher's expectations that he produce an account rich enough in detail that it would be possible to replicate. It is also an account that captures the essential concept of how thermometers work: The liquid goes up when the thermometer gets heated up by the warm water. Following Saville-Troike's (1982) notions of how the participants interpreted this event, teacher and student seem to be in accord. In terms of sociolinguistic competence this lab entry fulfills the core demands of the situation. John's account shows that he has learned that one key function of reports of experiments is to summarize the techniques of the experiment. The teacher described this entry as a model response for a monolingual English speaker.

In contrast, let's look at Dora's attempts at this genre, to demonstrate how informative language develops over time with examples where the level of competence still falls short of the requirements. Dora is a highly fluent English Language Learner, an engaged child, described by her teacher as "average, lovely child, excellent work habits in the bilingual program since kindergarten."

Dora - Entry 1 (early Fall)
We did weather
We measured that if you put a thermometer in ice the red liquid goes down and if you put the thermometer in warm or hot it goes up.

Note that the topic is highlighted at the very beginning. Clearly Dora is aware of an audience, of a need to provide a frame for the entry. The second sentence is quite complex but mal-formed, although there is an understanding of how in general thermometers work. The observation is rich enough to begin to replicate the experiment, although one key feature, water, is left out. The events of the experiment are sketched out but there is little cohesion. The writer seems to be writing as she is thinking. We can however, see at play causal cohesive devices, such as the *if–then* sequence (*then* is not expressed). The beginnings of discourse competence are clearly in evidence.

Focusing on the development of Dora's descriptive discourse in science, we can see by her second entry that she has internalized the vocabulary of science. BICOMP activities, including the Lab Sheet that scaffolds the report, have had an effect (note her beginning with *I observed*).

Dora - Entry 2 (mid Fall)
I observed that the cold balloon the air was sucking in into the bottle. The hot balloon is straight up and it has a little air.

This second experiment was designed to investigate how hot air functions in contrast to cold air. In this experiment, a balloon is placed on each of two bottles and the bottles are then placed in cans. Equal amounts of water are poured into each can. One can has hot water and the other cold water. Students watched the balloon on the hot water bottle blow itself up, while the cold water bottle balloon fell flat.

Dora's Entry 2 is short and outlines the experiment in very broad strokes, focusing on the last event of the experiment. The scientific conceptual understanding focuses on the movement of air but misrepresents the key concept of what happens to the air molecules. Note also the shift from past to present tense. The more dramatic event is presented in the present, although both events occurred in the past. In this account, she does not meet the teacher's expectation that she will record the experiment with sufficient detail so that it can be replicated. The only elements of the experiment that she includes are the bottles and the balloons and the fact that one is in a cold condition, the other in a hot condition. In Entry 2, Dora has focused on recording a single event at the conclusion of the experiment, but this entry does offer a window on Dora's false conception of the scientific principle at play. This gives the teacher a chance to see how Dora understands the experiment and in theory offers another opportunity for further clarification.

To be effective, these informal responses need an audience or interlocutor who interacts with the writer. If the responses are used as a kind of written conversation or dialogue, there is an opportunity for the development of strategic competence, for the teacher to probe and follow up when there are misconceptions and for the student to ask questions when there is a need for clarification. Given the structure of American schools, however, with very large class size, this kind of teaching is difficult to implement. Nonetheless, research in the use of interactive journals in other areas of the curriculum at the elementary level suggest that this type of dialogue could be promoted in science as well.

Dora's third lab report comments on an experiment in which students pour water into a bottle through a funnel, comparing the results when there is air space around the funnel and when the air space is covered with clay in a manner that prevents the air in the bottle from escaping.

Dora - Entry 3 (late Winter)
First we had a bottle and a funnel on top. Then we pored water into the funnel and it when (went) down to the bottle it when very fast and Mrs ___ said that water did not stay in the funnel. Then we put clay round the bottle so air would not get out then we put water in the funnel and it went really slow into the bottle.

It seems that in this entry, the audience is Dora herself. The presentation of the events is chronological and logical, and Dora provides most of the procedures necessary to replicate the experiment. Numerous cohesive ties now appear in this text. Most are temporal (*first*, *then*) or additive (*and*), but one (*so*) is causal. Dora's discourse competence has definitely evolved. She is now closer to what John was able to do with his very first entry, providing a detailed sequence of the experiment. Entry 3 has narrative features, including an indirect quote from the teacher. This is not expected in adult norms for formal lab reports (Braine, 1989). Nonetheless, if perceived as informal lab notes such as scientists might keep in journals designed for the purpose of remembering what went on during an experiment as well as reporting on the conversations around the task of experimenting, such comments are appropriate. With this last entry, she is even able to state the purpose of some of the procedures of the experiment, *we put clay around the bottle so air would not get out.*

From this qualitative analysis of the discourse of these two children, we see how the discourse of science develops over time in an English Language Learner. The schema for presenting an account of an experience in science is much richer in Dora's Entry 3 than in either Entry 1 or 2. More cohesive devices are used and the details of the procedures for the experiment are present. Although the point of the experiment is still not made explicit, Dora has progressed from very incomplete accounts of the procedures of an experiment to procedures that are completely replicable. In summary, Dora's writing shows a closer match with the function of lab notes as a genre designed to capture how an experiment is carried out. Dora still has far to go. There is no analysis, no connection to a scientific principle. This may be in part because this was a teacher-directed experiment designed to promote understanding of principles of air movement and pressure. We can infer some implied understanding of one scientific principle, that air takes up space, from Dora's statement about the function of the clay. However, she still has not learned how to relate the results of an experiment to a broader context. Such connections are complex, making the teacher's skill at teasing out concepts and generalizations through discussion with children extremely important.

In studies of monolingual written discourse, Witte and Faigley (1981) found that good writers tended to create a rich texture of cohesive ties in their writing. Recording Lab Notes for experiments calls for particular kinds of ties as pointed out by Meyer (1985). Structured writing through the scaffolding provided by the BICOMP activities can be very helpful for a child who begins the year without knowledge about the school's expectations for this genre. Dora, for example, has come to understand two key functions of the Lab Notes: Record with sufficient detail to replicate and explain why a particular procedure is followed. She has also learned how to link her account using cohesive devices. An analysis of her entries that focused on formal properties such as grammar or spelling would miss key features in the development of her sociolinguistic and discourse competence in this genre.

FORMAL LAB NOTES WHICH
REPORT ON AN EXPERIMENT

Next we turn to an analysis of scientific discourse in another classroom, using a more formal structure for the Lab Notes genre. For this purpose, we analyzed the BICOMP activity sheets that were used by the students to report their experimental findings. The activity sheets had this format: the problem, the hypothesis, the procedure, the recording of the data and the conclusion. These terms were scaffolded with visuals and presented in English and Spanish. The students responded on the form as the experiment unfolded, charting authentically the evolution of their thinking and their writing of scientific discourse.

This lesson was part of a unit on weather and weather forecasting. The students had measured temperatures throughout the school, looking for the hottest and coolest parts, and were now learning the causes of wind and how hot air and cold air interact to move weather fronts. They participated in the same air expansion experiment with hot and cold water balloons that figured in Dora's second entry. This is a classic experiment, presented as a demonstration in many elementary science curricula. In the design of BICOMP, the curriculum development team chose this experiment because it provides a motivating hook with something dramatic and because it provides an opportunity for students to come up with independent hypotheses of what might happen and verify their guesses very quickly. Finally, the experiment also offers the chance to explore a key element of weather prediction (i.e., how fronts move and change weather patterns).

Each component of the Lab Notes Activity Sheet, with the exception of the problem, which was commonly agreed on, was rated: the hypothesis, the procedures, observing/collecting data, and the conclusion. The focus of the analyses was two-fold: to unpack what the lab notes tell about the children's thinking as scientists and to analyze the discourse in terms of form and function. Our primary focus will be on (a) the scientific appropriateness of the responses, (b) the degree to which the responses conform to the expected discourse act, (c) the length of the response and (d) its grammatical accuracy. We included these elements because teachers of ELLs often target length and grammatical accuracy as the most important to rate, missing the richness of development in scientific conceptual understanding or in the use of scientific discourse. These examples are texts from students along the continuum of proficiency, including non-English speaking recent arrivals, limited English speaking students and fluent English speaking students who had been reclassified. The teacher allowed students to respond in the language of their choice, English or Spanish. In this part of the analysis, we focus on the texts of seven children. Two were classified by the schools as non English speaking (NES) and were recent arrivals to the school. Two who had been 2 years in the program were classified as Limited English Proficient (LEP), and three were classified as fluent in English.

HYPOTHESIZING AND PREDICTING

The element of hypothesizing or predicting was designed to cause reflection and socialize students in the practice of making educated guesses based on what they already know. The prompt accompanying this section contained the words: *if ...*, *then....* The idea was to stimulate thinking along the lines of causation. Predicting, a term most students were used to, was in parentheses to explain the more complex term hypothesizing. Teachers varied in how they used this segment and variation also occurred depending on the lesson. At times the predicting activity was done in a large group as a brainstorming of possibilities. Some times hypothesizing was tied to a group project such as building a solar oven based on the group's hypotheses about how best to use available materials. Other times it was presented as an individual reflection designed to promote individual, independent effort. An example of a student's prediction is: *when object move the shadow will move.* This response makes an accurate scientific generalization based on observation of shadows, made in the context of experimenting with a sun dial. Grammar and mechanics are still an issue, but the content of the message is fully conveyed. The prediction adheres to the structure of an *if ... then* statement, using *when*. Most importantly, it is a testable hypothesis.

The stimulus to hypothesize typically occasions clauses introduced in Spanish by the mental verb *yo creo* (I believe); in English by *I think.* All hypotheses were of this type. Examples in Spanish are presented first.

Diana is a non English speaker, recently arrived at the school.

Yo creo cuando el aire se calienta hace mas calor (10w, 3Cs).

(I think that when the air gets hot, it (the weather) is hotter.)

This response was categorized as being scientifically relevant at the macro level, because it represents a general scientific truth. The structure of the discourse is appropriate for stating a hypothesis that is testable. However, this hypothesis is not relevant to the situation in the air expansion experiment. The syntax and vocabulary are accurate, although an accent mark is missing. Contrast Diana's response to that of Jesus, a non-English speaker recently arrived at the school. Jesus produces a syntactically malformed response with a personalized irrelevant connection to the science of the experiment.

Yo creo que cuando el aire se calienta para secar la ropa. (12w, 3 Cs)

(I think that when the air gets warm it is for drying clothes.)

This hypothesis appears to have short circuited into a functional statement of what might happen when the air is hot, that is, that it will be easier to dry laundry (clothes). Vocabulary and spelling are correct, however. There are approximately three words per clause in this utterance, so Jesus' response has more words but fewer clauses than Diana's, thus more words per clause. This utterance might seem more complex than Diana's; nonetheless Diana's has more scientific relevance.

The most sophisticated hypothesis in the sample was produced by Jaime, an LEP child.

Yo creo cuando el aire se pone elado que se junta el aire. (13w, 3 Cs)

(I think when the air is cold, the air gets put together.)

This hypothesis shows an understanding about air molecules and how heat and cold affect them. Thus, we classified it as relevant at the micro level, in the context of this specific experiment. It has incorrect orthography, omitting the *h* in *helado*, but is syntactically correct. There are more clauses in this utterance than in the one produced by Jesus, and it is much more scientifically relevant. A teacher who focused on the accuracy of the form might consider Diana's response superior, but in fact Jaime shows a conceptually more appropriate understanding of the scientific principle.

The seven students' responses to the request for a hypothesis varied in length from 10 to 17 words. Only three were completely correct in form. The longest response, with 17 words and five clauses, produced by Elsa, was syntactically rich but less scientifically mature than Jaime's.

I think what's going to happen is it will go up in the balloon and desduv (dissolve). (17w, 5Cs)

Elsa seems to have made an analogy about air to ice, assuming that air will dissolve when heated. She has the framework of the hypothesis, however, linking one event to another. The discourse is more like a conversation about what might happen.

This analysis suggests several key generalizations. First, given a general schema for formulating hypotheses, children at all levels of proficiency are able to follow the schema in general and produce complex syntactic forms. Although teachers on the whole tend to focus on the accuracy of form in finished pieces, by viewing these texts from a scientific perspective, credit for conceptual understanding can be affirmed despite the errors in form. Teachers need to consider scientific relevance as well as the appropriate use of grammatical features used in scientific discourse as they teach students how to conceptualize and articulate a hypothesis in its appropriate syntactic frame. The discourse competence of these children is evolving and needs more overt attention to push it from conversational speculation to the expression on testable hypotheses.

THE PROCEDURES SECTION

Doing the experiment was the everyday English label given to the procedures section of the experiment. The students were told to make this section as complete as possible so that there would be an accurate record if the student wanted to report to others what was done in the experiment. Teachers emphasized the need for accuracy and completeness. They often suggested scaffolding the section in steps, numbering each one.

For some students, the procedures section of the experiment and the data collection/observation section merged. Most however, were able to use the procedures section to outline how they set up the experiment, although they varied in the number of elements that were included and in the detail in which they outlined their location. For this part of the analysis, we took a functionalist view, asking to what degree the procedures were sufficiently complete to replicate the experiment. Listed below are the elements mentioned by each student.

Element	N of Ss including it
Two bottles	7
Hot water	7
Two balloons	6
Cold water	5
Pan/pot to heat water	2
Ice for cold water	2
Placement of balloons	2
Purpose stated	1

Two salient features of the experiment, the bottles and the hot water, are included by everyone, but surprisingly not the balloons. Those elements most frequently left out, the pan and the ice, are incidental to preparing the cold and hot water and perhaps therefore implied. The placement of the balloons and most important, the purpose for the layout is most often left out.

The most important criterion to use in judging the adequacy of a procedures section is its replicability. Children need to be taught why procedures need to be replicable and how to make them so. In this sample, only one child, Elsa, a fluent bilingual student, came close to making the recording of the procedures replicable.

Two balloons

Two bottles

We put the two balloons in the top of the two bottles

And the water was hot in 1 bottle and cold in the other.

These procedures capture the experiment quite well, except for the detail of the bottles being in a can with hot or cold water. The events are delineated in sequence, although the prepositional phrase is malformed. Teachers need to give credit to students for adhering to a key convention of the task of writing procedures, that is, procedures should be complete enough to replicate the experiment. The fact that the prepositional phrase is malformed should be secondary in evaluating this response.

Perhaps we need to be more alert about how to create a context in which the need for replicability is clearly demonstrated. When students participate in a large group activity where everyone participates in the same experiment, the students may have a difficult time placing themselves in the situation of needing to know the procedures. One alternative might be to ask groups of students to participate in different experiments related to the same scientific phenomenon and thus create a more authentic opportunity to develop sociolinguistic competence about how the genre functions.

OBSERVING/COLLECTING DATA

The next section, observing and collecting data, was designed as the place where the students would summarize their data or results. Diana, with little experience in American schools and hands-on science, conceives this task as literally narrating what is going on in real time, as evidenced by her report:

estoy biendo como se esta inflando la bomba

(I am seeing how the balloon is blowing up)

cuando pones la bomba arriba de la botella adentro del agua fria

(when you put the balloon on top of the bottle in the cold water). (20ws, 3 Cs.)

Diana captures only one part of the experiment. For Diana, the schema of these different elements of the lab report is not yet clear. She interprets recording as observation, as focusing on the immediacy of the events, using the progressive *estoy *biendo* to record her observation, but leaves out the total sequence of events. Diana, then violates two principles seen in mature accounts of experiments as reported by Heslot (1982). She uses the present tense rather than the past and she does not present the complete sequence of events, reporting what happens in both conditions so that the data could be analyzed.

THE CONCLUSIONS SECTION OF THE LAB REPORT

A key element in becoming proficient in the use of scientific discourse includes developing a full understanding of the schema of an experiment. Recording experiments over and over again is one way in which students can actually internalize the schema. One of the most cognitively demanding tasks in a lab report is drawing defensible conclusions from the data collected. Such explanations are a form of persuasive language because they must be linked convincingly to the data collected. Diana, Maria, and Nora, however, seem to have interpreted this element as a report on the last event in the sequence of events in the experiment. Diana' response is the clearest illustration of this misconception:

> *Cuando pones la botella con la bomba en la agua caliente se infla y cuando la pones en el agua fria se desinfla.* (24w, 4 Cs.)
>
> (When you put the bottle with the balloon in the hot water it inflates and when you put it in the cold water it deflates.)

Diana's repetition of *and* shows the close links these notes have with oral language. One can almost hear her talking. However, her use of present tense creates the impression that this phenomenon is a consistent event in nature, almost as a statement of a scientific law.

The longest response, based on the number of words per clause and the variety of type of clauses in the sample, is Maria's. She uses causative and additive clauses but mistakenly assigns steam as the chief causative agent. Her response is syntactically malformed, with errors in orthography and vocabulary, principally not capitalizing and failing to mark accents. She is aware of needing to report all the features present in the hot water condition, but is uncertain of the cause.

> *la bomba se inflo porque tiene vapor tiene agua caliente y una botella de cristal y tiene la bomba encima y ya se paro.* (24w, 5 Cs)
>
> (The balloon inflated because it has steam it has hot water and a glass bottle and it has the balloon on top and it stood up)

Four of the children seem to have some inkling of the scientific phenomenon at play. Jaime's response targets the notion that air molecules are closer together when the air is cold, a very sophisticated observation. His conclusion is stated as a belief, a restatement of his hypothesis:

> Yo creo cuando el aire se pone elado que se junta el aire. (13w, 3cs)
>
> (I think when the air gets cold that the air gets closer together.)

However, because this statement does not elaborate how this happens and because there was no opportunity to probe, this response fails in showing convincingly a complete understanding of the scientific concept.

Elsa presents her conclusions as a generalization and a law. Although not yet sure of the technical vocabulary, (she writes *expanses*), Elsa seems to understand some of the rules of stating a law. Her generalization is stated in the present tense.

> Warm air expanses and the cold all shrinks. (8w, 2 Cs).

Again this conclusion falls short in linking data to the conclusion, detailing how it is that cold and heat affect air molecules. This represents another case where overt teaching about what is expected when scientists present their findings might help students to understand the demands of the task.

Structurally, the conclusions vary in length and complexity in interesting ways. Those children who interpreted conclusions as the ending event of a narrative of the experiment produced longer responses. Those who understood that the conclusion was a generalization about the phenomenon they had observed produced shorter syntactically less complex responses. This analysis affirms the need to consider complexity or maturity of syntax in relationship to the context. Cognitively more demanding, logically sequenced generalizations about a scientific phenomenon may appear syntactically less complex than less scientifically mature accounts of an experiment. Scientific terms such as *conclusions* that are also used in other contexts might need more elaborate explanation if students are to understand that to a scientific audience, it is not sufficient to state a law but to explain how it can be proven or how it was derived.

CONCLUSIONS AND IMPLICATIONS

The scientific discourse skills demonstrated by the bilingual learners in this study have begun to capture some of the essential features of the mature genre of lab reports. To varying degrees, the children seem to understand the role of the genre as a structured piece with its own set of rules. Some come close to giving rich accounts of the experiments they participated in, meeting the critical demand to be able to replicate the experiment from the accounts they present. In this aspect, these children have begun to understand what college-level students have to do in writing a lab report (see Schleppegrell, chap. 6, this volume). Some have an understanding of the role of discussion of findings. They understand that the conclusion must be linked to the data they collected. Some begin to articulate what they have learned from the experiment as a principle or natural law that communicates understanding of phenomena in the natural world. Some children, however, are still at the very beginning stages of understanding what the genre is about. Nevertheless, progress is being made in their development of advanced literacy.

In the bilingual programs in this study, designed to exit students at fifth or sixth grades, the choice for language of instruction often leans more toward English, but many times language choice for students' work is not specifically articulated (Ramirez & Merino, 1990). The teachers in this study allowed their students to respond in either English or Spanish, under the rationale that the focus of these activities should be on developing scientific conceptual understanding. This stance makes sense when we consider that these students were not used to writing about science at all. They had participated in science activities, but only as sporadic hands-on activities or as traditional science reports. But left to their own devices, students might always choose one language over another for all their writing activities. If there is a real commitment to maintenance of L1 with full development in L2, leaving the choice always in the hands of the writer will restrict the development of competence in writing in both languages.

Teachers have to become aware of the complexity of learning to write the discourse of science. They must understand that grammatical competence is only one aspect of what children are learning as they write. Sociolinguistic competence, defining the audience for whom they write and knowing how that affects how they write, is critically important. Teachers need to be aware that the discourse of science adheres to the rules of a culture of scientists. These rules are complex and involve not only grammatical competence, but also sociolinguistic, discourse, and strategic competence used in unique ways depending on the genre or task. Some tasks might approximate more closely what professional scientists do; others might reflect more what students of science are expected to do either in high school or college. Experiments defined by the teacher, designed to activate conceptual understanding about key scientific principles, might require a set protocol as a way to teach students how to communicate science in these settings. Experiments designed by the students in the form of models or projects such as building a solar oven might require a different writing approach. Depending on the audience, learning logs might function quite differently; they might be used for the benefit of the learner or for the benefit of the teacher or both. Formal lab reports also will vary with the audience and the nature of the task being reported.

Standards-driven curricula for English language development at the upper-elementary level often teach language within the context of language arts frameworks, emphasizing the reading and writing of narrative texts (California State Board of Education, 1999). Although narratives are valuable and easily accessible to students, they do not in themselves provide adequate preparation for the content-driven expository texts that students must use and produce in the later grades. Science is particularly suited for teaching academic language and advanced literacy because it provides hands-on, empirical experiences about which students can write. The thinking and writing required to be successful at science is rigorous and involves various discourse genres. Gergen (1995) suggests that language and conceptual development are relational and contextual. Hence, if ELL students are to be introduced to the language they need to succeed in science in later years, this language must be introduced in a meaningful context within the academic culture of science. In other words, language teaching cannot be separated from the teaching of content, and even beginning ELL students need content area instruction appropriate to their level. Teachers teaching content to ELL students need to exploit the opportunity science offers to teach advanced discourse skills.

REFERENCES

Baker, D. R., & Piburn, M. D. (1997). Constructing science in middle and secondary school classrooms. Needham Heights, MA: Allyn & Bacon.

Bentley, C., Ebert, C., & Ebert, E. S. (2000). The natural investigator: A constructivist approach to teaching elementary and middle school science. Belmont, CA: Wadsworth.

Braine, G. (1989). Writing in science and technology: An analysis of assignments from ten undergraduate courses. English for Specific Purpose, 8, 3–15.

California State Board of Education. (1999). English Language Learner Standards. Sacramento, CA.

Canale, M., & Swain, M. (1980) Theoretical bases of communicative approaches to second language teaching and testing. Applied Linguistics, 1, 1–47.

Collette, A. T., & Chiappetta, E. (1986). Science instruction in the middle and secondary schools. Columbus, OH: Charle E. Merrill.

Coughran, C., Hoskins, J., & Merino, B. (1986). BICOMP: Bilingual Integrated Curriculum Project. West Sacramento, CA: Washington Unified.

Crandall, J. A., Dale, T. C., Rhodes, N., & Spanos, G. (1989). English skills for algebra. Washington, DC: Center for Applied Linguistics/Prentice Hall Regents.

Cummins, J. (1981). The role of primary language development in promoting educational success for language minority students. In California State Department of Education (Ed.), Schooling and language minority students: A theoretical framework (pp. 3–49). Los Angeles, CA: National Dissemination and Assessment Center.

Cummins, J. (1999). Beyond adversarial discourse: Searching for common ground in the education of bilingual students. In I. A. Heath & C. J. Serrano (Eds.), Teaching English as a second language (pp. 204–224). Sluice Dock, CT: Dushkin/McGraw-Hill.

Delpit, L. (1995). Other people's children: Cultural conflict in the curriculum. New York: New Press.

Dubcovsky, L. (1999). Looking at the written structures of students in a dual Spanish immersion program. Unpublished M.A. Thesis. University of California, Davis.

Edelsky, C. (1986). Writing in a bilingual program: Habia una vez. New York: Ablex.

Gergen, K. J. (1995). Social construction and the educational process. In L. P. Steffe & J. Gale (Eds.), Constructivism in education (pp. 17–39). Hillsdale, NJ: Lawrence Erlbaum Associates.

Grabe, W., & Kaplan, R. B. (1996). Theory and Practice of Writing. London: Longman.

Heslot, J. (1982). Tense and other indexical markers in the typology of scientific texts in English. In J. Hoedt (Ed.), Pragmatics and LSP. Copenhagen, Denmark: Copenhagen School of Economics.

Koch, J. (1996). Science stories: Teachers and children as science learners. Boston, MA: Houghton Mifflin Co.

Merino, B., & Hammond, L. (1995). BICOMP Bilingual Integrated Curriculum Project. Title VII Program of Academic Excellence. Fourth Year Project Evaluation. Submitted to the U.S. Dept. of Education. West Sacramento, CA: Washington Unified School District.

Merino, B., & Hammond, L. (1998). Family gardens and solar ovens: Making science education accessible to culturally and linguistically diverse students. *Multicultural Education*, 34–37.

Meyer, B. (1985). Prose analysis: Purposes, procedures, and problems. In B. Britton & J. Black (Eds.), *Understanding expository text* (pp. 59–76). Hillsdale, NJ: Lawrence Erlbaum Associates.

Raimes, A. (1985). What unskilled ESL writers do as they write: A classroom study of composing. *TESOL Quarterly, 19*(2) 229–258.

Ramirez, D., & Merino, B. (1990). Classroom talk in English immersion, early-exit and late-exit transitional bilingual education programs. In R. Jacobson & C. Faltis (Eds.), *Language distribution issues in schooling* (pp. 61–101). Clevendon, UK: Multilingual Matters.

Saville-Troike, M. (1982). *The ethnography of communication*. Washington, DC: Center for Applied Linguistics.

Swain, M. (1975). *Writing skills of grade three French Immersion Pupils*. Toronto, Canada: The Ontario Institute for Studies in Education.

Swales, J. (1990). *Genre Analysis*. Cambridge, UK: Cambridge University Press.

Teachers of English to Speakers of Other Languages (TESOL). (1997). *ESL Standards for Pre-K–12*. Alexandria, VA: Author.

Tomkins, G. E. (1998). *Literacy for the 21st century*. Upper Saddle River, NJ: Merrill.

Ventola, E., & Mauranen, A. (1991). Non-native writing and native revising of scientific articles. In E. Ventola (Ed.), *Functional and systemic linguistics* (pp. 457–492). Berlin, Germany: Mouton de Gruyter.

Victor, E. (1985). *Science for the elementary school* (5th ed.) New York: Macmillan.

Witte, S., & Faigley, L. (1981). Coherence, cohesion and writing quality. *College Composition and Communication, 32*, 189–204.

13

Writing Backwards Across Languages: The Inexpert English/Spanish Biliteracy of Uncertified Bilingual Teachers*

Ofelia García
Long Island University

THE CONTEXT

As the United States raises educational standards for all students, the standards for teachers have also been set higher. Bilingual teachers in New York State, for example, have to pass three general certification exams with demanding English language essays, and two additional exams—one in English and another one in the language other than English (LOTE). The two language exams not only assess the teachers' bilingualism (listening and speaking), but also their biliteracy (reading and writing). In fact, for the first time, *advanced biliteracy* is required of these teachers, as measured by their ability to read decontextualized and isolated reading passages followed by multiple choice questions, and their ability to write an academic essay in both English and their LOTE. The balanced advanced biliteracy required of bilingual teachers is difficult for any bilingual individual to achieve, especially in the United States, a society that does not value bilingualism and whose schools do not develop biliteracy. And thus, in a city where 40% of residents are immigrants and over 50% speak languages other than English at home (García & Fishman, 1996), there is a shortage of qualified bilingual teachers (García & Trubek, 1999).

*My gratitude to the 12 dedicated bilingual teachers who taught me more about biliteracy than I ever taught them.

The reason why it is so difficult to find bilingual teachers who meet the new advanced biliteracy standards set by New York State has to do as much with the sociolinguistic difficulty of achieving advanced biliteracy in the United States, as with the history and nature of New York Latinos and their lives in the NYC public school system. Advanced biliteracy can only be developed if there are meaningful purposes and authentic audiences for which the two languages are read and written. But in the United States, there are few reasons why advanced literacy in Spanish is needed. Even students who arrive in the United States with good Spanish writing skills experience rapid Spanish literacy loss.

Approximately 30% of New Yorkers are of Latino ancestry, and of those, 40% were born in the United States (García & Fishman, 1996). New York Latinos born in Spanish speaking countries come mostly from Puerto Rico, the Dominican Republic, Colombia, Ecuador and Mexico (Zentella, 1996). For the most part, these New York Latinos arrive in the United States with Spanish literacy that often does not correspond to the advanced literacy uses in an increasingly complex and bureaucratic society with a huge academic testing industry. For example, they often have had little experience reading isolated passages followed by multiple choice questions or writing in ways that follow the essayist tradition, both prevalent activities in U.S. schools. The language barrier that they find in NYC schools is not limited to the language itself; for even if schools functioned in Spanish, these students would not have had experience using Spanish in the decontextualized literate academic ways of a U.S. school system.

Likewise, the English literacy of Latinos, both native born and foreign born, is sometimes less advanced than that of the white middle class. This has little to do with their Spanish language background, and more to do with social class, the poor quality of schooling that many receive, and the inability of the U.S. school system to build on the different literacy practices of the home (Delgado-Gaitán, 1990, Rodríguez, 1999).

Understanding that, for the most part, New York City Latinos have poor literacy development in their first language—whether English, Spanish or both—is of great consequence in understanding why claims about *transfer across languages* are of little consequence when gauging Latino college students', and especially bilingual teachers' writing. Instead of transfer from L1 to L2, these bilingual teachers with inexpert biliteracy end up *"writing backwards across languages"*. As we will see, both Spanish and English are written according to the English rhetorical perspective learned in U.S. schools. And both languages are written to communicate only with an inauthentic English literate audience made up of writing teachers.

This chapter analyzes the literacy views, experiences, and texts of 12 bilingual teachers who have been unable to pass the New York State Teacher Certification Exams. All the teachers speak English, as well as Spanish, fluently. As such, they are not traditional ESL students. As with the Chicanas in Anzaldúa's (1987) work on borderlands, these writers are socially situated in the margins of U.S. and Latin American discourse communities. Although they speak two languages, they have not had the sustained home and socio-educational conditions to be able to use writing in either language to explore complex ideas and texts at the university level. Their writing in the two languages, however, is being assessed within a U.S. higher education context, one that values standard English essayist literacy and does not recognize either a different Spanish literacy tradition or the different ways of writing that these borderland writers use.

ACADEMIC WRITING: DIFFERENCES ACROSS CULTURES AND TRANSFER ACROSS LANGUAGES

The high school and university literacy standards in the United States are clearly those associated with what Scollon and Scollon (1981) have called essayist literacy. Heath (1983, 1987) and Rogoff and Toma (1997) have shown how middle-class homes socialize their very young children in this essayist tradition even before they arrive in school. It is this literate tradition that is reinforced in U.S. schools and expected of middle-class adults (Gee, 1996, 1999). The features of English academic writing have been fairly well established (Biber, 1988; Halliday & Hasan, 1989; MacDonald, 1994).

Different cultures have also been shown to hold different views of critical analysis and to support evidence differently (Carson, 1992; Ramanathan & Kaplan, 1996; Scollon & Scollon, 1981). Different languages seem to structure their written products in various ways and have different textual features, including lengths of sentences, and different ways of drawing on metaphorical and personal language (Eggington, 1987; Hinds, 1987; Kaplan et al., 1983; Purves, 1988; Reid, 1990; Tsao, 1983). In general, researchers have found difference in academic writing depending on the culture and gender of the writer, on the topic addressed, on the genre or register of the writing, and especially on the language used.

Studies contrasting rhetorical patterns in, for example, Puerto Rican Spanish and English have shown higher proportions of coordinate structures, nonsequential sentences, additive constructions, and one- and two-sentence paragraphs in Spanish (Santiago, 1970; Santana-Seda, 1974; Streti, 1971; reported by Kaplan, 1976). The different discourse features of written Mexican Spanish have also been described (Montaño-Harmon, 1991). Writing seems to differ across cultures and languages.

That language abilities transfer across languages has been fairly well established, especially by Cummins (1979, 1981). Working with different language populations, researchers have tried to establish this transfer relationship for biliteracy in different languages and groups (Edelsky, 1982; Mace-Matluck, Dominguez, Holtzman, & Hoover, 1983 for elementary Spanish-English students; Canale, Frenette, & Belanger, 1988 for French English bilingual high school students). Moragne e Silva (1988) found that there is a high transfer of composing skills from L1 into L2. Connor (1996) has shown how writers draw on cross-linguistic and cross-cultural influences at the sentence, paragraph, and text level. Yet, Cummins (1979, 1981), among others, has shown that there is a *linguistic threshold* that must be reached in *the first language* before such transfer occurs. Parallel to Cummins' hypothesis, the *Linguistic Threshold Hypothesis* (*LIH*) in second-language reading research pertains to a threshold in *second-language* knowledge below which L1 reading comprehension skills cannot be transferred to reading comprehension in L2 (Alderson, 1984; Bernhardt & Kamil, 1995; Bossers, 1991).

Despite studies that confirm the literacy transfer across languages—provided that one has reached a linguistic threshold both in the first and the second languages—transfer in L2 writing remains under debate (Mohan & Lo, 1985). Carson, Carrell, Silberstein, Kroll, and Kuehn, (1990) have shown that reading ability transfers more easily than writing ability. But researchers seem to agree that there is some degree of transfer of writing ability across languages.

WRITING BACKWARDS ACROSS LANGUAGES: THE DOMINANCE OF ENGLISH IN INEXPERT BILITERACY

Our inexpert bilingual writers defy, as we will see, the findings of the literature on the differences in writing across cultures and transfer across languages. Situated in the borderlands, our writers do not have experience with two cultures and different discourse modes; rather, they write in two languages within the context of one dominant culture that imposes its rhetorical tradition. And they write in two languages solely within the U.S. university domain, where writing is only assessed according to well-defined cannons of U.S. English language essayist literacy. Furthermore, their audience when writing in the two languages is limited to the teachers and evaluators who read their essays.

As inexpert writers, these students have had many remedial writing courses in U.S. high schools and college. Thus, they have learned well the narrow *English essayist rhetorical tradition* that these remedial writing courses focus on. Yet, they have not developed other English written registers because they rarely write English for other than this schooling purpose. At the same time, they have either experienced loss of a very different Spanish essayist tradition or they simply never became familiar with it. Although the linguistic codes they use may differ, the rhetorical codes used in either language clearly come from the English essayist tradition that is valued in school.

Although these inexpert biliterate writers have acquired English rhetorical devices, they are unable to enter into authentic dialogue with a broad Anglo audience with whom they have had little verbal or literate interaction, even in real life. Both the English and the Spanish texts are written solely for the teachers and evaluators, all English speakers. These writers have had little experience socially with a broad range of English literate monolinguals who are not teachers, and little purpose to communicate with them, either orally or in writing. This has much to do with the continued patterns of social, residential and schooling segregation, and the little possibility of communication that these writers have with English speakers. Writing, as a productive language skill, needs an audience. And these inexpert biliterate writers have had little reason to establish written communication with an English monolingual audience, other than for purposes of schooling.

BACKWARD BILITERACY: THE WRITERS

The 12 female teachers involved in this study have lived in the United States for a minimum of ten years. Two of them were born in the United States and are of Puerto Rican background. Five of them were born in the Dominican Republic, with the rest of them coming from Colombia, Peru, and El Salvador. All have undergraduate degrees from colleges in New York City, and all but one had attended at least 2 years of high school in New York City.

The comments that follow were gathered through interviews with each of the teachers, as well as entries into journals that some kept for a course. The teachers' words are quoted in the language they used. Their views explain some of what we found in the limited biliteracy that they displayed.

Spanish Literacy: Positive Attitudes, Limited Use, and Audience

"Era muy buena escribiendo en mi país"

Almost without exception, the teachers who had been schooled in Latin America felt that their Spanish literacy was excellent. In fact, their attitude was indeed unrealistic, given the level of Spanish literacy that their essays revealed. What they said, however, makes evident the difference between how the Latin American school defined literacy and the literacy demands made by U.S. universities.

> *Era muy buena escribiendo en mi país. Se decía composición, y siempre sacaba buena nota. Allí no era como aquí. No hacíamos errores. Somos muy buenos en eso. Nos enseñaban las letras, las sílabas. Nos memorizábamos todo el libro. Allá no es como aquí en que los niños en quinto grado no saben ni leer ni escribir. Tenía una letra bonita y todos los días hacíamos páginas de letras.*

> [I was very good writing in my country. We called it composition, and I always got a good grade. There, it wasn't like here. We didn't make mistakes. We're great at that. They taught us the entire alphabet, the syllables. We memorized the entire book. There, it is not like here, that kids in the fifth grade don't know how to read and write. I had beautiful handwriting and every day we did pages of letters.]

It is clear that the act of writing that this student engaged in while in school in the Dominican Republic is different from that which she teaches students in the United States. Literacy there was about having beautiful penmanship, copying carefully, being a careful and correct writer. Writing was not used to support a thesis, to provide evidence, to express novel ideas, to convince an unknown audience. Writing was personal, an intimate transaction that one valued for its beauty and symbolism, for its mechanical correctness, more than for its cognitive challenges.

"En español el único problema es el bendito acento"

Because these teachers perceived Spanish writing to be a mechanical act, they evaluated it only in its surface features, especially its orthography. "In Peru," one of the teachers says, "the only rules in writing were the difference between b-v, s-c-z, and the accents [accent marks]. Here everything gets me confused. There's one word for a hundred meanings." Writers perceive that there's more to English writing than handwriting and orthography, including the choice of lexicon to express cognitively complex ideas.

"*En español el único problema es el bendito acento,*" says another student. ["In Spanish, the only problem is the lousy accent."] Again, only surface mechanical features of Spanish writing enter the picture.

"No es lo mismo escribirle a mi esposo, que a un padre hispano, que a un principal"

But it is not only the literacy tradition that writers perceive as different in Spanish, it is also that the readers of their Spanish writing have been less demanding than readers of their English writing. Thus, regardless of their level of Spanish literacy, these writers always feel more secure writing in Spanish. These writers have never taken standardized tests in Spanish writing, and their use of written Spanish is limited to those who are family, friends, or parents with limited education. A student says, *"No es lo mismo escribirle a mi esposo, que a un padre hispano, que a un principal."* ["It is not the same to write to my husband, as to a Hispanic parent, as to a principal."] The audience for whom Spanish is written is less powerful and less capable of literate judgement.

The security that these teachers feel in writing Spanish comes not only from their position of power vis a vis the readers of their writing, mostly poor immigrant parents, but also from the limited range that Spanish literacy has in the United States. Teachers claimed to read in Spanish nothing more than magazines such as *Vanidades* or *Cosmopolitan en español*. One told me that she read wonderful books in Spanish, and when questioned further, she replied: *"Sí, libros buenísimos en español, Sopa de Pollo."* ["Yes, wonderful books in Spanish, *Chicken Soup*."] Clearly, this was very undemanding literate material, making the teacher feel extremely competent in the act of reading Spanish.

English Writing: Negative Attitudes, Extensive Use, and Audience

"I feel illiterate in America"

These words were repeated in some sense by almost all of the foreign born teachers. *"Me siento analfabeta en inglés,"* said another one, in what was a nearly perfect translation of the quote above. Another student expressed it thus: *"Me siento frustrada. Estoy traumatizada. Yo aquí no quiero ser una ignorante."* ["I'm frustrated. I'm traumatized. I don't want to be an ignorant person here."]

Even the native-born teachers blame the English language itself for their difficulties. *"El inglés tiene demasiadas palabras,"* ["English has too many words,"] said one student, referring to the broader range of literacy use of English. Writers comfortable with the intimacy and limited range of Spanish language literacy seem to find the English language context far too broad for them to conquer. Spanish and English lexicon for these teachers manifest differences that have much to do with the contrast between the Latino world in Latin America and the United States, and the Anglo U.S. world. It parallels the difference between going to the Museo del Barrio in New York City or the Faro de Colón in the Dominican Republic, and the Metropolitan Museum in New York City. Whereas Latinos in New York City and Dominicans in Santo Domingo may become extremely familiar with all that the exhibit halls in the first two museums hold, no one ever truly becomes familiar with everything in the Metropolitan Museum. The books and experiences that these teachers have had in Spanish are limited, making their lexicon also limited. Likewise, the range of Spanish written lexicon that they have been exposed to in printed schoolbooks in Latin America and the United States can be controlled by these writers. But in the U.S. culture, with rich and powerful publishing houses, the lexicon explodes without any restraint, and it seems to these inexpert writers that it just has too many words.

Most writers not only expressed negative attitudes toward English writing, but also communicated their anxiety and doubts when writing English. "I worry that there's a mistake," said one teacher. And another one said, *"Me causa ansiedad porque tengo que tener algo que me toque para yo escribir,"* ["It causes me anxiety because I have to have something that really touches me in order to write"]. This teacher not only expresses her anxiety, but also communicates her feelings of alienation and separation when she has to write in English. Topics to be written in English simply don't touch her, she says. It's as if topics in English do not concern her, are outside of her, and are for others.

"Es difícil mantenerse en la mente del que lo está leyendo"

It is the difference between the Spanish-speaking and the English-speaking audience that seems to impact most strongly in these teachers' English writing. One teacher expresses it as follows:

> *Es difícil mantener el tópico, mantenerse en la mente del que lo está leyendo porque ése no es mi idioma. Si es español lo va a entender mejor porque uno conoce la mente de la gente.*
>
> [It is difficult to maintain the topic, to get oneself into the mind of the person who's reading because this is not my language. If it were Spanish it would be understood more easily because one knows the mind of people.]

This teacher has been told again and again by English writing professors that she needs to maintain the topic as she writes, but she claims that the problem is not one of holding the topic, but of entering and sustaining the interest of an Anglo mind. As far as this student is concerned, the problem lies with her audience. If she were writing for a Spanish speaking audience, she would have no trouble engaging them in her topic.

But it is not only the alienation from the English speaking audience that is the problem; it is also that the English language audience range is so vast. It is not limited to principals; it now goes beyond to Chat Rooms on the Internet. I was surprised by the number of teachers who mentioned their insecurity in entering Chat Rooms because they were worried about writing English to an unknown English-speaking audience with whom they have little interaction in real life.

Spanish and English Writing: Differences

"El español es más rico, más romántico. El inglés es más directo, más fácil."

All of these inexpert biliterate teachers, regardless of bilingual ability or the language they identified as their L1, identified emotionally with Spanish, and not English. This emotional attachment to the Spanish language was expressed by weighing Spanish with romanticism and sentimentality and portraying the English language as lacking these. The writer above referred to Spanish as richer, more romantic, whereas English was characterized as more direct and easier. Another student said, "As Spanish writers, we're more sentimental. Our feelings are deep. We tend to feel sorry or explain with a lot of words, to emphasize more. English writers go straight to the point. They tell you what it is, straight." And another one says, "*El inglés es más specific.*"

This feeling that English is a lot more direct than Spanish is also expressed by the student who says, "*El inglés es más directo que el español. En español se escriben muchas líneas, y darle vuelta, vuelta, y casi no decir gran cosas.*" ["English is more direct than Spanish. In Spanish you write many lines, and you go around and around, and you don't say much."] This teacher's intuition about the development of paragraphs in Spanish echoes Kaplan (1966), who describes the greater freedom of Romance languages to introduce extraneous material in complex digressions from the central idea. And yet, the written texts of these bilingual teachers, as we will see, all follow a more direct English rhetorical tradition.

These inexpert writers see English and Spanish writing only through the essayist tradition that they have been taught in U.S. schools. After many years of remedial English writing classes, they know the formula well, a formula they all seem to recite. This description was characteristic of what the teachers said: "You start with an introduction that is general. Then a body with the main idea and three paragraphs with supporting details and examples. You give first other people's opinion, what they said. Then you write your own opinion, and then the conclusion."

The functions of academic writing in school in Latin America were very different from those of schools in the United States. One of the teachers had attended high school in both Colombia and the United States, and she described the differences in this way: "In Erasmus [New York] you have to respond to reading in writing. In Colombia you discuss it, but you don't have to write about it. During a year and a half in Erasmus I did more writing than in Colombia. The problem is not school in Colombia, it is the lack of practice in writing." Writing is used differently, and assessed differently, in different societies. These teachers have written much more academic English than they ever wrote academic Spanish, and it is the English rhetorical tradition that dominates.

These teachers complain about the vastness of the English lexicon, but they're much more familiar with English rhetorical rules that they have drilled and practiced and that they control well. For them, it's as if the English world of words, represented in the vastness of published texts, is unmanageable as compared to Spanish. And yet, the English world of writing, represented by the essayist tradition, is much more manageable than the unstructured, more creative writing that some have once done in Spanish.

"Me parece muy frívolo en inglés cómo se dice"

These teachers feel the English language audience are less sympathetic, less emotive, more distant and cold, more alienating and alienated. Although these writers talk about rhetorical differences between Spanish and English, as we will see further on, in reality there are no rhetorical differences between their Spanish and English written discourses.

Describing her writing, a teacher makes the following insightful remark:

> The problem is when I write I don't think in Spanish, I think in English. *Quiero escribir lo que tengo por dentro, algunas veces en inglés es diferente de como yo lo siento. Me parece muy frívolo en inglés cómo se dice. Por ejemplo, 'I feel sorry for him.' Esa palabra es muy frívola, muy frívola, muy fría. En español, yo diría, 'Oye, qué mal te veo', pero yo creo, siento que debe ser distinto.*

> [… I want to write what I have inside, sometimes in English it is very different from what I am feeling. It seems very frivolous in English the way in which it's said. For example, "I feel sorry for him". That word is very frivolous, very frivolous, very cold. In Spanish I would say, "Listen! you really don't look good," but I think, I feel that it should be different.]

This teacher is feeling her alienation from an English-speaking audience. It is not the English lexicon itself that she characterizes as frivolous, it is the fact that her engagement with the audience is superficial, fleeting, cold, alienating. What she says in English and Spanish is of different import. In English, she does not directly address the English-speaking person, the target audience of her feelings and the written message. Instead, she directs her comments to her Spanish inner-self, speaking about the object of her remark in the third person. "I feel sorry for him," she says. The teacher comments that in Spanish she would have said, "Listen! you really don't look good!" In Spanish she directs her comments to the target audience directly. She becomes personal, direct, getting the attention of her audience with an imperative. In Spanish she doesn't simply express a feeling, as she does in English. Rather, she is direct with what she sees, the fact that the person she's talking/writing to doesn't look good, and she communicates that truth directly. It's as if, in Spanish, she's empowered to communicate, to act, to be personal, and to have an effect on the audience to which her remark is made. In English, however, she feels powerless, unable to directly address the person, able only to convey feelings indirectly, knowing that whatever she says, whatever she writes, will not have any direct effect. This is an insightful statement, one that conveys how important in the act of writing is the feeling of being able to reach and affect an audience, something that these inexpert biliterate writers feel incompetent doing.

BACKWARD BILITERATE TEXTS: SPANISH AND ENGLISH ESSAYS

A number of essays in both English and Spanish, written by these teachers throughout a semester, are the basis of our claim that the texts were composed backwards. The Spanish texts of these teachers show more Spanish writing loss than English influence. This is manifested by the support that English exerts in the mechanics and the rhetoric of writing in Spanish, and yet, the absence of the characteristic loans or loanshifts.

These writers are composing in Spanish not with their Spanish literate voices with which they have ceased to be familiar, or even with their Spanish oral voices that they use in their communities, nor with their popular English oral voices also used in their communities, but with a controlled and limited English literate voice that they have acquired in the many remedial writing courses. Their Spanish literacy is simply the lip-syncing of the English discourse.

Looking first at the loss of familiarity with Spanish writing mechanical and rhetorical conventions, the *bendito acento* [lousy accent], referred to earlier, is almost absent from these texts. These teachers, who use Spanish literacy rarely, have lost all ability to write Spanish accents. Likewise, the Spanish writing rules referred to frequently by the teachers and quoted previously, the difference between b-v, s-c-z, have been quite forgotten. We found both cases very frequently. Examples follow: *abanzada* for *avanzada*, *devido* for *debido*, *centarse* for *sentarse*, *ocacionan* for *ocasionan*, *nesesita* for *necesita*, *canzado* for *cansado*, *empiezen* for *empiecen*.

Their Spanish lexicon also follows English rules of capitalization. Teachers write: *Inglés* instead of *inglés*, *el Viernes* instead of *el viernes*. And English penetrates even the orthography at times. Some examples:

estoy the acuerdo for *estoy de acuerdo*

coger classes for *coger clases*

medios de comunication for *medios de comunicación*

exámen de inglish for *examen de inglés*

hablamos de education for *hablamos de educación*

el collegio for *el colegio*

Other times, English affects the structure of the writing. As in English, articles are omitted, as, for example:

[Los] *Estudiantes deben ser informados*

[Los] *Immigrantes necesitan apoyo*

[Los] *Programas de empresarios son importantes*

And the passive voice is used much more frequently than in texts of Spanish-literate Latin Americans. Some examples:

En esta sociedad es necesario preparar maestros

Estos estudiantes eran pasados por edad

But what most clearly characterizes these as backwards Spanish texts is that they're being composed from an English rhetorical tradition, following a rigid template. Although limitations of space prevent us from reproducing entire essays that follow the English rhetorical conventions, portions of a text, taken from one teacher's essay, help us understand this situation.

The teacher starts with an introductory paragraph paraphrasing the writing prompt, and she immediately gives her own opinion:

Los examenes regentes de las escuelas secundarias estan ocasionando controversias. Algunas personas estan de acuerdo y otras no. Yo estoy the acuerdo que los estudiantes de escuela secundarias tomen estos examenes y voy ha exponer mis ideas a continuacion.

[The High School Regents exams are causing controversy. Some people agree and others don't. I think high school students should be taking these exams and I'm going to present my ideas in what follows.]

Despite the lack of accents, some errors in orthography (for example, *ha exponer* for *a exponer*), and the loanshift in *exámenes regentes* for Regents exams, this paragraph is written in correct Spanish. What strikes us, however, is the orderly structure of the paragraph, the lack of elaboration of the idea or deviation from the main topic, the lack of poetic language, images and metaphors, the use of very controlled vocabulary, the few adjectives—all uncharacteristic of Spanish writing. This teacher, a fluent Spanish speaker, is composing her Spanish composition from the limited English rhetorical tradition she learned in remedial writing classes.

This introductory paragraph is followed by three perfectly structured paragraphs that make three arguments with a thesis sentence:

Primero, si los estudiantes pasan los regentes significa que estan preparados para ir a la Universidad.

Segundo, pasar los examenes regentes les beneficia los estudiantes.

Finalmente, pasar examenes de Regents ayudaria a la economia.

[First, if students pass the Regents it means that they're prepared to go to University.

Second, passing the Regents Exams benefits students.

Finally, passing the Regents exams would help the economy.]

And the essay concludes with a final paragraph, again, following all the conventions of the English essayist tradition—repetition of thesis statement and expansion of the introduction.

Finalmente, yo creo que es positivo que los estudiantes de escuelas secundarias pasen los examenes de Regentes para graduarse de High School. Esto es para beneficio de ellos y para la sociedad.

[Finally, I think that it is positive that high school students pass the Regents exams to graduate from High School. This is of benefit to themselves and to society.]

When we look at the teachers' English essays, however, we realize that their limited English literate voices are full of gaps, and that the voice that provided the discourse for the lip-syncing in the Spanish texts is only a whisper, limited to one register. Communication is sometimes impeded because the voice is timid and inauthentic and fails to engage an audience that, as listeners, has a much broader range of registers.

The English essays manifest all the mechanical errors that have been associated with developmental literacy—incomplete knowledge of punctuation, lack of sub-ject–verb agreement, unfamiliarity with past participles. But beyond the mechanical errors, they lack the normal flow of communication. Developmental native English writers often write just as they speak, with their writing showing a torrent of words and an informal, conversational tone. But the language in this writing is almost artificially controlled. The writers are not writing with their Spanish torrential voices, nor with those of the English in the streets; rather, their English writing is completely artificial. They have acquired a template in which they fit their voice, leaving no room for linguistic creativity and experimentation.

This artificiality in the flow of the text is also reflected in the difficulty that these writers have initiating written text. When composing, they freeze; they cannot find the words, those words that they cannot conquer. They write timidly, as if they were not the authors.

Yet, these teachers are bright and have a lot to say. They even like to write. One of the students wants to write a book. She says:

> I would like to write a book. I have a lot of ideas. I just don't know how to write them down. My thoughts became more and more complex, and then writing became complex and difficult. *I have many opinions to write, so it is difficult to arrange them.* (Emphasis mine)

And it is perhaps this image of many ideas and opinions and an inability to ar-range them that gives us a sense of what's happening with these inexpert biliterate writers. There have to be good reasons and meaningful functions for developing biliteracy. Experienced writers develop biliteracy as they experience an *expansion of functions* for which they write. But for these powerless inexpert biliterate writers, writing in the borderlands, the process is actually one of *contracting functions*. Two writing systems with distinct rhetorical traditions share one narrow function, that of the dominant U.S. academic society. And the purpose of the act of writing in ei-ther language becomes limited to the academic essay for an evaluative Eng-lish-speaking audience. Thus, these writers' multiple literacies, expressing the different contexts, realities and views of two cultural worlds, are forced and cramped into a limited space, a restricted function, a very narrow audience. The written biliterate text, rather than establishing a meaningful and airy dialogue in public with a literate audience in both languages, becomes suffocated and whispers only to itself within academic confines. Rather than communicate and open up dif-ferent worlds of possibilities, the use of the two languages in these academic essays restricts vision, as the essayist literacy they have learned funnels, limits, and forces acculturation to U.S. literacy patterns and world view.

IMPLICATIONS FOR U.S. SCHOOLS: EXPANDING THE DISCOURSE RANGE

In order to have advanced biliteracy and reap the benefits of transferring skills across languages, writers must have a broad *Discourse range* in the two languages;

that is, they must have opportunities to use different written varieties or registers for different social purposes and different audiences. (We use Discourse here in the sense used by Gee, 1999, and in this book).

If schools were really serious about developing advanced biliteracy, they would give students ample opportunity to read authentic texts and literature from both cultural traditions, as well as opportunities to write different genres in the two languages. As long as the books used in bilingual classrooms are mere translations of English texts, bilingual students will not develop familiarity with the range of texts and literacies of different cultural contexts. As long as the texts used in English language classrooms contain simplified vocabulary and structures, and the texts they write are solely academic essays, bilingual students will not be able to develop the richness in English language use that an English-speaking middle-class home supports.

Latino bilingual students need to engage in rich English language experiences in school that they cannot get in a Spanish-speaking home. Simplifying and reducing their language and literacy context in school may result in better scores in standardized tests in the early grades, but it will not get them to develop the advanced literacy needed for professional status as adults. Likewise, these Latino students need to read the rich literature of Latin America and delight in the richness of images and language of its poetry and fiction, as well as the vastness of its humanistic essays. Reading only academic texts that use Spanish to communicate content that is exactly the same as that in English texts leaves Spanish devoid of separate and different meaning and purpose, and makes Spanish and English completely redundant.

Unless advanced biliteracies, with different rhetorical traditions and functions are recognized as separate in U.S. schools, true biliteracy for U.S. citizens will elude us. And bilingual teachers will continue to compose backwards from a narrow English rhetorical tradition with English speaking academics as the sole audience, restricting not only their biliteracy, but also their professional and human possibilities.

REFERENCES

Alderson, J. (1984). Reading in a foreign language: A reading problem or a language problem? In J. Alderson & A. Urquhart, (Eds.), *Reading in a Foreign Language*, (pp. 1–27). London: Longman.

Anzaldúa, G. (1987). *Borderlands/La frontera: The new mestiza*. San Francisco: Aunt Lute Books.

Bernhardt, E. B., & Kamil, M. (1995). Interpreting relationships between L1 and L2 reading: Consolidating the linguistic threshold and the linguistic interdependence hypotheses. *Applied Linguistics, 16*, 15–34.

Biber, D. (1988). *Variation across speech and writing*. Cambridge, UK: Cambridge University Press.

Bossers, B. (1991). On thresholds, ceilings and short-circuits: The relation between L1 reading, L2 reading, and L2 knowledge. *AILA Review, 8*, 45–60.

Canale, M., Frenette, N., & Belanger, M. (1988). Evaluation of minority student writing in first and second language. In J. Fine (Ed), *Second language discourse: A textbook of current research*, (pp. 147–164). Norwood, NJ: Ablex.

Carson, J. (1992). Becoming biliterate: First language influences. *Journal of Second Language Writing, 1*, 37–60.

Carson, J. E., Carrell, P., Silberstein, S., Kroll, B., Kuehn, P. (1990). Reading-writing relationships in first and second language. *TESOL Quarterly, 24,* 245–266.

Connor, U. (1996). *Contrastive rhetoric: Cross-cultural aspects of second language writing.* Cambridge, UK: Cambridge University Press.

Cummins, J. (1979). *Linguistic interdependence and the educational development of bilingual children.* Bilingual Education Paper Series 3/2 (ERIC Document Reproduction Service No. ED 257 312).

Cummins, J. (1981). The role of primary language development in promoting educational success for language minority students. In *Schooling and language minority students: A theoretical framework,* (pp. 3–50). Los Angeles: Evaluation, Dissemination, and Assessment Center.

Delgado-Gaitán, C. (1990). *Literacy for Empowerment.* Bristol, PA: Falmer Press.

Edelsky, C. (1982). Writing in a bilingual program: The relation of L1 and L2 texts. *TESOL Quarterly, 16,* 211–228.

Eggington, W. G. (1987). Written academic discourse in Korean: Implications for effective communication. In U. Connor & R. B. Kaplan, (Eds.), *Writing across languages: Analysis of L2 text,* (pp. 153–168). Reading, MA: Addison-Wesley.

García, O., & Fishman, J. A. (1996). *The Multilingual Apple: Languages in New York City.* New York: Mouton.

García, O., & Trubek, J. (1999). Where have all the urban minority educators gone and when will they ever learn? *Educators for Urban Minorities, 1,* 1–8.

Gee, J. (1996). *Social linguistics and literacies: Ideology in discourses* (2nd ed.). London: Taylor and Francis.

Gee, J. P. (1999). The new literacy studies: From "socially situated" to the work of the social. In D. Barton, M. Hamilton, and R. Ivanic, (Eds.), *Situated Literacies: Reading and writing in context* (pp. 180–196). London: Routledge.

Halliday, M. A. K., & Hasan, R. (1989). *Language, Context and Text.* Oxford, UK: Oxford University Press.

Heath, S. (1983). *Ways with words: Language, life and work in the communities and classrooms.* Cambridge, UK: Cambridge University Press.

Heath, S. (1987). The literate essay: Using ethnography to explode myths: In J. Langer, (Ed.), *Language, literacy and culture: Issues of society and schooling* (pp. 131–140). Norwood, NJ: Ablex.

Hinds, J. (1987). Reader versus writer responsibility: A new typology. In U. Connor & R. B. Kaplan, (Eds.), *Writing across languages: Analysis of L2 text,* (pp. 141–152). Reading, MA: Addison-Wesley.

Kaplan, R. B. (1966). Cultural thought patterns in intercultural education. *Language Learning, 16*(1), 1–20.

Kaplan, R. B. (1976). A further note on contrastive rhetoric. *Communication Quarterly, 24,* 12–19.

MacDonald, S. P. (1994). *Professional academic writing in the humanities and social sciences.* Carbondale: Southern Illinois University Press.

Mace-Matluck, B. J., Dominguez, D., Holtzman, W., & Hoover, W. (1983). *Language and literacy in bilingual instruction.* Austin, TX: Southwest Educational Laboratory.

Mohan, B. A., & Lo, W. A. (1985). Academic writing and Chinese students: Transfer and developmental factors. *TESOL Quarterly, 19*(3), 515–534.

Montaño-Harmon, M. R. (1991). Discourse features of written Mexican Spanish: Current research in contrastive rhetoric and its implications. *Applied Linguistics, 74,* 417–425.

Moragne e Silva, M. (1988). Is the process of composing in a second language similar to composing in the first? *Texas Papers in Foreign Language Education, 1,* 16–25.

Purves, A. C. (Ed.). (1988). *Writing across languages and cultures.* Newbury Park, CA: Sage.

Ramanathan, V., & Kaplan, R. B. (1996). Audience and voice in current L1 composition texts: Some implications for ESL student writers. *Journal of Second Language Writing,, 5,* 21–34.

Reid, J. (1990). Responding to different topic types: a quantitative analysis from a contrastive rhetoric perspective. In B. Kroll (Ed.), *Second Language Writing* (pp. 191–120). Cambridge, UK: Cambridge University Press.

Rodriguez, V. (1999). Home literacy experiences of three young Dominican children in New York City: Implications for teaching in an urban setting. *Educators for Urban Minorities, 1,* 19–31.

Rogoff, B., & Toma, C. (1997). Shared thinking: Cultural and institutional variations. *Discourse Processes, 23,* 471–497.

Santana-Seda, O. (1974). A contrastive study in rhetoric: An analysis of the organization of English and Spanish paragraphs written by native speakers of each language. Dissertation. New York University, 1974. *Dissertation Abstracts International, 35,* 6681A.

Santiago, R. L. (1970). A contrastive analysis of some rhetorical aspects in the writing in Spanish and English of Spanish-speaking college students in Puerto Rico. Dissertation, Columbia University, 1970. *Dissertation Abstracts International 31,* 6368A.

Scollon, R., & Scollon, S. B. K. (1981). *Narrative, literacy, and face in interethnic communication.* Norwood, NJ: Ablex.

Streti, G. J. (1971). *A contrastive study of the structure of rhetoric in English and Spanish composition.* Unpublished Masters Thesis, McGill University.

Tsao, F. F. (1983). Linguistics and written discourse in particular languages: Contrastive studies: English and Mandarin. *Annual Review of Applied Linguistics, 3,* 99–117.

Zentella, A. C. (1996). Spanish in New York. In O. García & J. A. Fishman (Eds.), *The multilingual apple: Languages in New York City,* (pp. 167–201). New York: Mouton.

Author Index

Subject Index

A